A Glossary of Faulkner's South

A Glossary of

Faulkner's South

CALVIN S. BROWN

NEW HAVEN AND LONDON
YALE UNIVERSITY PRESS
1976

Contents

Acknowledgments

A work of this sort is even more dependent on external aid than most books, since the process of asking around until one finds someone who knows is an essential last resort. It is a pleasure to thank all those who gave me significant help on one matter or another, especially Jean Butler, E. Merton Coulter, Dick Dodd, Wilbur Duncan, Dan Kitchens, Robert Harrison, A. Q. Smith, Richmond Statham, and Gerald Walton. Astrid Fried, of the Old Sautee Store, and Sam H. Nickerson, of the Athens Hardware Company, gave me invaluable aid by the loan of old hardware catalogues. Cleanth Brooks, Frederic G. Cassidy, Harry Levin, and James Meriwether went considerably beyond the call of ordinary academic duty in helping with some knotty problems. Thanks are also due to the editors of *PMLA* and *Notes on Contemporary Literature* for their permission to reprint material which I had originally published in their journals.

Ellen Hudson Graham, of the Yale University Press, has been most helpful and cooperative in all the problems and details of publication.

Finally, I wish to thank my wife most of all, not only for a great deal of faithful proofreading and checking of references, but for providing both the carrot and the stick, the inspiration and the needling without which it is impossible to carry through a long-term project amid the alarms and excursions of daily academic life.

Introduction

In *Absalom, Absalom!* Quentin Compson and his Canadian roommate Shreve McCannon talk in their Harvard sitting-room late into a cold winter night, trying to reconstruct the story of Thomas Sutpen's abortive dynasty. At one point, Faulkner tells us, they imagine Judith Sutpen and Charles Bon strolling in a garden in Mississippi, "to disappear slowly beyond some bush or shrub starred with white bloom— jasmine, spiraea, honeysuckle, perhaps myriad scentless unpickable Cherokee roses—names, blooms which Shreve possibly had never heard and never seen" (pp. 294–95). Shreve is here in the situation of many readers of Faulkner all over the world. He is sympathetic, intelligent, and interested, but he is being called on to imagine and try to understand a world so foreign to his own experience that his imagination has little to work with. Even the names of the flowers may be as alien to him as the blooms themselves. The purpose of this book is to help the Shreves to understand what Faulkner is saying.

Faulkner makes his point by mentioning flowers common in Mississippi but not in Canada. He could equally well have made it in any number of other ways, for almost every reader is a Shreve in one way or another. The Mississippi cotton-farmer ought to be thoroughly at home in the agricultural references—but if he is under forty he will have grown up with tractors instead of mules, and loggerheads, trace-chains, hames, and buckheads will be as foreign to him as the flowers were to Shreve. If he is an elderly New England hill-farmer, he will probably understand plow-gear but not cotton or sharecropping. Anyone not from the South may need explanations of many words, usages, pronunciations, and customs which Faulkner takes for granted —things like the usage of *Miss* with a given name (even for a married woman), the pronunciation which Faulkner accurately represents as *Miz* (for *Mrs.*), and the use of fireworks to celebrate Christmas. Young people anywhere will be worried occasionally by such things as the

1

dead slang of the flapper era. Only the old-timer or antiquarian now
knows what a froe is, or how it is used, and hence only a few readers
know exactly what is going on in "Shingles for the Lord." It seems
obvious that a "yellin calf" is yelling, and a person who has never been
closer to a calf than an East Side delicatessen will not be puzzled by the
fact that calves do not yell. Few readers will realize, unaided, that it
is a yearling calf.

Such examples could be multiplied indefinitely. There are other
things in Faulkner which are even more restricted than the time-bound
or regional usages that have already been mentioned. In one sense,
only an old-time resident of Oxford, Mississippi, can get the full im-
pact of Jefferson and Yoknapatawpha County. To him, Hurricane
Creek, the big ditch behind the schoolhouse, the barber-shop that
operated at the northwestern corner of the square for more than half
a century (it moved in 1972), and the old jail (now gone forever) will
not be elements in a fictional world but the everyday realities that they
were for Faulkner himself. Things like this are here individually identified, as far as possible, and a separate appendix attempts to put them
together into a coherent whole.

One type of reader, all too often forgotten, has been constantly in the
back of my mind in the preparation of this glossary. Faulkner is not the
property of the South, or of American literature: he has definitely
become a part of world literature. He has readers all over the world
whose English is an artificially acquired second tongue. Many of them
have an excellent command of the standard literary language, but the
language of Faulkner, especially the dialogue, is an even greater stum-
bling-block for them than it is for New Yorkers and Londoners. A
German critic puts the case plainly enough. "If Faulkner's splendid
dialogues are ruined in translation, does one have to learn English in
order to be able to check them? It is worse than that: English would
not be enough. One would have to learn to handle Southern American
and decipher Negro dialogue, and to master the whole body of folklore
from Virginia to Louisiana, from Florida to Texas." The translators
themselves are frequently driven to ducking the issues. This same critic
inquires plaintively, "Just what might a 'Dogwoodbaum' be supposed
to be?"[1] It is partly in the interest of foreign readers and, especially,
translators that I have adopted the principle that, in case of doubt, it is
better to labor the obvious than to risk omitting the necessary.

1. Joachim Seyppel, *William Faulkner* (*Köpfe des XX. Jahrhunderts*, 24), (Berlin,
1962), pp. 9, 81. My translation.

One man's obvious is often another man's puzzle. *Light in August* begins: "Sitting beside the road, watching the wagon mount the hill toward her, Lena thinks, 'I have come from Alabama: a fur piece. All the way from Alabama a-walking. A fur piece.'" When the novel was first published, my sister was a graduate student at Cornell, earning her keep as housemother of a sorority house. One morning a bright girl from Brooklyn confronted her with Faulkner. She had been trying to read his new book, she said, but it just didn't make sense. Asked for an illustration, she cited the beginning. "Why should a girl sitting by a dusty Mississippi road on a blazing hot summer day be thinking about a fur-piece?"

This sort of misunderstanding is commoner than one might suppose. It is a notorious fact that Faulkner criticism is plagued by more than its share of blunders in matters of elementary fact, some of them committed by excellent critics.[2] It is impossible to know how many of these errors are due to misreadings which a glossary could have prevented, but there is no question that some of them are, and that others arise from a vague feeling that Faulkner's world is so strange and foreign that anything is possible there. (See NANCY for an incredible example.) Certainly the first business of any literary critic is to understand his text on the simplest literal level, and unless he does this he comments and interprets at his own peril. But many Faulknerians who will doggedly pursue a myth to the ultimate reaches of *The Golden Bough* never even pause to wonder what a laplink or a shikepoke may be.

It is true, of course, that such knowledge is not always necessary for adequate literary understanding. One can easily gather from the context that a laplink is an item of hardware and a shikepoke is some sort of bird, and perhaps that is all that really matters. But the precision is blurred, and no one will allow such an argument for things that he himself knows. The person who will contend that the difference between a buckboard and a buggy is a matter of antiquarian pedantry will probably also maintain that anyone who doesn't know a sedan from a convertible is ipso facto incapable of understanding contemporary fiction. The real point is that unless one understands something he cannot tell whether or not it is important. It may not matter that Faulkner's whippoorwills are actually chuck-will's-widows; but anyone who does not know the verb *to grabble* in the regional meaning that it has for fishermen is sure to miss an important link in the child Varda-

2. For an amusing collection of some of these howlers, see Floyd C. Watkins, "Faulkner and His Critics," *Texas Studies in Language and Literature* 10 (1968): 317–29.

man's confusion of his dead mother with a dead fish in *As I Lay Dying*. Precise knowledge of Faulkner's country will frequently lead to implications or insights that the critical reader without such knowledge is sure to miss.

On the other hand, knowledge can sometimes be a hindrance. Faulkner's insistence that he was not really a writer but just a Mississippi farmer who liked to write stories has long been recognized for the pose that it was, but it contains an important element of truth. He spun his books out of his head as he went along, not depending on outlines, notes, or, above all, research. The only novel for which he drew up a detailed plan in advance was *A Fable*—which turned out to be an impressive failure. Novelists like Zola and Thomas Mann did extensive reading and note-taking, and called on experts for help in fields where they were not sure of themselves. Faulkner never did this. When he needed something, he looked around in the "lumber room" of his head for something to serve his purpose.[3] He did not look in a library. There is a great deal of history in his work, but he was probably telling the truth when he said that he had read little history. He had picked it up from family traditions, reminiscences of Confederate veterans, and other oral sources,[4] and when he needed it he rummaged in his mental attic, not in reference books. What his history gains in immediacy easily makes up for occasional lapses in accuracy.

The same thing holds true in other fields. Faulkner knew the woods well, having roamed them as a boy and man and having done a moderate amount of hunting and a great deal of listening to hunters. But he was not a naturalist. His flora and fauna are fairly standard local knowledge. His birds, for example, are the obvious catbirds, mockingbirds, jays, bluebirds, and buzzards known to everyone in the region—not the crested flycatchers, anhingas, brown creepers, and prothonotary warblers familiar to even the most casual bird-watcher. Like most of his fellow-townsmen, Faulkner lumps the very different brown

3. This lumber room is a favorite metaphor of Faulkner's. For examples, see Frederick L. Gwynn and Joseph L. Blotner, eds., *Faulkner in the University: Class Conferences at the University of Virginia, 1957–1958* (New York, 1965), pp. 72, 109, 117.

4. He told Robert Cantwell, "I never read any history. I talked to people. If I got it straight it's because I didn't worry with other people's ideas about it. When I was a boy there were a lot of people around who had lived through it, and I would pick it up—I was just saturated with it, but never read about it" (Robert Cantwell, "The Faulkners: Recollections of a Gifted Family," in Frederick J. Hoffman and Olga W. Vickery, eds., *William Faulkner: Three Decades of Criticism* [East Lansing, 1960], p. 57). Note also Faulkner's statement at the University of Virginia: "As far as I know I have never done one page of research" (Gwynn and Blotner, p. 251).

thrasher and wood thrush together under the term *thrush*; and apparently he neither knows nor cares that a "buzzard" may be either a black vulture or a turkey vulture.

He treats his antiquities in much the same way, showing a great deal of knowledge of the clothing, implements, and general way of life of his country during the period of approximately a century which he covers, but never approaching these things as would an antiquarian or a researching historical novelist.

The result of all this is that, in spite of Faulkner's generally good memory and sharp observation, he slips up occasionally. Sometimes the error is his own. Often it comes from merely using something that is a matter of widespread misinformation, like the musky odor he attributes to the rattlesnake in "The Bear." It falls to the lot of a work like this glossary to indicate the occasional errors of this sort, lest they be spread further and, especially, lest they prove puzzling to readers who themselves know better.

One exception must be made to the general statement about the range and accuracy of Faulkner's knowledge. His Indians and their ways and customs are almost pure fantasy. Occasionally a bit of genuine lore turns up, as in the "Chief, Grandfather" applied to the ancient rattlesnake in "The Bear" (p. 330), but this sort of thing is exceptional. Some Choctaws remained farther south in Mississippi, but Oxford was in Chickasaw country (though Faulkner is inconsistent on this point). After the Chickasaws ceded their lands by the Treaty of Pontotoc in 1832, they departed for Oklahoma, leaving few stragglers and no sort of local oral tradition. My mother, who was some twenty years older than Faulkner and was named for his mother, was aware of this fact; and as a local historian she knew that the early records had nothing significant to say about the Indians. She once asked Faulkner where his Indians came from, and he frankly and simply replied, "Mrs. Brown, I made them up." Under the circumstances, it would obviously be pointless to try to gloss his ceremonial stick-burning or to explain the office of the Willow Bearer.

The material covered in this glossary is precisely indicated in the list of abbreviations and editions used. The general principle, as the title implies, is to deal with the works set in the South. The one apparent violation of this principle is the exclusion of *Pylon*, but it only appears to be an exception. The setting happens to be New Orleans, but it could equally well have been Cleveland or Buffalo or Seattle, for it is really the mechanical world of rootless barnstorming aviators. *Pylon* is in the

South, but not of it; and hence it is not included. The Southern short stories included in novels are not separately glossed: "Spotted Horses" is included only in the form that it takes in *The Hamlet,* and "Mule in the Yard" only as it appears in *The Town.* The story of the stolen race-horse, "Notes on a Horsethief," with its Southern setting, is glossed in the form that it takes in *A Fable,* though the rest of that novel, being set in France, is not glossed. On the other hand, the essentially Southern works are glossed as completely as possible, even when some of the action falls outside the region. Thus Bayard Sartoris's references to Jennys and Camels are explained, but World War I flying stories like "Ad Astra" and "Turnabout" are ignored.

Some explanations are tentative, or are even simply best guesses. Their status is clearly indicated, usually by words like *probably, presumably, apparently,* or *possibly.* One class of such guesses calls for special comment. These guesses have to do with things which I am convinced are errors not representing Faulkner's intention. I do not necessarily call them misprints, since they may well be accurate reproductions of uncaught errors in the manuscripts. Everyone knows that it is very easy, whether typing or writing longhand, to put down, say, *king* instead of *kind,* or *the* instead of *they.* Such readings would still be errors, in spite of being in the original manuscript. For this reason, I have not checked the few cases of this sort against the manuscripts, since they could not settle the question in any case.

Two examples will suffice here. In *Go Down, Moses,* a passage referring to Lucas's moonshining reads: "a business which he had established and nursed carefully and discreetly for twenty [years], ever since he had fired up for his first fun not a mile from Zack Edmonds' kitchen door" (pp. 34–35). This simply will not do. Operating a still is hard, hot work, and no one would call it fun. However, a *run* of a still is a standard technical term: filling the "kettle" of a still with mash and distilling it (once) constitutes a run. Faulkner knows the term, and uses it (*Sart.* 123). It is obvious that the passage was intended to read, "ever since he had fired up for his first run."[5]

The second example turns on a question of idiom rather than meaning. In *Sanctuary,* Gowan Stevens gets abominably drunk, spends part

5. Since writing this, I have found that James Meriwether reached the same conclusion, checked it, and found that the typescript had the same reading as the published version, but an earlier draft of the passage had the correct reading, *run* (Meriwether, "A Proposal for a CEAA Edition of William Faulkner," in *Editing Twentieth Century Texts,* ed. Francess G. Halpenny [Toronto, 1972], p. 24).

of the night passed out in his car, and finally wakes, aware that he is supposed to get Temple Drake off the special train at Taylor. He runs toward the station, falls, gets up, and runs on, "in his stained dinner jacket, his burst collar and broken hair" (p. 35). At the station he finds a Negro, who greets him with "Gret Gawd, white folks." Gowan asks about the special train, and the Negro replies, "Hit done lef. But five minutes ago." *But* would be perfectly appropriate here in the mouth of an educated Englishman, but Faulkner, with his fine ear for the nuances of speech, would have known that it is utterly impossible for a Mississippi Negro who greets a disheveled drunk with "Gret Gawd, white folks," and says, "Hit done lef." What he *would* say and what Faulkner doubtless intended, is " 'Bout five minutes ago."

Professional textual critics will probably disapprove of my practice here. I am, of course, aware of the principle of the *difficilior lectio* and of the dangers of cavalier emendations. On the other hand, I have undertaken to help the reader understand Faulkner's text, and the suggestion of a few emendations which seem to me clearly indicated is a part of the job. After all, I am not editing Faulkner and actually changing his text, but merely indicating how I believe it should be changed, and why.

Some problems remain entirely unsolved. I have no idea what Jason Compson means when he says, "I says you might send me to the state University; maybe I'll learn how to stop my clock with a nose spray" (*S&F* 243). I have never heard the expression, nor have any of the many people I have asked who are at home in Faulkner's period and idiom. A large number of reference books have been no help whatsoever. In this case I cannot even hazard a plausible guess except that, because of the context and the speaker, I feel sure that the general tenor of the remark is hateful, and probably nasty too. Words and phrases of this sort are listed here in the hope that they may thus come to the attention of someone who knows them and can explain them before it is too late.

Forms not Glossed. Because of limitations of space, widespread and easily recognizable substandard forms are not normally glossed. There is obviously no need to explain the use of *knowed* for *knew*, *went* for *gone*, or other familiar variants of the principal parts of verbs. The same principle excludes such obvious deviant pronunciations as *impident* for *impudent* or *extry* for *extra*.

Four large classes of variants are due to characteristics of Southern speech which can be explained once and for all and hence do not require separate listings for each instance.

1. The last of two or more final consonants is often dropped, as in *las(t)*, *nex(t)*, *tole (told)*, and *fine (find)*.

2. In substandard speech, initial *th* is often replaced by *d*, as in *dem (them)*, *den (then)*, and *dat (that)*.

3. "Dropping final *g*" (which is phonetically not a dropping of anything, but the substitution of a different phoneme) is very common in unstressed syllables: *goin (going)*, *writin (writing)*, etc.

4. As in the British received standard and in parts of New England, *r* is pronounced only before vowels: *fawty (forty)*, *waw (war)*, *lawd (lord)*. Sometimes the *r* vocalizes to form a separate syllable: *four* may become either *fo* or *foah*. And sometimes *r* disappears even before a vowel, as in *ma'ied (married)*, *thow (throw)*, and *fum (from)*.

Spellings indicating pronunciations of these four types are, in general, not glossed unless there is some reason to think that they may be misunderstood.

How to Find It. Since this is a glossary rather than an encyclopedia, the entries are, with a very few exceptions, Faulkner's own words. The exceptions occur in a few cases (e.g. BARN) where it seems easier to include a number of related terms under one general descriptive article than to deal with them separately. In such cases there are always cross-references from the specific words to the general article. A reader may occasionally have to try a couple of places to locate a phrase, when there is a question of what word to select as its beginning, but this will not happen too often.

Parts of speech are designated only when necessary. A word like *quoil* represents a pronunciation of *quarrel*, regardless of whether it is used as a noun or a verb. If the part of speech matters, and if the definition does not make it clear, then it is specifically stated.

All entries are arranged by alphabetical order in a single listing, ignoring hyphens, apostrophes, and word-separation; this is necessary for the user's convenience, since Faulkner's works are highly inconsistent in these matters. In *Sartoris*, a room contained "a wash-stand with a slop-jar beside it" (p. 108). This same description, in *Flags in the Dust*, has "a washstand with a slop-jar beside it" (p. 98). And in Temple Drake's room at Miss Reba's "sat a washstand bearing a flowered bowl and pitcher and a row of towels; in the corner behind it sat a slop jar dressed also in fluted rose-colored paper" (*Sanc.* 151). In *Go Down, Moses,* we find *canthooks* on p. 137, but only six pages later the word is *cant-hook.*

Faulkner is similarly inconsistent in his use of nonpossessive apostrophes. He has, after his earliest work, a strong tendency to omit them in such standard contractions as *cant* and *dont.* As a very broad generalization it can be said that in his works before and including *Sartoris* he indicated dialect pronunciations rather pedantically on the basis of standard spelling modified by apostrophes for the letters indicating the sounds not pronounced. In *Sartoris* we find *mont'* for *months,* for example (p. 290). A reader not thoroughly at home in the local speech and alert to the context is very likely to rhyme this with *don't* or with *font;* in either case he will be puzzled. In the same sentence, *wuz* for *was* (a respelling, where an apostrophe will not serve) is perfectly clear. The distracting use of apostrophes is illustrated by many words in *Sartoris:* '*a*' for *have* (p. 72), '*fo*' for *before,* and '*cep*' for *except* (both on p. 20). Even with this system, however, Faulkner is sometimes remarkably observant and accurate. The two versions of *towards* in *Sartoris,* Old Man Falls's *to'a'ds* (p. 21) and the *to'ds* of an unidentified Negro (p. 30) are not an inconsistency, but an indication of two different pronunciations. Old Man Falls characteristically makes the word two syllables, but in the Negro's speech it has only one.

Flora and Fauna. The plants and animals liberally mentioned in Faulkner's work are here identified, as far as possible, with brief descriptions aimed at making some sort of mental image possible and explaining any specific details needed for an understanding of Faulkner's references or implications. However, plants and animals are glossed only when they have some real relation to Faulkner's setting. There would be no point in explaining such universally known cultivated flowers as roses and geraniums. Very general references to large taxonomic groups, like the "crickets and frogs" of *Sart.* 45, are also passed over, since only the more or less universal characteristics of these groups are involved. On the other hand, it is desirable to gloss *beech,* since the American species is a larger tree than the European one. Similarly, purely literary and conventional references are passed over. *Mad as a hornet* (*Ham.* 15; *Mans..* 346) is a standard literary figure of speech having nothing particular to do with the Hymenoptera of Yoknapatawpha County, though they can get as mad as any. The same thing holds true when Faulkner himself compares Mink Snopes to a scorpion (*Mans.* 287) and to a krait and a fer-de-lance (*Mans.* 393). The fact that there are scorpions in Faulkner's country, but no kraits or fer-de-lances, does not matter: all three are literary comparisons. But when Ratliff, also speaking of Mink Snopes, says, "Only this here seems to be a different kind of Snopes like a cotton-mouth is a different kind of snake" (*Ham.* 91), the reference is immediate and local, and calls for explanation.

Frequency and Order of Citations. This glossary is not a concordance, and no attempt is made to list all occurrences of the words that are glossed. In general, three citations, involving two different works, are considered adequate. More are given if they add new information or raise new problems, or if the item itself is of especial importance or presents any particular difficulties.

The order of citations is designed to be as useful as possible. Beginning with *Sartoris*, they go through the novels in chronological order, and then pick up *Soldier's Pay, Mosquitoes*, those of the *Collected Short Stories* which are glossed, *Knight's Gambit*, and some miscellaneous items. This arrangement means that the most frequently cited and fully glossed works are the first half-dozen or so of the Yoknapatawpha cycle, which are also the most widely read and are generally considered the most important of Faulkner's works.

Place-names. With a few obvious exceptions like New York, Paris, and Heidelberg, Faulkner's place-names are glossed. It seems worth while to identify even such familiar places as Memphis, Little Rock, and Pensacola by giving their exact relationship to Oxford, Mississippi, which is, of course, Faulkner's Jefferson. Some places are given their right names in Faulkner and require only to be located. Others, like Mottstown (Water Valley, Mississippi) and Parsham (Grand Junction, Tennessee), must be both identified and located. Finally, there are place-names which are (to the best of my knowledge) fictional. They are not actual places, nor can they be identified with actual places. These are glossed as fictional places, along with any other relevant information. They may not be actually invented: local names, especially for things like creeks and sloughs, are highly variable and often do not get onto maps. For example, John Cullen believes that the name of Frenchman's Bend was adapted from Dutch Bend.[6] I have

6. John B. Cullen, in collaboration with Floyd C. Watkins, *Old Times in the Faulkner Country* (Chapel Hill, N.C., 1961), p. 64.

never heard of Dutch Bend, nor have I been able to find it on any map. But Cullen may well be right. Similarly, when Mink Snopes wants to buy two shotgun shells loaded with buckshot (to kill Jack Houston), he justifies the request by saying that a bear's track has been seen in the mud at Blackwater Slough (*Mans.* 32). This should be a slough (probably an old river cut-off) in the Yocona River bottom in the general area of Varner's Crossroads. I do not know of a slough so named, nor have I found it on any map. That is what is meant by glossing it as a fictional place.

Personal Names. Several listings of Faulkner's characters are readily available,[7] and no attempt is made to duplicate them here, especially since this glossary is concerned with the factual background of the fiction rather than the fiction as such. Nor is any attempt made to identify the real-life prototypes of the fictional characters. A few of these are quite plain: Gavin Steven owes a good deal to Faulkner's early literary mentor, Phil Stone; Deacon and his café (in *Sartoris*) draw heavily on Mr. Buffalo and his café, which was in about the middle of the western side of the square; the location of Christian's drugstore is shifted, but the institution and its proprietor are closely related to Chilton's Drug Store and "Uncle Top" Chilton. Most such identifications, however, are tenuous, and the fictional element usually outweighs the factual. The fact that everyone in Oxford has his own private candidate for the prototype of the Snopes clan simply underlines the fact that Snopesism is an endemic affliction. For all these reasons, Faulkner's characters are listed here only occasionally and for some exceptional reason.

Historical characters are listed unless such identification would be absurd, as in the cases of Hitler, Mussolini, and Franklin D. Roosevelt. Faulkner sometimes uses real people to create a background of verisimilitude: Paul Rainey, Horace Lytle, and Jim Avent, in *The Reivers*, are good examples. So are various historical characters in the Civil War, obsolete politicians like Vardaman and Bilbo, and various other groups. Such characters are listed under their last names, as in any biographical dictionary, with cross-references from the form in which Faulkner actually uses the name: e.g. the entry BED FORREST will direct the reader to (Nathan) Bed(ford) FORREST.

7. Cleanth Brooks, *William Faulkner: The Yoknapatawpha Country* (New Haven, 1963), pp. 453–87; Margaret Patricia Ford and Suzanne Kincaid, *Who's Who in Faulkner* (Baton Rouge, La., 1963); Robert W. Kirk, with Marvin Klotz, *Faulkner's People . . .* (Berkeley, 1963); Harry Runyan, *A Faulkner Glossary* (New York, 1964).

Tools, Guns, etc. It is a part of Faulkner's technique that he frequently uses precise or technical details, and the reader who does not understand such matters is often at a loss. This is true not only for obsolete or little-used things like froes and single-trees, but for contemporary ones as well. Many readers, for example, have little grasp of the difference between number six and number ten shot, or between a cartridge and a bullet. Most younger readers know nothing about passenger-trains. I recently discovered that not one of fifteen graduate students in a seminar understood what was meant when Quentin Compson, describing a trip on a Pullman, says, "I dragged my pants out of the little hammock" (*S&F* 107). A general attempt is made in this glossary to explain matters of this sort, especially because ordinary dictionaries, even when they define the word in question, seldom give the information needed for an understanding of Faulkner's reference. They tell what an adze is, for example, but not how one uses it, or that dressing lumber with it had already become a primitive way of working when Cash built Addie's coffin, in the first chapter of *As I Lay Dying*.

History (and Legend). Explanations in this field are confined to the specifically Southern or local, since Faulkner frequently assumes a greater knowledge than the average reader has. The Civil War, for example, is now more a matter of book-learning than of living tradition, and names like Shiloh, Spottsylvania, and The Wilderness no longer mean much to the unaided younger reader. (They have never meant much to readers outside the United States.) The ordinary historical knowledge of the mythical intelligent reader will take care of Faulkner's Helen and Attila and Caesar's wife, but it will not suffice for his Southern references and allusions, which are here explained or expanded wherever it seems necessary.

Abbreviations of Citations, Editions Used, and Material Covered

In general, the Random House hard-cover editions of Faulkner are the basis for this glossary, since they are likely to stay in print longer and be more generally accessible, in the long run, than paperback editions. An equal sign following one of these editions indicates another edition that has the same pagination, though not necessarily an absolutely identical text.

Following is an alphabetical listing of the abbreviations used and the editions to which the citations refer. Titles are indicated for the individual short stories in *Collected Stories* and *Knight's Gambit*, but not for *Go Down, Moses* or *The Unvanquished*, since Faulkner considered them novels rather than collections of stories.

Abs.   *Absalom, Absalom!* New York: Random House, n.d. (Photographically reproduced from first printing, 1936.)

AILD   *As I Lay Dying*, new edition, corrected and reset. New York: Random House, 1964. (Collated with original manuscript and typescript.)

CS   *Collected Stories of William Faulkner.* New York: Random House, n.d. Abbreviations of the individual stories that have a Southern setting and are glossed are given after a colon, as follows:

BB	"Barn Burning"
BH	"A Bear Hunt"
Court.	"A Courtship"
Dry	"Dry September"
Elly	"Elly"
Fox	"Fox Hunt"
Hair	"Hair"
Just.	"A Justice"

Lo	"Lo!"
MGM	"My Grandmother Millard and General Bedford Forrest and the Battle of Harrykin Creek"
MV	"Mountain Victory"
Queen	"There Was a Queen"
Red	"Red Leaves"
Rose	"A Rose for Emily"
SftL	"Shingles for the Lord"
SNP	"Shall Not Perish"
TES	"That Evening Sun"
TM	"The Tall Men"
TS	"Two Soldiers"
TWBF	"That Will Be Fine"
UncW	"Uncle Willy"

Dust   *Intruder in the Dust*. New York: Random House, 1948 = Vintage Books edition, V-792.

Fable   *A Fable*. New York: Random House, n.d. (Only the stolen-horse episode, pp. 151–204, is glossed.)

Flags   *Flags in the Dust*. New York: Random House, 1973. (This is the novel of which *Sartoris* is a revised and abridged form. The numerous minor revisions are ignored in this glossary, but the extensive passages which do not appear in *Sartoris* are glossed.)

GDM   *Go Down, Moses*. New York: Random House, n.d. = Modern Library, #175.

Ham.   *The Hamlet*, 3d ed. New York: Random House, 1964. (Collated with author's typescript and first two editions, with correction of errors. Includes some changes made by author in time references to avoid inconsistencies with the following volumes of the *Snopes Trilogy*.)

KG   *Knight's Gambit*. New York: Random House, n.d. Abbreviations of the individual stories are given after a colon as follows:

Error	"An Error in Chemistry"
Hand	"Hand Upon the Waters"
KG	"Knight's Gambit"
Monk	"Monk"
Smoke	"Smoke"
Tomo.	"Tomorrow"

LiA	*Light in August.* New York: Random House, n.d. (Photographically reproduced from first printing [Harrison Smith and Robert Haas, 1932].)
Mans.	*The Mansion: A Novel of the Snopes Family.* New York: Random House, 1959.
Miss.	"Mississippi," in *Essays, Speeches and Public Letters by William Faulkner*, ed. James B. Meriwether, pp. 11–43. New York: Random House, 1965. (An essay first printed in *Holiday*, April 1954.)
Mosq.	*Mosquitoes: A Novel.* New York: Liveright, n.d.
Race	"Race at Morning," in *The Big Woods*, pp. 175–98. New York: Random House, n.d.
Reiv.	*The Reivers: A Reminiscence.* New York: Random House, n.d.
RfaN	*Requiem for a Nun.* New York: Random House, n.d.
Sanc.	*Sanctuary.* New York: Random House, n.d.
S&F	*The Sound and the Fury.* New York: Random House, n.d. (Photographically reproduced from first printing, 1929.) = 1966 Modern Library Edition.
Sart.	*Sartoris.* New York: Random House, n.d.
SP	*Soldiers' Pay.* New York: Liveright, n.d.
Town	*The Town: A Novel of the Snopes Family.* New York: Random House, n.d. = Vintage edition, V-184.
WP	*The Wild Palms.* New York: Random House, n.d. = Vintage edition, V-262.
Unv.	*The Unvanquished.* New York: Random House, 1938.
WT	*The Wishing Tree.* New York: Random House, n.d.

The following abbreviations are used for secondary works that are cited several times.

Blotner	Joseph Blotner, *Faulkner: A Biography.* 2 vols. (New York, 1974).
Brooks	Cleanth Brooks, *William Faulkner: The Yoknapatawpha Country* (New Haven, 1963).
Faulkner in the U.	Frederick L. Gwynn and Joseph L. Blotner, *Faulkner in the University: Class Conferences at the University of Virginia, 1957–1958* (New York, 1965).
Johnson	Guy B. Johnson, "Double Meaning in Popular Negro Blues," *Journal of Abnormal and Social Psychology* 22 (April-June 1927): 12–20.

Meriwether   James B. Meriwether, "A Proposal for a CEAA Edition
             of William Faulkner," in *Editing Twentieth-Century Texts*,
             ed. Francess G. Halpenny (Toronto, 1972), pp. 12–27.
Mississippi   Federal Writers Project of the Works Progress Admin-
Guide   istration, *Mississippi: A Guide to the Magnolia State* (New
             York, 1938). (American Guide Series.)
My Brother   John Faulkner, *My Brother Bill: An Affectionate Remini-*
Bill   *scence* (New York, 1963).

Other Abbreviations

adj.	adjective	*poss.*	possessive
adv.	adverb	*p.p.*	past participle
E	east	*pro.*	pronoun
i.	intransitive	*p.t.*	past tense
infin.	infinitive	S	south
m.	mile(s)	*super.*	superlative
N	north	*t.*	transitive
n.	noun	*v.*	verb
OE	Old English	W	west

Arbitrary Symbols

′ foot, feet   ″ inch(es)   ° degree(s)

The Glossary

A

a (*AILD* 183; *Town* 80; *Fable* 189): have (sometimes pleonastic). Both usages are illustrated in a single sentence of Anse Bundren: "Because if He'd a aimed for man to be always a-moving and going somewheres else, wouldn't He a put him longways on his belly, like a snake?" (*AILD* 35).—Also '*a*' (*Sart.* 72, 224).

AA (*Mans.* 295): antiaircraft (shells).

A.A.A. (*Mans.* 306; *CS:TM* 58): Agricultural Adjustment Administration.

a-aggin' (*Sart.* 225): egging (on), with the initial *a* as in *going a-hunting*.

Aberdeen (*Miss.* 33): a town in NE Mississippi 60 m. ESE of Oxford and 15 m. from the Alabama line.

Ack (*Mans.* 207). This should be Harvard slang, but Professor Harry Levin, who has been at Harvard through the 1930s into the present, tells me that he has never heard it, nor have any of the other old-timers whom he has asked. He agrees that my guess that it means "academic costume" is as good as any.

active (*Mans.* 56): Ratliff's regular usage for *actual*, as explained in *Town* 142. It is shared by Mink Snopes (*Mans.* 435).

actively (*Town* 84, 142, 248; *Mans.* 52): Ratliff's regular usage (shared by I. O. Snopes), for *actually*. See ACTIVE.

A.D.C. (*Town* 42): aide-de-camp.

adze (*AILD* 4; *RfaN* 41): a tool with a handle like that of an ax, and a curved, axlike blade set at right angles to it, like the blade of a hoe. It is used to smooth timbers and boards. The fact that Cash uses an adze to make boards for Addie's coffin indicates the primitive way of life of the Bundren family, since this type of hand-work was already archaic at the time of action of this story. The chips among which Cash stands were made by the adze.

aggravoke (*WT* 44): a blend of *aggravate* and *provoke*.

Agnes Mabel Becky (*S&F* 61; *Mosq.* 347). The most popular contraceptive early in the century was a brand of condom called the Merry Widow. It was sold in circular metal boxes, three to a box. The top of the box bore the legend: THREE MERRY WIDOWS   AGNES MABEL BECKY. The top of one of these boxes is the "bright" thing that Luster finds under a bush and hands to Quentin's red-tied suitor—which is why he comments, of her other suitors, "Damn if one of them didn't leave a track."

agoment (*Town* 255): apparently a blend of *agony* and *torment*.

aguer (*AILD* 179): ague (two syllables).

19

aguh—(*CS:TES* 301): a strange representation of the first two phonemes of *again*, as the word is cut off by Nancy's "Hush."

Ah (*GDM* 136, 138): I.

a-hickin' (*CS: BH* 78): making the sound of hiccuping (a nonce-word).

a-holt (*Mans.* 52, 54, 62): hold, in the expression "get a-holt of."

a-horseback (*AILD* 119): on horseback.

ahrn (*Mans.* 414): iron.

ahun (*S&F* 5): iron. As in AHRN, the *h* is not pronounced but merely indicates the pronunciation of the first syllable, like the exclamation *ah*.

aidge (*Sart.* 51): edge.

aihy (*S&F* 141, 142). See ERE A.

aim (*AILD* 178, 229; *S&F* 12): intend.

ain't: 1. Negative or interrogative of almost any form of the auxiliary verbs *to be* or *to have* (*Sart.* 53; *Unv.* 126; *CS:MGM* 689). This form was once perfectly acceptable and was regularly used, especially by cultivated old ladies like Miss Jenny and Rosa Millard, well into the present century, with no implication of ignorance or ill-breeding. Cf. modern British *Aren't I?* **2.** doesn't; don't (*Unv.* 5, 6, 70; *CS:Queen* 729, 743). **3.** didñ't (*CS:MV* 755).

ain't gwine skip it (*Sart.* 82): (I'm) not going to skip it; I won't fail to do it—a smarty catch-phrase of the post-World-War-I era.

aint it? (*Mans.* 20): a general interrogative formula at the end of a statement (like *nicht wahr?* and *n'est-ce pas?*). Here it takes the place of *doesn't he?*

aint only (*Mans.* 56; *CS:Dry* 170): am only.

air. 1. any (from *e'er*: ever) (*Sart.* 224; *Flags* 217). **2.** are (*Sart.* 225, 311; *Abs.* 87). **3.** is (*Ham.* 343).

airy (*Sart.* 235; *AILD* 193): any (from *e'er a*).

Akrum (*Reiv.* 303): Acheron.

Ak. W. (*Sart.* 44): evidently a plane already obsolete by the last years of World War I, but I have not been able to identify it. Jane's *Fighting Planes* is of no help. Faulkner mentions the Ak. W. again in an unpublished poem (Blotner, pp. 1131–32).

alder (*Ham.* 183): a large shrub or small tree (*Alnus rugosa*), common on stream-banks and swamp edges. The buds of *Abs.* 323 are leaf-buds, since the flowers are catkins.

Algonquian (*Miss.* 11, 13): a widespread stock of American Indians and Indian languages. As a matter of fact, the Chickasaws, Choctaws, and most of the other tribes of Mississippi were not Algonquian but Muskogian.

all-day singing (*Ham.* 128; *CS:BH* 63): a summer church festival devoted largely to hymn- and gospel-singing, with the congregation bringing lunch, which is eaten picnic-style in the churchyard.

All folks talkin' 'bout heaven ain't gwine dar (*Sart.* 42): part of the refrain of the spiritual "I Got a Robe." It is usually sung in the form "Everybody talkin' 'bout heaven ain't goin' there," though there are, of course, no definitive texts of spirituals.

alligator (*RfaN* 101; *WP* 255; *Mosq.* 277). The alligator (*Alligator mississippiensis*) does not range as far north as Oxford, and never did. In *RfaN* 101 Faulkner is speaking of the whole untamed area of what is to become Mississippi. The alligator's "lovesong" (*Mosq. 171*) is the male's hoarse bellow (*WP*264), which is audible for more than a mile. It also makes a threatening hiss (*WP* 259). Its tail is heavy and rough, and when swung sidewise it makes a dangerous weapon (*WP* 258).

alphea (*CS:Red* 322): presumably an error for ALTHEA, which is used for SNUFF-STICKS.

Althea (*LiA* 52): rose-of-Sharon (*Hibiscus syriacus*), a summer-blooming shrub up to 8' high bearing flowers of various colors (according to variety) about 3" across.

Aluschaskuna (*GDM* 341, 360). This name seems to be taken from the earlier form of the name of the Skuna River, which flows into the Yalobusha River some 5 m. NE of Grenada. A map of 1845 labels it "Loosa Schoona Cr."

ambeer (*Town* 298): tobacco-juice, as spit by tobacco-chewers. The word is a corruption of *amber*, referring to the color.

and-bush (*CS:MGM* 684): ambush.

animal crackers (*WP* 134): sweetish little cookies, in various animal shapes, sold in a box depicting circus animals in cages and having a narrow ribbon for a handle, so that it can be used for a toy handbag, etc.

animal magnetism (*AILD* 78): an old name for forces supposedly involved in mesmerism and hypnotism, and sometimes for the phenomena themselves. It is doubtful whether Cash is at all clear himself as to just what he means by it.

another hog in this wallow (*Reiv.* 108, 164): another person meddling in this business.

A.P.M. (*GDM* 292): Army Provost Marshal.

Appomattox (*RfaN* 233, 234; *CS:TM* 54): Appomattox Court House, Virginia, 75 m. WSW of Richmond, where the Civil War ended with Lee's surrender to Grant on April 9, 1865.

apron (*Abs.* 151). Farm women traditionally gather eggs and carry them to the house in their aprons.

ar (*GDM* 148): there (pleonastic in use with *that*).

ara (*Unv.* 199; *Town* 252, 253; *Mans.* 24): e'er a; any.

Aransas Pass (*RfaN* 172) an inlet on the Texas coast just above Corpus Christi Bay.

arctioned (*Town* 34): auctioned.

Arkansas (*Mans.* 278): the language, dialect, of Arkansas.

Arkansaw (*Sanc.* 244; *Unv.* 52; *Mans.* 291): Arkansas.

Armstead (*Dust* 195). See GARNETT.

arra (*Abs.* 284, 290): e'er a; any.

arr'nd (*Sart.* 107): errand.

artermatic writing pen (*CS:TS* 91, 97): fountain pen.

artillery . . . creek bottom (*Unv.* 35). The Colonel is speaking of his own artillery, not that of the enemy. His point is that if the cavalry are still around when the artillery gets to the creek, they and their horses will be pressed into service to help drag the cannon through the mud.

ary (*CS:SftL* 43): e'er a(n); any.

ash (*GDM* 319, 340; *RfaN* 101): either white ash (*Fraxinus americana*) or green ash (*F. pennsylvanica*), two generally similar trees having compound leaves and reaching heights of about 80'. Both grow in low woods and river bottoms.

Ashby (*GDM* 286): Turner Ashby, Confederate cavalry leader under Stonewall JACKSON. Faulkner's reference to him must be oral legend. He *was* killed while leading infantry (not his own regular cavalry forces) against a force of hidden Federal riflemen, but he was on regular duty at the time and the troops had been assigned to him for this mission.

askeered (*Unv.* 59): a blend of *afraid* and *skeered* (scared).

ask me another (*WP* 214): a catch-phrase growing out of a mania for general and specialized quizzes as parlor games, radio entertainments, etc. It was the title of at least one book of such quizzes.

ast (*CS:Fox* 602): asked.

astink (*LiA* 364): stinking; in a stink.

a-tall (*Sart.* 8, 80; *S&F* 381): at all. The *a* is pronounced like the name of the first letter of the alphabet, and both syllables are stressed.

Atchafalaya (*WP* 172, 240): a river in Louisiana paralleling the Mississippi and for some distance quite close to it. Its whole basin was under water during the 1927 flood. It is now used as a flood-relief channel for the Mississippi and Red rivers.

a-teelyer (*Mans.* 54, 55, 57): Montgomery Ward Snopes's attempt at French *atelier*.

Atlanta (*Mans.* 52, 60): Atlanta, Ga., the site of a federal penitentiary.

a-trodding (*AILD* 69): treading. The initial *a* is that in expressions like *a-hunting* (originally OE *on*). The form of the verb is not, I believe, standard usage, but is Cora Tull's attempt to use a biblical word that she can't quite handle.

attaboy (*SP* 246): that's the boy (a familiar formula of approval and encouragement).

atter (*CS:BH* 78): after.

Aunt (*Town* 248; *Reiv.* 34): a title of respect used, with a proper name, in addressing an elderly Negro woman.

aunty (*Sart.* 345; *LiA* 411; *GDM* 371): a respectful form of address used, without a proper name, to an elderly Negro woman.

automobiles, law against (*Town* 11, 164, 166; *Mans.* 34; *RfaN* 242). In 1916, Oxford passed a law forbidding the operation of automobiles on its streets. The law was never enforced, but remained on the books as an interesting curiosity for many years.

awda (*WP* 214): ought to.

ax (*Sart.* 24; *Unv.* 85; *Ham.* 162): ask; asked. Similarly, *axed* (*Sart.* 63; *GDM* 75; *CS:MV* 757) and *axes* (*GDM* 121, 148).

axe-morticed (*RfaN* 16). Roughly or crudely mortised with an ax. The logs of a LOG HOUSE do not need to be precisely mortised, since the spaces between them will be chinked with mud or clay anyway.

axle-grease (*Ham.* 261, 272; *GDM* 327): a thick black grease used where the wheels of wagons turn on the axles. It is also used in some forms of medication, both to keep out air and infection and as a vehicle for other medication.

axletree (*Sart.* 205, 312; *Ham.* 286). See WAGON.

B

baby buggy (*Mans.* 114): baby carriage, perambulator.

back (door) (*Abs.* 232; *GDM* 45; *CS:MGM* 674): normally the same thing as KITCHEN DOOR. For its social significance, see FRONT DOOR.

back house (*CS:MGM* 676): privy. Because of its general size and shape, it is called a sentry-box.

backing strop (*CS:TS* 95): synonym for BRITCHING STROP on the preceding page. See DOUBLE-JINTED BACKIN'-UP STROP for an explanation of the meaning here.

backin'-up strop (*Sart.* 5). See DOUBLE-JINTED BACKIN'-UP STROP.

backlog (*Dust* 10): a large log burned at the back of a fireplace. It serves the double function of holding the fire when (as here) it is not being very actively tended, and keeping an active fire to the front of the fireplace so that more of the heat will be thrown out into the room instead of going up the chimney.

back porch (*Sanc.* 41: *LiA* 220): similar to a FRONT PORCH but often smaller and used primarily as a work-area rather than for relaxation or social purposes. In farmhouses it frequently has a shelf with a pan and water for washing one's hands and face (*Sanc.* 44).

back the plow out (*GDM* 58). At the end of a row, the plow is engaged in the ground, and the plowman must pull it backward far enough to free the point before turning around.

bad-eyed horse (*Mans.* 7): not a horse with defective eyes, but one whose eyes suggest to a judge of horses that he is a vicious or dangerous animal. Cf. The Man's words to Doom: "O Sister's Son, your eye is a bad eye, like the eye of a bad horse" (*CS:Just.* 346).

baff room (*SP* 102): bathroom.

bag (of a cow) (*Ham.* 179, 187): udder.

bagging twine (*Reiv.* 296). See COTTON BAGGING.

bah——(*LiA* 291): first syllable of *bastard*.

bail (*CS:SftL* 39): the wire handle of a lantern or bucket.

bait (*AILD* 81, 110; *Abs.* 135): a feeding, meal.

baling wire (*Ham.* 289; *Mans.* 11, 190); the thin, flexible wire with which bales of hay are fastened. It is the general-purpose light wire for temporary or clumsy repairs about a farm.

balloon (*Abs.* 230–235). See KATZENJAMMER KIDS IN THE FUNNY PAPER.

balloon pants (*Mosq.* 123, 257): pants with wide legs and slightly flaring bottoms, popular in the mid-1920s.

band (*S&F* 244): mourning band, a strip of black cloth worn around the arm as a formal indication that a person is in mourning.

bandsaw (*Unv.* 224): a power-saw with a blade in the form of a continuous band running, like a belt, under tension, over two wheels. A bandsaw band (*Unv.* 163) is one of these blades, and the point of the lieutenant's sarcastic humor is that if the obliterated brands on the mules are to be passed off as TRACE GALLS, they can be explained only if old bandsaw blades have been used as TRACES.

bang, n. (*Sart.* 182; *S&F* 360): a fringe of hair cut across the forehead in a straight line.

bank-and-railroad bandits (*Fable* 162): Jesse James and his gang, who operated in this general area.

banloo (*Mans.* 62): Ratliff's quotation of Gavin Stevens's use of French *banlieu*.

banty (*Reiv.* 114): bantam.

baptisings (*Ham.* 128). Those of country Baptists, with total immersion in some creek or lake, are elaborate social as well as religious events.

barbed wire (*Reiv.* 28, 86). This barbed wire is to be used for fastening the block and tackle at the ends. Barbed wire is used because the barbs make it easy to loop it so that it won't slip, and also probably because it is readily available.

Barksdale (*Unv.* 17): William Barksdale. Though he was born in Tennessee, Mississippi "did own" him in that he had been a Congressman from Mississippi, 1853–61. He rose to the rank of brigadier general in the Confederate army, and was killed at GETTYSBURG.

bark tea (*Sart.* 151). See SASSAFRAS.

bar'l (*Unv.* 182): barrel.

barn. A barn may be anything from a small shed with a feed-room and a single stall to a large and elaborate structure, but there is a general pattern to which most barns of any size conform. Seen from the end, the outline is essentially that of the façade of a Gothic cathedral, with the HALLWAY occupying the nave; the stalls or stables, CRIBS, feed-rooms, etc., corresponding to the various chapels in the aisles; and the (hay)loft in the clerestory. The hallway has a large, square entrance, runs the entire length of the barn, and is large enough to accommodate a large wagon with plenty of clearance on both sides and the top. The stalls and other rooms have doors opening off this hallway, the stalls having dirt floors, and the cribs and feed-rooms wooden floors raised a foot or two above ground level. Cribs and feed-rooms are sometimes

built as tight as possible in a vain attempt to keep our rats, but they often
have openings in the wall just above the MANGERS (feed-boxes) on the walls
of the adjoining stalls, so that stock can be fed without having to enter the
stalls. In the place of some stalls there may be sheds for wagons, CULTIVATORS,
etc., and these are open to the outside of the barn. The loft is entered through
one or more TRAPS, or permanent openings in the floor, and each of these is
reached by means of a ladder made of slats about 1" × 2", nailed to studs on
the wall of the hallway. The loft also has a large opening in the gable at each
end through which hay is loaded into it from wagons. One may easily fall
through the rotten or loose boards of an old loft. Tommy warns Gowan about
this possibility (*Sanc.* 45), and later (*Sanc.* 90) it actually happens to Temple.
Sunbeams shining into the gloom of a barn through cracks and knotholes
produce interesting effects, especially since anyone who is there to see them
will have stireed up motes of dust. These facts explain the "yellow-barred
gloom" (*Sanc.* 45) and Benjy's perception that "the slanting holes were full
of spinning yellow" (*S&F* 13).

barrel (*Sanc.* 121: *Ham.* 165; *WP* 63): the body, trunk (chest, belly, and loins)
of a horse, cow, etc.

barrel-slat hammock (*Ham.* 350): BARREL STAVE HAMMOCK.

barrel stave hammock (*Abs.* 125, 228; *Ham.* 16): a standard sort of homemade hammock. A few inches from each end of each stave there are two wires
which are twisted (not woven) a couple of times before the next stave is put
between them. The two sets of twisted wires are then brought together and
fastened to a support at each end. The staves have enough curvature so that
the weight of a person is below the wires, and hence the hammock is reasonably stable. If straight boards were used, the hammock would easily flip over.

barren clown (*Abs.* 200); mule. Being a hybrid (jackass and mare), the mule
is sterile.

barrow-pit (*GDM* 320; *Reiv.* 65; *WP* 61): borrow pit, a pit or ditch along a
road or levee from which earth has been borrowed for fill. (This form is
probably originally a hyper-correction, formed on the assumption that
borrow pit is derived from the common unlettered pronunciation *wheelborrow*,
rather than from the verb *to borrow*.)

Basin Street (*Fable* 165): a street in the "restricted district" of New Orleans
which was open for legal prostitution from 1897 to 1917. Basin Street was the
site of the palatial brothels, as opposed to the squalid "cribs" on some other
streets. It was also a sort of center of the underworld.

basket phaeton (*Unv.* 245): a very light, four-wheeled vehicle seating two
people, with a seat made of wickerwork and hence suggesting a basket.

baskets of food (*Abs.* 211). Neighbors regularly took baskets of food to neighbors in times of serious illness or death, when they could not be bothered
with cooking. The same thing was sometimes done, secretly and tactfully,
for people in need, as is Miss Rosa. Etiquette demands that the dishes, nap-
kins, etc., be washed and returned or (if secretly given) left where they were

found. Miss Rosa's refusal to wash them is an attempt to pretend that she neither needs nor accepts her neighbors' help, even when she obviously does both.

bastud (*Unv.* 8, 86): bastard.

Batesville (*Mans.* 377): a town 25 m. W of Oxford, on the main highway between Jackson, Miss., and Memphis.

Baton Rouge (*WP* 172): the capital of Louisiana, on the Mississippi River, 130 m. below Vicksburg on an air-line, and much farther as the river flows.

Battenburg (*KG:Smoke* 29): a fictional town on the road between Jefferson and Memphis.

battercake turner (*Dust* 108): kitchen spatula.

bawn (*WT* 27): born.

bay, *v.t.* (*GDM* 8, 193): to bring to bay.

bayou-rat (*WP* 256): SWAMP RAT.

Bay St. Louis (*Reiv.* 18, 41): a town on the Mississippi Gulf coast, 50 m. NE of New Orleans.

ba'ytone (*Sanc.* 111): baritone.

bead (*Ham.* 49): the small bubbles made by shaking a bottle of whiskey. Their size, duration, etc., are indicators of the quality of the whiskey.

Beale Street (*S&F* 289, 329; *LiA* 199; *Town* 72): a street in Memphis famous as the high point of the city's low-life. Since it runs east and west, it was officially Beale Avenue until the name was changed to match the common usage. The most notorious section of the street, just off Main Street, was razed a few years ago. There is now (May 1975) a scheme to rebuild it for tourists.

bean blower (*WP* 260): a section of CANE cut between two joints, so that it is hollow for its entire length, and used as a blowgun to shoot beans, DOGWOOD berries, etc. It is a child's plaything with which one can annoy other children, but do no actual damage.

bean-pole (*AILD* 124): a pole stuck in the ground for bean-vines to climb on. A country bean-pole is usually a sapling about 1″ or more in diameter at the base and 6′ high, with the side branches cut off so as to leave stumps several inches long.

bear (*GDM* 3; *Reiv.* 20): American black bear (*Euarctos americanus*), formerly abundant in northern Mississippi. The largest males may be over 4′ high at the shoulder and weigh more than 500 1bs. Bears do not hibernate in Mississippi, as they do in colder climates. They are omnivorous, and will attack green corn (*GDM* 223).

bearded cypresses (*Mosq.* 82, 83): CYPRESSES draped with SPANISH MOSS. In the same sense, cf. "beards of moss" (*WP* 166) and "bearded trees" (*WP* 170).

bear's grease (*LiA* 237): grease rendered from the fat of bears—a standard multipurpose grease in the early days.

beat (of a county) (*Ham.* 5): an administrative district of a county. Lafayette

County has five beats, and though the lines have recently been revised, the numbering and the essential areas included have not changed. Since Faulkner's use of beat numbers is *always* wrong for the actual county, he plainly intended to avoid specific local reference. He even has a Beat Nine (*Mans.* 61) as the home of the Gowries, though in *Dust* (27, 30, 36, etc.) he repeatedly has them living in Beat Four. Actually, the Gowries are plainly indicated as living in the northeastern part of Yoknapatawpha County, but Beat Four is in the southwestern part of Lafayette County. However, Faulkner seems to be thinking in terms of the actual beats and merely changing their numbers: "five miles from town and he would cross . . . the invisible surveyor's line which was the boundary of Beat Four" (*Dust* 94) is perfectly accurate except that it should be Beat Two.

beaten biscuit (*Sart.* 26; *S&F* 358; *CS:MV* 760): a sort of BISCUIT made with slightly different ingredients from the ordinary kind. The distinctive thing about it is that the dough must be beaten vigorously for about half an hour. A rolling-pin may be used, but careful cooks like Dilsey use a special mallet (*S&F*, 358). Beaten biscuits are not really very good, but they are always appreciated because of the labor that goes into making them.

beatin'es' (*Sart.* 27): beatingest. "De beatin'es' man" indicates general astonishment and approval: "the most amazing, remarkable man."

beat one's time (*AILD* 237; *Town* 342): to intrude as a competitor into an established male-female relationship.

beat up (*Mosq.* 291): to round up, beat the bushes for (Briticism).

Beauchamp (last name of Lucas in *GDM* and *Dust*). This name should probably be given the common pronunciation of *Beecham*.

beaver (*Abs.* 45): a beaver hat, top hat, whether made with beaver fur or not.

be dawg if (*Mans.* 407; *CS:BH* 66, 68). See I BE.

bed (of wagon). See WAGON.

bed (*GDM* 42; *CS:TS* 82): to plow land so as to make alternate seed beds (rows) and MIDDLES.

Bed Forrest (*CS:MGM* 684, 686): (Nathan) Bed(ford) FORREST.

bed-rid (*AILD* 84); bedridden. *Hurt himself bed-rid* means "hurt himself in such a way that he would have been bedridden," i.e. a permanent invalid.

bedrode (*Mans.* 428): bedridden.

bed-ticking overalls (*WP* 67). Bed-ticking is made in striped patterns like the traditional convict's stripes. The overalls may have actually been made of bedticking.

beech (*Sart.* 138; *Sanc.* 3; *CS:BB* 20): American beech (*Fagus grandifolia*), growing at the foot of hills along the edges of creek and river bottoms, and often associated with springs. It is similar to the European beech (*F. sylvatica*), but has larger and more sharply serrated leaves and lighter-colored bark, and grows over twice as high (up to 100'). Beeches tend to grow just at the junction of hills and creek bottoms, and since they seek out underground water, springs frequently flow from under their roots.

beef, *v.t.* (*Ham.* 158, 202) : to slaughter for beef.

been to the bushes (*Mans.* 404) : had a bowel movement (a country euphemism). Cf. *AILD* 217.

beggar lice (*S&F* 300; *Mans.* 57; *Dust* 157) : stick tights, beggar's ticks (*Bidens frondosa*), a weed whose tick-sized flat seeds stick to the clothes of anyone who brushes against them. In Oxford they go through two generations in one season, so that they can be a nuisance both in the spring and in the fall, but April 6 (*S&F* 300) is really too early for them.

behime (*WT* 44, 56) : behind.

bejesus (*Town* 208; *Mans* 210, 217) : a vague noun-oath used in such expressions as "why the bejesus . . ." and "beat the bejesus out of . . ." It is derived from *by Jesus.* *Hell* can always be substituted for it with no appreciable change of tone or meaning.

belike (*LiA* 154) : perhaps, probably.

bell, *v. i.* (*GDM* 176, 354) : to bay.

bell, *n.* **1.** a small handbell, rung when meals are ready, standard in most Southern homes during Faulkner's era (*S&F* 345; *Ham.* 82; *GDM* 313). The bell can be heard all over the house and yard, and thus saves the trouble of notifying everyone separately. It may be called a dinner bell, breakfast bell, or supper bell when only the sound is in question, but the object itself is usually called a dinner bell (*Ham.* 282). **2.** (*Ham.* 193; *GDM* 48) : a large bell, 8″ to 1′ high, hung on a post outdoors and used on farms to call workers in from the field to meals. **3.** (of locomotive) (*Unv.* 112). Steam locomotives have, in addition to a steam-whistle, a brass bell rung by a cord extending from the cab. The bell is suspended on top of the locomotive, where it is clearly visible, "tossing" as it is swung by the cord. **4.** (*CS:Lo* 402) : a bell-pull. **5.** (*Sart.* 349; *S&F* 364–365) : a contraption of accordion-pleated paper, usually red, which opens out to form a three-dimensional bell used as a Christmas decoration.

beller (*S&F* 17, 41, 66) : to bellow.

bellyband (*Fable* 157, 191) : a strap or girth passing around a horse's body and under his belly.

belly up (*Mosq.* 274) : to belly up to the bar—i.e. press one's belly against it (an old saloon term). The extended meaning is "come to be served."

bench leg (*LiA* 307). A leg of one of the "overturned benches," or pews, had been knocked off in the commotion already, so that Christmas could pick it up and use it for a weapon.

Bend (*AILD* 176; *Ham.* 325) : FRENCHMAN'S BEND.

bent (*KG:Hand* 63) : tied, fastened (as with the knot known as a fisherman's bend).

bevel (*AILD* 74) : to cut at an angle other than a right angle. Instead of making butt-joints, with the edge of one board against the side of another, Cash will make 45° mitred joints, like those at the corners of a picture frame. Since the coffin itself is not rectangular (see Faulkner's diagram, p. 82), this process will require fairly complicated and time-consuming compound miters. This method of construction is what Cash calls making the coffin "on the bevel" (*AILD* 77).

be white a little while longer (*Unv.* 23). The meaning is that, even though old relationships are breaking up, Louvinia, as a house-servant, will have to be on the side of her master's family for a little while longer, reporting news from the black community which they need to know.

bib (*Town* 21; *CS:UncW* 236): bibcock, a stopcock with a bent-down nozzle. (An ordinary faucet is one form of bibcock.)

bib (of overalls) (*Mans.* 261, 273; *Dust* 12; *Reiv.* 7): the panel of cloth extending from the waist up to the shoulder-straps.

bib pocket (*Mans.* 434). See FOB POCKET OF HIS OVERALLS.

bicycle-racer (*Fable* 187): Henry Ford.

Big Bottom (*GDM* 173; *Town* 43): originally the TALLAHATCHIE RIVER bottom, after it has broadened out into a real wilderness. Major de Spain's hunting camp (NW of Oxford and now under the Sardis Reservoir) was in the Big Bottom. But the Big Bottom is not a fixed place so much as an idea: the untamed river bottom inhabited by big game and relatively unmolested by human tampering (*GDM* 350).

big boy (*GDM* 87,147): a smarty-contemptuous form of slang address.

biggity, *adj.* and *adv.* (*S&F* 17; *Dust* 19): brash, pompous, and conceited, or in a manner indicating brashness, etc. The idea is that of making oneself *big*.

Big Harpe (*RfaN* 5). See NATCHEZ TRACE.

big house (*LiA* 87; *Abs.* 98, 210; *Miss.* 42); the main house, where the owners of a plantation live, as distinguished from slave quarters, Negro cabins, or tenant houses.

Big River (*CS:Just.* 346, 351; *Miss.* 11, 24): the Mississippi River.

Bilbo (*Town* 37; *Mans.* 161, 301; *Miss.* 13); Theodore G. Bilbo (1877–1947), twice governor of Mississippi and three times U.S. Senator. Bilbo, like VARDAMAN, was typical of the shrewd, ruthless, rabble-rousing politician. (It is significant that the Gowrie twins, in *Dust*, were named for Bilbo and Vardaman.) Bilbo did serve a sentence for contempt of court (*RfaN* 249), but the matter was juicier than Faulkner's account implies. The paternity suit in which he refused to testify was brought against a former lieutenant of his, turned a political rival. The rumor was that Bilbo did not actually know anything about the matter and that his testimony would have meant nothing; but by refusing to testify he gave the impression both that he was protecting a former friend and present rival and that his testimony would be ruinous if he were to give it.

b'ilin(g) (*Sart.* 115; *KG:Smoke* 8): boiling.

bill (*CS:UncW* 240): the peak, beak, of a cap.

Bill Sunday (*Fable* 181): the evangelist William Ashley Sunday, usually known as Billy Sunday.

billy-O (*KG:KG* 202): almost confined to the expression *like billy-O*, meaning "to an extreme degree." The usage is more British than American.

billy sale (*GDM* 93): bill of sale.

birch (*Dust* 18): river birch (*Betula nigra*), a tree of wet lowlands growing to 80′ high and 3′ in diameter, with an irregular crown. It has the easily recognized characteristics of birches in general.

bird colonel (*Mans.* 308): full colonel, with eagle insignia, as opposed to lieutenant colonel.

bird dog (*Sart.* 34): a dog used for hunting QUAIL, either a setter or a pointer. A well-trained bird dog freezes to a point instantly when he locates a bird, since he is supposed to point it out but not to flush it or make it run. This fact explains why Jody Varner "Paused in midstride like a pointing bird-dog" (*Ham.* 317).

bird-dog trials (*Reiv.* 119): the Grand National field trials, held annually at Grand Junction, Tenn. (Faulkner's Parsham). Field trials differ from ordinary bench shows for dogs in that the dogs are judged on their performance of an exacting job rather than on arbitrary "points" of shape, color, etc.

birds (*Sart.* 330; *Mans.* 230; *Reiv.* 69). In a hunting context, this always means QUAIL. It is not even used for other game birds like ducks and doves.

bird-shot (*GDM* 324, 325): #7–#8 shot (see SHOT SIZES), for birds like quail and doves. Shooting a bear with such a load would be about like attacking a bull with a fly-swatter.

Birdsell (*AILD* 33): apparently a good make of wagon. Wood swells when the humidity is high and shrinks when it is low. A sorry, ramshackle wagon like the Bundrens' would always rattle, but not a good, tightly built wagon. Thus "a rattling wagon is mighty dry weather, for a Birdsell" means "It's evidence of mighty dry weather when even a Birdsell wagon rattles." (I am convinced that this is correct, even though I have not been able to run down any evidence of a make of wagon so named.)

biscuit (*S&F* 322, 344: *GDM* 11; *Mans.* 23): a quick bread made from flour, baking powder, salt, shortening, and milk, cut into circles about 2″ in diameter and served hot with butter to accompany the main course of a meal. *Biscuit* (like *loaf* and *pone*) is the name of an object, not of the material of which it is made. The word is sometimes used, without a final *s*, as a sort of collective plural (*GDM* 113). Biscuits are often cooked only until they are beginning to brown and the inside is still doughy. This is especially common in Negro and poor-white cooking: hence the "half-cooked biscuits" of *Dust* 13.

biscuit board (*Sart.* 38): bread board, a wide, smooth board on which dough is kneaded, rolled out with a rolling pin, and cut into small circles with a metal cutter to make BISCUITS.

bison (*RfaN* 101): the American "buffalo" (*Bison bison*). Originally it ranged almost to the Atlantic coast, but it had been exterminated east of the Mississippi by about 1825.

bit (*GDM* 8): the metal mouthpiece by which a horse is controlled. The bits which could be seen shining in the sun (*Unv.* 159) were the ends of the bits on each side of the horses' mouths and the rings on them to which the REINS are attached. If a horse can get the bit in his teeth, as Acheron did when he "had the bit" (*Reiv.* 237), it cannot be used to pull on his mouth, and he can hardly be controlled. When Ned was "at the bit" of the horse (*Reiv.* 274), he was holding the horse by the ring at one end of the bit.

bitch (*WP* 88, 93, 287): to fornicate, copulate. Since I have never heard this usage and have been unable to document it, I believe that Faulkner invented it for Charlotte.

bit-ring (*Dust* 91): a metal ring at either end of a horse's BIT.

bitt (*Town* 182): bit, mouthpiece of a pipe.

bitted (*Ham.* 214). See UNBITTED.

bitted bridle-curb (*Abs.* 139): not a standard term. *Curb* belongs with *bit*, not with *bridle.* The phrase seems to be a condensed form of something like "bridle equipped with a curb-bit."

bitterweed (*Ham.* 26): a weed 1'–2' high (*Helenium tenuifolium*) bearing bright yellow flowers and blooming in the summer and early fall. It is intensely bitter and makes the milk bitter when cows eat it. Once it is well up, they avoid it, but in the early spring they cannot single it out and milk often tastes of it.

black (*Sart.* 14): a black horse.

black-and-tan (*Dust* 5): a type of black-and-tan coonhound, usually considered to be a distinct breed.

blackberry (*Reiv.* 248; *SP* 128). See BRIER PATCH.

black blood (of Negro) (*LiA*, 205, 440). These two passages have caused some confusion. I know of no sort of folk belief that the blood of Negroes is black. Folk beliefs do not fly in the face of elementary and easily observed facts in this way. But the term *black blood* is used for Negro ancestry, just as *blue blood* is used for noble ancestry. Max is simply making a grim, heavy-handed joke: Joe told Bobby that he has black blood (figuratively); we'll check it by drawing blood from him (literally). The second passage is quite different. Certainly Faulkner does not mean, after keeping the question of Joe's possible Negro blood open throughout the book, to step in as an omniscient narrator at Joe's death and settle the matter. Words meaning "black," in many languages (including English: see next entry), can also be used in the sense of "dark," and in this usage "black blood" is an ancient literary commonplace. Homer, for example, uses it frequently: e.g. *hâma kelainòn* (*Iliad* 1. 303) and *mélan hâma* (*Iliad* 11. 98). Similarly, Ovid has "nigrescunt sanguine venae" (*Ars Amatoria* 3. 503). When Faulkner speaks of the black blood rushing out after Joe is castrated, he is simply following this literary tradition.

black-complected (*KG:Tomo.* 100): having a dark complexion.

black cotton land (*Mans*, 49): the rich black alluvial soil of the DELTA, producing excellent cotton crops, as contrasted with the poor red-clay hills of Yoknapatawpha County.

black-gum (*Mans.* 176): black tupelo (*Nyssa sylvatica*), a tree of river bottoms and swamp edges, growing to 90' high and 3' in diameter, and having bright red leaves in the fall.

blacking-box (*CS:SNP* 104): shoe-shine box.

black iron pots (*Dust* 4). See WASH POT.

Black Jack (*Mans.* 75): nickname of General Pershing, Commander-in-Chief of American forces in Europe in World War I.

blackjack (*Sanc.* 45; *LiA* 402; *Town* 369): blackjack oak (*Quercus shumardii*). Faulkner's "stunted blackjacks" (*Sanc.* 32) is misleading. As individual specimens, the trees are not stunted; the blackjack oak is naturally small, growing on poor soils and reaching a maximum height of about 30'.

black man (*Sanc.* 40, 47): man in a black suit, i.e. Popeye.

black powder (*Ham.* 218; *Mans.* 105): the gunpowder used before the invention of smokeless powder. It exploded more suddenly and violently and produced dense clouds of smoke.

blacksnake whip (*Ham.* 274; *GDM*, 278): a long whip made of braided leather.

Blackwater Slough (*Mans.* 32): a slough in the vicinity of Varner's. The name is Faulkner's invention, so far as I know.

blades of the sights (*Mans.* 86): the sharp edges of the front sights of pistols.

Blankton (*Fable* 178): Blank-Town (a nonce-word). The lawyer has asked and been told which town had the nearest big jail (pp. 176–77). Since any such town would do, the turnkey now calls it Blankton.

blind *n.* (*LiA* 73): a place of concealment, like a hunter's blind. The word may also have overtones of *blind tiger* and *blind pig*, both of which designate distribution centers for illegal liquor.

blind tiger (*Reiv.* 290): an illegal saloon or bottle-shop.

bline side (*Sart.* 5): blind side, the side of a train on which passengers are not being loaded and unloaded.

blister (*Ham.* 306): to apply a blistering ointment to a horse as a form of veterinary treatment.

block (*Abs.* 301, 307): a clog tied to an animal to impede its movements.

block signal (*KG : Smoke* 12). A railroad track is divided into blocks, usually about a mile in length, and a block signal is a semaphore-and-light signal which shows whether there is a train in that block or in the next one.

blockade runners (*Unv.* 281). During most of the Civil War the Confederacy suffered from a Union naval blockade, and many essential supplies had to be slipped through it by blockade runners, who were a daring but mercenary lot. Since they functioned well only on very dark nights, to a blockade runner "No bloody moon" (*Unv.* 282, 285) is a toast to or prayer for good luck. Blockade runners could be either the men or the ships that ran the blockade (*GDM* 310).

blooded (*CS: Fox* 590): pedigreed, pure-bred.

blooden (*AILD* 246): by blood. In using this term, Anse Bundren is not raising any questions about the parentage of any of his children, but is simply harping on the family obligation of his children to him.

bloody (*WP* 20). "Why bloody can't I?" is a vague Briticism presumably picked up by Charlotte in the cosmopolitan artistic and social circles in which she has moved. Proper British usage would require *bloody well*.

blotting paper (*AILD* 230). The usual color of blotting paper was an ashy gray with a slight tinge of blue.

blouse (*Reiv.* 66, 102): a boy's normal upper garment before boys started wearing shirts. The blouse was full at the waist above a tight waistband, and had no tail to tuck in.

blow. 1. *v.t.* (*GDM* 18): to allow (a horse) to catch his breath. **2.** *v.i.* (*Race* 182): to catch one's breath.

blow-down (*GDM* 238): an area cluttered with trees blown down by a storm. Cf. *GDM* 211.

blow in (*Abs.* 239; *RfaN* 19): to call in by blowing hunting horns.

blowing his head off (*Sanc.* 202): blowing off at a great rate. The . . . *ing one's head off* is a regular intensive, as in expressions like *yelling his head off*, and it is here used with the expression *to blow off*, with the *off* doing double duty.

blowing-off (*CS: Rose* 127): display, ostentatious ceremony.

blow the gaff (*Town* 314): to give away a secret, to let the cat out of the bag. (Originally gamblers' and carnival slang. The *gaff* is the trick or gimmick which keeps the sucker from winning, and to blow the gaff is to reveal it.)

blue-and-white daisies (*Ham.* 172): almost certainly not daisies, but any of several species of *Aster*.

bluebell (*Town* 332). This name is so widely used for such a variety of cultivated and wild flowers—almost anything with a blue, bell-shaped blossom— that it would be pointless to try to link Gavin Stevens's association with any specific plant, especially since the whole passage is erotic, rhapsodical, and literary rather than accurately descriptive.

bluebird (*WT* 77): not the mythical Maeterlinckian bluebird, but the common Eastern bluebird (*Sialia sialis*), a small thrush (about 5″–6″ long) with a bright blue back, a ruddy breast, and a white belly.

bluegum (*S&F* 84, 85; *CS: Just.* 343, 344): a Negro whose gums are blue rather than pink. In folklore he is viewed with that mixture of reverence and fear which constitutes awe. He has many strange properties, such as a fatal bite, and he is a particularly adept and powerful conjuror. I know of no exact parallel to Versh's story, but it is the general sort of tale frequently told about bluegums.

blueless guns (*GDM* 236). The metal parts of guns are blued as an ornamental finish. This finish wears off in time unless it is renewed—as it would not be on the guns of the SWAMP RATS.

bluetick(ed) hound (*Ham.* 62; *Mans.* 7, 10): a hound TICKED with blueish markings.

blump (*AILD* 148; *LiA* 274): apparently an imitative nonce-word of Faulkner's invention.

boa'din-place (*Sanc.* 176): boarding-place, here a place to live rather than a place to take meals.

board tree (*CS: SftL* 27): a tree of straight-grained, easily split wood, intended to be split up into boards or shingles. This particular tree has already been felled and cut up into BOLTS.

bobbasheely (*Reiv.* 177): apparently a somewhat fancy and flippant word for *walk* or *go*, much like *sashay*, but this is simply a guess from the context. I have not heard the word used, or found it attested elsewhere.

bob-wire (*Ham.* 31, 32; *Mans.* 48; *Reiv.* 283): barbed wire.

bofe (*S&F* 335; *Unv.* 80; *GDM* 139): both.

bogue (*Mosq.* 278): a stream, creek, river. (From Choctaw *bok*, "stream.")

bohunk (*WP* 128): a central European, especially an unskilled laborer.

boiled shirt (*Sart.* 290; *GDM* 373; *Town* 72): starched, stiff-fronted shirt.

boiled whiskey (*RfaN* 102; *Miss.* 14): presumably whiskey made in a POT STILL, in which the mash is boiled.

boiling (*Town* 333): group, batch, gang; usually in the phrase *the whole boiling*, or the even more standard *the whole* KIT-AND-BILING.

Bolivar, Tennessee (*CS: Hair* 142): a town 55 m. NNE of Memphis.

boll (*Ham.* 148): COTTON BOLL.

bollix (up) (*Mans*, 52, 131): confuse.

boll-weevil (*S&F* 235; *Miss.* 14): a small gray weevil (*Anthonomus grandis*) whose larvae infest cotton-bolls and are the most serious pest of the cotton industry. Boll weevils are estimated to destroy more than a tenth of the crop annually and to be responsible for an annual loss of over $100,000,000.

bolt (*CS: BB* 19; *CS: SftL* 31): a piece of a log, cut off square at both ends, for splitting into shingles, etc. A shingle-length bolt makes a convenient seat. In the making of homemade shingles ("shakes"), after a straight-grained, easily split tree has been felled and the top and branches removed, there are three processes. Assuming that the shakes are to be 18″ × 8″, the log will first be sawed into CUTS 18″ long. These cuts will then be split ("rived") into bolts having faces 18″ × 8″ and a depth of approximately the thickness of the original log, or varying, if one cut will make several bolts. Then the individual shakes will be split from the bolts by means of a MAUL and a FROE.

bone (*Reiv.* 118): bone of contention.

bone-buttoned cuffs (*Ham.* 324): cuffs fastened with cuff-links made of bone.

bone-gaunted (*AILD* 108): thinned (GAUNTED) down to the bone.

bone in its teeth (*WP* 65): a nautical metaphor. A boat or ship is said to have a bone in its teeth when it is moving fast enough to make a white, foamy wave under the bow. The point here lies in the application of a nautical metaphor to a truck in a flood.

bone or two in your forearm (*Reiv.* 28). One or both bones in the forearm were frequently broken in cranking cars. This happened when a cylinder fired before the piston had reached the top of its stroke, forcing the piston back down and turning the crankshaft backward. If this happened on the upward pull (and a car was supposed to be cranked with short, upward single pulls, though the cranker often got desperate and "spun" it), and if the cranker did not have a very firm grip on the crank, it would be snatched out of his hand, make a half-revolution, and strike on the back of his forearm about halfway between wrist and elbow. If the cranker had not remembered to take the car out of gear, there was a much greater danger: it could start and run over him.

boneyard. 1. (*S&F* 399): cemetery, graveyard (adolescent jocular). Luster's reply is probably a nonce-use of the word for *crap game*, where the "bones" are rolled. **2.** (*Ham.* 148): a remote place where dead livestock can be dumped.

bonnet (*Sart.* 36; *LiA* 138): a brimless hat, fastened under the chin by a ribbon. Bonnets were often elaborate affairs trimmed with lace and ribbons. An ordinary bonnet does not have the flaring, tunnel effect of a SUNBONNET. Note that Mrs. McEachern wears a bonnet when dressed for church, but when it gets too late to go to church and she is going outdoors, she changes into a sunbonnet (*LiA* 141).

bonnet (of a car) (*RfaN* 241; *Reiv.* 26): hood. One of Faulkner's Briticisms.

booger (*Mans.* 378): bogeyman, monster. This is a standard Southern usage apparently arising from a blending of *bugger* and *bogey(man)*.

boom (*Town* 83): to manipulate by means of the boom of a derrick. The watch-chain is described as being as big as a heavy logging chain. *Boom* is deliberately somewhat misapplied in *Dust* 220: since Crawford Gowrie's body is treated like a log in being tied to the running gear of a log truck with log chains, it is described as being similarly "boomed" onto the truck.

booming (*Ham.* 224, 229): a word used to designate the deep calls of bullfrogs.

boot (*Reiv.* 120): apparently betting money. The context makes this clear, but it is not standard usage.

Booth, William (*Fable* 181): the founder (1878) of the Salvation Army, of which he was the "general."

bootleg. 1. *v.t.* (*Town* 154): to provide or sell illicitly, as a BOOTLEGGER sells whiskey. **2.** *adj.* (*Mans.* 355): illicitly transported or sold.

bootlegger(-ing) (*Sanc.* 237; *LiA* 42, 74; *Mans.* 356): a transporter and seller of illegal liquor. Many people nowadays confuse *bootlegger* and MOONSHINER, but Faulkner always keeps the distinction accurate.

bor'd (*Sart.* 52, 346): borrowed.

bore (*AILD* 70): borne, endured.

bore, *v.i.* (of a horse) (*Unv.* 74; *GDM* 238; *Mans.* 39): to pull against the bit (when he is being held back) by putting the head forward and low. The word can be extended to any other animal advancing in the same position.

born. 1. *v.i.* (*LiA* 330): to be born. **2.** *v.t.* (*LiA* 371, 403; *Abs.* 339; *KG:Tomo.* 101): to see to, preside over, the birth of.

borried (*Reiv.* 146, 232): borrowed.

borrying (*Reiv.* 12): borrowing.

boss-man (*GDM* 152): a common form of address from Negro to white, even when the white is not actually the Negro's boss. In this case the night-watchman is not Rider's boss, though he is in authority at the sawmill at night.

bot (*GDM* 321): apparently a misprint for *bolt*.

bottom (*Sart.* 214, 330; *Unv.* 221; *GDM* 37): the floodplain of a creek or river, often heavily timbered and overgrown with vines and undergrowth.

bottom (*Sart.* 326; *GDM* 108): stamina, endurance.

boudoir cap (*Sart.* 24; *Town* 237; *CS:Dry* 173): a woman's cap adorned with lace and ribbons, worn over curlers, etc., or as part of a negligee.

box (*Abs.* 103; *KG:KG* 233, 234): the driver's seat of a coach or carriage.

boy (*LiA* 446): a male Negro servant, regardless of age. There is no offense intended in compounds like *yardboy*. As a form of address to a Negro or white man, it is sometimes deliberately contemptuous (*Reiv.* 172, 192), though not necessarily so (*Sanc.* 118).

brace (*WP* 67, 254): a pair of dogs leashed together. Cf. COUPLED.

brake-lever (*GDM* 321). A wagon with a built-in brake has a lever within the driver's reach which operates a brake-shoe pressing against the rim of the off-rear wheel. Wrapping the lines around this is a dangerous practice, since it means that if the team bolts, it will pull against the brake at the same time, throwing the wagon out of line and out of control.

brakeman (*Reiv.* 130, 135; *KG:Monk* 55): a man who manages the brakes and serves as general assistant to the CONDUCTOR of a train.

brake-pole (*GDM* 322): BRAKE-LEVER.

brake-rod (*Dust* 205): in prehydraulic car-brake systems, a rod making the mechanical linkage between the brake pedal and the actual brakes. Having the brake-rod snap is like having the master cylinder burst on a modern brake system.

branch (*S&F* 5; *GDM* 143): a small stream (considered as a branch of a larger stream). A typical branch will run from a spring to a creek, will be anything from a couple of hundred feet to a mile long, and will be something that an able-bodied man can jump across.

brand-blotted (*Unv.* 157): with the identifying brand-marks blotted out.

brass bucket-lids (*Ham.* 315): Ratliff's term for cymbals.

bread board (*S&F* 336): BISCUIT BOARD.

break. 1. (*Sart.* 6; *Ham.* 313; *GDM* 42): to plow, harrow, etc., a field, in preparation for planting. **2.** (*LiA* 406): to give way suddenly, as in *to break and run*. The figure is that of a team about to panic and run away.

break (a gun) (*Ham.* 229; *GDM* 56; *Mans.* 292): to BREECH.

break a leg (*Reiv.* 278): to suffer heavy losses, to go broke.

break cover (*Ham.* 96; *GDM* 14, 178): to come out of hiding, to come out into the open (a hunters' term, applied to game).

breast-yoke (*AILD* 53; *Ham.* 298, 352; *CS:Just.* 344): a piece of iron-bound wood used to support the TONGUE of a wagon or carriage. It is shaped much like a WHIFFLETREE, being about a yard long and usually slightly tapering at the ends. It is fastened to the end of the tongue by a swivel-eye at its center, and each end is suspended from the collar of one of the horses by a short strap or chain.

breathing (*Ham.* 21): slowing down in order to catch breath.

breech, *v.t.* and *v.i.* (of a gun) (*Ham.* 229): to open at the breech, for loading and unloading, by releasing a latch and swinging the rear end of the barrel or cylinder (of a revolver) upward on a pivot. Synonym: *break*.

breech-loader (*GDM* 202, 205): a gun that can be loaded at the breech, as contrasted with a muzzle-loader, in which the charge must be rammed in from the muzzle with a ramrod. At the time of "The Bear," muzzle-loaders were still in use, though breech-loaders were replacing them. The breech-loader uses "paper shells" (*GDM* 202: see SHELL) instead of loading CAP, powder, shot, and wadding separately.

breed (*WP* 217): to give birth: "I take easy and breed hard" means I conceive easily and have a hard time in labor.

breshin' (*Sart.* 236): brushing.

Brice's Crossroads (*Miss.* 17). On June 10, 1864, at this place, Gen. FOR-REST routed a Federal force over twice as large as his which had been sent against him in order to protect SHERMAN's supply lines. The site of the battle is 18 m. E of New Albany (Faulkner's birthplace), the same distance N of Tupelo, and about 50 m. ENE of Oxford.

brick coping (*Abs.* 188). The vaults of Thomas and Ellen Sutpen were made with a rectangular wall of brick a foot or two high, with a marble slab lying flat on top of it, a construction quite common in old cemeteries. I have seen one like this, complete with the small-animal entrance described by Faulkner, in an old cemetery in the north Georgia mountains.

bricks (as footwarmers) (*Abs.* 103: *Unv.* 173: *CS:MV* 756). When traveling by carriage or wagon in the winter, the gentry often kept their feet warm by resting them on hot bricks wrapped in cloth. When the bricks got cold, they would stop and have the servants build a fire and reheat them. Faulkner had seen bricks used in this way in early cars. See Blotner, p. 639.

bridal wreath (*Sart.* 169): a deciduous ornamental shrub (*Spiraea prunifolia*), often planted in borders and along driveways, where it forms a solid wall of white flowers in the spring.

bridge nail (*WP* 248): a huge (7″–12″ long) flat-headed nail used to fasten the flooring of wooden bridges to the supporting beams. The largest size would have a head 3/4″ in diameter.

bridlerein (*WT* 15): one of the REINS. They are attached to the bridle, and may be called bridle-reins, especially to distinguish them from such things as CHECK-REINS.

brier (*LiA* 402; *GDM* 325: *Mans.* 404). See BRIER PATCH.

brier patch (*Sanc.* 263; *Unv.* 69): a patch of wild blackberries (*Rubus argutus*). They have sharp, small thorns which have a habit of breaking off in the flesh of their victims. In the early summer they produce a good, edible fruit. Though the word *briers* includes all sorts of thorny, low-growing plants, a "brier patch" is regularly a patch of blackberries, since they form dense thickets 4'–7' high of the sort in which Brer Rabbit was "born and raised."

britch (*Race* 191): breech.

britching (*Reiv.* 148): breeching or breeching strap, a strap around a horse's buttocks to take the load when he is backing up or holding back on a downgrade. The meaning here is: loop the switch behind his hocks, as a breeching strap is looped behind a horse's buttocks.

britching strop (*CS:TS* 94, 98): BRITCHING. See DOUBLE-JINTED BACKIN'-UP STROP for the meaning here.

britch-loader (*Dust* 53; *Town* 79: *Race* 178): BREECH-LOADER. Will Legate's double-barreled shotgun can fire only twice without stopping to reload. It is here compared, by implication, with a repeating rifle or PUMP-GUN (both loaded from the side into a magazine instead of at the breech directly into the chambers of the barrels), which could get off far more shots without reloading.

broad hats and heeled boots (*Fable* 160). Eastern Oklahoma, like eastern Texas, is an extension of the South. The cowboy hats and boots indicate that the location is far enough west to be a part of the West.

broadhorn (*RfaN*, 104): a large, shallow-draft flatboat used for freight. The name comes from two long oars sticking out near the bow.

broke my manners (*Reiv.* 72): behaved in an unmannerly fashion, committed a breach of etiquette.

broken-backed cabin (*Ham.* 18, 72), ~**log house** (*Flags* 258): one with its roof badly sagging in the middle.

broken hair (*Sanc.* 35). The fashion was for hair to be plastered down and slick. (Sears sold a preparation for the purpose called Hair Slik.) Hair groomed this way can, of course, be actually "broken" when the slicked-down surface cracks. Cf. "breaking his hair loose" (*Sanc.* 307).

brooder lamp (*Town* 366): an oil lamp supplying heat for young chicks kept in a brooder.

brung (*Sart.* 332; *AILD* 183; *Ham.* 45): brought.

Brunswick stew (*GDM* 204): a hunters' stew in which the primary ingredient is the meat of wild game. Most people hold that squirrel is essential for the genuine article, but there are many schools of thought, and besides, the recipe depends partly on what meat is available. These facts explain why Gen. Compson is making it, "with Uncle Ash to quarrel with about how he was making it."

brush-hook (*Ham.* 192): bush-ax, an axelike implement with a blade having an edge about 10″ long, with a hooklike curve at the tip. It is used for clearing weeds and brush too large for a SCYTHE and too small for an ax.

Bryan (*Fable* 181): William Jennings Bryan.

bub (*SP* 101); a more or less patronizing form of address to a boy (an abbreviation of BUBBER).

bubber (*S&F* 137; *CS:UncW* 230): brother (a nursery-term).

buck (*GDM* 324): BUCKSHOT.

buckboard (*Sart.* 98, 377; *AILD* 80; *LiA* 232): a light four-wheeled carriage with the seat mounted on a long, flexible board connecting the front and rear wheels, instead of on a sprung body.

bucket (*Mans.* 280): helmet.

buckhead (*GDM* 293): the metal end of a wooden PLOWSTOCK, to which the SINGLE-TREE is attached. The single-tree and buck-head are joined by a CLEVIS, and the buckhead has two or more metal loops to which the clevis can be attached, according to the depth of plowing desired.

buck-nekkid (*Sanc.* 139): buck-naked, stark naked.

buck saw (*Mans.* 266): a woodcutting saw with a thin ribbonlike blade kept in tension by a wooden frame. (The modern bowsaw is simply a bucksaw in which a metal bow has been substituted for the wooden frame.)

buckshot (*GDM* 225, 247; *Mans.* 30; *Race* 190); heavy lead pellets, about 1/4″ to 1/3″ in diameter, used in shotguns for big game.

buckskin (*Dust* 171): yellowish gray (color of a horse).

buck vine (*Race* 179, 186; *Miss.* 11); a woody vine (*Brunnichia cirrhosa*) that climbs high into trees by means of tendrils. It has shield-shaped leaves about $1\frac{1}{2}$″ long, and the stems grow to $\frac{3}{4}$″ thick. It is common along the banks of creeks and rivers.

Bucyrus, Ohio (*Fable* 157–158); a town about 60 m. SE of Toledo.

bud (*Flags* 343): a familiar form of address to a man or boy.

buddy (*Mans.* 75): an American soldier in World War I.

buddy-boy (*Reiv.* 145): intimate friend, close companion.

buffalo (*Miss.* 11): American bison (*Bison bison*), a large, dark brown, hoofed animal with a huge head and a hump on the shoulders. Large bulls may weigh a ton. The bison is usually associated with the western plains, where it roamed in huge herds late in the nineteenth century, but it formerly ranged over practically the whole United States. John Bartram visited a huge buffalo-lick in north Georgia in 1773. Buffalo Hill, near Laurel, Miss., is another old buffalo-lick.

buffalo grass (*Miss.* 17): grama grass (*Boutelous curtipendula*), a pasture-grass growing in the prairies of northeastern Mississippi.

bugged out (*Mans.* 62): bulged out, bulging. Cf. "buggin' their eyes" (*Sart.* 225).

buggy (*AILD* 54: *Sanc.* 56: *LiA*, 134): a light, four-wheeled carriage. Most buggies were one-horse vehicles, but Dr. Peabody's was drawn by a team.

buggy whip (*Town* 100; *Mans.* 123, 126): a very light, semirigid whip. Because of its lightness, the butt end was weighted with lead to keep it from bouncing out of the WHIP SOCKET in which it was carried, and this loaded end made a usable blackjack.

buh——(*Sanc.* 250): not a syllable, but merely a representation of the initial *b* of *bitch.*

bulb-stacked (*RfaN* 225): having a smoke-stack with a bulbous enlargement at the upper end, as early locomotives regularly did.

bull (*Mosq.* 162): policeman, detective—here specifically the railroad police who patrol for hoboes and knock or throw them off trains.

bull bat (*Sart.* 144): common name for the common nighthawk (*Chordeiles minor*), a goatsucker (not a hawk) that feeds on flying insects, flying erratically to catch them—hence the "bullbat" name. After achieving an altitude of several hundred feet, the nighthawk swoops almost vertically, turning up close to the ground with a booming hum of the wing-feathers that is audible for up to a quarter of a mile.

bullet (*Unv.* 286; *Mans.* 337, 346; *CS:Court* 374): the projectile fired from a rifle or pistol. As a hunter and a man who knows guns, Faulkner usually distinguishes between a cartridge and a bullet, though *bullet* is used loosely for *cartridge* in *Mans.* 292. A cartridge is the unit that is loaded into the breech of a gun, and consists of a metal case, primer, powder, and bullet. The bullet is what comes out of the muzzle of a gun when this cartridge is fired. "Both bullets" (*Abs.* 33) is indicative of the fact that Sutpen's pistols, at that time, would be single-shot weapons: he had a pair of pistols, and shot both bullets, one from each. Before the modern metal cartridge, bullets were separately loaded. When Drusilla says "I can't shoot you all, because I haven't enough bullets (*Unv.* 102), she means just that. She might have enough powder and CAPS, but she does not have many bullets. The same point applies to *Abs.* 189. When the hunters find, under Old Ben's skin, "the old bullets (. . . fifty-two of them, BUCKSHOT rifle and ball)" (*GDM* 247), the word is used to include (as it usually does not) pellets and single balls fired from a shotgun.

bulletin board (*Sanc.* 170): the blackboard at a small railroad station, with train arrivals and departures painted on it, and spaces to add in chalk any information on lateness, etc.

bullet mold (*Abs.* 229). The pioneer used bulk lead to cast his own BULLETS. The usual bullet mold was made like a pair of heavy-jawed pliers, with half the cavity in which the bullet was formed located in each jaw. The jaws were held shut and the cavity was filled with melted lead. As soon as it had cooled enough to be solid, the jaws were opened and the bullet dropped out. Since the bores of early guns were not standardized, a good rifle had its own bullet mold that went with it.

bull-goaded (*Ham.* 143): extremely pestered or irritated, as by a bull (ox) GOAD.

bull pen (*GDM* 158): a large jail-cell in which a number of prisoners are kept.

Bull Run (*Abs.* 119). See MANASSAS.

bully boy (*Mans.* 267): a form of address implying a mixture of familiarity and contempt.

bumf (*Mans.* 191): official papers. (British slang. The word was originally schoolboy slang for "toilet paper," and was an abbreviation of *bum-fodder*.)

burd (*GDM* 269): buried.

burial association (*Fable* 169). The Negro burial association is a sort of mutual-insurance organization to provide money for the funerals of its members, but it often has religious and social functions as well. It is not unlike a mediaeval religious guild.

burke (*RafN* 124: *Dust* 107). The normal meaning of this word is "to strangle, to dispose of silently." It comes from the name of one of the principals in what De Quincey calls "the sublime episode of Burke and Hare"—two men who lured good physical specimens to their apartment, strangled them, and sold their bodies to medical schools for dissection. Faulkner evidently uses it to mean "to balk, to refuse to accept," but this is an idiosyncratic use.

burn (*Sanc.* 248): electrocute. Since Lee Goodwin is later burned alive by a mob for the murder of Tommy (which he didn't do), there is the possibility of a misunderstanding here; but there would be no notion of a lynching to punish a gangster murder within gangland.

burned out on (*Town* 168): BURNT-OUT ON.

burning of Jefferson (*Unv.* 216: *Town* 306; *RfaN* 46; *Dust* 50). Union troops under Gen. Andrew J. Smith burned the business section of Oxford (including the courthouse) and several of the larger homes on Aug. 22, 1864. Faulkner has the correct date in *Unv.*, but puts it a year too early in the other references.

burnt-out on (*Town* 106; *Mans.* 38, 99): jaded about, satiated with.

burn . . . up (a truck) (*LiA* 478–479): to ruin the engine by overheating. Car and truck engines required a long and careful breaking in at slow speeds. The furniture dealer had left home not intending to drive faster than 15 m.p.h. (p. 468), but he is now determined to get to some town where he can deposit Lena, even if he has to ruin his engine doing it.

burr-headed (*Dust* 19; *CS:UncW* 235, 245): having short hair standing up like the spines on a burr. (One of my classmates at Oxford High School was nicknamed Burrhead.)

Burtsboro Old Town (*Ham.* 311): an imaginary place. *Old Town* enters into a number of Mississippi place-names, indicating the earlier site of a town that has either moved or been abandoned.

burying money (*KG:Hand* 68): possibly actual cash saved up and deposited, but more likely a burial-insurance policy for which the storekeeper is the agent.

burying society (*Sart.* 373): BURIAL ASSOCIATION.

buster (*Mans.* 272, 352): a familiar-contemptuous form of address.

bust out (*AILD* 122: *CS:TS* 82): BREAK, prepare for planting. The addition of the intensive *out* may imply that the land in question is "new ground," being plowed for the first time.

bustskull (*GDM* 156: *CS:BH* 75): a regular *adj.* (and *n.*) for poor-quality MOONSHINE whiskey. (*Popskull* is a common synonym.)

but (*Sanc.* 35): evidently a printer's error for '*bout* (about). See Introduction, pp. 6–7.

Butler, General (*Mosq.* 324): Union General Benjamin Franklin Butler, who was in charge of the forces occupying New Orleans in 1862. He is chiefly remembered as the author of the notorious order that any woman showing disrespect for any Union officer or soldier should be "held liable to be treated as a woman of the town plying her avocation." Because of this order, in the South he was generally known as Beast Butler.

butter and soot (*AILD* 214): a standard homemade ointment. If there was bleeding to be stopped, cobwebs were often added to it.

butterfly. Faulkner's repeated image making Ellen Coldfield Sutpen a butterfly is quite clear and effective in its general intent but uses some strange misinformation. In spite of *Abs.* 69–70 (and *Faulkner in the U.*, p. 36), butterflies *do* have organs corresponding to stomachs, and they do not shrink before dying (*Abs.* 85). In the case of the "butterfly" discovered in the swamp by Pat (*Mosq.* 171), Faulkner was doubtless thinking of a large moth, like a luna or polyphemus, newly hatched and drying its "damp, lovely wings" in the sun. Many butterflies (the mourning cloak is a conspicuous example) are attracted to excrement and carrion (*CS:Court.* 379).

butternut (*RfaN* 18): a large tree (*Juglans cinerea*) belonging to the same genus as the black walnut and closely resembling it. Steeped in water, the hulls of the nuts made a yellowish-orange dye used by pioneers to color their homespun fabrics.

buttoned shoes (*Town* 233). "Mens shoes which buttoned" were already obsolete at the time of *Town.*

buy . . . on my word (*AILD* 127): buy on credit, charging it to me.

buy or sell (*Unv.* 259). A standard way of dissolving a partnership was for one party to name a price that he would either give or take, at the option of the other. In this case the two parties seem to have agreed on the price, with either one having the option of paying it.

buy yourself a hoop (*Sanc.* 307): an allusion, suited to the circumstances, to the slang formula of contemptuous dismissal, "Go roll a hoop," which is equivalent to "Go fly a kite," "Go jump in the lake," "Get lost," etc.

buzzard (*AILD* 14, 112: *S&F* 40): vulture. Both the turkey vulture (*Cathartes aura*) and the black vulture (*Coragyps atratus*) are common in Mississippi, the former with a 6' wingspread and the latter with one up to 5'. An experienced eye can distinguish the two species at a great distance by differences in the shape of wings and tail and manner of flight (the black flaps more and soars less than the turkey, for example). People without specific ornithological interests (including Faulkner) do not normally differentiate the two, calling them indifferently "buzzards," and many are not aware that there are two species. Hence a composite description is in order. Both species are predominantly black and sail, often at great heights, on thermal currents. Both are graceful in the air and clumsy on the ground, where they move with an awkward hopping and flopping motion. Both feed entirely on carrion, which they can locate from great distances. Vardaman never learns where they spend the night. Actually, they usually congregate in groups of 20 or 30 at well established "buzzard roosts." Like other vultures, they have bare heads and necks, "like a old bald-headed man" (*AILD* 112). They also have a habit of sitting around waiting for a sick or injured animal to die (*AILD* 14). They sit and move with a hunched posture: "It kind of hunkered up when I come in. . . . It looked around and saw me and went on down the hall, spraddle-legged, with its wings kind of hunkered out" (*AILD* 112). Buzzards often circle high in the sky: "circling and circling for everybody in the county to see what was in my barn" (*AILD* 177). This is the motion of the "coiling buzzards" of *Ham.* 192.

buzzer (*GDM* 329) : the rattle of a rattlesnake.

by dad (*CS:BH* 75) : a vague euphemism for *by God.*

by Godfrey (*Unv.* 57, 138; *Town* 56; *CS:MGM* 690) : a euphemism for *by God.*

by ordinary (*Sanc.* 151 : *LiA* 3, 113 : *Mans.* 419) : ordinarily.

by-road (*Sanc.* 6) : side road, field road.

Byron Society (*Town* 51, 310) : obviously a women's book club. It has all the earmarks of being a cover-name for the actual Browning Club, which flourished in Oxford (as did others in many other towns) in the first third of this century.

C

cabbage palm (*WP* 36, 209) : cabbage palmetto, the only native tree-palm of the eastern United States (*Sabal palmetto*), growing to 80' high and 2' in diameter, with leaf-stems some 7' long. On younger trees the old leaf-bases remain attached to the trunk, giving it a cross-hatched appearance; hence the "scaling palm trunks" (*WP* 227). Unless some imported species is specified (e.g., coconut palm), in Mississippi *palm* normally refers to this species. It is common on the Gulf coast and is the tree which gives *The Wild Palms* its title.

cabin (*S&F* 330; *LiA* 32; *CS:TES* 289); a small house, almost invariably a Negro house (see *KG:KG* 241), and especially a servant house in the backyard of a large house. It is frequently a "dog-trot cabin"—a two-room structure with an open-air hallway between the rooms (*Ham.* 219).

Cahline (*S&F* 9, 37) : Caroline.

cahy (*S&F* 231): carry. The *h* is not pronounced; it merely indicates that the word has two syllables.

ca'iage (*Sart.* 25): carriage.

caint (*Sanc.* 44, 70; *Flags* 258): can't.

Cajan (*WP* 253, 256. 260); a French-speaking inhabitant of Louisiana or south Mississippi. The word is derived from *Acadian* and is usually spelled *Cajun*.

Caledonia (*Unv.* 143): a Mississippi town about 80 m. SE of Oxford and almost on the Alabama line.

Caledonia Chapel (*Dust* 69, 220): an imaginary rural church. The name is selected to emphasize the Scots ancestry and the clannishness of the inhabitants of Beat Four.

calf rope (*S&F* 166; *GDM* 109). One child seizes a handful of another's hair (probably originally a girl's pigtail) and keeps pulling until the victim says "calf rope." From this usage, to *say calf rope* gets the general meaning of to "give in, surrender, admit defeat."

Calhoun County (*Ham.* 360): the county lying just S of the eastern half of Lafayette Co., and hence only a few miles from Frenchman's Bend.

call (*Reiv.* 128): recall.

callacanthus (*Sart.* 42)/**callicanthus** (*KG:KG* 234): Faulkner's misspellings of *Calycanthus florida*, or sweet shrub, a bush growing wild but frequently cultivated in gardens. It bears fragrant chocolate-colored flowers in early spring.

Callina (*GDM* 266; *CS:Queen* 732; *CS:Fox* 590): Carolina.

Cal'line (*SP* 170): Caroline (the formal name of Callie).

Camel (*Sart.* 45): Sopwith Camel, a fighter plane of World War I. It was highly maneuverable but notoriously unstable and dangerous to fly.

camphor (*S&F* 214; *Abs.* 26): spirits of camphor (placed on a handkerchief and used much like smelling-salts).

cane. 1. (*AILD* 134; *Ham.* 3, 222): either of two species of reeds with hard, jointed hollow stems, growing along creeks and in river bottoms. Switchcane (*Miss.* 17), or small cane (*Arundinaria tecta*), grows to about 10' high and has leaf-blades up to 8" long. Large, or giant-cane (*A. gigantea*), is, to the nonbotanist, simply a much larger version of the same thing, growing to a height of over 30' with leaves up to 20" long. It is regularly used for fishing poles, BEANPOLES, children's whistles, POPGUNS, etc. It typically grows in crowded stands and forms dense CANEBRAKES. The two species are normally not distinguished and are simply lumped together as "cane." The "snapping and hissing cane" as the hunters ride through it (*GDM* 239) refers to the snapping when stalks are broken and the hissing sound of the leaves as the riders brush against them. **2.** (*Sart.* 278, 279): the jointed stems of SORGHUM, so called by analogy with sugarcane (see 3, below). **3.** (*WP* 332): sugarcane. This is *Saccharum officinarum*, the non-native plant from which sugar is made. It can be grown in southern Mississippi and Louisiana but not in north Mississippi. That is why, when the other convicts understand *cane* only in sense 1 (above), the tall convict calls it sorghum, since that is something similar which they know. The distinction between sorghum and true sugarcane ("cane for sugar") is emphasized in *Miss.* 32.

canebrake (*Abs.* 233; *Race* 175): a dense thicket of CANE.

Canfield (*WP* 127): a type of solitaire sometimes used for gambling.

canna (*Ham.* 199; *GDM* 49; *SP* 315): a plant of the banana family, genus *Canna*, with broad green leaves and large scarlet (or sometimes yellow) flowers. It is usually grown massed in solid beds.

cannonball (*Reiv.* 198, 199, 237): a popular name for a crack express passenger-train.

can of soap (*Unv.* 169). Home-made SOFT SOAP is a viscous liquid, and hence must be kept in a container.

Canton (*Miss.* 32): a town in central Mississippi, 25 m. N. of Jackson.

cap: a detonator that sets off the charge of powder in a gun. It is fired by the percussion of the hammer. In early guns the cap was a separate object (*LiA* 281; *Abs.* 265; *Unv.* 29). See CAP AND BALL REVOLVER. In more modern guns, the cap is built into the base of the CARTRIDGE or SHELL (*GDM* 58).

Cap (*Sanc.* 33): Captain (a somewhat patronizing term of respect).

cap-and-ball revolver (*LiA* 267, 281; *CS:MV* 753): the common type of revolver in the Civil-War era. It used separate percussion CAPS. The CHAMBERS of the CYLINDER were loaded with powder and BULLETS from the front. At the back of each chamber was a raised, hollow "nipple" over which the cap was fitted. The striking hammer detonated this cap, which in turn ignited the powder. Joanna Burden had evidently loaded the pistol recently, since only two chambers were loaded, "For her and for me," as Joe says (*LiA* 270). But the pistol and caps had presumably belonged to her carpetbagger grandfather, and it is no wonder that a cap over sixty years old did not fire (*LiA* 270, 281). Faulkner knew the Civil War cap-and-ball revolver intimately. When he was a bit over ten years old, he and his brothers found an old one and managed to load it up and fire it in an astonishing manner. See *My Brother Bill*, pp. 54–57.

Cape jasmine (*Sart.* 42; *SP* 315): gardenia (see JASMINE).

Cap'm (*Sart.* 21; *LiA* 109, 269; *Mans.* 97): CAPTAIN.

captain. 1. (*LiA* 307; *GDM* 82): a vague term of respect, used to a man. **2.** (*LiA* 412): Lucas Burch's attempt to write *capturing*.

Captain Joe Thoms (*Miss.* 37). See THOMS, CAPTAIN JOE.

Captin (*CS:UncW* 243): CAPTAIN.

captive (*Unv.* 143): to capture.

captured warships with cavalry charges (*Abs.* 346). Gen. FORREST's cavalrymen captured several gunboats at Paris Landing on the Tennessee River in the fall of 1864—though not exactly by cavalry charges. Faulkner attributes this exploit to MORGAN (*GDM* 288).

carbide headlight (*CS:SNP* 105): a light worn on the forehead for night hunting. It is fueled by acetylene, which is generated by water dripping on calcium carbide.

carcasses (*Town* 84): caucuses.

Carnarvon (*WP* 239, 246): Caernarvon, La., on the eastern bank of the Mississippi, 14 m. below New Orleans. The LEVEE was dynamited here at noon on April 29, 1927, in order to ease the strain on the levee at New Orleans. This plan was announced several days in advance, and the inhabitants of the bayou country that was to be flooded were evacuated to an armory in New Orleans (*WP* 275). Faulkner follows the history of the flood scrupulously except for some chronological liberties. Actually, the Atchafalaya basin was flooded by breaks in its levees more than three weeks after the dynamiting of the Mississippi levee at Caernarvon.

Carolina wren (*Sanc.* 7): a large wren (*Thryothorus ludovicianus*) with a conspicuous white line over the eye. It is common in thickets and undergrowth and has a very loud three-note call, usually repeated four to six times without pausing, though occasionally one hears it once only (*Sanc.* 3). The song does sound mechanical "as though it were worked by a clock" (*Sanc.* 5). It is rare for Faulkner to call a bird by its official ornithological name. The point here seems to be that Horace Benbow knows the book name but has trouble recalling the popular name, *fishingbird*. It is fortunate that Faulkner gives us the identification: I have never heard this name and cannot find it attested anywhere.

Caroline (*Miss.* 16, 39): Faulkner's "Mammy Caroline Barr," to whom he dedicated *GDM*.

carpet-bag (*Abs.* 175; *GDM* 303; *RfaN* 109): a large bag made of carpet-material—a cheap type of luggage. The CARPETBAGGER derived his name from arriving with all his possessions in a carpet-bag.

carpetbagger (*LiA* 235; *Abs.* 161; *GDM* 278): a YANKEE adventurer in the South after the Civil War.

carpet slippers (*LiA* 189): house slippers made of carpet-material.

carriage- and wagon-rims (*KG:KG* 230): the tires, or rims, of carriage and wagon wheels. They are narrow metal bands heated and shrunk onto the wooden wheels. See WAGON.

Carrollton (*WP* 245, 246): a Mississippi town 40 m. SE of PARCHMAN.

carry (*Sart.* 281): to take, accompany, escort. (This usage was standard eighteenth-century English.)

cartridge. 1. (*Ham.* 277; *GDM* 58): the single unit (metal case, primer, powder, and projectile) constituting one round of ammunition for a modern pistol or rifle. (The similar unit for a shotgun is a SHELL, and the two terms are usually distinguished, though sometimes they are used interchangeably.) Cartridges are lubricated to facilitate passage of the bullet down the barrel and ejection of the empty case (*GDM* 237). **2.** (*Abs.* 265; *CS:MV* 750): a container for the powder and bullet used in a muzzle-loading "percussion" rifle or pistol. It was usually made of paper, and the percussion CAP was separate from it.

case (*Sanc.* 10, 21): a person, viewed with amused condescension or indulgent disapproval. Cf. SIGHT.

case (*S&F* 364; *Unv.* 6, 90): because. (Pronounced *kaze.*)

cash ... on the barrel-head (*Mans.* 269): a standard expression for cash demanded and paid instantly and without quibbling.

cast (*Abs.* 243): a trip made by a dog or other tracker in an attempt to pick up a trail.

cast (*LiA* 310; *GDM* 14): to cause (dogs) to seek a trail.

cat (*CS:Red* 331; *CS:Just.* 345): WILDCAT.

catacorner(ed) (*Dust* 74, 221): diagonally.

catalpa (*RfaN* 213): southern catalpa (*Catalpa bignonioides*), a tree growing up to 60′ high and 3′ in diameter. It bears profuse clusters of white flowers, marked with yellow and purple, in the spring, heart-shaped leaves up to 1′ long, and bean-shaped seed-pods even longer.

Catalpa Street (*Mans.* 277; *Reiv.* 139, 151). There is a very short Catalpa Avenue in Memphis, but it is 4 m. from the red-light district. Faulkner probably invented the name for the location of Miss Reba's brothel (its real-life prototype was on MULBERRY STREET—Blotner, p. 838), and happened by accident on the name of an actual street. He had invented MANUEL STREET for the same purpose earlier, and that is where he located Miss Reba's place in *RfaN* 141. The contradiction (unless we assume that the house was on the corner of these streets) is good evidence that the names are fictional. The fact that Ned "left us in front of Miss Reba's . . . and walked around the corner to Beale Street" (*Reiv.* 290) is conclusive proof that Faulkner did not intend the real Catalpa Avenue.

catbird (*Sart.* 169): a slender, dark gray bird (*Dumetella carolinensis*), named for its mewing scold-note, a good singer, in general has habits much like the brown thrasher and MOCKINGBIRD. Since it nests only a few feet high in dense thickets, Faulkner is in error in having Isom "hauling his overalled legs into a tree about which two catbirds whirled and darted"—presumably trying to protect their nest (*Sart.* 373).

catch (*Ham.* 307; *Mans.* 17): to conceive, become pregnant. (The opposite verb is MISS.)

cat-crib (*Reiv.* 159): rustic or small-time brothel. The word seems to be a blend of CAT HOUSE and CORNCRIB.

catfit (*Sanc.* 44): a violent fit (figuratively).

cat house (*RfaN* 141; *Mans.* 74; *Reiv.* 208): brothel, whorehouse.

cattle chute (*Reiv.* 296; *Fable* 160): CATTLE-LOADING CHUTE.

cattle-dip (*CS:SNP* 105): any of various compounds used to treat cattle for ticks and other skin infestations.

cattle-loading chute (*Reiv.* 165): a narrow cleated ramp with sturdy sides, leading from the ground up to the level of a railroad cattle-car's floor, so that when a car is placed by it, cattle or other stock can be driven directly onto or off the train.

cattle guard (*Reiv.* 61) a series of spaced planks (about 2″ × 6″) set on edge, or of steel pipes, level with a road and running at right angles to it, with a shallow ditch underneath them. Cattle will not try to cross such a device, and it eliminates the need for getting out of a car to open and shut gates.

cattycorner (*Mans.* 414): diagonally.

cattymount (*AILD* 98: *Mans.* 117; *CS:BH* 66): catamount. See PANTHER.

caught that bear (*Ham.* 70): caught the proverbial bear by the ears, i.e. got hold of something dangerous that one can't get rid of or turn loose. Ratliff is fond of this type of allusion to proverbial sayings. The GRAZED UP of the rest of this speech implies a necessity to seek greener pastures.

Cause (*Reiv.* 234): Lost Cause: the Confederacy, the Civil War.

caze (*CS:MV* 753, 755, 756): because.

ca'y (*SP* 313): carry.

ca'yin (*Sart.* 287): carrying.

C.C.C. (*RfaN* 242; *Mans.* 306): Civilian Conservation Corps, a government agency during the depression of the 1930s which set up camps for unemployed men to work on public projects such as recreational lakes, trails, etc.

Cecelia Farmer April 16th 1861 (*RfaN* 229). Faulkner's account of this inscription is a mixture of fact, legend, and invention. The name of Jane T. Cook was scratched on the window pane of a house on South Lamar St., the pane now being preserved in the MARY BUIE MUSEUM (*RfaN* 253). The story is that Jane Cook came out and berated the retreating Confederate forces and that one of them was so impressed by her loyalty that he came back when he had a chance and married her. It is a fact that Jane Taylor Cook (born 1847) married the son of Nathan Bedford FORREST, and that he had retreated through Oxford. For a concise account of the facts and legends, see E. O. Hawkins, "Jane Cook and Cecelia Farmer," *Mississippi Quarterly* 18 (Fall 1965): 248–51.

cedar (*Sart.* 169; *S&F* 67): Eastern redcedar (*Juniperus virginiana*), an evergreen with fragrant heartwood used for cedar chests and water buckets (*AILD* 10; *LiA* 142; *CS:BB* 20). Cedars shed their small needles a few at a time and gradually build up a brown blanket of them on the ground (*Abs.* 158, 190, 210). Cedar shavings, used as packing, protect things from most insects (*CS:Red* 320).

Celia Cook (*Unv.* 17). See CECELIA FARMER.

celluloid like a drummer (*S&F* 114). A celluloid collar was easily cleaned with a damp cloth and hence represented a sort of fake elegance, as compared with a starched linen collar. Drummers (traveling salesmen) habitually wore celluloid collars.

cementless chimneys (*GDM* 91). Many old chimneys were made of bricks or fieldstones with red clay between them instead of mortar. This works perfectly well below the roof, where the chimney is not exposed to rain; but when the roof of an abandoned house with such a chimney falls in, the chimney collapses fairly rapidly.

cemetery. In Negro cemeteries and, to a lesser extent, in those of poor whites, graves were regularly outlined and decorated with bits of broken pottery, old bottles, brickbats, etc. (*KG:Hand* 70). It is generally considered that these decorations have occult ritual significance, such as the "killing" of the deceased's plates and cups, and Faulkner (*GDM* 135) agrees with the *Mississippi Guide* on this point. But since flower beds, yard paths, etc., are often adorned in exactly the same fashion (*GDM* 49, 118), the degree of ritual significance is at least open to question. See Newbell N. Puckett, *Folk Beliefs of the Southern Negro* (Chapel Hill, N.C., 1926), pp. 104–07.—In *Abs.* 187 and 213–14, Luster, knowing of the earlier murder and the somber history of the Sutpen cemetery, is superstitiously afraid to go near it.

Cemetery Ridge (*GDM* 286): a ridge on the battlefield of GETTYSBURG, the scene and objective of PICKETT's charge.

center pole (*WP* 63). A haystack is regularly built around a pole in the center of it.

Central (*Mans.* 387, 391): the telephone switchboard-operator, who, in a small town, knew people's habits and friends and could usually find a person for a long-distance call no matter where he happened to be.

'cep' (*Sart.* 20; *LiA* 306): except.

chain-gang (*S&F* 288, 398; *GDM* 158; *Fable* 175): convict gang, formerly chained together when used for work on roads.

chalk-line (*AILD* 150, 153): a heavy cord used by carpenters and masons. It is rubbed on a cake of blue chalk and then pulled taut and held or tacked at the points marking the ends of, say, a horizontal line. When it is pulled back and released, it snaps against the wall, leaving a visible mark along its entire length. It is because of the blue chalk-dust on it that the chalk-line is called "the blue string" (*AILD* 154).

chamber (of a gun) (*S&F* 200; *LiA* 281): the place where a CARTRIDGE (for rifle or pistol) or a SHELL (for a shotgun) rests when it is fired. Automatic or repeating weapons put a new round into the chamber for each shot. A revolver has chambers in the CYLINDER, which rotates to bring them one by one in line with the barrel.

chameleon (*Abs.* 27). This may be simply a literary reference, but it may also be a local reference to the American "chameleon" (*Anolis carolinensis*), a graceful lizard 5″–8″ long which is common in shrubbery and runs through color-changes from light green through light brown almost to black.

Chancellorsville (*GDM* 286; *CS:TM* 54): a Civil-War battle fought May 1–4, 1863, about 50 m. N of Richmond, Va. It was here that Stonewall JACKSON was mortally wounded, by mistake, by his own forces.

chanceso (*LiA* 362): accident.

chap (*Sart.* 138; *AILD* 29, 110; *LiA* 15): child—by extension, offspring (*Sart.* 329).

chapping (*AILD* 165): breeding, producing children. Cf. CHAP.

chartered whiskey (*Mans.* 13): presumably bonded whiskey. Unless artificially colored, corn whiskey is clear, or "white," as in "white hill whiskey" (*Ham.* 133). Bourbon gets its amber ("red") color from the charred white-oak kegs in which it is aged.

Chartres and Toulouse and Dauphine streets (*RfaN* 104): streets adjoining the Mississippi River in New Orleans.

Chatauqua (*GDM* 284). Originating with Lake Chatauqua, N. Y., this term generalized to designate almost any series of (often outdoor) lectures, entertainments, etc.

Château-Thierry (*Mans.* 280): a town which played a prominent part in the Second Battle of the Marne in World War I.

Chatter Teary (*SP* 29): CHÂTEAU-THIERRY.

check-rein (*Ham.* 248, 352): a short strap used to hold a horse's head up or back.

cheekstrap (*S&F* 397): one of the side straps of a bridle, running along the horse's cheek to the BIT. Dilsey takes it to hold the horse for a moment without having to get into the surrey and take the reins, or hitch the horse.

cheer (*Sart.* 20, 310): chair.

cheese begun to bind (*Mans.* 67): see WHEN THE CHEESE . . . .

Cherokee rose (*CS:BB* 10): a climbing rose (*Rosa laevigata*) with simple white flowers about 3″ across. The savage thorns plus the fact that there are no long stems make it "unpickable," but it has a delicate fragrance and is not "scentless" (*Abs.* 295). In spite of its name, it is a native of China, but it had been taken across Asia and then (by the Arabs) across Africa and into Spain, and to the southeastern part of this country by the Spaniards, so that the English colonists found it growing here as a wild plant.

cherry (*SP* 288): maidenhead.

chew (*AILD* 85): a chew of tobacco.

Chickahominy (*Reiv.* 285). See WADE HAMPTON.

Chickamauga (*Miss.* 12, 15): a battle fought in the extreme NW corner of Georgia, Sept. 19–20, 1863.

Chickasaw (*Abs.* 34: *Ham.* 171; *GDM* 164): the Indian tribe inhabiting north Mississippi at the time of white settlement. The Chickasaws ceded their territory to the United States in 1832 and moved to Indian Territory (Oklahoma). For this reason there was little contact between whites and Indians in this section, and practically no tales or traditions of the Indians survived. Knowing this, my mother, who had done a good deal of work on Lafayette County history, once asked Faulkner where he got his Indians from. "Mrs. Brown," he answered, "I made them up." In *Town* 11, Faulkner erroneously gives the date of the departure of the Chickasaws as 1820.

chicken run (*SP* 157): CHICKEN WALK.

chicken walk (*Reiv.* 147, 149): plank with cleats nailed across it every six or eight inches, serving as a walkway for chickens from the ground to nest-boxes or to roosting poles. The term is jocularly applied here to a much larger ramp built on the same principle. The same comparison is used, with the synonym *chicken run*, in *SP* 157.

chicken-yard (*Sart.* 112): a wire-fenced enclosure for chickens. Most houses in Jefferson would have their own chicken-yards and keep their own chickens.

chico (*LiA* 233): boy (Spanish).

Chief . . . Grandfather (*GDM* 330). See RATTLESNAKE.

Childs (*Sanc.* 270): a vast chain of restaurants.

chillen(s) (*S&F* 37, 63; *Unv.* 84): children.

chilluns (*Sart.* 11): children.

chimbley (*GDM* 69; *Town* 257): chimney. In the first of these references, the meaning is really "fireplace."

chimney (*Sanc.* 52, 60; *Unv.* 44). See LAMP.

chimney-sweep (*GDM* 304): folk name for chimney swift (*Chaetura pelagica*), a long-winged, short-bodied bird that is especially conspicuous in the early morning and late evening, flying erratically and twittering as it catches insects on the wing. It nests in colonies in chimneys, making shelflike mud-and-stick nests which are attached to the sides. Elsewhere, Faulkner calls these birds SWALLOWS though they are not. They evidently had a colony at the Old Frenchman place since the chimney there was "foul now with bird-droppings" (*Ham.* 357).

chinaberry (*Ham.* 304; *Reiv.* 167): an Asiatic ornamental tree (*Melia azedarach*) often grown around houses. It has doubly compound leaves, fragrant smoky-purple flowers in the spring, and round fruits about 3/4″ in diameter that turn yellow when ripe, and fall and are squishy underfoot.

chine knucklebone (*Unv.* 161): the rounded butt-end of a hambone.

chink (*Ham.* 286): to provide a LOG HOUSE with CHINKING. Something can be excellently concealed by putting it between the logs and chinking over it.

chink (*WP* 128, 187): Chinese.

chinkapin (*Unv.* 13): Allegheny chinkapin, or chinquapin (*Castanea pumila*), a small species of chestnut, seldom growing over 30′ high.

chinking (*AILD* 4; *CS:MV* 748, 749): material used to fill the chinks between the logs of a LOG HOUSE or similar structure. The traditional chinking is red clay, but mortar is sometimes used.

chipmunk (*Ham.* 160): Eastern chipmunk (*Tamias striatus*), an attractive, striped, golden-brown ground squirrel about 10″ long. It is not common in Faulkner's country, which is about the southern edge of its range.

Chippeway (*Miss.* 13): an Indian tribe living N and W of Lake Superior. It was from their territory that Jacques Marquette and Louis Joliet set out in 1673 and explored the Mississippi River to about the mouth of the Arkansas, thus traversing about the northern third of the boundary of what is now Mississippi. Actually, their party consisted of five men in two canoes.

Chi (pronounced "shy") **syndicate** (*Mans.* 86): Chicago gang of murderers.

chitterlings (*CS:Court.* 372): small intestines (usually of pigs), cooked and eaten.

chock (a wheel) (*AILD* 150): to put a wedge, stone, log, etc., under it in order to keep it from rolling; to scotch it.

chocks (*GDM* 143): wooden wedges driven under the logs at the edge of the bed of a log-truck, to keep them from rolling.

Choctaw (*Abs.* 101; *RfaN* 21; *Miss.* 12): the tribe (and language) of Indians immediately to the S of the CHICKASAWS of Faulkner's country. Faulkner's Indians are largely the creatures of his fantasy, and he doesn't bother about petty details like making The Man a Choctaw chief (*CS:Just.* 344) when he should have been a Chickasaw.

choker (*S&F* 381): hand-choke on a car.

choke strop (*Ham.* 16): choke strap, a strap fastened at one end to the bottom of a horse's collar, passing between the front legs, and fastened at the other end to the belly-band. It keeps the collar from riding up on the horse's neck to where it can choke him.

chomp (*Reiv.* 205): champ, chew.

chop cotton (*Sart.* 141; *AILD* 123; *GDM* 33; *RfaN* 50): to thin out (and incidentally to weed) a new stand of cotton with a hoe.

chopping block (*Sart.* 107; *KG:Tomo.* 103): a piece of wood, usually a section of a log, used in chopping and splitting wood. Small pieces to be chopped are laid or held on the block; large pieces, to be split, are stood up on the block or leaned against it. The block serves two purposes: it stabilizes and supports the wood that is being cut, and it keeps the ax from going into the ground and being dulled by sand or stones. Chopping and splitting are not the same thing. Chopping is across the grain, and splitting is with the grain.

Christmas Day, *1865* (*Town* 288). This is apparently chosen simply as an approximate date for the complete end of the antebellum world, but the choice may be influenced by the fact that the 13th Amendment to the Constitution, abolishing slavery, was proclaimed on Dec. 18, 1865.

Christmas gift! (*Abs.* 105). If I say this to you on Christmas Day before you can say it to me, you owe me a gift. This custom has always been more of a game than a fact, the flow of gifts not being materially affected by it. The "white men and youths . . . giving nickels and dimes and quarters to negro lads who shouted 'Chris'mus gif'! Chris'mus gif'!' as they passed" (*Sart.* 349) would not have shouted it first to the lads, or, if they did, it would have been a joke and they would not have expected to collect. This is plainly seen in Bayard's childhood memories which follow this passage: Simon would let the children catch him, but no gift is mentioned as a consequence. Similarly, when Quentin Compson catches a Negro with the phrase, he proceeds to tell the Negro that he'll "let him off this time," and gives him a quarter (*S&F* 107).

chuckle (*CS:MV* 753). When a CAP-AND-BALL REVOLVER is cocked, it makes a series of clicks something like the sound of a ratchet. Causing it to make this sound seems to be what is meant here by *chuckle*.

Chuesday (*SP* 8): Tuesday.

chunk. 1. (*S&F* 26, 343; *GDM* 151; *CS:TES* 290): to throw; to throw at. **2.** (*S&F* 33, *Dust* 233): to build up (a fire) by putting chunks of wood on it.

Churchill Downs (*Fable* 191): the track in Louisville, Ky., on which the Kentucky Derby has been run every May since 1875. Racing at Churchill Downs is to a horse what playing at Wimbledon is to a tennis-player—a symbol and evidence of high standing in the sport.

church singing (*WP* 338): ALL-DAY SINGING.

churn (*S&F* 243; *Abs.* 146; *GDM* 79): a cylindrical container in which milk is churned into butter. It is made either of wood or of stoneware (usually the latter), and comes in various sizes. The common four-gallon size stands about 16″ high and is 10″–12″ in diameter. The churn has a lid with a hole in the center a bit larger than a broomstick. The dasher is a stick some 3′–4′ long with two crossing pieces of wood, each slightly shorter than the inside diameter of the churn, fastened across one end. The milk is put into the churn; then the dasher is put in, and then the lid is put on, with the stick of the dasher projecting up through the hole. Then the dasher is moved up and down, so that the pieces on the end agitate the milk. When the butter begins to "come" (i.e. to cohere in small lumps), this fact can be known by the feel and the sound of the churn (*CS:SNP* 103). A churn makes a handy container for water or any other fluid (*Reiv.* 267).

cicada: any of a group of large insects (up to 2″ long) with transparent, heavily veined wings. Some of these are the so-called seventeen-year locusts of the genus *Magicicada*. (The Southern species have a life cycle of thirteen, not seventeen, years.) The larva develops underground, sucking the sap from the roots of trees, for thirteen years. Then the immature insect crawls up a tree trunk and splits down the back, and the mature insect emerges. The old brownish translucent shell is left clinging to the bark of the tree, and is the "transparent and weightless shell" of *LiA* 34. The males make a very loud, shrill, strident sound which can be almost deafening when there are large numbers of them (*Sanc.* 162, 179; *KG:Tomo.* 97), and a few of them may survive into the fall (*CS:TM* 54). Both the use of pesticides and the cutting of forests have greatly reduced the number and noise of cicadas in recent years. The "dog-day locusts" (genus *Tibicen*), with life cycles of two to five years are generally similar to those with longer life cycles.

'cide (*Univ.* 105, 131): decide.

cinch strop (*Race* 186, 187, 191): GIRTH STRAP, saddle girth.

circuit rider (*LiA* 229): a preacher who makes a regular circuit of country churches, preaching at a different one each Sunday.

Citizens Council (*Reiv.* 169): White Citizens' Councils, organized in opposition to the desegregation decision of the Supreme Court. Faulkner is lining up irreconcilable pairs, and contrasting the truculent conservatism of these councils with the gushing liberalism of Eleanor Roosevelt.

civilian-military act (*LiA* 426): the National Defense Act of 1920, which reorganized the National Guard and made it essentially a branch of the regular army.

Cla'ence (*Sanc.* 169): Clarence.

clamb (*Sart.* 62; *S&F* 357): to climb.

clam up (*LiA* 470): to shut up (like a clam).

Clarksdale (*Mans.* 104, 377): a DELTA town 20 m. from PARCHMAN on the main road to Memphis, which is 65 m. farther on.

claw-hammer coat (*Town* 72): tail-coat, formal "tails." The name comes from a comparison of the tails to the nail-pulling claws of a hammer.

claybank (*Unv.* 9, 84; *WP* 250): brownish yellow (as color of a horse). The term is conventional and not an actual comparison, the clay of north Mississippi being generally much redder than this.

clay chimney (*GDM* 277): a chimney actually built up of pure clay, without bricks or stones. Such a chimney cannot survive long, of course, in a rainy climate.

clay-daubed fieldstone chimney (*Dust* 10). The chimney was probably put together with clay instead of mortar. It also had, in the fireplace, an inner lining of clay.

clay-eaters (*CS:Fox* 587): a term of contempt for poor rural whites. It comes from the fact that one of the symptoms of a heavy infestation of hookworms is a craving for clay, which is frequently actually eaten.

clay mortar (*RfaN* 41): not a special type of mortar, but simply clay, used as mortar.

clay road and sand (*Sanc.* 132). The hills are clay, but the creek bottom and the area below the spring are sand. This fact is used several times: "down the clay road and into the sand" (*Sanc.* 132): "the sand ceased" (*Sanc.* 6).

cleated ramp (*Reiv.* 146): an inclined plane made of planks with cleats nailed across them at right angles to serve the double purpose of holding them together and giving solid footing to a person using it.

clematis (*Mans.* 264; *CS:Elly* 214): any of several ornamental flowering vines, the commonest being the white-flowered *Clematis paniculata*. The vines appear to be dead in the fall and winter, but grow very fast in the early summer.

clevis (*GDM* 293): an approximately U-shaped piece of metal with holes through the ends and a pin which is passed through these holes and a hole in another object placed between the prongs, as a means of coupling. A clevis often has a 90° twist in it. Clevises come in various forms and sizes, but in this context Faulkner doubtless refers to the small twisted clevis used to connect a BUCKHEAD to a SINGLE-TREE.

Click. Snick-cluck (*Race* 190). See PUMP GUN.

climb the wheel (of a wagon) (*Ham.* 362). Since the bed of a wagon is high off the ground and the wheels are high, a lady is likely to get in by stepping up onto one of the more-or-less horizontal spokes of the wheel.

close-coupled (*Dust* 17): SHORT-COUPLED.

clost (*Sart.* 235): close.

clubhouse (*CS : Hair* 141): almost certainly an error for *courthouse* because: (1) there is no clubhouse in the story, nor was there one in Oxford which could be meant: (2) the courthouse yard in Oxford was the place where idle men amused themselves PITCHING DOLLARS; (3) Faulkner always locates this activity in the courthouse yard (*Sart.* 167; *Sanc.* 157, 160), even in the entirely fictional town of Charlestown, Ga. (*SP* 112).

clumb (*LiA* 306; *Ham.* 44; *CS:SftL* 29): climbed.

Coahoma (*Miss.* 23): a village about 60 m. S of Memphis and a few m. N of Clarksdale. It is a few miles E of US 61.

coal house (*RfaN* 266): a small house in the back yard (usually 8′ or 10′ square) for storing coal.

coal oil (*S&F* 142; *Ham.* 17, 62): kerosene. It is used not only as a fuel for lamps and lanterns, but as an all-purpose solvent and medicine about the farm, for disinfecting wounds, delousing heads, cleaning excess or old grease from machines, and as an internal medicine, with various additions. In *GDM* 53, 58, the coal oil is to be used by a lynch-mob to burn Lucas.

coasters (*Sart.* 348): various types of toy wagons used by children for coasting down hills.

coat sweater (*Town* 233): cardigan, a sweater buttoning up the front.

cob pipe (*Sanc.* 168: *LiA* 419; *Ham.* 6). See CORN-COB.

cob stopper (*GDM* 147). see CORN-COB

cock (a gun) (*Unv.* 29): to draw the hammer back until it catches, so that a pull of the trigger will release it and fire the gun. The hammer of an old-style percussion musket had to be pulled back against a strong spring. It was too strong for the fingers of Bayard and Ringo, and that is why Bayard had to use the weight of his body to cock it.

cocked hammer (*LiA* 267). See SINGLE ACTION PISTOL.

cockle-burr (*Ham.* 287; *CS:Red* 333): the spiny seeds of either of two species of *Xanthium*. They are distributed (and make nuisances of themselves) by sticking to clothing and to the hair of dogs, the manes and tails of horses, etc.

cock of the hammer (*Mans.* 416): the position of the hammer when the revolver is cocked. When the trigger was pulled and the hammer fell, this reflected point of light disappeared—"flicked away." It is also possible that, in an unorthodox usage, Faulkner is referring to the curved extension of the hammer, into which the thumb is hooked to cock it, as the "cock of the hammer."

Cockrum (*Unv.* 63): a Mississippi town about 40 m. from Oxford, between it and Memphis, though not on a main route.

coffin (*AILD* 75): the regular and ancient name for the box in which a person is buried. The modern *casket* (originally a small and elegant jewel-box) is simply a morticians' euphemism. The old coffin was the shape shown in Faulkner's diagram (*AILD* 82). The head went toward the shorter end, so that the shoulders were at the widest part; but Addie Bundren was put in "head to foot" (*AILD* 83) so that the widest part would accommodate the flared-out bottom of her wedding dress.—The coffin of a baby's funeral (*Ham.* 145) would be carried on someone's knees because a still-born infant, or one that lived only a day or two, would normally be buried quietly without such trappings as a hearse.

coffin money (*CS: TES* 308): burial insurance.

cold meat (*Sart.* 44): easy prey.

Cold Water (*GDM* 264): Coldwater, Miss., a town in the DELTA 40 m. NW of Oxford.

cole (*Sart.* 113; *CS:Fox* 587): cold.

collar (*LiA* 137, 343). The collar was normally a separate unit from the shirt, and was fastened to it by studs or collar-buttons, so that the collar could be changed more often than the shirt. It could also be left off for comfort or convenience when it was not needed, Cf. *collarless* (*LiA* 230, 324; *Ham.* 6).

collar (of a horse or mule) (*Sart.* 278; *GDM* 78; *Reiv.* 84); a heavily padded oval of leather which fits around the animal's neck and against the shoulders. Most of the pulling is done against the collar through various attachments, according to the type of harness.

collard greens (*Dust* 13); greens made from collards (the plural is usually used). The collard is a variety of kale growing on stalks. Collards are typically a Negro and poor-white food.

colonel (*Town* 10, 137; *KG:Monk* 59): often a purely honorific title going with a purely honorific position on a Southern governor's staff. Also handed down as a hereditary title among the descendants of Confederate officers. Faulkner's great-grandfather was actually a Confederate colonel, but he mentions Mammy Callie Barr "calling his grandsire 'colonel' " (*Miss.* 16).

color (*LiA* 470): apparently "signs, appearances," though the usage here does not fit any standard meaning of the word. In Bret Harte's "The Luck of Roaring Camp," when a group of prospectors are looking at a newborn infant, they make remarks including "Mighty small specimen" and "Hasn't more'n got the color." Both of these are gold-hunters' jargon, *color* being tiny specks of gold in the pan, too small to collect, but indicating the possibility of larger dust or nuggets. Since both Bret Harte's and Faulkner's passages deal with the appearance and age of an infant, I would guess (though of course there is no proof) that, consciously or unconsciously, Faulkner took over the word from Harte, intending the phrase to mean "Not if I know the signs," "Not if I'm any judge of appearances."

colored-picture charts (*CS:SftL* 40): gaudy illustrations of biblical scenes, etc., of the sort that were widely used for church decorations and Sunday-school prizes.

colored waiting-room (*Sart.* 350): the separate waiting-room provided for

Negroes at railroad stations, hospitals, etc., during the time of racial segregation.

Columbia, Tennessee (*Ham.* 55): a town some 200 m. NE of Oxford.

Columbus (*Mans.* 325; *Miss.* 33, 35): a Mississippi town 90 m. SE of Oxford and almost on the Alabama line.

columns (*Unv.* 267; *Ham.* 213; *Mans.* 366). Columns are an essential part of all but recent Southern houses, simply because the climate demands a porch, and columns are required to support its roof. Like other architectural features, they are more or less fitted to the size and pretensions of the building. Wash Jones's shack had its porch, just as did Col. Sartoris's mansion, and both had the roof supported in the same way. A minor element of elegance is required before the supports are called columns—crude ones are called posts (*Abs.* 287; *Ham.* 12).

colyums (*Town* 352; *Mans.* 154): COLUMNS.

come into the bridle (*Reiv.* 237): to begin to move or pull forward,

come up (*Ham.* 19, 50): a command to a horse to get moving or to move faster.

commissary (*Abs.* 229; *GDM* 78; *Mans.* 92): the store operated by a plantation for its tenants. It may issue clothing, tools, etc., as needed, on a slave plantation. Later, it sells on credit to SHARE-CROPPERS, against their share of the crop—sometimes at reasonable and honest interest and sometimes at exorbitant rates, depending on the character of the owner. It may serve a double function: the Virginia commissary in *Abs.* 235 supplied the slaves free and exacted "exorbitant credit" from the poor whites.

commonality (*Sart.* 25): commonalty, the common people.

commonist (*Mans.* 93, 243, 414): ignorant version of *Communist*.

companionate marriage (*Sanc.* 172): a system of trial marriage for young people proposed by Judge Benjamin Lindsey in 1927. It imposed the conditions of childlessness and divorce by mutual consent, unless or until a permanent union was contracted. The idea was widely discussed, and the term for it inevitably degenerated into a loose designation for any sort of liaison or affair.

company room (*GDM* 285): guest room.

compress (*Town* 319). See COTTON COMPRESS.

Compson's Creek (*RfaN* 220): Burney's Branch, a stream 5/8 m. E of the Oxford courthouse, crossed by Miss. 6 the same distance E. of South Lamar. It would flow through the eastern part of the Compson's square mile.

comvenient (*WT* 47): convenient.

conduck (*WT* 54): conduct.

conductor (*Sanc.* 165: *Reiv.* 130, 136): the man who is in command of a train, as a captain is of a ship. One of his duties is the collection of tickets and fares from passengers. When there is a separate Pullman conductor, the man in charge of the whole train is called the train conductor (*SP* 15). The conductor calls the stations for the passengers shortly before the train arrives at them

(*KG:Monk* 48). He also waves his hand (or a lantern, at night) to the engineer to signal that the train is ready to start (*Mans.* 35).

Confed bank note (*Unv.* 207). By this time the Confederacy had fallen and Confederate bank notes were utterly worthless.

Confederate monument (*Dust* 49). Every Southern county seat has its Confederate monument. The one at Oxford is in front of the courthouse, facing down South Lamar—and there has been a good deal of wit expended on the spectacle of a Confederate soldier with his back to the north (*RfaN* 240). This is the monument at which Luster turned the wrong way, throwing Benjy into a bellowing panic (*S&F* 400).

Confederate Park (*Mans.* 285–286): a park on the bluff overlooking the Mississippi River in Memphis, between Jefferson and Madison avenues.

Confedricy (*CS:MGM* 686): Confederacy.

Confed'rit (*Unv.* 137): Confederate.

confer (*S&F* 123): Deacon's attempt at *defer*.

congress boots (*Mosq.* 67): high, elastic-sided shoes for men, popular in the early twentieth century.

conjure (*AILD* 184; *S&F* 38): to put a spell on, literally or figuratively.

conscripted levee gangs (*WP* 28). In real emergencies, all able-bodied men may be forced by public opinion—backed up by shotguns, if necessary—to work on the levee. In the flood of 1937, a reporter from Memphis (which is safe on a high bluff) went down into the Mississippi DELTA to do a story on conscripted levee gangs. After he had piled sandbags for eight hours and the crest of the flood had passed, he was allowed to go home and write his story.

Consolidated (*CS:TS* 81, 82): consolidated school, a name used when local rural schools began to be abandoned for big complexes to which students were bussed.

contrack (*Town* 244): contract.

contracted stage (*GDM* 276): a stagecoach operating on a regular schedule.

convict camp (*Ham.* 220). Convict labor was frequently leased by the state to private individuals who were, of course, free to hire other labor as well. Mink was a hired laborer here, not a convict (see *Ham.* 236).

cookin' place (*Sart.* 290): a place where one is employed as a cook, a job as a cook.

cooling tub (*Town* 37): a tub of water used by a blacksmith to cool (and temper) hot iron. This is the "tub" of *Ham.* 64.

cool out (*Reiv.* 185): to exercise (a horse) gently while he cools off after strenuous exercise.

'coon (*Sart.* 121, 286; *Sanc.* 69; *GDM* 171): raccoon (*Procyon lotor*). The full name, with the initial *rac*—, is used only by pedants and zoologists. The coon is a stocky animal with a bushy, ringed tail, a black "mask" on the face, and a general grayish-brown color. The average weight is about 20 lbs., the maximum, 50 lbs. A coon has black paws that look and are used very much like human hands (*Mans.* 415). Coons are hunted with dogs, which must be good fighters as well as good trailers and runners, since a big male coon is a match for several dogs. When a coon takes refuge in a hollow tree, he is smoked out (*KG:Smoke* 32).

coon hide (*Univ.* 88, 213). Coon hides (or any others) are nailed to the barn door, partly to dry out, but also as hunting trophies and as warnings to other vermin. This is what the Yankees might have done to Bayard and Ringo, and what these two eventually did to Grumby.

coon-hunting (*GDM* 337, 353): a deliberate equivocation on the two senses of *coon*: (1) raccoon and (2) Negro.

Coop (*Sanc.* 28): a collective student name for Ricks and Ward Halls, the two women's dormitories at the University of Mississippi at this time. They were on the site now occupied by the Ole Miss Union. The name comes from the idea of a chicken-coop. The *oo* is pronounced like the *oo* in *took*.

cooter (*GDM* 8; *Mans.* 291, 406, 429): slider, any of several species of turtles of the genus *Pseudemys*, especially *P. concinna*. These are turtles with broad, flat shells, typically about 1' long and 8" wide. They are often seen sunning on logs in sloughs and rivers.

copper (*S&F* 157): copper cent.

copper snake (*CS:Just.* 357). Since this snake is evidently dangerous, the copperhead, or highland moccasin (*Agkistrodon mokasen*) is doubtless meant. It is a copper-colored pit-viper with darker saddles on the back, and usually lives on high ground. Adults measure $2\frac{1}{2}'$ to 4'.

cops and robbers (*Dust* 132): a children's game of make-believe which, like cowboys and Indians, has no set rules and is improvised as it goes.

Co'pul (*SP* 171): Corporal.

corduroy, *v.t.* (*Reiv.* 81): to make (a road through mud) roughly passable by laying poles or logs split into halves side by side across it.

Corinth (*Abs.* 339; *Unv.* 5, 24; *Miss.* 15): a town in NE Mississippi, near the site of the Battle of SHILOH. There was also a Battle of Corinth, Oct. 3–4, 1862.

corn (*Mans.* 13; *CS:MV* 757; *Race* 197, 198): CORN WHISKEY.

corn bread (*Sart.* 21, 330; *LiA* 23): a kind of bread made from corn meal, shortening, baking powder, salt, and water. A richer variety substitutes milk for water and adds eggs and sugar. A primitive fisherman's variety consists of corn meal, salt, and water, cooked in a SKILLET. There are many variants, but proper corn bread is never crumbly or sweet, as are most Northern and restaurant imitations of it.

corn cakes (*LiA* 231): pancakes containing kernels and juice of fresh corn.

corn-cob: the round central shaft of an ear of corn, to which the individual grains are attached. A corn-cob is typically about 1" in diameter and 8" long. It is very light when dry, and very rough. Since there is no important use for corn-cobs, there are always plenty of them around barns (*Sanc.* 91). Broken into halves (they break easily), they can be used as stoppers for JUGS (*Sart.* 138, 142). Hollowed-out sections of them are used for rustic—and some commercial—pipes (*Sanc.* 168; *Town* 182, 223). The impotent Popeye uses a corn-cob as the instrument with which to rape Temple Drake (*Sanc.* 276, 280).

corncrib (*RfaN* 7): a CRIB specifically for the storage of corn. It may be fastened shut by a heavy plank sliding in or dropped into slots on either side of the door (which opens to the outside). Such a fastening has, of course, no effect on possible thieves; its purpose is to keep the livestock from learning to open the crib. Such a bar would, however, make it impossible to force the door open from the inside.

corn nubbin (*CS:SftL* 39): a stunted or undeveloped ear of corn.

corn pone (*Sart.* 98): a broad, flat piece of CORN BREAD, either rectangular or circular. A pone is an object, not the material of which it is made. Thus *pone* is to *corn bread* as *loaf* is to *bread*.

corn shucks (*Sart.* 319): SHUCKS.

corn-silk (*Ham.* 323): the fibers (like silk thread) growing out the end of an ear of corn.

corn whiskey (*Sanc.* 261; *Mans.* 231; *CS:UncW* 236): MOONSHINE whiskey, "white lightning." Though bourbon is made from corn, the term normally refers to moonshine whiskey only, even when bonded bourbon is legally available.

co'se (*Sart.* 208): (of) course.

co't (*Sart.* 236): court.

cotch (*CS:BH* 79): caught.

cotton bagging (*Unv.* 155; *Reiv.* 271): not bagging *of* cotton, but bagging *for* cotton: the coarse hemp or jute fabric used on the outside of COTTON BALES. It is so loosely woven that it is called "bagging twine" in *Reiv.* 296.

cotton bale (*Abs.* 197). The COTTON GIN compresses the ginned cotton into bales with jute bagging and metal strapping, weighing some 500 lbs. each.

cotton boll (*Ham.* 142): the pod which bears the fiber and seed of cotton, and which opens when it is ready for picking.

cotton compress (*Unv.* 173; *WP* 65): a place where cotton intended for distant shipment is compressed much more heavily than can be done at an ordinary COTTON GIN. However, the term is also used for the part of an ordinary gin that compresses and bales the ginned cotton.

cotton gin (*Sart.* 129; *Abs.* 50; *Unv.* 234): a mechanized processing-plant for separating the fibers of cotton from the seed and compressing the fibers into bales. It is normally housed in a fairly large building with walls and roof of corrugated sheet-iron. A wagon loaded with cotton is driven onto scales, weighed, unloaded by a suspended SUCTION PIPE, and then weighed again.

cotton house (*Sart.* 340; *AILD* 3; *LiA* 311): a small house in the fields or by a road, used for storing cotton between the time when it is picked and when it is taken to the gin. A typical cotton house will be about 10′ square and have a sheet-iron roof.

cotton-mouth (moccasin) (*Ham.* 91; *CS:Red* 330, 334): a dangerous venomous snake (*Agkistrodon piscivorus*) which lives in or on the edge of water and swamps and attains a length of 6'. The name comes from the dead-white lining of the inside of the mouth and the snake's habit of opening the mouth wide when confronted by an enemy. See also MOCCASIN. The "sluggish thick serpent" which Pat harried with a switch (*Mosq.* 171) was presumably a cotton-mouth: one of the harmless water snakes would be spryer and more easily alarmed.

cotton pen (*Unv.* 189): COTTON HOUSE.

cotton pickers' sacks (*KG:KG* 158). See COTTON PICKING.

cotton picking. Cotton was, until recently, picked by hand into a long, narrow white bag or sack which was dragged on the ground by the picker as he moved down the row of cotton (*AILD* 25–26; *Ham.* 149). Cotton pickers employed for the job were paid by the hundred pounds picked, not by the hour (*Mans.* 371), and when the Negro tells Mink that he is paying "six bits," this is understood to mean that he pays 75 cents per hundred pounds. Cotton must be dry when picked, and the general lack of dew during the cotton-picking season is an advantage (*Mans.* 403).

cotton sack (*Unv.* 200): the long, narrow sack into which a cotton-picker puts his cotton. The standard sack is 29" wide and from 4.5' to 10.5' long. It is dragged down the rows behind the picker.

cotton-seeds (*Sanc.* 208): Temple Drake's error for COTTONSEED-HULLS. She neither knows nor cares about such rural matters.

cottonseed-hulls (*Sanc.* 80, 197). After cotton has been through the COTTON GIN, the cottonseed oil and cottonseed meal are removed from all the seed not kept for future planting. Then the outside casings of the seeds (hulls) are ground up coarsely to be used as stock feed. Cottonseed-hulls are gray and springy and are very comfortable to lie on.

cotton shed (*Miss.* 28): COTTON HOUSE.

cotton spindles (*Ham.* 172): spindles of textile mills, usually made of DOG-WOOD because the firm, close-grained wood has little tendency to abrade the thread.

cottonwood (*GDM* 40): eastern cottonwood (*Populus deltoides*), a tree of low-lying land, with large, toothed, roughly triangular leaves. It grows to a height of 100' and a diameter of 4'.

Council of Dancing Rabbit (*RfaN* 106): the council leading to the Treaty of Dancing Rabbit Creek (1830), by which the Choctaws sold to the United States all their Mississippi lands remaining after the treaty of DOAK'S STAND (1820).

country, the (*Ham.* 9, 11, 34; *RfaN* 42; *CS:BB* 5): not the nation or even the state, but the community, in a large sense. When a man "leaves the country" he simply goes far enough to get away from the people who know about him. The deer "leaving the country" (*Race* 179) left the area where there would be any hunting.

county town (*Miss.* 11): county seat, a town which is the governmental capital of a county.

coupled (*GDM* 14): leashed together in pairs. Since Chaucer's day this has been the standard way of taking dogs to the field.

courtjury (*LiA* 283). When a jury is trying an important case and must be kept together and locked up at night, it is evidently put up at Mrs. Beard's; hence the jury, as a unit, may be passing through her hallway.

Court Square (*Mans.* 286–87; *Reiv.* 141): a small park in Memphis, on South Main St. between Jefferson and Madison avenues. It is only a short block from CONFEDERATE PARK.

Cousin John (*Unv.* 220). Drusilla is actually John Sartoris's first cousin once removed, but that is not the point. There are two possible points, but they are not mutually exclusive. (1) Since Aunt Louisa is insisting that Drusilla and John be married, she doesn't want the kinship emphasized. (2) *Cousin* has so often been used as a euphemism for *lover* that the use of the term could compromise Drusilla even more than her riding in John's cavalry troop has already done.

covey (*Ham.* 172): a group (usually 10–30) of QUAIL. They pair off to breed in the spring, and assemble into covies in the fall and winter.

cow's horn (*Sart.* 281): a hunting horn 1′–2′ long made by cutting off enough of the tip of a cow's horn to open up the interior cavity so that it can be blown with lip-vibration, like a bugle or trumpet. It is slung over the shoulder on a cord. There are no special horn-calls or signals. The horn simply provides a sustained, far-carrying sound, and when the dogs hear it they are supposed to return to the hunters.

crabapple (*LiA* 137): southern crabapple (*Malus angustifolia*), a small tree (up to 30′ high) bearing profuse fragrant pink flowers about 1″ across in the early spring, and fruits about the same size later on.

cramp (a wheel) (*Ham.* 353; *Reiv.* 244, 259): to steer the horse or team as far to one side as possible, so that the front wheels are jammed against the body of the wagon. This makes it impossible for a sudden start of the team to throw or injure a passenger in the act of getting in. Since the bed of a wagon is high, it is frequently entered by climbing over a wheel, using a horizontal spoke like the rung of a ladder, and it is especially important, of course, that the wheel not turn while this is being done. This is how Lena gets into Armstid's wagon (*LiA* 9). He does not cramp the wheel because he has hold of the reins and apparently has complete confidence in the steadiness of his team and his control over it. A BUCKBOARD has a step for getting in, but Ratliff cramps the wheel for Varner (*Ham.* 26) because he is not himself in the buckboard holding the team.

crane (*CS:Red* 338): in common usage, a heron. A "white crane" could be a common egret, a snowy egret, or (in late summer) an immature little blue heron.

craned silk and satin (*CS:Rose* 125): silk and satin curtains hung on drapery cranes. These were curtain-rods mounted much like the old fireplace-cranes for cooking-pots, so that the draperies could be swung forward to the window or back from it. (I have not found this use of *crane* listed in any dictionary, but have confirmed it from old hardware catalogues.)

crank (*CS:Fox* 603). Early, hand-cranked cars had a crank permanently installed at the front of the car, in line with the crankshaft of the engine.

crape myrtle (*Sart.* 25; *LiA* 52): a small tree of Chinese origin (*Lagerstroemia indica*), growing to a height of about 30'. It has profuse masses of small pink flowers throughout the summer. (Bred-up varieties are also blue, white, etc.) It is a common yard-plant and often marks the site of a former house.

crawfish (*Town* 38): crayfish.

craws (*Sart.* 279): crops (of birds).

creakwheeled and limpeared avatars (*LiA* 5). The first epithet refers to the wagons in which Lena rode; the second to the mules that pulled them.

Creek (*CS:Lo* 396): a southeastern Indian tribe, one of the "five civilized tribes," living largely in Georgia and Alabama, but having some contact with the CHICKASAWS.

crepe-myrtle (*SP* 196, 209): CRAPE MYRTLE.

crib (*S&F* 25, 168; *Sanc.* 81, 95; *Abs.* 153): a room in a BARN, usually for the storage of corn, often built as tight as possible in an effort to keep out rats. A crib may also be a separate small building (*Ham.* 17).

crick (*GDM* 264, 267): creek.

cricket (*S&F* 186; *Sart.* 41; *Sanc.* 179). There are various species of grass and tree crickets, and they produce various sorts of songs and chirpings. Almost any unidentified insect-sound at night is likely to be attributed to crickets. The best-known species, and the one that Faulkner probably usually has in mind, is the common field cricket (*Acheta assimilis*), which lives throughout the United States and is prized by fishermen for bait.

crimp (*CS:MV* 749): not used here in the technical sense applying to ammunition. These are Civil War CARTRIDGES made of paper and containing both powder and bullet. The "crimping" apparently consisted simply of flattening one end of the paper cartridge so that it would stand upright.

crimp (*Sanc.* 9). The most plausible of several underworld meanings seems to be "a cheat."

critter. 1. (*AILD* 65; *Sart.* 224): a horse. **2.** (*Sart.* 226; *LiA* 469; *Ham.* 202): any other creature, including a human being.

crittur (*Sanc.* 66): CRITTER (2).

croaching (*Abs.* 37; *WP* 284; *Mosq.* 294). This word is a mystery. In *WP* it seems to be an aphetic form of *encroaching*. It is not a standard word, and dialect dictionaries give nothing helpful. In *Abs.* and *Mosq.*, Faulkner seems to be using it to mean something like "cracking and peeling off in flakes."

crokersack (*Unv.* 101, 173; *Ham.* 41; *Mans.* 284): tow sack.

crooked (*S&F* 332): one syllable: *p.p.* of *v. to crook*. This is the standard method of carrying an "arm-load" of wood. Cf. "Philadelphy . . . over at the woodpile, stooped, with an armful of wood already gathered into the crook of her elbow (*Unv.* 4–5).

crop-duster (*Mans.* 254); one who dusts or sprays crops with insecticides from a plane.

crope (*Sart.* 63): crept.

cropper (*Mans.* 90, 91): sharecropper. See SHARES, FARMING ON.

cross-cut saw (*Ham.* 236): strictly speaking, any saw made to cut across the grain, as contrasted with a rip-saw, which cuts with the grain. In general usage, though, a cross-cut saw is a two-man saw with a blade 5'–6' long and a handle at each end, used for felling trees and cutting logs into sections. One does not literally "swing" his end of such a saw; the verb here is used in the sense of "manage, take care of."

Crossman County (*Dust* 104, 115, 188): Faulkner's name for Pontotoc Co., lying on the eastern border of the southern two thirds of Lafayette Co., of which Oxford is the county seat. Chick Mallison's fantasy about Miss Habersham being carried through four counties by the flood of traffic (*Dust* 188–89) uses fictional names for the counties, but is otherwise accurate. Oxford (Jefferson) is in the middle of Lafayette (Yoknapatawpha) Co., which is an approximate square. (All the county lines involved in this passage run due north-south or east-west.) Pontotoc (Crossman) Co. is another square of about the same size, to the E, but its northern border is about two-thirds of the way up Lafayette Co., and hence its southern third is below Lafayette. Calhoun (Mott) Co. and Yalobusha (Okatoba) Co. both lie S of Lafayette, with the north-south boundary between them striking at about the middle of the southern boundary of Lafayette. The southwestern corner of Pontotoc takes out what would be the northeastern corner of Calhoun (exactly as Wyoming does with Utah). Miss Habersham's fantasy ride follows a square course. From Oxford she goes due E across Lafayette Co. and into Pontotoc Co. Then she turns S and continues into Calhoun Co. Here she turns W and crosses the line into Yalobusha Co., where she heads N into Lafayette Co. and straight on to Oxford.

cross my heart and hope to die (*WT* 39): a child's solemn asseveration that he is telling the truth. Crossing the heart was presumably originally making the sign of the cross over it, but in north Mississippi, at least (where practically no one knows how to cross himself anyway), a child making this affirmation simply draws an X over his heart with his right forefinger. The second part of the phrase is elliptical: "I hope to die if I am not telling the truth."

cross-tie (*Unv.* 254; *KG:KG* 237): one of the timbers laid at right angles to the line of a railroad track, to which the rails are fastened by spikes.

cross-tie it up (*Fable* 196): tie a horse up with ropes running in several directions, so as to immobilize it completely.

crow-bait (horses) (*Unv.* 107–08, 139; *Ham.* 285): horses good only for carrion to attract crows into range for shooting.

crum (*Mosq.* 257): a vague slang term for a person considered to be a misfit, or inadequate, or simply not "with it." The newer *square* is a rough equivalent.

The *n.* has practically disappeared, but the *adj. crummy* survives as an epithet of vague condemnation.

C.S.A. (*Reiv.* 74) : Confederate States of America.

cub (*WP* 88) : to work as a novice (cub) reporter on a newspaper.

cucklebur (*Mans.* 57) : COCKLE-BURR.

cuckolry (*Town* 24) : Mr. Harker's attempt at *cuckoldry.*

cud. 1. (*AILD* 91) : the food regurgitated from a cow's first stomach for a second chewing. **2.** (*Abs.* 135) : anything similarly chewed (by a "brute") : e.g. Wash Jones's chew of tobacco.

cuh—— (*Sanc.* 257) : the first syllable of *couldn't* (*say*). The *u* is pronounced as in *full.*

cu'i's (*Sart.* 232) : curious, strange.

cuiser (*S&F* 366) : curiouser, stranger.

cullud, *adj.* (*Sart.* 62, 64) : colored, Negro. Until fairly recently, Southern Negroes preferred to be called colored folks.

cultivator (*AILD* 180; *S&F* 235; *LiA* 7; *Mans.* 26) : any of several types of mule- or tractor-drawn implements used for cultivating plants after they have come up and reached a fair size.

Cumberland Gap (*Abs.* 189; *RfaN* 7) : a pass through the mountains, on the main route of the pioneers moving from the Atlantic seaboard to the west. It is located almost at the junction of Virginia, Tennessee, and Kentucky.

Cunnel (*Sart.* 2, 20; *CS:Queen* 728) : Colonel.

cup towel (*Dust* 108; *CS:MGM* 674; *SP* 123) : dish towel.

curb (*Sart.* 121; *Mans.* 39; *Dust* 91) : an attachment to a horse's BIT enabling the rider to produce great pressure on the mouth by a relatively slight pull on the reins. Also, a bit so rigged. It is used to control unruly horses.

curdled (of milk) (*Ham.* 29) : separated into curds and whey. Ratliff has already used the standard metaphor that Ab Snopes is soured. Now he carries it one step further, since milk first sours and then curdles.

curl-papered (*Ham.* 211) : having the hair in curl-papers—strips of paper which were formerly used much like the various elaborate plastic rollers of today.

curry (a horse) (*Unv.* 10) : to clean and rub with a CURRY-COMB.

curry-comb (*Sart.* 51; *AILD* 174; *Abs.* 45) : a comb made up of several serrated metal plates, used to groom horses. When Simon calls his hoe a curry-comb, he implies that the edge is badly nicked—and that hence he will have to sharpen it a long time before he can be expected to use it.

cur'us (*WT* 57) : curious, peculiar.

cuss. 1. (*AILD* 37; *Abs.* 282; *Unv.* 81) : to curse. "Cussed him quiet" (*CS:BH* 67) means "cursed him into silence." **2.** (*CS:MGM* 683) : a curse. *I don't give a cuss* is a euphemism for "I don't give a damn" (*S&F* 23). **3.** (*LiA* 446, 476) : a person viewed with affectionate or amused derogation.

cussin (*Sart.* 97) : cursing, swearing.

cussing (*Abs.* 282) : a bawling-out, a calling-down. Wash Jones certainly knew enough of the Sutpen household and of upper-class manners to know that it was inconceivable that Ellen would actually curse Sutpen.

cuss word (*Race* 175): oath, piece of profane language. (In popular use this term often includes obscenity as well as profanity.)

customers serving themselves (*Ham.* 25). Customers in country stores were often trusted to serve themselves and pay for what they bought, without any check from the proprietor. At a country store in Oglethorpe Co., Georgia, in the 1960s, I was talking with the owner when several customers (white and black) came in. I told him that he had better leave me and see to them, but he said they could see to themselves. They got what they wanted, rang it up and put the money in the cash-register (making change if necessary), nodded to the owner, and departed.

cut (*CS:SftL* 31, 35): a section of a log sawed off square at each end, the length being determined by the purpose for which it is to be used. See also BOLT.

cut and run (*KG:Tomo.* 99): to get away quickly.

cut-bank (*Ham.* 45): the bank of a cut. In *Sart.* 165, it is the deep railroad cut just south of the railroad station in Oxford. The old power-plant was on the town side of the railroad at the beginning of this cut.

cutdown underwear (*LiA* 143, 145). The underwear had been bought for McEachern and then cut down to fit Joe approximately.

cute (*AILD* 179): shrewd and devious.

cut-out (*Sart.* 149; *Town* 58, 195; *CS:BH* 71): a device operated from the driver's seat which lets a car's exhaust bypass the muffler and emerge directly into the air, making an unholy racket. Cut-outs were widely used on early cars, until they were generally outlawed. They are still sold by some dealers in accessories. The "unmuffled engine" of *Sart.* 118–19 is due to an open cut-out. Manfred de Spain's cut-out was operated by a pedal on the floor-board of the car (*Town* 59, 60).

cut-over (*Race* 188): an area that has been logged (cut over) recently enough so that the effects are still obvious. This particular area had presumably been logged several years before, since it is now grown up in dense thickets (*Race* 186).

cut the pot for the house kitty (*Mans.* 69): take a part of the stakes in a gambling game as the share of the house, i.e. the casino, dealer, or whoever sponsors and operates the game.

cutter (*CS:BB* 16): colter, a blade fastened to a plow-beam, serving to cut the ground ahead of the plowshare and to cut vines, grass, etc., which would otherwise foul the plow.

cutting (*Sanc.* 30): cut. The cut through which the railroad runs just S of the station at Oxford is the deepest on the entire line between Chicago and New Orleans. The bridge over it is on University Boulevard.

cyar (*Sart.* 87): car.

cyarpet-baggers (*Sart.* 22, 235): CARPET-BAGGERS.

cylinder (*S&F* 200): the cylinder of a revolver, which holds the cartridges and revolves to bring them one by one into line with the barrel and under the hammer or firing-pin. Some revolvers have a hinged frame so that the barrel and cylinder swing up as a single unit for loading; others (like this one) have a rigid frame and a catch which can be released so that the cylinder is swung out to one side for loading. The revolver in *GDM* 56 is of the hinged-frame type, as indicated by the use of the verb BREAK. The chamber at the top of the cylinder, directly under the hammer, is often left empty, as a sort of safety, so that an accidental blow on the hammer cannot fire the gun. When the gun is cocked or the trigger is pulled, the cylinder is automatically rotated so that it brings a cartridge under the hammer. In most revolvers the cylinder rotates counterclockwise, as seen by the shooter, but this direction is not invariable. This fact explains why Lucas, handling an unfamiliar weapon, puts the empty chamber at the bottom, "so that a live cartridge would come beneath the hammer regardless of which direction the cylinder rotated" (*GDM* 56). Mink Snopes (*Mans.* 415) has tried out his revolver and knows which way the cylinder turns. Hence, when it misfires on his last cartridge, he raises the hammer slightly to disengage the turning mechanism, and knows which way to turn the cylinder by hand to bring the same cartridge back under the hammer for another try.

cypress (*Sanc.* 3; *Unv.* 221; *Ham.* 3): baldcypress (*Taxodium distichium*), a tree of river bottoms and permanent swamps. Old specimens grow to a height of 125′ and a diameter of 7′. The base is flared and buttressed, and the shallow root-system produces "knees"—woody knobs or spires which rise anything from a few inches to several feet above the normal surface of the water (*SP* 311; *Mosq.* 174). Being very resistant to rotting, cypress makes excellent shingles (*Ham.* 17). Though deciduous, it is a conifer and has needles instead of leaves (*Mans.* 104).

cypress knees (*CS:Red* 328). See CYPRESS.

D

da——(*CS:TS* 91): the beginning of *damned*, which is suppressed out of deference to the ladies.

daddy longlegs (*Reiv.* 181): harvestman: any of a number of species of spider-like insects with very long, thin legs, belonging to the Order *Phalangidae*.

Dagoes (*Ham.* 151): Italians.

dam'f (*Mosq.* 256): damned if.

damp towsack (*GDM* 21, 144). Evaporation will keep something wrapped in a damp towsack cool, on the same principle as that of a desert water-bottle.

Dancing Rabbit (*Miss.* 33). The Treaty of Dancing Rabbit Creek (1830), by which the CHOCTAWS ceded their remaining lands in Mississippi, was negotiated at a meeting held between the two prongs of this creek, in what is now Noxubee Co., Miss. There is no town or settlement called Dancing Rabbit.

dandelion (*Ham.* 200): the common European weed, *Taraxacum officinale.* Faulkner's "burrs of dandelion blooms" is a strange designation for the spherical heads of parachutelike seeds which follow the flowers and which children love to blow, scattering the seeds.

dang (*Sart.* 23): euphemism for *damn(ed).*

Dan Patch (*Reiv.* 233): a famous coal-black harness horse (a pacer), who sold for $60,000 in 1903. The next year he cut his own world record for a mile by a quarter of a second to 1:56 flat. In 1905 he claimed a new record of 1:55¼, but since this was made under special conditions, it was never officially recognized. It stood unofficially until Billy Direct set an official pacing record of 1:55 flat in 1938. Dan Patch became a sort of popular hero and was a great drawing-card at tracks and shows.

dar, *adv.* (*S&F* 120; *GDM* 136, 379): there.

dark lantern (*WP* 25, 248): a lantern equipped with a shutter which can conceal the light when it is not in use.

darky (*S&F* 116, 126; *Unv.* 126; *GDM* 375): Negro—an indulgent and affectionate term, not a contemptuous one.

darning egg (*Ham.* 33; *Town* 61; *Dust* 138): an egg-shaped piece of porcelain which is slipped inside a sock, etc., to facilitate darning.

das (*Abs.* 215): that's.

dashboard (of a wagon) (*LiA* 321): the plank forming the front wall of a wagon bed.

dasher (*CS:SNP* 103). See CHURN.

dash pocket (*CS:TWBF* 272). The vertical board at the front of a carriage, which prevented dirt and mud thrown up by the horse's hoofs from being scattered over the driver and passengers, is the dashboard. It often had a pocket in it that served the same general purposes as the glove compartment in a car.

dass (*GDM* 152): that's.

dassent 1. (*AILD* 25; *Town* 260; *Mans.* 263): dare(s) not. **2.** (*Town* 81): did not dare.

Dasso (*Sart.* 216): That's so.

dast. 1. (*S&F* 393; *Unv.* 199): to dare. **2.** (*Mans.* 385): dared.

dat ere (*CS:MV* 757): that there, that.

day coach (*Sanc.* 163; *Town* 359, 371; *Reiv.* 198): a railroad passenger-car without sleeping arrangements, in which people traveling at night sleep as best they can.

Deacon, the. Quentin comments on this Negro parasite on Harvard students: "his manner gradually moved northward as his raiment improved" (*S&F* 120). His language does the same. The speech on p. 120, with things like "hit'll be done got cold dar" (it will have already gotten cold there), shows an exaggerated Southern Negro idiom, but it takes him only two pages to get to a condescending, almost British schoolmaster "my boy" (pp. 122, 123). His language is a deliberate pastiche skillfully combining servility and pomposity.

Dead-eye Dick (*Ham*. 308): a dead shot, an expert marksman. Since the term has western associations, Ratliff applies it satirically to the Texan who auctioned off the ponies.

dead-fall. 1. (*Ham*. 159; *GDM* 193; *Miss*. 37): a trap made with a log between two rows of stakes. One end of the log is raised and supported by a device triggered to drop the log on an animal when he pulls at the bait tied underneath it. The usage in *GDM* 216, when Sam Fathers "made a dead-fall" of the door of the corn-crib to catch Lion, is peculiar. A dead-fall would have been built to fall on Lion and crush him. What seems to be meant is that Sam rigged an arrangement like that of a dead-fall, by which the door would fall to and fasten itself when Lion, inside the crib, tugged at the bait. **2.** (*CS:Fox* 598): a gambling or drinking establishment.

decking (*CS:SftL* 39): in the roof of a house, the parallel planks, with spaces between them, which run at right angles to the rafters, and to which the shingles are nailed.

decorious (*Mans*. 146): decorous.

deef (*S&F* 60): deaf.

dee-neweyment (*Mans*. 117): dénouement.

deep-barreled (*Unv*. 245). See BARREL.

dee-po (*Sart*. 5; *Town* 365: *CS:TS* 89—also *deepo*, *Town* 33, 101): depot (meaning railroad or bus station).

deer (*Abs*. 39; *GDM* 3): Virginia deer, or white-tailed deer (*Odocoileus virginianus*), which, in various subspecies, ranges from southern Canada to Peru. In flight its raised short white tail ("scut," *WP* 176) is conspicuous. Deer have sharp hooves which can be used as dangerous offensive weapons (*GDM* 164).

deer thongs (*CS:Red* 322, 324): thongs cut from deer-hide.

deir'n (*S&F* 372): theirs.

Delsarte-ish (*Sanc*. 261). François Delsarte invented a once-popular system of exercises, etc., including elocution, which were supposed to produce grace and charm—hence the application of the *adj*. to the phony diction of long-distance operators.

delta (*S&F* 292; *Sanc*. 15; *GDM* 335): a frequently misunderstood term. In the geological sense, the Delta of the Mississippi is the land that has been built out into the Gulf of Mexico by silt carried by the river and deposited at its mouth. This is a relatively rare, technical usage. The Mississippi delta, or simply the Delta, is that part of the flood-plain of the river which lies in the state of Mississippi. It is roughly lens-shaped and extends from the point almost on the Tennessee line where the bluffs swing away from the river to the point where they return to it just north of Vicksburg, giving an area almost 200 m. long and some 60 m. wide at its widest point. This is flat land with rich black alluvial soil and many bayous, sluggish streams, and oxbow lakes. It is traditionally cotton country farmed in large plantations, first by slaves, then by sharecroppers, and now by large corporations using a high degree of mechanization. Both in terrain and in way of life the delta is quite different from the red-clay hills of Yoknapatawpha (cf. Faulkner's "Delta Autumn," in *GDM*, and Eudora Welty's novel *Delta Wedding*). *Sanc.* 15 refers to the Indian mounds in the delta. In some places the hills give way to the delta gradually, but in others the transition is sudden, and one can tell to within a foot where the hills stop and the delta begins (*GDM* 335, 336). Faulkner illustrates the delta schematically with an (inverted) capital Greek *delta* (*GDM* 343).

den (*Abs.* 245): to stop for the night, "hole up," like an animal retiring to its den.

deny (*Abs.* 284): to refuse (to do something).

depot (*S&F* 254; *Sanc.* 33; *LiA* 339): railroad station.

Depot Street (*Abs.* 209): the old name for what is now Jackson Ave. in Oxford.

deppity (*Sanc.* 305): deputy (sheriff).

derringer (*Sart.* 17; *Abs.* 338; *Unv.* 268): originally a .41-caliber pocket pistol with a 3″ barrel, made by Henry Deringer (note difference in spelling). The word soon generalized to a designation for any short-barreled, large-bore pocket pistol. Most derringers had one or two barrels, but three-barreled ones, like Col. Sartoris' (*Sart.* 91), and even four-barreled ones were manufactured. On the other hand, "John's got two shots in the derringer" (*Unv.* 237) sounds as if the colonel's derringer was an ordinary double-barreled one.

des (*S&F* 363, 374; *Abs.* 215): just.

deseyer (*CS:MV* 763): these here, these.

despair (*Ham.* 291, 292). I have never heard this use of the word, nor found it attested in any glossary or dictionary. But my colleague, Mrs. Tyus Butler, tells me that about 1920 she had an old Negro nurse who had been brought up near Griffin, Ga. (about 40 m. S of Atlanta), who frequently said of someone: "He ain't got no more to spare than to" do something foolish. The word to be understood after *more* was something like *sense, gumption,* or *brains*. I feel certain that this is the expression intended here, and that *to spare* was mistaken for *despair* somewhere along the line of transmission.

despaired (*Mans.* 274): desperate.

dey (*Sart.* 63, 64): there (expletive).

dickey (*Ham.* 200): a detachable or fake shirt-front.

diddle (*Ham.* 143, 201): to have sexual intercourse with, to screw. Also, in a figurative sense, to cheat, swindle (*Mans.* 59).

didies (*Mans.* 332): diapers.

different breed of cat (*S&F* 250): different sort of person, horse of another color.

digger (*Mans.* 21, 22): post-hole digger.

dinner (*Ham.* 265, 350; *GDM* 302; *SP* 226): except on very formal occasions, the noon meal. This usage is made unmistakable in the reference to Belle Mitchell's afternoon teas: "It had taken Belle some time to overcome Jefferson's prejudice against a formal meal between dinner and supper" (*Flags* 167–68).

dinner horn (*GDM* 9): a horn used to summon people to dinner.

dip (*AILD* 17; *LiA* 12): to take or use snuff.

dipper (*AILD* 11; *Sanc.* 51; *Unv.* 169): a cup on a handle, used for drinking from a spring or a well-bucket. Traditionally it is made from a GOURD, but it may also be of tin, with a metal or wooden handle.

dirt dobber (*Mosq.* 234): dirt dauber, mud dauber. A wasp of the tribe *Sceliphronini*. It makes a sort of nest of clay or mud in a sheltered place, and the pupae develop in it. When the adults emerge, they have to make holes in the nest through which they come out.

dirt farmer (*Unv.* 55; *Ham.* 115; *Town* 344): a farmer who does his own field-labor, instead of having it done by slaves, sharecroppers, or hired hands.

dirt-floored (*KG:Smoke* 5): unfloored. The cabin was built directly on the ground, so that the ground formed its floor.

Dirty Spoon (*Mans.* 192): Greasy Spoon, a generic name for a small, poor restaurant.

disc (*KG:KG* 239): a disc-harrow or disc-cultivator, which breaks up clods or cultivates the soil by rolling a gang of sharp steel discs over it.

dishing (wheels) (*Ham.* 364). When a wagon-wheel is made, it is deliberately "dished," i.e. made with one side concave. This is the side toward the wagon, and the structure of the wheel is such that it is straightened into one plane by the addition of weight. See Eliot Wigginton, ed., *Foxfire 2* (New York, 1973), pp. 118–19, 122–23. But the wheels of these ramshackle wagons are not dished, but dishing: they are becoming concave on the outside, and will soon fall apart.

dispatch box (*GDM* 51): a small rectangular metal box for carrying and storing important papers.

disyer (*CS:MV* 753, 754): this here, this.

ditching the dyking machinery (*GDM* 342): error for *ditching and dyking machinery*. See *Meriwether,* p. 24.

divining machine (*GDM* 81, 89, 123). The modern reader immediately thinks of a metal-detector of the type now used for locating treasure, antiques, etc., but this instrument was a product of World War II. The instrument referred to here, however, was a fake, and selling such treasure-finders was a standard form of confidence-game. In the 1920s my father saved a Negro man who sometimes worked for us from being taken in by this swindle—not by convincing him that it was a fraud (which he was unable to do), but by refusing to lend him money for it. Since the Faulkners were our close neighbors at the time, they may well have been similarly approached.

Division (*CS:Hair* 137): a fictional town on the Mississippi-Alabama line.

division (*Town* 235): a large administrative unit (and area of the network) of a railroad. A "train schedule for the division" would give the times of freight as well as passenger trains, and the freights were being used to kill the mules.

division point (*LiA* 162): a town in which a railroad DIVISION headquarters is located.

division superintendent (*Reiv.* 130): the supervising officer of a DIVISION.

dizzent (*Sanc.* 261): doesn't.

Doak's Stand (*RfaN* 105): a treaty by which, in 1820, the CHOCTAWS sold to the United States a large tract of land in the southwestern part of their holdings.

doan (*GDM* 136): don't.˙

doc (*Ham.* 271): abbreviation of *doctor*, familiar but implying some position of authority or dignity in the person addressed. A voice from the crowd can call Jody Varner this at Frenchman's Bend, but Jody would never address, say, Mink Snopes in this way.

Doddsville (*Mans.* 400): a small DELTA town 15 m. S of PARCHMAN.

do for (*AlLD* 25, 163; *Mosq.* 11): see to, provide for.

dog (*CS:Fox* 600, 601): a race- or hunting-horse, especially (but not necessarily) a sorry one.

dog-cart (*Ham.* 95): a light, two-wheeled carriage with back-to-back seats (and originally a compartment for carrying hunting dogs).

dog fennel (*S&F* 68; *Ham.* 26): mayweed, an acrid, rank-smelling weed (*Anthemis cotula*) bearing a daisylike flower. It is mentioned in *Sart.* 153 because it bears no resemblance whatever to SASSAFRAS.

doggery (*Abs.* 224): a low tavern or grogshop.

dog-robber (*Sart.* 63): orderly (World War I slang).

dog-trot cabin (*Mans.* 399; *Reiv.* 167): two-room cabin with an open breezeway between the two rooms.

dogwood (*Sart.* 6; *S&F* 95; *Sanc.* 133): flowering dogwood (*Cornus florida*) a small tree with showy white "flowers" about 3″ across in the early spring, and red fruits ("berries") in the fall. A bred-up variety has pink flowers (*Town* 310). The "flower" is actually a cluster of tiny flowers surrounded by four large petal-like bracts. The wood is used for the spindles of textile mills (*Ham.* 172). The twigs of a branch lie pretty much in the same horizontal plane (*SP* 158).

dollar watch (*Sanc.* 6, 305; *LiA* 160; *Ham.* 245): a large, sturdy, open-faced nickel-plated pocket watch. There are several makes of them, and for years the standard price was one dollar. They are still made, but now cost about $5–$7.

done. 1. (*Sart.* 65; *Unv.* 50; *GDM* 150): auxiliary *v.* equivalent to *have* or *had*. It is originally pleonastic (*Town* 99, 157; *Fable* 191), and then the original auxiliary verb is dropped. The typical development runs from *I have seen him* through *I have done seen him* to *I done seen him*. There is a similar pleonastic use with the *v. to be*: "He's done already asleep" (*AILD* 111). The *v.* may even be entirely dropped; "Marse John done home" (*Unv.* 212): "We're done out" (*WP* 152). "We done caught now" (*Sanc.* 191) is passive: "we have now been caught; we are now caught." So also "done damned" (*LiA* 55). **2.** (*Mans.*

45; *Fable* 154); did. **3**. (*AILD* 125; *S&F* 392; *Town* 248): through, finished.

dont want to smell the mules (*GDM* 179): must not be allowed to smell the mules.

Dorothy Mackaill (*Mosq*. 204). See MACKAILL, DOROTHY.

double (*Ham*. 355): to get around, get to the other side of.

double-ended feed-basket (*Ham*. 282). This could be a basket with a partition so that two sorts of feed could be separately carried in it—but this is a mere guess.

double-ender (*WP* 152): a boat so constructed that either end can serve as the prow.

double-jinted backin'-up strop (*Sart*. 5): double-jointed backing-up strap. Simon describes a Sam Browne belt in terms of a horse's harness, which is much more familiar to him. A backing-up strap is a breeching strap, which goes around a harness-horse's buttocks and takes the thrust when he backs up.

double tree (*Ham*. 33; *Reiv*. 84, 88): a crossbar attached to a wagon or similar implement, to each end of which one of a SPAN of mules is attached by a singletree, or WHIFFLE-TREE.

dove (*Sart*. 136; *Unv*. 97; *Dust* 146): mourning dove (*Zenaidura macroura*), a slender dove with a plaintive, far-carrying call. It is a swift flier and is hunted as a game-bird in the fall and winter. In *Ham*. 316, the bird is simply being given its full name: *mourning* is not a descriptive epithet here.

down. 1. (of tree, timber, etc.) (*Sart*. 288; *GDM*. 45, 208; *CS:Red* 334); fallen. **2**. (of an animal) (*GDM* 218, 242): lying down and unable to rise because of weakness or injury.

down-slanted (*GDM* 253). As a careful and responsible hunter, even in an emergency situation like this, McCaslin automatically points the gun toward the ground while unloading it, in case of an accidental discharge. A gun is also regularly carried slanted up or down, for the same reason. Cf. Walter Ewell, "slanting the . . . barrel of his rifle downward to walk with it again" (*GDM* 181).

downwind (*GDM* 181, 211): in the direction toward which the wind is blowing. "Five miles is still Hogganbeck range, even if we wasn't downwind" implies that Boon Hogganbeck could be heard (and smelled) five miles away even against the wind. In the expressions UPWIND and downwind, the wind is simply a stream of air and the relationships are the same as in *upstream* and *downstream*.

drag. 1. (*KG:KG* 239): harrow. **2**. (*Ham*. 321): any device for locking a wheel of a wagon or carriage making a steep descent. Cf. *Sart*. 205–06. The use here is metaphorical. When Ratliff is getting excited and almost frantic, Bookwright's "Hook your drag up; it aint nothing but a hill" means "Calm down; it's a routine matter that can be dealt with easily, and there's no need to get excited."

dragging a stick along the fence (*S&F* 140). If one presses a stick against a picket fence while walking or running alongside it, the stick will strike against each separate PICKET and make a hellish noise, much beloved by children.

Dragon (*Mans.* 301, 302): an official of the KU KLUX KLAN.

drag one's foot (*GDM* 11, 12; *Reiv.* 100): to make a deep, formal bow. One begins standing upright, with the feet equally advanced; then, as one bows at the waist, the right foot is dragged back about 18″ or so.

drained marsh in December (*S&F* 105). The point of the comparison is that, in the summer, with all the undergrowth around it, a drained marsh will hardly be visible. But in December the bare bottom of the marsh will correspond to the jeweler's bald spot, and the parting of his hair to the ditch through which the marsh was drained.

draw (a lady's) chair (*Unv.* 265): pull it back from the table so that she may take her seat in it. This is, of course, a gentleman's or escort's duty, and is not left to a servant.

draw-bar (*GDM* 322): the bar to which the couplings at each end of a railroad car are attached. It carries the main pull of the train.

drawing room (*Reiv.* 199): a luxurious private compartment on a PULLMAN.

drawn (*Flags* 218): tracked down. Faulkner extends the normal meaning of the *v.*, which is (in this sense) "to search (a thicket) for game," or "to track by scent." There may also be an element of the bird-dog man's use of *draw*, meaning "to advance cautiously, so as to get closer to game without flushing it."

draw time (*LiA* 40, 49): to be paid for the time that one has worked.

dreened (*Town* 18): drained.

drench (*Ham.* 306): to make (a horse, cow, etc.) drink a medicine.

dressing sacque (*S&F* 350; *Town* 361): a woman's hip-length dressing-gown.

drew the loads (*CS:Court.* 374): unloaded. This term applies only to a muzzle-loading gun, in which it is a fairly elaborate job to remove the cap, and then the powder, bullet, and wadding which have been rammed down the barrel. Because both the CAP and the powder (through the NIPPLE) are exposed to atmospheric moisture, a muzzle-loader that has been loaded for any considerable time is highly unreliable.

drive (of a horse) (*Unv.* 74; *Dust* 97): to exert himself in running.

drive *v.t.* (*Abs.* 36; *Mans.* 31): to go through (an area), driving game to waiting hunters.

driving rods (*Unv.* 112): the rods transmitting the power of a steam locomotive from the pistons to the circumferences of the DRIVING WHEELS.

driving wheels (*WP* 69): the big wheels of a steam locomotive, to which the power is transmitted by a complex of piston-rods, or DRIVING RODS.

drove (*Ham.* 32). The general meaning of the whole phrase is clear enough, but I have never heard this use of *drove*, or found anyone who has, or any dictionary or glossary that gives any help.

drover (*Abs.* 51, 57): a dealer in livestock, or one who drives herds to market.

drowned fish (*WP* 235): presumably fish killed by lack of sufficient oxygen in the water, either from stagnation or from fouling with mud. I have not found this usage attested elsewhere.

drug my foot (*Reiv.* 100). See DRAG ONE'S FOOT.

drugstore (*Mans.* 32; *SP* 145). Old-time drugstores invariably kept in their show-windows one or more large glass globes, jars, or urns filled with colored water.

drummer (*Sart.* 5; *S&F* 114, 217): traveling salesman, commercial traveler.

druther (*Town* 295): rather (with a modified vowel and an initial sound added from the *had* which normally precedes it).

dry heifer (*Reiv.* 75): since a dry cow is one that has no milk, and a heifer is a young cow that has never borne a calf, "dry heifer" is redundant.

dry up (*Reiv.* 53: *Mosq.* 50): shut up.

dulcimer (*CS:MGM* 670, 674, 687): not the dulcimer of European musical history, but the Appalachian dulcimer, also known as the "folk zither." It is a long, narrow instrument with (usually) three strings: a melody string and two drone strings. It is played on a table or on the performer's knees, with the right hand "picking" the strings and the left hand stopping them.

dumbness (*Mosq.* 74): a form of address to, or name for, a person accused of stupidity. It was fairly widespread in the 1920s. (It was the playful nickname of a very bright girl in my class at Oxford High School.)

Dumfries (*Sanc.* 37, 53, 135): a fictional town on the route between TAYLOR and the OLD FRENCHMAN PLACE. Actually, there is nothing resembling a town between these two sites, which are only about 15 m. apart by road. But since Taylor is located with respect to Faulkner's "Oxford" and the Old Frenchman Place with respect to his Jefferson (see Appendix), there has to be a considerable stretch of fictional territory between them.

dummy (*Sanc.* 10: *KG:Hand* 72): a dumb person, a mute.

durnation (*CS:TS* 95): apparently a blend of *durn* and TARNATION.

durn his tightfisted time (*CS:Hair* 136). *Durn his time* is standard as a vague not-too-serious condemnation, something like *Confound him.* The insertion of a modifier for *time* is unusual and humorous.

dusk-dark (*CS:Queen* 733): late twilight.

dust. Unpaved north Mississippi roads become very dusty in summer, and the vegetation along a road is often visibly weighted down with the dust which has settled on it (*Abs.* 175). This dust on the ground, often a couple of inches deep, can easily be picked up by handfuls, as in *Unv.* 7. In this passage the boys are not having a dust-fight: they are using the dust as a stage-prop to reproduce the clouds of smoke that hung over battles when black powder was in use.

dust-dark (*AILD* 58, 105; *Town* 34, 108): late twilight. The expression is a folk eytmology derived from DUSK-DARK.

dust-dawn (*AILD* 69; *Town* 245): early dawn. Cf. DUST-DARK.

duster. 1. (*Sart.* 3, 4; *Abs.* 24): a "long shapeless throat-close neutral-colored garment" (*Reiv.* 29) worn to protect the clothes of riders in carriages and early cars from dust. **2.** (*Sart.* 241): anything used for dusting furniture—most likely a feather-duster, a sort of little, one-hand broom made of turkey feathers.

dynamite (*Abs.* 306). Dynamite is nitroglycerin in some absorbent material, wrapped into a cylindrical package. This dynamite is nitroglycerin in sawdust, wrapped in paper. Dynamite in the Civil War (*Town* 306) is an anachronism.

E

eagering, homing, barning (*LiA* 135). Horses normally perk up as they get close to home and their stalls at the end of a trip.

Earl Sande (*Reiv.* 233). See SANDE, EARL.

Early, Gen. Jubal A. (*CS:MGM* 673): a Confederate general famed for his bitter loyalty to the Confederacy after the Civil War and for his invariable and picturesque profanity. Since Early died in 1894 and the former Confederate general Joseph Wheeler was not commissioned into the U.S. Army (as major general) until the Spanish-American War in 1898, Faulkner's anecdote is obviously impossible, though true to Early's views and character. The tale is told in many forms, all more or less apocryphal. A more plausible version has an old Confederate soldier at Wheeler's funeral, seeing the body lying in state in its Federal uniform, saying, "Wall, by gee, gen'ul, when you get on to'ther side and Jubal Early catches you in them togs, I'm bettin you'll get the puttiest cussin' that ever cum your way!"—Quoted from Millard K. Bushong, *Old Jube: A Biography of General Jubal A. Early* (Boyce, Va., 1955), p. 1.

easy rider. "This apt expression is used to describe a man whose movements in coitus are easy and satisfying. It is frequently met both in Negro folk songs and in formal songs. 'I wonder where my easy rider's gone.' is a sort of by-word with Southern Negroes. There is an interesting circumstance connected with this expression which throws light upon the question of how vulgar meanings get over into art songs from folk songs. W. C. Handy . . . noticed the widespread use of 'easy rider' as well as the existence of various folk songs based on that theme. He wrote a song, *Yellow Dog Blues*, in which he used the phrase. In this song there is a race horse and jockey . . . involved. The jockey deserts his horse, goes back South, and the horse wonders 'where my easy rider's gone' " (Johnson, p. 16). Since *Yellow Dog Blues* was published in 1914 (the same year as Handy's *St. Louis Blues*), and since the dance where the phrase occurs (*SP* 198) is a white dance that would be using commercial popular music rather than authentic folk blues, this is doubtless the song Faulkner had in mind. But it is worth noting that, whether by accident or design, all three of the songs quoted in his account of the dance have covert sexual meanings. See SHAKE IT AND BREAK IT and SHIMMY.

eating and drinking: racial etiquette. Whites and Negroes were not expected to eat and drink together *socially*. The strength of the convention depended entirely on the nature of the occasion; it did not hold at all for a casual snack on a job or on a hunt. (In the 1960s, during a racially tense time when the Jackson, Miss., airport was under heavy police guard because of the invasions of "freedom fighters," I saw one of the white police guards and a black employee of the airport sitting side by side on a bench, drinking Coca-Colas and chatting. This would have astonished outsiders, but was not even a matter for notice to anyone who understood the conventions.) As the number of persons involved or the formality of the occasion increases, the taboo comes into effect. Minnie and Miss Reba would drink together if they wanted to, but in a larger group Minnie carried her glass back to the kitchen because "she declined to drink with this many white people at once" (*Reiv.* 113). When a group of whites had breakfast at the sheriff's, "they left Aleck Sander [black] with his breakfast at the kitchen table and carried theirs into the diningroom" (*Dust* 114). Similarly, Bayard Sartoris has to insist that the Negro family eat Christmas dinner with him instead of waiting until he has finished (*Sart.* 347), just as Ned sets aside the drink which Colonel Linscombe pours for him in the company of a group of whites in the colonel's office, and will not drink it until told to do so (*Reiv.* 285).

eave-cat (*Ham.* 162): a cat climbing about the eaves: i.e. a tomcat in the act of TOMCATting.

. . . ed (*Mans.* 281): fucked.

Ed Pinaud (*Sanc.* 305): a proprietary line of toilet preparations widely sold at the time of *Sanc.*

efn (*GDM* 150, 151): if.

eggsuckers (*LiA* 312): a term of abuse for dogs. A badly trained and undisciplined dog may learn to "suck" (actually, to break and eat) eggs.

egvice (*S&F* 372): advice.

egvised (*Sart.* 64): advised.

Egypt (*Miss.* 32): a town in eastern Mississippi, 75 m. S of Tennessee and 30 m. W of Alabama. The *Mississippi Guide* says that it "was named for the variety of corn grown here." It was a center for collecting corn for the Confederate army until Federal troops burned both the corn and the town. "The town has grown but little since that time."

elbers (*Ham.* 345): elbows.

elbow units (*CS:SftL* 36): a nonce-word making elbow-grease (a standard term for physical effort) parallel to the work-units and dog-units already in the discussion.

elder (*Sart.* 138, 140; *CS:MGM* 678, 680): American elder (*Sambucus canadensis*), a large bush or small tree growing along watercourses and the edges of swamps. A wine is made of its flat-topped "pale clumps of tiny bloom," and a different wine is made of its purplish fruits.

elefump (*S&F* 399; *WT* 27, 63): ignorant pronunciation of *elephant.*

elm (*Sanc.* 137; *SP* 174, 315): a large tree (*Ulmus americana*) frequently planted along streets. When Quentin says "Elm. No: ellum. Ellum" (*S&F* 154) he is humorously correcting his own Southern and standard English pronunciation (*elm*) and conforming to the New England rural one (*ellum*).

embusque (*Abs.* 169): one who shirks or evades military service.

E.M.F. (*Town* 58, 116, 187; *Mans.* 129): a make of car manufactured from 1908 to 1912, when it was bought by Studebaker.

empty plow (*Ham.* 32): plow from which the PLOW STOCK has been removed.

end-gate (*Ham.* 304): normally the same thing as TAIL GATE, but Faulkner is clearly using the word here to designate the vertical plank forming the *front* end of the wagon box.

end of the row (rhymes with *no*, not with *now*) (*KG:Hand* 78): final point, as far as one can or will go. When a farmer plowing or chopping cotton reaches the end of the row he either stops, or turns around and starts back down the next row. "This is the end of the row" has exactly the same figurative meaning as "This is the end of the road (or line)." See *AILD* 26 for the decisiveness of the end of the row in Dewey Dell's life.

English sparrow (*RfaN* 44): SPARROW, house sparrow (*Passer domesticus*). Since this species was introduced into the United States, in Brooklyn in 1850, the sparrows that moved in on Jefferson as soon as it was founded are an anachronism and a good example of what Aristotle calls a probable impossibility.

Enkyew! (*Sanc.* 261): Thank you!

enough ... to fat a calf (*LiA* 336): a small amount, since a calf being fattened for veal is not large enough to eat very much.

Episcopal church (*Town* 306). Faulkner is clearly referring to St. Peter's Episcopal Church in Oxford, which was built in 1851 and is the only Oxford church of any architectural distinction or interest. It is by no means "the oldest extant building in town," though it was doubtless built primarily by slave labor. The gold cross on the spire (*KG:KG* 241) is accurate. The spire is here seen from what used to be "Stone's Crossing," the intersection of the railroad and Washington Ave.

equinox (*Unv.* 244, 246). In "An Odor of Verbena," Faulkner uses this word to mean, not the astronomical phenomenon (all of October is after the equinox), but the change of weather from late summer to fall which is connected with the old idea of equinoctial storms.

(')ere (*Sart.* 20, 21, 332; *AILD* 83): there (pleonastic) in the expression *that 'ere*.

ere (*Sanc.* 39; *Town* 239; *WP* 253): e'er, any.

ere a (*AILD* 16, 65): e'er a, any.

ergain (*Sart.* 367). again.

eunuch race (*WP* 158). Being hybrids, mules are very rarely fertile.

evening (*Reiv.* 225; *Flags* 299): afternoon.

even though and in August (*GDM* 57). The cultivation of corn is normally finished by August (see LAY BY). The sense is plain here, but there is a textual problem of an obvious omission, after *though*, of some phrase like *the spring had been late* or *planting had been delayed*.

ever(') (*Sart.* 20; *AILD* 68; *LiA* 336) : every.

ever body (*Town* 82, 101) : everybody.

exhaust (of a locomotive) (*LiA* 417; *GDM* 318). The steam locomotive could send its exhaust steam through the firebox and out the smokestack, thus helping to blow the fire and producing (when the train was running slowly) a series of loud puffs. The description (*LiA* 416) won't quite work when it speaks of shortening the stroke of the engine on a grade. Since the pistons are fixed, there is no way for a locomotive to shorten its stroke. The sound will become heavier as the puffs slow down and are heard individually, but the strokes will remain the same and the time between them will be lengthened.

express truck (*Sanc.* 170; *KG:KG* 243) : a four-wheeled, hand-propelled truck with a platform the height of the floor of a railroad express car, used to load and unload express shipments from trains.

F

fahr (*CS:BH* 67, 75) : fire.

family woman (*S&F* 84) : woman "in a family way," pregnant woman.

fancy-work (*Sart.* 151) : any sort of ornamental needlework.

fare-you-well, to a (*Town* 245) : to an extreme degree.

farm-furnish stores (*Town* 216) : stores selling supplies for farms. See FURNISH.

far offest (*WT* 48) : most distant.

far piece. 1. (*AILD* 206; *Ham.* 327; *GDM* 130) : a long way. **2.** (*Ham.* 46) : far piece of land, remote field.

fatback (*Mans.* 105, 274) : SIDE MEAT, SOWBELLY, salt pork.

Father of Waters (*WP* 158) : the traditional translation of the original name of the Mississippi River, though apparently the Algonquin *Missi Sipi* means something more like "great river."

fault. 1. (*AILD* 162) : to make a mistake, blunder, err. **2.** (*Abs.* 238; *GDM* 18) : to lose the trail (hunting term).

favor (*Sart.* 26) : to look like, resemble. *He jes' don't favor hisself* means "He just doesn't look like himself."

fawty-one Colt (*Dust* 69) : a .41-calibre Colt pistol. This is the exact bore of a so-called .410 shotgun, but is utterly archaic as a pistol bore.

fed at the same breast (*Unv.* 7). A white child's Negro "mammy" was often his wet-nurse as well. Cf. Molly Beauchamp, *GDM* 45 ff.

federal courthouse (*GDM* 63) : the old brick building, containing both the court and its offices, on the NE corner of the Oxford square. The Oxford water-tank used to stand immediately behind it. The court has now been moved to the new Federal Building (on the site of the old Oxford school building), and the old federal courthouse building is now being used as the

Oxford City Hall.—Moonshining involves Federal authorities because of the failure to pay federal excise taxes on the liquor produced.

Federal officers (*Ham.* 4): enemies of MOONSHINERS because they do not pay the excise taxes on the whiskey they make.

feeb (*Sanc.* 9, 10, 124; *KG:Hand* 65): feeble-minded person.

feed, *v.i.* (*LiA* 150; *Ham.* 364; *CS:SftL* 27): to feed the livestock.

feed box (*LiA* 140, 141): a box sitting on the floor of a stable, in which feed is placed—not a manger, which would be attached to the wall too high for a man to lower himself to the top of it.

feed corn (*Ham.* 243): mature, hard corn kept for stock-feed. Such corn is not normally edible for people unless ground into meal and made into bread, but in desperation it can be parched and eaten.

feed lot (*Mans.* 10): enclosure in which livestock is fed.

feed room (*KG:Error* 128): a room in a barn for storing feed. It normally has a floor raised a couple of feet above the ground in order to keep the feed from getting damp and moldy; hence it would be possible to crawl under it and bury a body clumsily, and the burial would be visible from the outside. (The terms *feed room* and *crib* are sometimes used interchangeably: when Ruby took Temple Drake to the barn, she "guided her up a single step into a floored room" [*Sanc.* 80], into the crib.)

feice (*Ham.* 159, 249): a singular or a strange plural form of FICE.

fellow in the cap (*KG:Monk* 48). The CONDUCTOR of the train, wearing the official cap that was a part of his uniform, regularly called out each station as the train approached it.

Female Academy (*RfaN* 225; *Mans.* 195): FEMALE INSTITUTE.

female compound (*Town* 313): patent medicine for FEMALE TROUBLE.

female dope (*AILD* 189): patent medicine for FEMALE TROUBLE.

Female institute (*RfaN* 45). See JEFFERSON ACADEMY.

female trouble. 1. menstruation. **2.** any pains, cramps, irregularities or other troubles connected with menstruation. These were widely used euphemisms in patent-medicine ads. The drugstore clerk in *AILD* 233 plays on these two meanings: "Have you got 2, or do you want 1?" with a hint of a third meaning: the trouble of an unwanted pregnancy.

fence panel (*Abs.* 279): a section of fence between two posts, or whatever other supports are used.

fence picket (*S&F* 328; *LiA* 314): one of the vertical and usually pointed slats about 1″ × 3″ which are nailed, a couple of inches apart, to two horizontal rails to make a picket fence.

fence rail (*Town* 196; *CS:TM* 51; *KG:Error* 111). See RAIL.

fender (*Sart.* 135, 137): running board—a somewhat unusual usage. The youth that "clung" to the fender was riding the running board, i.e. standing on it and holding on to the top of the car. When cars had running boards this was a standard method of carrying one or more extra persons on a relatively short haul.

fer (*CS:TS* 97): far.

Ferginny (*Unv.* 58, 60; *RfaN* 28; *CS:MV* 753): Virginia.

fetch. 1. (*Sart.* 204; *Abs.* 151; *GDM* 46): to go and get and bring back. **2.** (*Sart.* 80): to arrive at. **3.** (*LiA* 476): to produce.

fetch up (*AILD* 12): to come to a stop.

fetlock (*AILD* 55): the joint just above a horse's hoof.

F.F.V. (*Sanc.* 24): a member of one of the First Families of Virginia.

fice (*S&F* 233, 354): a small mongrel dog.

fiddle-head horse (*Ham.* 287): a horse with a large, coarse, ungainly, or ill-shaped head.

field hand (*Ham.* 8; *GDM* 270; *CS:MV* 746): agricultural laborer.

field niggers (*Sart.* 234; *Dust* 15; *CS:MV* 764): Negroes who do agricultural labor and who are socially held to be considerably beneath "house niggers" or domestic servants. Lucas's refusal to let Molly have her portrait made with a HEADRAG (*Dust* 15), because "I didn't want no field nigger picture in the house" is part of his general pride and orneriness, since house-servants frequently wear headrags.

field peas (*Ham.* 61; *KG:Tomo.* 91): a type of pea often planted with corn in cornfields (*LiA* 217). They can be either broken and eaten pod and all, like snap beans, or shelled, like black-eyed peas. They are often cooked with molasses.

field rat (*LiA* 312): cotton rat (*Sigmodon hispidus*), a medium-sized native American rat of thickets and abandoned fields.

field trial (*Town* 362; *WP* 67, 254): a competition in which bird dogs are judged on their actual skill in the field instead of on "points" of shape, color, etc., as in a bench-show. "A field trial pointer or setter" would be one good enough at least to make a decent showing in such a competition, and hence a valuable dog.

find (someone) **in** (something) (*Abs.* 306): to provide someone with something.

fined (*Mans.* 243): find.

f——ing (*LiA* 204): fucking.

firebox (*S&F* 356): the part of a stove in which the fire burns. The "door to the firebox" is the same thing as the FIRE-DOOR.

fire (of corn) (*Ham.* 255, 336; *GDM* 125). Corn fires (or is fired) when the leaves turn yellowish as the ears mature.

firedog (*Sanc.* 86; *Unv.* 207; *Reiv.* 216): andiron.

fire-door (*S&F* 68, 72; *Sanc.* 49): the metal door, about 6″ × 8″, which opens into the long, narrow FIREBOX of a kitchen range, and through which it is stoked. The door is hinged at the bottom and opens downward. When it is open, a person sitting in front of the stove can see the fire, as Benjy does. Luster torments him by reaching from behind him with a piece of wire and closing the door, so that the fire disappears. Benjy finally reaches out and touches the hot fire-door.

firefly 82

firefly (*LiA* 240; *Abs.* 31; *Ham.* 29). The fireflies, or lightning bugs (family Lampyridae) of Faulkner are pretty much like the other members of the family in temperate zones all over the world. Faulkner knows that the flashing lights of fireflies are sexual signals: " 'Yes, sir,' Jenny agreed, passive in the darkness, like an erotic lightning bug projecting [to Major Ayers] that sense of himself surrounded, enclosed by the sweet cloudy fire of her thighs, as young girls will" (*Mosq.* 222).

fire road (*Race* 178, 192): a road serving the double purpose of being a fire-break in a forest and providing access for fighting forest fires.

fire siren (*LiA* 435). This was not a siren on a fire engine, but a permanent installation at the power plant, used as a general community alarm. It was a large steam whistle built like the toy musical instruments known as slide whistles. The whistle extended through the roof and sounded on the outside of the building, but the slide that changed the length of its column of air was operated by a pole hanging down into the building. Under favorable cir- cumstances, this siren could be heard four miles away.

fireworks (*Sart.* 348–49; *S&F* 108; *CS:TWBF* 266, 278). Christmas, not the 4th of July, is the traditional time for fireworks in the South.

firing-pin (*GDM* 58; *Mans.* 429): the pointed device that strikes the cap of a modern cartridge or shotgun shell and detonates it. It may be either a point on the hammer itself or a separate horizontal pin which the hammer drives against the cap. Since the firing-pins of cheap guns are easily broken or damaged and since a gun will not function without one, the "firing-pinless pistols" in a pawnshop (*WP* 121) can be used to represent the idea of useless junk in general.

First Manassas (Miss. 16): the First Battle of Manassas (Bull Run), July 21, 1861.

first pop (*GDM* 92): the first time, on the first attempt.

first Saturday (*Reiv.* 14, 17): the first Saturday of the month.

fish-blooded (*Mans.* 206, 215): cold-blooded to a superlative degree.

fish-grabblers (*Town* 80). See GRABBLE.

fishingbird (*Sanc.* 7): CAROLINA WREN.

fish-line (*Race* 192): a series of unattended hooks set out for fish. Cf. TRAP- LINE. A fish-line can consist of several TROTLINES, or individual set-hooks, or a mixture of both.

fitten (*Sart.* 2; *AILD* 85; *LiA* 119): fit, suitable.

Fitz-John Porter (*Reiv.* 285). See WADE HAMPTON.

Five Hundred (*Dust* 60): a card game (a form of euchre) in which the first person to score 500 points is the winner.

fixed bull (*Reiv.* 26): castrated bull.

flac-soled (*S&F* 330). The off-white color of the palm (sole) of Dilsey's hand is apparently being compared to the similar color on the bellies of many fish. All attempts to explain the root or the exact application of *flac* to this concept, however, have failed. *Flax-soled* is a remote possibility.

flagman (*Reiv.* 130, 135): a man who signals with flags, lanterns, etc., on a train in a railroad yard. He has more responsibility and status than a BRAKEMAN.

flags (*S&F* 163): flagstones.

flapping apron (*Dust* 141). A woman driving hens deliberately flaps her apron at them to shoo them along.

flash (*Mans.* 277): flashy.

flat (*GDM* 8, 14): a level stretch of ground; hence, in Faulkner's country, often a section of creek or river bottom, as opposed to the surrounding hills.

flat city pistol (*Fable* 192): an automatic, as opposed to the revolvers favored in rural areas.

flatform (*Reiv.* 144): presumably a misprint for *platform*.

flatiron (*Sart.* 155; *S&F* 98, 105; *Mans.* 80): a heavy pressing iron heated on a kitchen range. It is sometimes called a sadiron.

flat racer (*Reiv.* 144): a racehorse that runs on ordinary tracks, as distinguished from a jumper or steeplechaser.

flenching-knife (*GDM* 262): apparently a variant form of *flensing-knife*, a long-bladed knife on a long handle, used to strip blubber from whales. It seems to be a strange comparison in the Yoknapatawpha context.

flintlock rifles (*Ham.* 4): early rifles that used a hammer to strike a spark (on the flint-and-steel principle), which ignited the powder.

flivver (*Mosq.* 215): a contemptuous term for a small, cheap car, here applied to a similar motorboat.

float (*Ham.* 306): to file down the points (of a horse's teeth).

flood year 1927 (*WP* 23). In 1927 there was a disastrous flood of the Mississippi River, which broke through the LEVEES on the Mississippi side and flooded the whole DELTA, including a number of fairly large towns like Greenville.

Florence, Alabama (*CS:Hair* 142): a town 30 m. from the NW corner of Alabama.

flou' bar'l (*Sart.* 208): FLOUR BARREL.

flour barrel. Flour was bought by and shipped to individual house-holders in barrels weighing 196 1bs. (*Sart.* 208). To "keep the flour barrel full" (*S&F* 243, 258) is to provide for a household, to keep the wolf from the door.

flour gravy (*Mans.* 29): gravy thickened with flour, white gravy.

floursack. When not bought in barrels, flour was bought in cloth sacks of from 20 to 50 1bs. These sacks, like some feed sacks, were often deliberately made with attractive patterns so that they could be used eventually for towels or even dresses (*LiA* 13, 237; *GDM* 138). During the Civil War, coarse (un-adorned) flour-sacking was often the only fabric available (*Unv.* 155; *CS:MV* 748).

flour sacking (*LiA* 72; *Abs.* 172): the unpatterned, grayish-white material of which flour sacks are often made.

flush. 1. *v.t.* (*Ham.* 287): to scare up (a bird) so that it flies. This is a hunting term, and when applied to anything other than a game-bird, it always implies a comparison with one. **2.** *v.i.* (*GDM* 8, 14, 41): to be scared up and forced to fly or to reveal one's presence.

flying jenny (*Mans.* 317): merry-go-round, carrousel.

flying squirrel (*GDM* 159): a small arboreal rodent (*Glaucomys volans*), gray above and white below, with a furry membrane joining its front and hind legs and its sides, and a flattened tail. It cannot actually fly, but by leaping from a tree and extending its legs, it can make fairly long downward glides. Hence a space between two trees "that a flying squirrel could not have crossed" (*Abs.* 239) is a considerable space.

flywhisk (*Abs.* 31): a bunch of horsehair or feathers mounted on a handle and used to shoo or brush flies away.

fob pocket of his overalls (*Mans.* 30, 261): a pocket over the left chest. It is sewed on $3\frac{1}{2}$ sides, with only the top half of the right side remaining open.

Fokker (*Sart.* 45): a German military airplane (biplane or triplane) named for the manufacturer, Dutch-born Anthony Herman Gerard Fokker.

foot (*GDM* 83, 124, 206; *Mans.* 32): footprint.

foot (of a car) (*Sanc.* 35): the foot-and-leg space of passengers, the space above the floor and below the level of the seats.

footlog (*Dust* 5): a log spanning a creek or ditch and used as a bridge. It may be felled or placed for the purpose, or may be a windfall used simply because it happens to be there.

footstool (*Mans.* 35). At railroad stations without loading-platforms, the porter or conductor sets a light metal stool on the ground to make it easier for passengers to negotiate the considerable distance between the ground and the firrst step of the railroad car.

forage cap (*CS:MV* 754): a small cap with a round, low crown, worn with un-dress uniform.

ford (*AILD* 118, 119, 141). **1.** Since the ford is a shallow place in the river, even when it is deep under floodwater it creates eddies and catches the branches of floating uprooted trees, so that it is possible to locate it by watching the floating debris. See also p. 138. **2.** (*KG:Monk* 41): Ford car (a capital is needed). The creeks in Faulkner's country have bottoms of mud, sand, or quicksand, and cannot normally be forded by cars.

fore God (*Town* 239, 241, 369): before God (an exclamation somewhat like "by God," but, unless used in a solemn asseveration, it contains an element of pleasant excitement or surprise).

Forest, N. B. (*GDM* 264): FORREST. (This misspelling of the name is commented on later, *GDM* 272.)

forge (*Ham.* 267; *CS:Just.* 358): the place where a blacksmith heats metal to be hammered into shape. It is a raised metal table with side-walls in which smoldering coals are kept, and is equipped with some sort of bellows (usually a crank-driven fan or blower) that supplies a draft from beneath to generate fierce heat when it is needed.

fork (*Ham.* 285, 286): to bestride (a horse).

forked peach branch (*Ham.* 344): a divining rod. The charms used with such
a rod (in this case, the gold-filled tooth) are optional and highly idiosyncratic,
but the forked twig itself is standard and invariable.

form (*LiA* 112): a long, backless bench (Briticism).

forrader (*Reiv.* 59): forwarder, further along.

Forrest (*Sart.* 174; *Abs.* 152; *Unv.* 17, 171; *Mans.* 17): Gen. Nathan Bedford
Forrest, Confederate cavalry leader. He was successively a cattle-dealer,
slave-trader (*GDM* 263), and planter before he volunteered in the Confederate army as a private and turned out to be a military genius. His activities of immediate concern in Faulkner's world are his fighting in the vicinity
of Oxford at HURRICANE CREEK and TALLAHATCHIE CROSSING, his raid into
MEMPHIS when it was held by Federal forces, and the fact that at one time
he had his headquarters in Oxford.

Fort Moultrie (*Sart.* 10): a fort in the harbor of Charleston, S.C. Faulkner's
reference is very loose. When South Carolina seceded, the fort was occupied
by U.S. troops. Their commander, seeing that Fort Moultrie was very vulner-
able, spiked its guns and moved his forces to Fort Sumter, which was much
stronger. Long negotiations for the surrender of Fort Sumter to the state
(and then to the Confederacy) finally fell through, and the Confederate
bombardment and capture of Fort Sumter (when Federal ships were approaching to reinforce and provision it for determined resistance) marked the
beginning of the Civil War.

forty (*Mans.* 5): a forty-acre piece of land, usually a field.

forty-ones (*Mans.* 292): .41-caliber cartridges.

fotch (*Sart.* 224; *GDM* 67, 122; *Unv.* 213): *infin.* or *p.t.* of FETCH.

fotched (*GDM* 119); fetched.

Four-F (*Mans.* 267, 313): a person exempt from the draft because of failure to
meet the physical standards of the armed forces.

four-five (*Mans.* 272): four or five.

four-footed gait (*Dust* 92): a pace of four time: one in which each of the
horse's hooves strikes the earth at a different time, so that there are four
hoofbeats to each stride.

fox, *v.t.* (*Ham.* 143; *Town* 207): to trick, deceive, outwit. To fox oneself is to
outsmart oneself.

fox-grape (*Unv.* 251): one of the more edible species of WILD GRAPE (*Vitus
labrusca*) growing in thickets on low ground and ripening in the fall.

fox-horn (*GDM* 9, 17; *RfaN* 19): a horn used for, or such as might be used for,
fox hunting.

fox hunting. Mississippi fox hunting is essentially a spectator sport. It is done
at night, and the participants may ride horses from place to place trying to
intercept the pursuit (*Sart.* 331), but usually they simply build a fire on a
commanding hilltop and stay by it with a jug of whiskey (*KG:KG* 158). In
either case, their principal pleasure is in following the chase by ear and

admiring the "music" of the hounds. This is what Henry Sutpen is doing in *Abs.* 315, and Sam Fathers and the boy in *GDM* 170; similarly, *CS:SftL* 27. In Virginia, fox hunters ride to hounds in the English manner.

fox squirrel (*Sart.* 288): a large squirrel (*Sciurus niger*), about a third larger than the ordinary gray squirrel. There are several color phases, but in Faulkner's country fox squirrels are usually black with white nose and ears.

fox trot (*Sart.* 306; *Abs.* 32): a gait of a horse, between a trot and a walk.

'fraid cat (*S&F* 64; *SP* 95): fraidy cat, coward. This is a children's term, and is usually used to designate someone who is afraid to do some specific thing on a particular occasion rather than one who is timid or cowardly in general.

frail (*Sart.* 85; *AILD* 20; *LiA* 229): to strike, beat. When an officious publisher's editor, after several other patronizing "corrections," wanted to change this word in *LiA* to *flail*, Faulkner wrote in the margin: "O.K. as set and written. Jesus Christ" (*Blotner*, p. 784).

frantic running (*Dust* 4). When a hog is butchered, he is knocked in the head or shot and then hung up by the heels, after which his throat is cut and he is singed, disembowelled, etc., in this position.

Fraser's Store (*Dust* 27): an imaginary country store in Beat Four of Yoknapatawpha Co.

Freedman Town (*LiA* 106; *Dust* 39): a Negro section of Oxford bounded by Jackson Ave., N. Seventh St., and the railroad, and extending N past Washington Ave. See Appendix.

free paper (*GDM* 265): the documents (the phrase is usually used in the plural) certifying the free status of a manumitted slave, so that he will not be bothered by PATROLLERS, etc.

French Lick (*S&F* 117, 126): a resort town in southern Indiana.

Frenchman's Bend (*Sart.* 24, 172; *Ham.* 3; *RfaN* 33): a settlement in southeastern Yoknapatawpha Co. See Appendix, p. 233, and map, p. 228.

Frenchmen (*LiA* 473): Alphonse and Gaston, two characters in the comic strip of the KATZENJAMMER KIDS, who regularly behaved as here described, especially when they came to a door.

freqump (*WT* 54): frequent(ly).

freshen (*Mans.* 8. 10): (of a cow) to bear a calf, and hence start a fresh supply of milk.

Frisco depot (*Reiv.* 115). Memphis has two railroad stations, about half a mile apart. The Grand Central Station, out of which the Frisco line operates, is often called the Frisco Depot.

frockcoat (*LiA* 232, 443; *Abs.* 35; *Unv.* 155): a knee-length, double-breasted dress coat. The tail of such a coat often contained capacious pockets (*Fable* 165, 169).

froe (*CS:SftL* 27, 29): an implement for splitting shingles. (It rhymes with *go*.) It has a blade about 1' long, wedgeshaped in cross-section, and a handle at right angles to it. The blade is not supposed to be sharp, since it is used for splitting rather than cutting, and "dull as a froe" is a standard rural simile.

The blade is placed on top of a BOLT, the thickness of a shingle away from the face of the bolt. It is then driven in with a MAUL until the wood begins to split; then a pull on the handle pries the shingle off. This is the proper way to do the job, and is what Solon and Homer were doing; but "Pap" was splitting the shingles off with a heavy blow of the maul, so that they were whirled off as missiles.

frog: a general term for batrachians, including toads. The frog in *S&F* 26 is evidently a toad, since he is on the brick walk in the yard, far from water, and since it is to toads, which themselves have warty skins, that folk belief attributes the property of making warts on those who handle them. Since frogs hibernate, none would be available in November (*S&F* 83). Faulkner's "young frogs" (*LiA* 149) are not necessarily newly transformed adults but are merely small species of peepers, cricket frogs, and chorus frogs, of the genera *Hyla*, *Acris*, and *Pseudacris*. An adult of the best known of these species, the spring peeper (*Hyla crucifer*), is only about 1″ long. In the "booming and grunting of frogs" (*Ham.* 224), the grunting might come from several species, but the booming can be only bullfrogs. When diving from an elevation, frogs enter the water with a clean, head-first dive, but if they are sitting at the water's edge, many of them (including the big bullfrogs), leap parallel to the surface and more or less run along it until they sink (*Ham.* 230–31). When Ringo leaps onto Grumby, "looking exactly like a frog, even to the eyes" (*Unv.* 210), the reference is to his extended legs and spread arms, like those of a frog diving from a bank into the water, and his eyes bulged out with excitement.

frogstools (*Race* 183): toadstools.

front door (*Abs.* 229, 232; *CS:MGM* 674). Until recently, the front door was for visitors and social equals and the back (or kitchen) door was for tradesmen and social inferiors. The distinction was one of caste, not race. The ragged, mountain white boy Sutpen was not admitted to the front door of a Tidewater plantation house (*Abs.* 229–32); and, in an extreme case, the poor white Wash Jones was not even allowed to *approach* Sutpen's house from the front, and was not allowed *into* it even from the back (*Abs.* 134, 183, 281).

front of her dress (*CS:Elly* 209): a traditional place of intimate concealment with women. Here the indication is hidden cigarettes and surreptitious smoking.

front porch (*S&F* 236): a porch, usually large, across part or all of the front of a house, protected from rain by a roof supported on columns. These may be anything from warped two-by-fours to Corinthian columns 6′ in diameter. For well over half the year in Faulkner's country the front porch can be used for outdoor living.

fruit jar (*LiA* 137; *GDM* 63; *Town* 241): a glass jar used for putting up fruit, preserves, etc. The standard form ultimately became that of the Mason jar. Fruit jars are sealed with separate gaskets of pale red rubber: Drusilla's mouth was "pale as one of those rubber rings women seal fruit jars with" (*Unv.* 275).

full dark (*Unv.* 15; *GDM* 17, 118; *Town* 64): fully dark; i.e. night instead of twilight.

full daylight (*GDM* 65): broad daylight. Cf. FULL DARK.

full night (*Reiv.* 72): FULL DARK.

fun (*GDM* 35): a misprint for RUN. The distilling of one batch of mash constitutes a run of a still. See Introduction, p. 6, and n. 5.

furnish (*Ham.* 8). This is both *n.* and *v.*, and the use here could be either: "[We] furnish out of the store here" or "[You get] furnish out of the store here." In *Ham.* 11 it is used once as a *v.* and once as an *adj.* derived from the *n.* The store or commissary furnishes (supplies the needs of) the sharecropper on credit while he makes a crop, and the bill is settled when the crop is sold in the fall. The *n.* can also be used to mean simply groceries or necessities (*Town* 167), or to mean furnish bill (*Mans.* 28) or payment in kind as part of wages (*WP* 334). It is in this last sense that Edmonds tells Lucas (who wants to retire), "But you can't expect me to furnish a house and wood and water to a family that ain't working any land" (*GDM* 43).

fur piece (*LiA* 1): a long way. "I would a got a fur piece quick trying to tell him that" (*Mans.* 163) is sarcastic and means "I would have gotten nowhere."

fuzz (*AILD* 206, 207): to appear fuzzy. Mr. Gillespie's boy is old enough to have hair on his legs, which makes them look fuzzy in the moonlight.

fyce (*GDM* 15, 18; *Mans.* 316): FICE.

G

Gaines' Mill (*Reiv.* 285). See WADE HAMPTON.

galled mules (*Town* 282): mules afflicted with TRACE GALLS.

gallery. 1. (*Sanc.* 137, 138; *Abs.* 12; *Fable* 190): a porch, especially a long, narrow one. **2.** (*Unv.* 153): a slave gallery built upstairs in the back of a church, much like the gallery in a theater, with a railing or balustrade across the front.

galluses (*Town* 138; *Dust* 113; *CS:BH* 68): suspenders, braces. In *Unv.* 200 the three pairs of suspenders are fastened together to make an improvised cat-o'-nine-tails.

gap (*Fable* 191): a term used in the southern Appalachians for what is called a "notch" in New England and a "pass" in the West and internationally. It is a word "which we didn't have in Mississippi" (*Unv.* 17) because the state has no real mountains.

G. A. R. (*S&F* 101): Grand Army of the Republic, the Northern Army during the Civil War.

gar (*WP* 308; *Fable* 156): garpike, any of a number of fish with a heavy armorplating of scales, a long, cylindrical body, and a long snout. The most sensa-

tional of these is the alligator gar (*Atractosteus tristoechus*), which reaches a
length of well over 15′.

garage hammer (*Mans.* 385): the ball-peen hammer mentioned a few lines
above, called a garage hammer because it is used largely for metal-work, as
opposed to a carpenter's claw-hammer.

garbled (*LiA* 111): apparently a misprint for *gabled*.

gardenia (*Mosq.* 16). See JASMINE.

Garnett and Kemper and Armstead and Wilcox (*Dust* 195). These men
were all involved in PICKETT's Charge at GETTYSBURG, the first three glorious-
ly. Gen. Richard Brooke Garnett was killed outright, Brig. Gen. James
Lawson Kemper was critically wounded, and Brig. Gen. Lewis A. Armistead
(Faulkner misspells his name) was mortally wounded. Brig. Gen. Cadmus
Wilcox conducted his troops with great inertia and uselessness.

gash (*Reiv.* 145): gap.

gas-jet (*Sanc.* 59, 269): the slightly tapering, rigid-metal pipe bringing gas
into a room. A rubber tube is slipped over it to connect it to a portable hot-
plate, heater, etc. The point here is that Ruby had no such appliance but
had to cook awkwardly over a flame from the jet itself.

gasoline (*Reiv.* 48). The description is typical for the early equivalent of a
filling station. Gasoline was pumped by hand into a graduated glass reservoir above head-level and drained from there by a hose into the car. The gas-
tank of a car was under the front seat; engines had no fuel pumps, but used
a gravity-feed. There were also no fuel gauges, and a marked or notched
stick, dipped into the tank, was used to measure the gasoline supply.

gasoline lever (*CS:Fox* 594): throttle of a car—probably not an accelerator
on the floorboard, but a lever mounted on the steering column, as on a
modern tractor.

Gaston (*Reiv.* 96). At the time of *Reiv.* this hotel (long since gone) stood on
Court St. at COURT SQUARE in Memphis.

gates (*Abs.* 25). The Southern plantation house stands well back from any
public road and is approached by its own driveway, often a long one. Sutpen's driveway was half a mile long (*Abs.* 365). There is some sort of formal
gateway where the driveway leaves the road. Such a gateway is often only
that, with no actual gates (*GDM* 9). Sutpen evidently had gates, as their dis-
appearance is commented on (*Abs.* 364). However, they apparently were not
normally closed, since there is never any mention of opening them. Essentially, the gates stood open and served merely as a gateway and formal entrance.

gather (*Ham.* 9–10, 11): to harvest. This is a general term, applied to cotton,
corn, etc. If cotton specifically is meant, the *v.* is always *pick*.

gather (of a horse) (*Ham.* 173; *GDM* 14): to bring the feet close together in
preparation for a sudden leap or effort.

gathering time (*Ham.* 11, 16): harvesting time, in the fall.

gathering with horses and dogs (*Abs.* 289). Gathering thus equipped will
show that they assume that Wash will not stand his ground but will have to

be run down by a posse. This is the point of "these it was whom he was expected to run from," lower on the same page.

gaunted. 1. *adj.* (*AILD* 193; *LiA* 58; *KG:Tomo.* 99): gaunt, thin. **2.** *p.t.* and *p.p.* of *gaunt* (*Unv.* 12; *GDM* 218): made thin, emaciated.

Gayoso. 1. (*S&F* 289; *Mans.* 62): an avenue in Memphis, once elegant but sadly decayed by the 1920s. **2.** (*Sanc.* 183; *Reiv.* 95, 96): the Gayoso Hotel, once the leading hotel of Memphis. It operated until about 1960. The red brick building (now painted white) still stands on Front St. betewen Main and Gayoso, and is now used as an annex of a department store. There is a persistent legend that Gen. FORREST rode his horse into the Gayoso lobby in search of a Union general, who escaped out a window in his underwear (*GDM* 234). The facts are somewhat more entertaining than the legend as Faulkner tells it. When Forrest made a surprise raid on Memphis, his brother, Capt. William Forrest, did ride his horse into the lobby of the Gayoso. Gen. Washburn, who was in bed, cleared out through the back door without stopping to dress. Gen. Forrest sent his clothes to him under a flag of truce. Washburn, not to be outdone, had Forrest's tailor make a fine new uniform to Forrest's measure, and sent it to him with his compliments. See Andrew Lytle, *Bedford Forrest and His Critter Company* (New York, n. d.), pp. 324–25.

gear (*Unv.* 270; *GDM* 47, 48; *RfaN* 278): a collective term for a horse's or mule's harness, bridle, saddle, etc.

geared-up mules (*Reiv.* 74): mules with harness, trace-chains, etc., already put on them, so that they are ready to be hitched to an implement immediately.

gear-up (*Dust* 96): to put harness, trace-chains, etc., on a horse or mule in preparation for working him.

gee and haw (*Reiv.* 82, 83): words used to order draft aminals being driven without reins to go to the right and the left, respectively.

gee dee (*Town* 61): G.-d., euphemism for *God-damned.*

geese (*Mans.* 30, 320): Canada geese (*Branta canadensis*), resident and hunted in Mississippi in the winter.

geese and ducks (*Unv.* 187). Faulkner's country is in the Mississippi Valley flyway for migrating birds. Flocks of waterfowl are sometimes seen by day, but much more often are heard passing over at night. There were, of course, far more of them at the time of *Unv.* than now, and they would have been much more audible to people sleeping out in the silence of the winter woods.

gempmuns (*CS:Fox* 590): gentlemen.

general (*Unv.* 85): to lead and maneuver (someone), as a general does his troops.

General Booth (*Fable* 181): See BOOTH, WILLIAM.

General Early (*CS : MGM* 673). See EARLY, GEN. JUBAL A.

General Smith (*Unv.* 137, 145; *CS:MGM* 689): Union Gen. Andrew J. Smith. He did fight FORREST around TALLAHATCHIE CROSSING and HURRICANE CREEK. He also burned Oxford.

General Wheeler (*CS:MGM* 673). See WHEELER, GEN. JOSEPH.

Genl (*GDM* 324; *CS:MGM* 689): General.

Genl Fawhrest (*CS:MGM* 689): Gen. FORREST.

gentle, *v.i.* (*Ham.* 273): to respond to taming and training.

Gentle-men (*Dust* 241). The hyphen is Faulkner's way of indicating a second stress, on the last syllable—a very noticeable characteristic of most Negro speech in such words as "govern*ment*" and "presi*dent.*"

Gentlemen, hush (*Town* 241, 256). See HUSH.

George Peyton (*Reiv.* 194): a well-known handler of bird dogs. From 1917 to 1941 he handled one or more dogs almost every year in the NATIONAL TRIALS.

Georgia, hog in (*KG:Hand* 65). See OR THERE AIN'T A HOG IN GEORGIA.

Germantown (*Reiv.* 194): a town (now on the edge of Memphis) 35 m. W of Grand Junction (Parsham).

get (*Mosq.* 68): understand.

get a-holt (*Mans.* 89, 136; *CS:TM* 51; *CS:TES* 300): get a hold, get a start.

get done (*S&F* 30; *Sanc.* 61; *CS:MGM* 672): finish.

get my alley (*Flags* 173). In tennis (doubles) one gets the alley of the person playing net by putting the ball past him into the alley on his side of the court.

get-out (*Ham.* 307), or **all~**: an extreme, as in "hurt like all get-out."

get out of the sun (*Fable* 170): get out of the way; don't obstruct.

get shed of (*CS:BH* 72): GET SHUT OF.

get shet of (*Unv.* 138): GET SHUT OF.

get shut of (*Sart.* 293; *AILD* 183; *Sanc.* 20): get rid of.

Gettysburg (*GDM* 286): a decisive battle fought near Gettysburg, Pa., July 1–3, 1863. The high point of the battle, and the "high-water mark of the Confederacy" was PICKETT's Charge. Faulkner's inclusion of "Longstreet too at Gettysburg" among the senseless misfortunes of the Confederacy is a reference to a still-acrimonious debate about Longstreet's delay in engaging his troops there.

get up (*Dust* 125): to mount a horse.

get up. 1. (*S&F* 11): a command to a horse or mule to start moving or to move faster. **2.** (*Ham.* 15). Ab would be expected to stand up when addressed by and answering his landlord.

ghy (*Sanc.* 111, 219; *LiA* 411; *Unv.* 22): GWINE, going to. (Pronounced like *guy.*)

Gilbert, John (*Sanc.* 220). Minnie doubtless refers to the romantic movie star (1897–1936), not to the actor of the same name (1810–89).

gillymus (*WT* 73): GILLYPUS.

gillypus (*WT* 25, 57, 58): an imaginary animal (?) invented by Faulkner— or by the little old man.

gimmit (*Unv.* 62): give me it.

gin (*Sart.* 277; *Unv.* 95; *GDM* 341): COTTON GIN.

gin (*S&F* 237; *Ham.* 56): to put (cotton) through a COTTON GIN.

ginned-up (*Sanc.* 237): drunk—not necessarily on gin.

ginney (*Sanc.* 303): strictly speaking, an Italian. The rural Alabamians in the courtroom are not Italians, but *ginney* is a term of contempt, and that is all that Popeye means or wants. He is no more concerned about their nationality than he is about the actual names of the people he contemptuously calls Jack (e.g. *Sanc.* 6, where Horace Benbow has just told Popeye his name).

girth-strap (*Dust* 91): a strap that passes under a horse's belly and holds the saddle in place.

git (*Unv.* 76; *Ham.* 167, 175): get, in the sense of "go away, clear out."

Git a horse! (*Reiv.* 77). Beginning as a jibe at an early motorist having car-trouble, *get a horse* soon became a general catch-phrase applicable to almost anything connected with a car.

git up with (*AILD* 43): get up with, catch up with.

Give-me-lief (*Mans.* 430): Give me leave. At the bottom of this page, because of the nature of the game here described, *lief* extends from meaning "leave, permission" to mean "chance, turn."

Give me your foot (*CS:BB* 14). See THREW ME UP.

give one the air (*Mosq.* 344): to get rid of, or run out on, a person.

give twenty or thirty pounds (*Town* 90): to fight an opponent weighing 20 or 30 lbs. more (boxing jargon).

gizzle (*S&F* 79): Caddy's attempt at *gizzard*. It is fairly standard to threaten to slit someone's gizzard.

Glasgow (*Dust*, 63, 115, 223): a fictional town in Crossman (Pontotoc) Co. (There is an actual Glasgow, Miss., 55 m. SE of Jackson, but this fact is evidently accidental since it is 200 m. from where Faulkner places his Glasgow.)

globe. 1. (of a lamp) (*LiA* 143): an ornamented glass globe fitting over the chimney of a fancy "library lamp." McEachern has removed the globe to light the lamp, and as he replaces it the light shines through his hand. **2.** (of an electric light) (*Abs.* 89, 128): a frosted globe, about 8″–10″ in diameter, put over the bulb of a porch-light to diffuse the light. During the summer it has not only become stained by insects flying against it, but it is "bug-fouled" by a considerable mass of small insects dead in the bottom of it.

glugging (*Sanc.* 105): an imitative nonce-word: making a sound imitating that of whiskey being poured from a jug.

go' (*SP* 313): going to.

goad (*Sart.* 206; *Reiv.* 83): a stick sharpened at one end, used to prod mules, and especially oxen, into action. It is sometimes considered a cheap substitute for a whip.

goan (*GDM* 136): going.

gobble talk *Fable* 154, 199): French.

go-cart (*S&F* 260): hand-cart, pushcart. Jason is assuming that Caddy resents his having any inheritance and wants him to be a penniless street-peddler.

goddam (*S&F* 229) : not standard usage as a *n*. Miss Quentin is only seventeen, and she has the spirit of profanity but has not yet mastered the idiom.

God dawg (*Race* 185, 191) : God dog (euphemism for *God damn*).

godfrey (*GDM* 14, 21, 22) : euphemism for *God*.

Go Down, Moses (title) : a Negro spiritual, with the refrain, "Go down, Moses, way down in Egypt's land, and tell old pharaoh to let my people go." (This is as I remember hearing it from my early childhood. A spiritual, being a work of genuine oral art, has no definitive text or score.)

going wump-wump-wump inside (*Sanc.* 203). The belly-rumbles of horses are notorious. Faulkner frequently refers to those of Will Varner's horse— e.g. "the rich, sonorous organ-tone of its entrails" (*Ham.* 157).

goin' on (*WT* 41) : foolishness, nonsense.

Golden Gloves (*Town* 183, 187, 285) : regional, state, and national amateur boxing contests, and the awards given to their winners.

gold stars(*Sart.* 120). A gold star was the heraldic emblem of a mother who had lost a son in World War I.

gole waiter (*LiA* 451) : gold waiter (i.e. serving-tray).

gone (*Fable* 196) : have gone.

gonter (*Unv.* 26, 41; *GDM* 13, 76; *Reiv.* 12) : going to. (The *o* is pronounced as in *no*.) Sometimes a redundant *to* is added, much like the *us* in *let's us*, to produce *gonter to* (*CS:MGM* 689).

good girl (*Sanc.* 34). There may be an allusion here to a standard undergraduate distinction of the time of *Sanc.* between a nice girl ("won't let you put it in") and a good girl ("will put it in for you").

go out (*GDM* 9, 14) : (of a horse) to begin to run at full speed.

Gordon Hall (*Sanc.* 165) : the men's dining-hall at the University of Mississippi in the 1920s. It was on the site of the present School of Engineering.

gorilla (*Sanc.* 124) : gangster. There is no implication of either great size or strength : Popeye had neither.

go to earth (*GDM* 18) : to seek out and stop in a place of refuge, as a fox in his den.

gots. 1. (*GDM* 74) : get. **2.** (*GDM* 136) : got, have.

gots to (*GDM* 121) : got to, must.

gouge (*Abs.* 29; *Mans.* 118; *Miss.* 19) : to gouge out an eye with the thumb, or try to, in a rough-and-tumble fight. In *S&F* 113 the idea goes with the "no holds barred" in making the world's championship of sitting around a violent affair.

gourd (*AILD* 4; *Unv.* 40; *CS:Red* 341) : a dipper made from a gourd. A special variety, known as a dipper-gourd, is grown for this purpose. It bears a fruit with a handle about 1″ thick and 15″ long, on the end of which is a spherical enlargement the size of a grapefruit. One side of the sphere is cut out to make a dipper, which is used to drink from a spring or well-bucket. A loop of string through a hole bored in the end of the handle is used to hang the dipper from a nail or branch.

Governor Smith (*Town* 314): Al (Alfred E.) Smith, governor of New York, and Democratic presidential candidate in 1928.

gown (*S&F* 90): nightgown, NIGHTSHIRT.

grabble (*AILD* 143, 144; *Ham.* 232; *Reiv.* 6): to feel for and grasp by feel. Grabbling is a standard method of fishing in which a person wades along the edge of a creek or river, groping in holes, under logs and overhanging banks, etc., and seizing any fish that he can. Because of this way of fishing, Vardaman knows that Darl "is the best grabbler" in the family (*AILD* 143). The fishing reference also explains the passage on the following page: " 'Where is ma, Darl?' I said. 'You never got her. You knew she was a fish, but you let her get away.' " The "grabble and snatch" (*CS:TM* 58) of government agencies like the WPA ("three-letter reasons for a man not to work") is a graphic way of picturing loafers groping for any possible handouts and snatching anything they find.

Grand- and Petit Gulf (*Miss.* 28). In 1700, Iberville gave the names *Grand Gouffre* and *Petit Gouffre* to two dangerous whirlpools in the Mississippi River. Half-translated, these names were then applied to the settlements on the banks adjoining these spots. The whirlpool of *Grand Gouffre* was formed by a combination of the mixing of the currents of the Mississippi and the Big Black rivers and the effect of a sandstone bluff jutting out into the stream. A settlement was established on the plain above this bluff in 1828, and Grand Gulf became a leading cotton market, with big luxury stores, banks, a theater, and its own newspaper. It was destroyed by the river and the Yankees. The river began to undercut the bluff, taking some of the town along with it. Then, during the Vicksburg campaign, Federal troops burned most of what was left. Then the river moved the other way and abandoned the ruins. There is still enough of it to be shown on maps. It is 25 m. S of Vicksburg, and a couple of miles below the junction of the Big Black and the Mississippi. Petit Gulf was 15 m. SSW of Grand Gulf and 23 m. N of Natchez. It was important enough to have one of the leading strains of cotton named for it. It occupied the approximate location of the present village of Rodney. The outlaw "Little Harpe" (see NATCHEZ TRACE) was captured and hanged at Old Greenville, near Petit Gulf.

Grand National Trials (*Reiv.* 194). See PARSHAM.

Grant (*Sart.* 223): Federal Gen. Ulysses S. Grant is important in Faulkner largely because of his movements in northern Mississippi in connection with the Vicksburg campaign. He made his headquarters in Oxford for most of December 1862.

grape vine (*WP* 149, 232; *CS:BB* 5; *Race* 184). The vines of the WILD GRAPE are the regular improvised swings of country children and the improvised ropes of adults. On one occasion during the Civil War, FORREST used them to build pontoon bridges on which he took cavalry and artillery across a river.

graphophone (*AILD* 225, 247): phonograph, gramophone. This was for a time the standard term: all such devices in the 1902 Sears catalogue are called graphophones.

grass (*Mans.* 4): spring. The native grasses (not the improved modern pasture ones) of Faulkner's country are killed to the ground by the first frost and are replaced by new green growth in the spring.

grass rope (*Ham.* 185): rope made of any vegetable fiber except cotton: hence sisal rope, manila rope, etc.

grate bars (*S&F* 332): the bars that make the grate in a stove. They have a handle by which they can be shaken to shake down the ashes, and this process is a noisy one.

grate screen (*SP* 221): a large-meshed screen in front of a fire-grate, to keep coals from popping out on the floor.

grave-filling (*S&F* 249; *GDM* 135). It was customary for friends and relatives to fill the grave after a funeral.

gravel (*GDM* 83, 84; *Town* 291; *Mans.* 103). Before roads were paved, main ones often had a gravel surface to help avoid skidding and miring down in wet weather. The material used around Oxford was natural gravel from beds at the edge of the DELTA, not crushed stone. Later, main roads were paved and secondary ones were gravel (*GDM* 341).

grazed up (*Ham.* 70): grazed until there is no grass left; i.e. exhausted the possibilities of profit. The phrase implies a need to seek greener pastures.

green-and-ruby gleams of switch points (*Reiv.* 144): reflections of railroad signal lights on the tapered, movable rails at switches.

Greenbury (*KG:KG* 192, 193): a fictional hotel in Memphis. Because of the phonetic resemblance and the metrical equivalence of the names, I suspect that both the Greenbury and the Teaberry are pseudonyms for the PEABODY. The statement about Mississippi beginning in the lobby (cf. the first sentence of *Miss.*) was normally applied to the Peabody.

greens (*Sart.* 27; *AILD* 39; *GDM* 139): any leaves that can be or have been boiled for eating. *Greens*, used alone, implies cooking. If the leaves are to be eaten raw, they are called *salad greens*.

greenshaded reading lamp (*LiA* 71): a lamp with a porcelain shade, green outside and white inside. This was a standard type of desk or floor lamp for reading.

Greenville (*Mans.* 103, 325; *Miss.* 28): a town in the DELTA where there is a bridge across the Mississippi.

Grenada (*Sart.* 223; *Unv.* 186): a Mississippi town about 45 m. SSW of Oxford.

Grenier County (*Ham.* 9, 77): a fictional county near the southern edge of Yoknapatawpha Co.

gret (*S&F* 400; *Sanc.* 35; *Unv.* 159, 237): great.

grew man grown (*LiA* 367): grown into a grown man.

grift (*Sanc.* 112, 265): business, profession (underworld slang). Goodwin wants his child given a start in life as a newsboy selling papers on the street.

Grinnich Village (*Mans.* 151, 159): Greenwich Village.

grip (*AILD* 249; *S&F* 120; *Town* 97): valise, small suitcase.

grits (*RfaN* 253; *Mans.* 276; *Reiv.* 171): a characteristically Southern dish made of corn, which is hulled, coarsely ground, boiled, and served hot, with butter or gravy.

grooved barrel (*RfaN* 218): rifled barrel. The rifle was a considerable improvement, not only over the bow and arrow, but over the old smooth-bore guns as well.

grove at the University (*Abs.* 95): the grove lying to the right as one crosses the bridge from Oxford onto the campus of the University of Mississippi and goes straight ahead. The drive encircling it is now called Grove Loop.

grub contractor (*Mans.* 64): a person who makes a contract for the feeding of convicts.

Gulfport (*Flags* 345): a Mississippi town on the Gulf of Mexico, some 270 m. from Oxford.

gully (*GDM* 60, 77). Much of Lafayette Co. is badly eroded. The hills are largely what is known geologically as the Lafayette formation: a layer of loam some 4′–8′ thick, overlying sand. Washes start on the slopes of abandoned fields, deepen slowly at first, and then sensationally when they get down to the sand. Many gullies exist in which a two-story house could easily be concealed. Cf. the "deep ditch" of *LiA* 435, and see Appendix on it. They are variously called gulleys, ravines, SAND-DITCHES, etc., but are all essentially the same phenomenon. With extensive reforestation, the gullies are not now nearly so prominent as they used to be.

gum (*Sart.* 6, 276; *Sanc.* 3; *Ham.* 278). Any of several species of trees of the genera *Nyassa* (BLACK-GUM) and *Liquidambar* (SWEET GUM or redgum). All are large trees, tending to grow around the edges of lowlands and river bottoms. Their leaves turn bright red in the fall. Black-gum twigs are often used for SNUFF-STICKS (*CS:Red* 322).

gumbo (*WP* 4, 5): a soup thickened with unripe okra pods and (on the Mississippi coast) normally made with crabs, shrimp, etc.

gum branch (*LiA* 478): a branch of a GUM, used as an improvised broom.

gun rag (*S&F* 228): a rag used to clean, oil, and polish a gun—hence a dirty, oily rag.

guttering (*Sanc.* 53): in normal usage, the running of wax down the side of a candle. Faulkner seems to have made a two-stage transference of meaning, first to the blowing of the flame sidewise which causes guttering, and then to the sound made by a flame so blown.

gutting (*Mosq.* 253). I have found no clue as to what this may mean. Presumably *somebody's* and *anybody's* are possessives rather than contractions, and in that case *gutting* must be a *n.* or gerund; but that does not give much help.

gwinter(*Unv.* 25): going to. (The *i* is pronounced as in *fine*.)

gwup (*SP* 298): go up.

gyard (*Sart.* 226): guard.

gyarden (*Sart.* 50): garden.

gymnasium shoes (*Sanc.* 85; *Ham.* 290): shoes with rubber soles and canvas tops, tennis shoes, sneakers.

H

hack (*S&F* 249, 254; *Reiv*. 24; *CS:TWBF* 269): a hired (or for hire) carriage or coach.

Hadley (*Ham*. 232): a make of shotgun.

haid (*Sart*. 63): head.

hair made into a frame (*CS:Hair* 139). The hair would be tightly plaited to make the frame. Rings, brooches, pictures, etc., made of human hair were an elaborate international handicraft in the nineteenth century. Hawkshaw's mail-order frame was about the last gasp of this dying business.

hair trigger (*Unv*. 257): a trigger or (more properly) a lock mechanism that is very easily fired with the slightest pull.

Haley bottom (*AILD* 176): a fictional creek or river bottom.

half a quarter (*Race* 175, 176, 179): half a quarter of a mile, furlong, 220 yards.

half-bred colt . . . with Morgan on the bottom (*Reiv*. 183): a colt with one high-quality parent and one nondescript one, and a basis (doubtless the good parent) of the MORGAN breed.

half-length doors (*Ham*. 281): the doors of the HALLWAY of a barn, which are high enough only to hold in the livestock, and hence roughly half as high as the actual hallway.

half-size axe (*CS:BB* 16): a boy's axe, a standard implement used both to teach a boy to use an axe and to let him cut wood effectively long before he can wield a man-sized axe.

half-starved (*Mans*. 374). When Ratliff applies this description to Mink, he is probably referring to the latter's diminutive stature.

hall (*AILD* 112): the central passageway of a BARN, usually called a HALLWAY.

Halleck, General (*Sart*. 13). In July 1862, Lincoln made Henry W. Halleck general-in-chief of the Union armies, and made Gen. John Pope (*Sart*. 10, 13, 19) head of the new Army of Virginia under him. This is evidently the situation at the time of Bayard's escapade.

hallway. 1. (*Sart*. 137; *Sanc*. 79, 96; *Unv*. 82): the central passageway of a BARN. **2.** (*Ham*. 219; *GDM* 45): the open space between the rooms of a DOG-TROT CABIN.

halter (*Unv*. 137; *Ham*. 44; *GDM* 83): any sort of rope and head stall for leading or tying a horse, cow, etc. "Bucking at the halter" (*Sanc*. 26) is trying to slip out of it. A halter-rein is the line attached to the headstall for leading an animal, and the "two halter-reins" (*Ham*. 194) are one each for the mule and cow the farmer is leading.

halter rein (*Fable* 196). See HALTER.

halvers (*LiA* 394; *WP* 255): claiming and getting a half-share. Two children may agree to "go halvers" on some project, i.e. to divide the proceeds equally. Similarly, when one child finds something, a companion may exclaim "Halvers!"—thus putting in a claim for an equal share in it.

hames (*Ham.* 16; *GDM* 78; *Reiv.* 84): two curved, rigid, wood-and-metal or all-metal pieces that fit into the flare of a horse-collar, one on each side, and against which the actual pull is exerted. They are held together at the top and bottom by HAME STRINGS, and the TRACES by which the horse pulls are attached to them. They are equipped with various rings for these attachments. Hames are often ornamented with brass balls at the tops.

hame string (*S&F* 242, 264; *Abs.* 82). Strictly speaking, the HAMES may be fastened together above and below a horse's collar either by hame strings (leather thongs, which are tied) or by hame straps (leather straps, which are buckled). In practice the distinction is often ignored, and Faulkner uses *hame string* for either system. A hame strap would be a handy thing to thrash someone with, being a fairly heavy strap 26″ or 21″ long for the top and bottom straps, respectively.

hammer (of a gun). See CAP-AND-BALL REVOLVER and SHOTGUN.

hammer double gun (*GDM* 342): double-barreled hammer (as opposed to hammerless) shotgun.

hammer-headed . . . horse (*RfaN* 27): a horse with a bony ridge between the ears and, supposedly, a low mentality.

hammer-lock (shotgun) (*Ham.* 232): one having external, hand-cocked hammers (see SHOTGUN), as opposed to a modern "hammerless" gun.

hammer mill (*CS:TM* 47): a mill in which feed is pulverized by small hammers revolving at high speed.

hammock (*S&F* 107): a little hammock-shaped net in a PULLMAN berth in which the occupant puts his clothes when he undresses.

hammock made of barrel staves (*S&F* 393): BARREL STAVE HAMMOCK.

Hammond (*WP* 56): a Louisiana town 35 m. NW of New Orleans, N of Lake PONTCHARTRAIN. It is some 60 m. by rail, around Lake Pontchartrain ("the larger lake," *WP* 58) and along the isthmus between it and Lake Maurepas. The two lakes are joined by a waterway crossed by a trestle.

Hancock (*GDM* 286). See STUART, James Ewell Brown.

hand (*Reiv.* 125): four inches. The basic unit of measurement (at the withers) for the size of horses. Thus, this horse, "not even sixteen hands," was less than 5′4″ high at the highest part of the back, between the shoulder blades.

hand (*Ham.* 8; *Reiv.* 293; *Race* 194): laborer, employee.

hand gallop (*Reiv.* 170): a moderate gallop or a gait between a canter and a gallop. It is a relaxed pace on a loose rein.

hand-grip (*AILD* 248; *Ham.* 78): GRIP, valise.

handkerchief about his head, and earrings (*LiA* 348): the regular get-up of a gypsy traveling about the country with one or two trained bears.

hand me your foot (*Reiv.* 171, 181). See THREW ME UP.

hand-polished cane (*Ham.* 331): not given any special polishing, but simply polished in the natural course of events by the hand that carried it.

hand satchel (*Sart.* 109; *CS:TS* 91): a rustic's term for a lady's handbag.

hant (*GDM* 215; *Town* 238; *Reiv.* 270): haunt, ghost, any supernatural creature.

happen-chance: 1. *n.* (*Reiv.* 64): possibility. **2.** *v.i.* (*Reiv.* 66): to arrive or come along by accident.

Hard Shell Baptist (*Mans.* 53, 58, 181): member of the Primitive Baptist Church, an extremely rigid, severe fundamentalist sect.

Hare (*RfaN* 103, 104; *Miss.* 14): Joseph Thompson Hare, an early Mississippi outlaw omitted from Faulkner's earlier list of those operating on the NATCHEZ TRACE (*RfaN* 5). Governor Claiborne, an early Mississippi historian, describes him as "a more blood-thirsty villain even than the celebrated Mason."

harness strap (*LiA* 139): a generic rather than a specific term. It could be a specific strap from a harness—a hame-strap (see HAME STRING), CHOKE STROP, etc.—or a strap for making or repairing harness. All that the term really indicates is a piece of pretty heavy leather strap.

Harpes (*RfaN* 5, 16, 102; *Miss.* 14, 28). See NATCHEZ TRACE.

harrow teeth (*Ham.* 25). A harrow is used to break up clods and prepare a seed-bed for planting. A tooth-harrow consists of a flat, rectangular metal frame in which teeth connected to stiff springs are mounted. These teeth are sharp spikes about 6″ long which break up the clods as the frame is dragged along. The frame is practically indestructible, and new teeth are bought separately and installed from time to time.

harrycane (*CS:BH* 75): hurricane.

Harrykin Creek (*Town* 53; *Reiv.* 68; *CS:MGM* title and 697): HURRICANE CREEK.

hasp: a hinged metal plate used to padlock a door. The hasp is fastened to the door or doorjamb, and the hinged part has a slot which fits over a staple fastened opposite it. If the hasp and the staple are not well aligned (as by sloppy mounting, or by sagging of the door), a person can be locked inside a room simply by forcing the hasp over the staple, without putting a pin or padlock through it. This is what happened when Temple was in the crib and heard Tommy "drive the hasp to" (*Sanc.* 97). Strictly speaking, one does not snap a padlock through the hasp, but through the staple (*Reiv.* 31).

hatrack (*Town* 298): a highly variable article of furniture, ranging from an upright stand with hooks on it, through a mirror with hooks on the sides of the frame, to an elaborate piece of furniture with a bench-seat and a flat back containing a mirror in the middle and hooks at the sides. Since a hatrack is placed right by the front door, it is an obvious and standard place to leave a message.

Hattiesburg (*Miss.* 32): a town in south-central Mississippi, 70 m. from the Gulf.

have (*CS:Fox* 602): sometimes, as here, entirely redundant.

hawberries (*Race* 183): the hard, bright red fruits of various species of haw (thorn), genus *Crataegus*.

hawg-lot (*Sart.* 22): hog-lot, a fairly large enclosure, perhaps an acre, for hogs.

hawg-trough (*Dust.* 71): hog-trough, a trough in which hogs are fed. Primitive ones are made by splitting a hollow log and nailing boards across the ends. Later ones have two planks nailed together with the edges at right angles, with a board across each end to serve both as an end and as a support, so that the trough is simply a **V**.

hawk (*Unv.* 75). The hawk of this striking simile is clearly a marsh hawk (*Circus cyaneus*), which winters in the South and hunts in the manner described here, flying just above the tops of grass and weeds in winter fields.

Hawkhurst (*Unv.* 91, 97, 217): a fictional town in fictional Gihon Co., Ala.

Hawkshaw (*CS:Hair* 141): originally, the name of a detective in Tom Taylor's play *The Ticket of Leave Man* (1863). The subliterary use of the name comes from Gus Meyer's comic-strip *Hawkshaw the Detective*.

hawm (*GDM* 148): harm.

hawss (*Sart.* 344; *CS:MV* 746; *WT* 12): horse.

hay baler (*Reiv.* 33; *CS:BH* 69, 74): a machine for compressing hay into bales and fastening them with HAYWIRE. Early hay balers, often homemade, had a box into which the hay was pushed by hand. It was then compressed by turning a crank, and the slack was taken up by a coarse ratchet. It is the sound of this ratchet, coming at intervals as the crank is turned, to which the sound of hiccups is compared.

hayfork (*Mans.* 13): pitchfork used for moving hay.

hayrack (*Unv.* 82): a container built onto a stable wall, making a **V** with the wall at the bottom of the rack. It is made of widely spaced slats, so that hay put into the rack can be pulled out between them. It is different from a manger, which is a solid, flat-bottomed box for such feed as oats and corn.

haywire (*Mans.* 230): to go haywire is to go wrong, go wild, act as if crazy.

haze (*Unv.* 165): to drive, with whatever inducements may be necessary. The verb implies that there will be a good deal of shouting, waving of hats, swinging of sticks or whips, etc.

he (*S&F* 47, 369; *CS:BH* 79; *CS:MV* 746): his.

head-and-head poker (*Unv.* 53): two-man poker, poker with only two players.

headcloth (*GDM* 100): a cloth worn wrapped around the head like a turban. It is often worn by elderly Negro women at work, and is sometimes called a HEADRAG. Faulkner also calls it a turban (*S&F* 330).

head-kerchief (*GDM* 70): HEADCLOTH, HEADRAG.

headrag (*LiA* 243; *Abs.* 214, 368; *Unv.* 8): HEADCLOTH. For *Dust.* 15, see also FIELD NIGGERS.

head-stall (*Unv.* 120; *Ham.* 35; *GDM* 233): the part of a bridle that fits over the head.

He ain't only going to Buffalo (*SP* 14): He is going only to (as far as) Buffalo.

heap (*Town* 350; *Fable* 188): large quantity, considerable number.

heap rather (*Dust* 80): a heap rather, much rather.

heard its feet bunch (*S&F* 201). A running horse, suddenly reined in, bunches its feet close together, almost skidding to a stop. Cf. *AILD* 12, 13.

heat (*CS:MGM* 682): the glow of red-hot iron.

heaven trees (*Sart.* 165, 352; *Sanc.* 110, 120): not the botanists' tree of heaven (*Ailanthus altissima*), but a local name for the princess tree, or royal paulownia (*Paulownia tomentosa*). This oriental tree, now escaped from cultivation in many places, grows 30'–60' high and 1'–2' in diameter. It has large leaves, and in the spring is covered with pyramids of mauve flowers, trumpet-shaped and about 2" long, which have an almost sickeningly sweet odor. The flowers are somewhat sticky, and when they fall off they are squishy underfoot, exactly as described in *Sanc.* 122, 130. There were formerly heaven trees by the old city power plant in the railroad cut at Oxford (*Sart.* 165)—there are still some in this general vicinity—and in the jail-yard (*Sanc.* passim). Stark Young's novel *Heaven Trees* is set on a plantation bearing this name, and the trees which give it its title are presumably the same species, though Young never describes them in sufficient detail to establish the fact.

hedge bush (*Reiv.* 147): PRIVET.

heel, *v.t.* (*CS:SftL* 34): to urge (a horse or mule) on by striking him in the side with one's heel.

heel-bolt (*GDM* 293): a heavy (nut and) bolt used to fasten a SWEEP or other PLOWSHARE to a PLOW STOCK. The nut is a tail nut, i.e. one having a tapering "tail" on one of its sides, curved around to form a rigid ring. By inserting any strong stick in this ring, one can tighten or loosen this nut without having to use a wrench.

heeler (*WP* 88): one who serves as a general flunkey for a publication, hoping to get a regular place on the staff. This meaning (not found in dictionaries) is confirmed by Sinclair Lewis's story from the same period, "Young Man Axelbrod," in which one Yale student says of another, "Thinks he's literary, they say, and yet he doesn't even heel the 'Lit' like a regular literary fellow."

he——hope to breakfast (*CS:TS* 91). The Law starts to use the standard *from hell to breakfast*, but out of deference to the ladies changes in mid-word to a nonce-euphemism.

Held, Anna (*Mosq.* 240): a pert, beautiful, widely publicized music-hall singer and comedienne of French-British extraction (1873–1918). For Faulkner's simile, see LAMP.

hell a mile (*Ham.* 264; *WP* 271): a more emphatic form of *hell*.

Hellaw (*Reiv.* 115, 252): Hello (as pronounced when it is shouted).

Hell Creek (*Reiv.* 68, 78): Spring Creek, which flows into the Tallahatchie and which the road from Oxford to Memphis crosses between this river and Waterford. Faulkner seems to have borrowed the name from an actual Hell Creek which flows in a parallel course to Spring Creek, near New Albany, but it is clear off the route followed in *Reiv.* or any other reasonable route from Oxford to Memphis.

hell-full (*Sanc.* 245): unpleasantly full, crowded with. (*Hell* simply serves as an intensive.)

He'll have a gun now (*LiA* 311). Any Negro cabin will have a gun of some kind, and the sheriff assumes that Joe will now have it.

hem up (*RfaN* 278): to corner, surround.

hen-coop (*GDM* 277; *WP* 157; *Dust* 181): a small structure, something like 3' square and 18" high, usually made of slats, in which one or two hens are shut up temporarily. It is much smaller than a HEN-HOUSE. The simile in *Dust* 181 is that of hen-coops swept along on a flood, as described in *WP* 157.

hen-hawk (*Ham.* 319): any large hawk, but especially the red-tailed hawk (*Buteo jamaicensis*) or the red-shouldered hawk (*B. lineatus*). Since most farmers shot all large hawks on sight, they became very wary and quick to take flight.

hen-house. 1. (*Ham.* 83; *Reiv.* 203; *WP* 244): a small house, 8'–10' square, in which hens roost. It usually has nest-boxes for laying, though hens often ignore them and lay in various hideouts around the barn instead. A henhouse is often entirely enclosed by wire and the chickens are shut into it at night, in an attempt to protect them from POSSUMS and other vermin. **2.** (*Sanc.* 187; *GDM* 23): any place where women live, or are available.

hen nest (*Mans.* 7). Hens are supposed to lay in nest-boxes in the HEN-HOUSE, but they often prefer to find their own hidden places. Finding the secret nests and collecting the eggs from them is one of the jobs of the farm wife. It is also a good pretext for straying off into hidden places (*Ham.* 140).

heron (*Town* 206). Faulkner does not distinguish the species here, but the comparison would indicate that he is probably thinking of the great blue heron (*Ardea herodias*), which stands about 4' high.

Heyo (*Sart.* 348): an exclamation of general cheerfulness or celebration (probably derived from *heigh-ho*).

hibiscus (*Mosq.* 14, 324): a genus of ornamental plants, including some that are fairly hardy well to the north. When used unqualified, however, *hibiscus* normally refers to *H. coccinneus*, which grows on the Gulf coast. It has widely flaring trumpet-shaped scarlet flowers 3"–4" across.

Hickahala bottom (*Unv.* 151): the bottom of Hickahala Creek, which flows in a westerly direction between Senatobia and Coldwater, Mississippi. Ab Snopes would therefore have been hiding out about 25-30 m. from Sartoris.

hickeynuts (*S&F* 5): HICKORY nuts.

hickory (*Sart.* 206; *LiA* 324; *GDM* 342): any of several species of the genus *Carya*. Some provide nuts good for food, and all are medium to large trees with wood that is very tough and consequently used for things like toolhandles. The leaves turn golden-yellow in the fall (*Sart.* 276; *Unv.* 167). Hickory makes excellent firewood but has a tendency to pop out sparks more than most woods (*Unv.* 16).

hickory shirt (*Fable* 196): a work-shirt, usually blue, made of heavy cotton twill.

high (*Mosq.* 37): high gear. With early cars and largely ungraded roads, to "take a hill in high" (i.e. without having to shift down) was often an achievement, and the expression came to mean "to have great power, to have surplus energy."

high brown (*LiA* 66; *Reiv.* 164): a Negro (usually a woman) with a good deal of white blood and a light tan complexion.

high-school graduating classes ... caps and gowns (*Town* 123). This is an anachronism since the time is right after World War I, but the high-school aping of baccalaureate regalia did not come until well after my graduation from Oxford High School in 1925. Faulkner was probably thinking of the University High School commencement of 1951, at which he made the address.

hill-billy (*Sart.* 21; *WP* 244, 256): a yokel, rustic. A backwoods inhabitant of the red-clay hills. There are no mountains in Mississippi, and it is an error to confuse the Mississippi hillbilly with the Appalachian mountaineer, as many critics have done. The term can also be applied to real mountaineers (*CS: MV* 771).

hill-gully (*Ham.* 79): a gully located, as most large ones are, on the side of a hill.

'hind (*Unv.* 63): behind.

hipering (*Town* 126): bustling, hurrying.

Hiram (*LiA* 172): Hiram (Hayseed), traditional contemptuous name for a rustic.

hiring his crop gathered (*Ham.* 11): hiring people to gather his crop, paying for the gathering of his crop.

his (*GDM* 175): obvious misprint for *him*.

hishing (*S&F* 94): an imitative nonce-word.

hit (*Sart.* 80; *AILD* 42, 193): it.

hitching-block (*Sart.* 25): not a standard term. Since the block is referred to, a few lines later, as "the post," it presumably is simply a synonym for *hitching-post*.

hitching chains (*Sanc.* 160): "the continuous iron chain looping from wooden post to post along the circumference of the courthouse yard, for the farmers to hitch their teams to" (*RfaN* 243).

hitch-rail (*Miss.* 11): a rail, usually about a yard high and supported on posts, to which horses, mules, and teams are hitched.

hitch-rein (*AILD* 53, 55; *Ham.* 302): hitching strap, a strap that was used for hitching a horse to a post, tree, etc., but was not a part of the regular harness.

hitch up (*S&F* 310; *Unv.* 95; *GDM* 42): to harness horses and mules and attach them to the vehicle or implement they are to pull.

hit's (*Mans.* 113): its. (The apostrophe is an error.)

H'mawn, dawg (*Sart.* 283): Come on, dog.

ho (*Ham.* 175): a command: "Stop!"

hog (*KG:KG* 156). A hog is "deadliest of all" livestock for a motorist because it is so compact and close to the ground. A car will throw a horse or cow off the road but is likely actually to run over a hog, and to turn over as a result.

Hog Bayou (*Race* 181, 183): a bayou near the Sunflower River in Sharkey Co., Miss. Faulkner went on a hunt in this vicinity just after receiving news of the award of the Nobel Prize.

hog, bleeding like a (*Ham.* 332). When a hog is butchered, he is first killed (either knocked in the head or shot) and then he is immediately hung up by the hind feet and his throat is cut.

hog for punishment (*S&F* 315): one who seems to try to get into more than his fair share of trouble.

hog-trough (*KG:KG* 157). The hedge-jumps for the Harriss horses are planted in troughs like those used for hogs (see HAWG-TROUGH) so that they can be moved from place to place.

hog wallow (*S&F* 169–170). By rooting up the soil and lying in the muddy troughs so excavated, in wet weather hogs build up areas of some extent covered to a considerable depth with semiliquid, stinking mud. In his boyhood Faulkner once tricked another boy into jumping into a hog wallow. See *My Brother Bill*, pp. 121–22.

'ho'-house (*Sanc.* 199): whorehouse.

hoick (*Town* 293; *Dust* 17; *Mans.* 393): to urge on (hounds) with the traditional cry of "hoicks!" This is the standard meaning, but Faulkner regularly uses *hoick* to mean "to grab, snatch."

holding his money (*S&F* 43). I have never heard the superstition here credited to Versh. Faulkner once implied that he had invented it (*Faulkner in the U.*, p. 263).

Hold me, big boy; I'm heading for the henhouse (*Sanc.* 187). This was a standard formula of the period in which various substitutions could be made, according to circumstances. A fairly common version, applicable to anything from a bucking horse to a well-hit baseball, was, "Hold 'er, Newt; she's headed for the briar-patch."

hold up (*Ham.* 22): wait, stop.

holland (*Sart.* 59; *Reiv.* 196): an upholstery fabric, also used to make removable dust-covers for infrequently used furniture.

holl'in (*S&F* 337): hollering, shouting.

Hollow, the (*Dust* 39): NIGGER HOLLOW.

holly (*Abs.* 105; *GDM* 340; *CS:Fox* 604): American holly (*Ilex opaca*), generally similar to European holly, and standard in Christmas decorations. In favorable locations, such as river bottoms, it grows more than 50' high and 2' in diameter.

Holly Branch (*CS:MGM* 695): a fictional stream or town, unless it is a disguised form of HOLLY SPRINGS, 30 m. N of Oxford.

Hollymount (*Dust* 63, 221, 223): a small town, apparently fictional, in the general vicinity of Jefferson.

Hollyknowe (*KG:KG* 162; *Race* 187): apparently a fictional small town in *KG*. In *Race* it may represent Holly Bluff, a village on the Sunflower River in Sharkey Co., in the general area of this story.

Holly Springs (*Sart.* 226): a town 30 m. N of Oxford. It occurs several times in Faulkner's work without being named. For example, it is where Bayard Sartoris and his companions serenade a girls' school in *Sart.* 147–48.

holp (*Sart.* 208; *AILD* 85; *Ham.* 38): helped (the **l** is silent, and the word is pronounced *hope*). The form goes straight back to the OE *p.p. holpen*.

hol' up (*WT* 45): HOLD UP, wait, stop.

Holy Roller (*Town* 297): a contemptuous name for a member of any of several sects whose worship involves violent physical manifestations. These sects are considered outside the pale by the standard, established churches.— Since Mrs. Varner was a Methodist (*Town* 343), her hatred of Baptists was automatic.

homemade lye (*CS:BB* 13): lye made by leaching wood ashes with water. This process gives a strong alkaline solution, and there is no control over its exact strength or chemical composition.

Home, Sweet Home (*Sanc.* 29): regularly played as the last number at a dance, to indicate that it is time to go home.

Homochitto (*GDM* 341): a tiny town in Copiah Co., Miss., some 250 m. SSW of Oxford.

honey (*Town* 245, 250, 254): often used as a term of friendly address without any idea of particular endearment. As used by Cally (*SP* 170), it is a holdover from Donald's infancy.

honeysuckle (*Sart.* 26; *S&F* 117, 394): a Japanese vine (*Lonicera japonica*), evergreen, bearing tubular white flowers with an almost oppressive fragrance in the spring. It has run wild and become a great nuisance, forming dense thickets, overrunning trees, etc.

honnymonning (*WP* 339): honeymooning.

hoo (*Unv.* 44): a mild exclamation, usually expressing surprise or incredulity.

hooded furniture (*Sanc.* 116—cf. *Sart.* 59): furniture covered with dust-covers.

hoof-parings (*CS:BB* 19): parings of a horse's hoof made with a knife, coarse rasp, or any of several special paring tools used in fitting shoes to horses.

Hooker, Gen. Joseph (*GDM* 286): Union general whose flank was turned at CHANCELLORSVILLE by a concealed march of Stonewall Jackson's forces across the front of Hooker's.

hook your drag up (*Ham.* 321). See DRAG (2).

hoops (*CS:MGM* 695): the hoops supporting a hoop-skirt. This absurd garment had a tricky way of tilting up at the back to produce an indecorous exposure of its wearer. Hence "spreading her hoops back" was not merely the spreading of the skirt that frequently accompanied a curtsy, but a precautionary measure as well.

hoops (*Abs.* 31, 328): hoop-skirts.

hope (*GDM* 148, 150): helped.

Horace Lytle (*Reiv.* 166, 194): J. Horace Lytle, a Dayton, Ohio, advertising executive and sportsman and writer on dogs. He served as one of the three judges of the National Field Trials in 1933. Among his books are *Bird Dog Days* (1926) and *Breaking a Bird Dog: A Treatise on Training* (1931).

horn. 1. (*Mans.* 118): saddle-horn, the high pommel of a saddle. **2.** (*CS:Court.* 364): drinking horn.

horny (*Reiv.* 201): sexually excited, having an erection.

horse (*Abs.* 286; *GDM* 213): when contrasted with *mare*, a male horse, stallion.

horse block (*CS:BB* 15): a block of wood, or, more elaborately, brickwork or masonry, placed in front of a house and used as a platform for mounting or dismounting from a horse.

horse-box (*WP* 251): a box in which a horse can stand comfortably without rattling around, used for transporting a horse on a train or truck. Hence a cabin "a little larger than" this is very small indeed.

horse-cars (*GDM* 231): horse-drawn streetcars.

horse lot (*CS:BB* 20): an enclosure used for the keeping or selling of horses.

horse pistol (*Abs.* 338; *Unv.* 53): a large pistol designed to be carried by a man on horseback. The U.S. cavalryman of 1850 had two heavy, single-shot .54-caliber pistols slung across the saddle in a double holster. They were designed to be used as clubs after they had been fired. Confederate forces used the same weapon. The Colt "dragoons" (for mounted infantry) were .44-caliber pistols weighing more than four pounds each.

horsing. 1. (*Town.* 206): horsing around, indulging in horse-play. **2.** (*Reiv.* 255): behaving like a stud-horse.

hostler (*Sart.* 130; *Abs.* 45; *Ham.* 132): a person in charge of horses. By folk etymology, it is frequently pronounced "horseler."

hotchachacha (*CS:Fox* 598): a frenetic exclamation or refrain of the Jazz Age (usually with only two *cha*'s), and hence an *adj.* to describe a hot night-spot.

hot irons (*Dust* 224): a metaphorical allusion to the expression that someone "has too many irons in the fire," i.e. is involved in too many diverse activities.

hot mamma (*AILD* 232): slang for a fast or available girl. A popular song of the 1920s, "Red Hot Mamma," drew on and contributed to the vogue of the expression.

hot salt water (*Unv.* 194): used as a disinfectant. Gunshot wounds are particularly liable to infection, especially when the bullet has gone through dirty clothing, as Uncle Buck's must have been. Running the rag wet with hot salt water through the hole cleans it and disinfects it at the same time.

hound (of a wagon) (*Ham.* 65): a reinforcing bar used in the running-gear.

house (*LiA* 54; *Reiv.* 99, 127): whorehouse, brothel. Cf. Polly Adler's *A House Is Not a Home*.

houseman (*Mans.* 203, 423; *Reiv.* 283): a rather vague term for a male house servant. It is parallel to YARDMAN, and may even designate the same individual when he is working indoors. On the other hand, the houseman of *Mans.* 363, being in an elaborate establishment, seems to be essentially a butler. Faulkner refers to his own houseman in *Miss.* 41, 42.

house negroes (*Abs.* 31, 47): Negroes employed at the BIG HOUSE—personal servants with a considerably higher status than field Negroes. This is why "house-servants" cannot be ordered to do manual labor (*RfaN* 34).

house-servant (*RfaN* 34). See HOUSE NEGROES.

housework (*Flags* 66). At this time, a town white woman who had any social pretensions or status would have a Negro servant (usually a combined cook and maid) who did most of the housework.

Huey Long (*Mans.* 301, 305; *KG:KG* 229). See LONG, HUEY.

hull (*Sart.* 223): whole.

hull (*Mans.* 429): the empty brass case remaining after a CARTRIDGE has been fired.

hulls and meal (*Ham.* 182): COTTONSEED-HULLS and cottonseed meal, both regularly used as cattle-feed.

hum on (*Dust* 171): come on.

humming (*LiA* 130): the audible power-hum of the electric motor of a street-car, even when the car is not moving.

humming bird (*Fable* 171). The only hummingbird east of the Mississippi is the ruby-throated hummingbird. Its pure white egg is $\frac{3}{8}'' \times \frac{1}{2}''$—roughly the size of a bean in a can of pork and beans.

hummock (*Fable* 154). Such an "island" is not necessarily always, or even usually, surrounded by water, but it is definitely a patch of higher ground. In Florida the word is *hammock*.

hum up (*S&F* 10, 11; *GDM* 229): come up, get up; a command to a horse to start moving or to move faster.

hunker: to squat, sitting on the heels. Faulkner uses *hunker* also in a special sense which seems to be influenced by *hunch*, to describe the hunched and awkward movements of BUZZARDS on the ground (*AILD* 112) and the position of the arthritic Alex Holston in front of his fire (*RfaN* 219).

hunker down (*S&F* 319; *Unv.* 96): to assume, come into, a squatting position, sitting on one's heels.

hunky (*WP* 188, 189, 198): an east central European, especially a Hungarian. Cf. BOHUNK.

huns (*Mans.* 191): a name (usually capitalized) used for the Germans by Allied propaganda in World War I.

hunting case (*Dust* 75): a watch-case with a metal cover that snaps shut over the crystal and protects it.

Hurricane Bottoms (*RfaN* 6): HURRICANE CREEK bottom.

Hurricane Creek (*CS:MGM* 697): a creek flowing in a general northwester-ly direction into the Tallahatchie River. The road between Oxford and Holly Springs crosses it about 5 m. N of town. It runs a mile or two N of Sartoris, and is the creek, creek bottom, etc., often mentioned in connection with that plantation. There are many other references to it in Faulkner, though usually not by name. For example, in *Mans.* 404 Mink Snopes leaves the truck at the highway crossing of this creek.

hush (*S&F* 371): an exclamation of satisfaction and admiration. It is related to "Gentlemen, hush!" (*Town* 241).

hustle (*Sanc.* 264): to obtain by prostitution.

hustling (*Sanc.* 9): prostitution, whoring.

Hwup (*Sart.* 206, 209): a contraction of COME UP, addressed to horses and mules.

I

I be: I will be, in expressions like "I be durn" (*AILD* 67, 183) and "I be dog" (*AILD* 109; *Mans.* 316; *CS:SftL* 35).

I bound (*AILD* 36; *S&F* 91; *LiA* 397): I will be bound (that), will guarantee (that).

ice-cream pants (*Ham.* 132): pants the color of vanilla ice cream, i.e. white flannels.

I.C. Railroad (*Mans.* 88): Illinois Central Railroad. It is normally called by the initials, and Mink has obviously never heard it called anything else.

I godfrey (*GDM* 14, 17; *CS:SftL* 28, 43): euphemism for *by God*.

I'm a good mind to tell (*AILD* 192): I'm seriously considering telling.

immortal (*Reiv.* 177): Butch's blunder for *immoral*.

in course (*GDM* 324; *Reiv.* 118): of course.

————ing (*Town* 197; *Mans.* 280, 281): fucking.

injector (*Town* 17): the device that injects more water into a steam-boiler. Injecting water will lower the temperature and hence the steam-pressure.

in season (of a cow) (*Mans.* 10): in heat, ready to breed.

insects. Northerners, and Europeans even more, are often surprised by the chorus of insect voices heard in the deep South at night. Faulkner often refers to this phenomenon: see *Sart.* 85; *Sanc.* 215; *LiA* 85. This chorus has been much reduced in recent years by the wholesale poisoning of the environment. It falls off rapidly as summer passes into fall (*Mans.* 418).

Integer vitae, etc. (*SP* 57): Horace *Odes* 1. 22. It is incredible that the first two stanzas of this familiar poem should have been printed and reprinted in this grammatically, metrically, and typographically garbled form, since Faulkner clearly does not intend any misquotation.

Internal Revenue Department liquor licenses (*Mans.* 220). Since national prohibition had been repealed, Jakeleg Wattman chose to be a legal operator with respect to the Federal government in order to avoid trouble with the "Feds," though he was still a bootlegger and a criminal according to state law.

interrupted with out-looking (*LiA* 460). Passengers going down the aisle to get off the train were stopping to bend down and look out the windows, presumably for people who would meet them, and delaying those behind while they did so.

intervoke (*Sart.* 25): a pompous coinage of Simon's, intended to mean "obstruct."

Inverness (*AILD* 176): a town in the Mississippi DELTA, about 90 m. SW of Oxford.

Irey (*Fable* 170): a pronunciation of the proper name Ira.

iron (*GDM* 7, 18): stirrup.

Iron Bridge (*Reiv.* 73, 79). In actual fact, this was a bridge on the Oxford-Sardis road (Miss. 314), now blocked by the Sardis Reservoir, but Faulkner has shifted it here to the Memphis road. See Appendix.

iron plate (*CS:BB* 8): a plate made of tinned or galvanized iron, commonly called a tin plate.

iron-riddle (*Abs.* 352): apparently "riddled with iron (gray)."

is. 1. (*S&F* 19): have. **2.** (*Unv.* 44): are.

Ise (*Sart.* 51; *WT* 41): I am.

it: often used in place of the expletive *there*: "It likely won't be no need" (*AILD* 31); " 'Taint no rush" (*AILD* 32); "It ain't no end to bad luck" (*AILD* 223); "It was another office behind that un" (*CS:TS* 95).

it ain't none of my red wagon (*Dust* 245): it's not my lookout; I'm not responsible.

itch, *v.t.* (*Ham.* 198): to irritate, annoy, offend.

It'll be a po' day in de mawnin' (*SP* 170): it will be a poor day in the morning; i.e. a sad time, with the implication that it will never happen.

It's about (*AILD* 82). The meaning of this laconic statement of Tull is clear, but it is impossible to know what exact word is to be understood. Three obvious possibilities are *time, ready,* and *finished.*

Iuka (*Reiv.* 193): a town in the northeastern corner of Mississippi, 60 m. ESE of Grand Junction, Tenn. (Faulkner's Parsham). It is not in any real mountains but is close to the highest elevation in Mississippi—808'.

I wonder where my easy rider's gone (*SP* 198). See EASY RIDER.

J

Jack (*Sanc.* 6, 308; *Mans.* 267; *WP* 298): a familiar and somewhat contemptuous form of address to one whose name the speaker does not know or does not bother to remember.

jacklight (*Sanc.* 30): a lamp or spotlight used for hunting. Faulkner here applies it to a spotlight mounted on a car.

jack-lighting (*Mans.* 340): hunting at night with a JACKLIGHT.

Jackson (*Sanc.* 170; *S&F* 328; *AILD* 242, 243): the capital of Mississippi, 150 m. SSW of Oxford. The state insane asylum is located there.

Jackson, Gen. Thomas J. (*GDM* 286; *CS:TM* 54): Confederate Gen. "Stonewall" Jackson. He conducted a brilliant campaign in the Shenandoah

Valley in 1862. He was shot by his own men in the confused fighting at CHANCELLORSVILLE on the night of May 2, 1863, and died of the wound about a week later.

Jackson, Tennessee (*LiA* 469; *GDM* 156): a city about 80 m. NE of Memphis and 50 m. N of Mississippi.

jail (*Sanc*. 122 and passim; *Dust* 49 and passim). The Oxford jail was very much as Faulkner describes it and exactly where he locates it, a short block off the square on North Lamar. The present jail is an entirely different sort of building, built in the 1960s on the site of the old one.

jake (*Race* 194): contemptuous term for a man, probably from *country jake*, "a yokel."

jake (*Mans*. 376; *WP* 211): all right, in order. (Used primarily in the phrase *Everything's jake*.)

Jakeleg (*Mans*. 220). The nickname is significant. During Prohibition, JAMAICA GINGER, known as "jake," "jakey," "jakers," etc., was widely used as a beverage among alcoholics. Jakeleg was a form of paralysis attributed to its habitual use.

Jamaica ginger (*CS:UncW* 234): an alcoholic ginger extract made for flavoring. Since the alcoholic content was high, it was used as a beverage during Prohibition by those who were sufficiently tough or desperate.

japonica (*WP* 227): Japanese quince (*Chaemomela lagemaria*), a shrub bearing brilliant scarlet flowers that appear before the leaves in the spring, and yellowish fruits later.

jar of milk in the spring (*AILD* 132). A spring is regularly used for refrigeration, whether with a spring-house (see SPRING), or, more simply, by setting milk, etc., in jars in the cold water. A hermetically sealed ("tight") jar will, of course, keep the milk much better than one open to the air. Also, a "powerful spring" (one with a large flow to replenish the cold water constantly) will be a more effective refrigerator than one with only a small flow. So far, Tull's analogy is clear. From this point on, there are several possible interpretations, none of them necessarily correct. I believe that the looseness of the analogy from this point on is a part of the effect: Tull is turning the comparison over in his mind, but he does not work it out in strict and impeccable logic.

jasmine (*Sart*. 25; *LiA* 148; *Abs*. 295): Cape-jasmine, a common name in the South for what is more widely known as gardenia (*Gardenia jasminoides*), a small evergreen shrub with large, white, very fragrant flowers.

jawbreaker (*Sanc*. 109): a ball of hard candy about 3/4″ in diameter.

jay (*Sanc*. 261): a rustic, hick.

jaybird (*S&F* 331; *WT* 63, 65): the standard common name of the blue jay (*Cyanocitta cristata*), a brightly colored, large-crested blue, white, and black bird, very common around houses. It is a large bird (10″ long) with a raucous cry resembling its name, as well as many other calls and warblings. It is a generally flamboyant bird, a great scolder of cats, owls, and snakes, and a great robber of other birds' nests. Luster's remark on *S&F* 335 refers to the folk legend that jays are the devil's spies and that once a week they fly to hell to make their reports. I was brought up to believe that they do this on Friday, but Luster's jays apparently report on Monday.

jazzing (*Sanc.* 57; *Mans.* 78): fornicating, screwing.

jean clothes (*CS:MV* 747): clothes made of jean, a tough twilled cotton fabric long used for work clothes. Jean was originally used in solid colors or stripes. The plural, *jeans*, originally meant "fabrics of the jean type"; then it came to mean "pants of jean," and now to most people it means "pants of blue denim." Faulkner's usage here is strictly accurate for the period at the close of the Civil War.

Jeb Stuart (*Sart.* 10). See STUART, James Ewell Brown.

Jefferson (*S&F* 115, 141; *AILD* 18; *Sanc.* 5): the fictional county seat of Yoknapatawpha Co., modeled closely on Oxford, Miss. (see Appendix). In *LiA* 340, line 1, *Jefferson* is an error for *Mottstown*.

Jefferson Academy (*Mans.* 354). The Oxford Female Academy, incorporated in 1838, operated under various names and auspices until 1911, when a fire destroyed its buildings. It was in the vicinity of Eighth St. See *Town* 287 for Faulkner's estimate of such schools.

jelly (*Sanc.* 25): a girl-friend, a girl whom one dates. Cf. JELLY-BEAN.

elly-bean (*Sart.* 154; *S&F* 229, 298; *SP* 228): slang of the 1920s for a slick-haired, self-consciously fashionable adolescent—a "drugstore cowboy."

Jenny (*SP* 47): a World War I training airplane, the Curtiss JN-4.

jest lief (*Sanc.* 46): just as lief, just as soon (as not).

Jesus H. (*Mosq.* 202): abbreviated form of *Jesus H. Christ!*

Jim Avant from Hickory Flat (*Reiv.* 194): James Monroe Avent (1860–1936), of Hickory Valley, Tenn., was a "hound man," but he could hardly have considered himself slumming among bird dogs. He owned and handled the first National Field Trial winner in 1896, and handled seven other winners. He was a charter member of the Field Trial Champion Association, and his skill and canniness as a handler earned him the nickname "the Fox of Hickory Valley." Faulkner's misspelling of his last name is probably influenced by the Avant family of Oxford.

jimber-jawed (*GDM* 40, 74): prognathous, having the lower jaw protruding.

Jim Crow car, smoker, etc. (*Sanc.* 164; *GDM* 364; *Reiv.* 198, 199): a segregated railroad passenger-car for Negroes.

jimson weed (*Sart.* 22, 138; *S&F* 5, 61): Jamestown weed, common thorn-apple (*Datura strambonium*), a large, rank-smelling, poisonous weed, common around barns.

jitney (*Town* 58, 101; *Mans.* 35): a cheap, informal, small-town taxi.

John Held (*Mosq.* 230): an artist whose indulgently satirical caricatures of the "flappers" of the 1920s were widely popular.

John Moissant (*Miss.* 38). See MOISANT, JOHN.

johnny-jug (*CS:TM* 51, 52): demijohn.

Johnston (*Sart.* 174: *Abs.* 276; *RfaN* 233): Confederate Gen. Joseph E. Johnston. He is the "Old Joe" of *Abs.* 346, 355.

Jones County (*Miss.* 32, 33): a county lying some 60–75 m. SE of Jackson, Miss. LAUREL is the county seat and principal town.

joogled (*Reiv.* 71): shaken (from *juggled?*).

judas tree (*Sart.* 6; *Abs.* 323; *RfaN* 213): redbud (*Cercis canadensis*), a shrub or small tree bearing profuse pink flowers in the early spring. The name comes from the botanically impossible legend that this was the tree on which Judas hanged himself.

jug (*Sart.* 139): typically, a gallon jug made of glass or glazed earthenware. Except for a brief period during the Prohibition Era, when Mason jars became popular, it has been the standard container for illicit whiskey. Since the neck of such a jug is just a bit smaller than an average CORNCOB, a corncob is frequently used as a stopper. (I knew one enterprising Lafayette Co. moonshiner who, having built up a good local name for his product, was solicited by some wholesale buyers from Memphis. He let them sample some of his best whiskey, and then sold them a hundred gallon jugs with corncob stoppers that had been soaked in this same whiskey—but the jugs contained pure spring-water). There is a ritual technique to drinking from a jug, which is described in *Sart.* 139—only the fact that a finger is hooked through the ear of the jug is not mentioned. This omission is remedied in two other descriptions of the ritual (*SP* 310; *Miss.* 38).

juke joint (*CS:SftL* 30): a cheap restaurant or cabaret with music furnished by a jukebox.

julep (*S&F* 184; *Town* 310): mint julep, a drink made with bourbon whiskey, fresh mint, crushed ice, and sugar. The exact recipes are infinitely varied and highly controversial. See *SP* 97 for one version.

jump. 1. *v.t.* (*GDM* 14, 207): to start (game), to find it and cause it to jump up and run. **2.** *n.* (*Race* 177, 180): the act, fact, or occasion of game being caused to jump from a place of concealment and run.

jumper (*Reiv.* 9, 254): a blue denim jacket worn over, and matching, a pair of overalls.

Junction, the (*Mans.* 284, 396): MEMPHIS JUNCTION (HOLLY SPRINGS).

June tenth (*RfaN* 250): I know of no such holiday or celebration among Mississippi Negroes. The closest thing to it seems to be June 19th, known as "June teenth" and celebrated by Texas Negroes as the anniversary of the emancipation of slaves in Texas.

just fo gittin (*GDM* 74): just before getting, just about to get.

K

kag (*Town* 357): keg.

kahysene (*CS:MV* 757): kerosene.

katydid (*Mans.* 36). These include two subfamilies of long-horned grasshoppers, the true katydids (*Pseudophyllinae*) and the false and bush katydids (*Phaneropterinae*). True katydids are seldom seen but are often heard at night singing from trees a refrain vaguely resembling "Katy did; Katy didn't." The false katydids sing both day and night from trees and bushes; they include the often-seen green, flat katydids. Faulkner probably had the true katydids in mind, since their song is much better known.

Katzenjammer kids in the funny paper (*LiA* 335). *The Katzenjammer Kids* was a popular comic strip originated by Rudolph Dirks, in which two brats of German extraction, by traps and trickery, performed various sorts of mayhem against their father and the other characters. The balloon with a face and hat was one of their favorite ruses; they would paint balloons with their own features and then tie them up as if peering over a fence or hedge in order to avert suspicion while they themselves were off performing some sort of devilment. Faulkner seems to have had this balloon-trick in mind in the recurring imagery of the slick, unreal, nonhuman balloon-face in *Abs.* 230–35.—Because of the anti-German hysteria of World War I, the comic strip was, for a while, entitled *The Shenanigan Kids*; after that, it became *The Captain and the Kids*.

Keeley (*CS:UncW* 241): a Keeley Institute. Dr. Leslie E. Keeley professed to have found a cure for alcoholism, and set up a flourishing and lucrative chain of "institutes" for the treatment and rehabilitation of alcoholics. The one referred to here would be the one on the southern edge of Memphis.

keeper (*Dust* 91): a loop, like those on men's belts, which holds the loose end of a strap beyond the point where it is buckled.

keeping batch (*Sanc.* 197): living as a bachelor, keeping house for oneself.

keep let him alone (*S&F* 392). As it stands, this expression is impossible from the points of view of both idiom and meaning. I would hazard a guess that Faulkner wrote *keep him* (i.e. take care of him) and then revised it to *let him alone* (i.e. don't tease or irritate him)—or vice versa—and that he failed to strike out the words he wanted to cancel.

keer (*Sart.* 329; *AILD* 43; *S&F* 249): care.

kee-wee (*SP* 23, 47): a nonflying member of the Air Force (from *kiwi*, a flightless bird of New Zealand).

Kemper (*Dust* 195). See GARNETT.

kept (*CS:MV* 756): keep.

kettle (of a still) (*Sanc.* 123; *GDM* 37; *Town* 317): the metal container in which the mash is boiled. The term is sometimes used loosely for the whole still (*GDM* 60).

Kiblett (*Reiv.* 155, 179): a fictional town in Arkansas.

kick up (quail) (*Sart.* 282): to FLUSH, more or less accidentally, by walking near or among them.

kiddo (*Reiv.* 102): a smarty-familiar form of address from a man to a girl.

kike (*S&F* 155): derogatory term for Jew.

kind of cave (*Abs.* 233): "kind of" because this cave was not in the earth but in the vegetation. The "uptorn roots" of the oak would form a disk some 6'–8' in diameter, holding the trunk off the ground at its base, as the branches did farther out. Hence the space under the oak, walled in on both sides by the cane, is in effect a cave.

king's crown (*Ham.* 246): in checkers, the man put on top of another to crown him, or make him a king.

Kingston (*CS: TWBF* 279): a fictional town, possibly representting Oakland, on the main line of the Illinois Central Railroad some 20 m. W of Motts-town (Water Valley). It clearly has nothing to do with the actual Kingston, Miss., which is a village 22 m. SE of Natchez.

Kinston (*Sanc.* 5): a fictional town in the Mississippi DELTA. It could well be intended as the same place as KINGSTON.

kissing one's elbow (*Sanc.* 209). Children are told that if you kiss your elbow, you will change sex. The joke is that it takes them some time to find out that kissing one's elbow is impossible.

kit-and-biling (*Mans.* 165): group. The sense is always derogatory, and the expression is almost always used, as here, in the form "the whole kit-and-biling of them."

kitchen door (*GDM* 45): BACK DOOR. See also FRONT DOOR.

K.K.K. (*LiA* 66; *Mans.* 161; *SP* 281): KU KLUX KLAN.

Klavern (*Mans.* 301): a local chapter of the KU KLUX KLAN.

klaxon automobile horn (*Mans.* 241): mechanical automobile horn (originally a trade-name). Faulkner is probably referring to the famous "oo-gah" of the early Fords.

Kleagle (*Mans.* 301, 302): the top official of a local chapter of the KU KLUX KLAN.

knickers (*Sanc.* 28, 84): girl's bloomerlike undergarment.

knife-gnawed wooden bench (*Ham.* 53). Everyone carries a pocket-knife and, when idle, is likely to amuse himself by whittling or carving on whatever is handy.

Knight, Newt (*Miss.* 33). Leader of the hill-men of JONES COUNTY, who were not slave-owners and who opposed Secession. They organized the Jones County Free Staters, called the county the Free State of Jones, and declared war on the Confederacy. This is the standard legend, and the exact amount of truth that it contains has been endlessly debated. It is certain that Knight was at the head of a band of freebooters that raided Confederate lines and supplies, and that the group was more or less broken up by Confederate forces in the spring of 1864. But no one knows for sure how much of Knight's activity was prompted by political or moral principles and how much was mere brigandage and opportunism. Nor is it certain whether there was ever any secession from the Confederacy or declaration of war against it.

knobnot (*S&F* 42). See SKIZZARD.

knock out *v.t.* & *i.* (*Town* 311): to toss a baseball into the air and bat it to someone else, who then has a chance to field it.

knock up (*Town* 297; *Mans.* 70, 268; *WP* 212, 214); to make (a woman) pregnant.

knotted up one rein (*Ham.* 35). The team would have one rein from the left side of the left animal and one from the right side of the right one. In order to ride one animal, it was necessary to loop his rein around and fasten it to the other side, and also to shorten it, since it no longer had to go back to a driver in a wagon.

know'm (*S&F* 335; *Town* 310; *CS:Queen* 729): know, ma'am.

Kosciusko (*Miss.* 32): a town 90 m. S of Oxford, named for Tadeusz Andrzej Bonawentura Kosciuszko, a Polish soldier who volunteered into the American Revolution and fought with distinction as a colonel and brigadier general. The name is pronounced (in Mississippi): KAH-zi-ES-ko.

ks (*Town* 122): quais.

Ku Klux Klan (*Mans.* 300): a secret, night-riding, terrorist organization first organized to control unruly elements (largely, but not entirely, Negro) during Reconstruction. It was revived during the present century, although, as Faulkner indicates, it had no real power or following in Lafayette Co. "The sheets and hoods and night-galloping horses" that Sutpen refused to join (*Abs.* 166) were those of the Klan. Faulkner's clear distinction between the original Klan as a desperate expedient for a desperate situation and the twentieth-century revival of the Klan as a base monstrosity (*Miss.* 19) is the view of most responsible white Southerners.

kyo (*CS:BH* 78): cure.

L

Labove (*Ham.* 103 ff.). A contemporary of Faulkner's in Oxford had this as a given name. It rhymes with *stove*.

lace leather (*Unv.* 190; *Ham.* 318): leather cut into narrow, flat strips and used for such jobs as lacing the edges of saddles together.

lack (*GDM* 139): to like.

ladder (of a BARN) (*Sart.* 137; *S&F* 167; *Sanc.* 84): a permanent ladder, nailed to the side of the HALLWAY, by which the loft is entered.

lady's watch (*Unv.* 190). This is really a misplaced modifier. Uncle Buck did not wear the pistol "stuck into his pants like a lady's watch," but "on a loop . . . around his neck . . . like a lady's watch."

La Grange (*Reiv.* 194): a town 2 m. W of Grand Junction (PARSHAM).

Lake Cormorant (*Mans.* 259): a small town in Mississippi some 35 m. S of Memphis.

lamp (*AILD* 57; *Sanc.* 52): kerosene lamp. A lamp stands on a flat base containing a reservoir for the fuel. On the round opening at the top of this base fits a metal ring holding a wick which extends into the reservoir and a finger-wheel for adjusting the wick upward or downward to control the height and smokiness of the flame (*Unv.* 284). On this ring, or within prongs extending upward from it, is fitted the chimney, a glass cylinder constricted toward the top, and admitting a small amount of air at the bottom (*Sanc.* 52, 60). One lights a lamp by removing the chimney, turning the wick down low, and putting a match to it; after it is lit, the wick is turned up to the desired height (*Abs.* 309, 369). A lamp must be carried upright to keep from spilling the oil; hence the Yankee "riding around the corner with a short carbine, carrying it in one hand like a lamp" (*Unv.* 82) was holding the gun just behind the trigger-guard, with the barrel straight up. Labove's lamp, "the brightest lamp the village had ever seen . . . with valves and pistons" (*Ham.* 110), was not a kerosene lamp but an incandescent gasoline lamp. Ornamental lamps often had chimneys with vaguely female hourglass shapes, or, more often, achieved the same effect by having one globe on the lamp-stand and another on the chimney, with a narrow waist between them. This is the point of the comparison in *Mosq.* 240.

lamp oil (*CS:MV* 757): coal oil, kerosene.

lantana (*Abs.* 113; *WP* 37; *Mosq.* 14): any of various ornamental plants of the genus *Lantana,* largely semitropical, with clusters of showy flowers. "Lantana with its clotted wounds" (*Sart.* 169) seems to refer to the masses of orange-and-red flowers of one variety which Faulkner mentions, in a letter home from Hollywood, as "the normal orange with red center which I know at home" (Blotner, p. 1185).

lantern (*Sart.* 281; *S&F* 141; *Sanc.* 104): a portable kerosene LAMP, differing from a table lamp in having a larger and shorter chimney, a wire frame to protect the chimney, a metal top, and a handle by which it is carried. In *AILD* 73 the lantern must be sheltered from the rain because water striking the hot glass of its chimney will probably crack it.

lantern-jawed (*Mans.* 69): having long, thin jaws, or, more specifically, a protruding lower jaw.

lap-link (*Ham.* 318): repair link for chain, a metal ellipse solid at one end and open at the other in a horizontal plane, so that when the links of a chain have been slipped on and the opening has been hammered shut, the two curves of the open end will overlap.

lard bucket (*LiA* 39): a gallon bucket with a bent-wire bail for carrying. Lard was regularly sold in such buckets, and the empty ones were used for lunch-pails and various other such uses.

latch, on the (*Town* 312): not locked, but closed, so that one can open it from outside by turning the knob and releasing the latch.

later (*GDM* 158): obvious misprint for *lather.*

lathering horsemeat (*Ham.* 143): riding or driving a horse so hard that he gets into a lather.

lattice (*S&F* 46). Many large old Southern homes have the ground floor 8'–10' above ground level, reached by a large flight of steps leading up to the front porch. Such houses have an above-ground basement enclosed by lattice in order to allow air to circulate under the house.

laurel (*Dust* 171; *CS:MV* 772, 776; *Fable* 195): mountain laurel (*Kalmia latifolia*), a shrub or small tree with tough, evergreen leaves and pink flowers in the late spring. It has gnarled and twisted branches, and in the Appalachians it usually forms dense thickets known as laurel hells. It is often mixed with rhododendron. It is not common in Lafayette Co.

Laurel (*Miss.* 32): a town in southern Mississippi, 90. m. from the Gulf and 35 m. W of Alabama.

law (*Sanc.* 21; *LiA* 338, 357; *Reiv.* 186, 255): one or more law-enforcement officers.

Lawd a mussy (*WT* 44): Lord have mercy.

lawn mower (*SP* 104): an old-fashioned, hand-powered reel-mower without a grass-catcher, so that the blades throw the cut-off grass-ends back onto the legs of the man pushing it.

law something out of me (*Town* 243): get something out of me by legal action.

lay by (*AILD* 3; *Ham.* 11): to finish cultivating (a crop). Corn and cotton are laid by about midsummer, when there is no need to cultivate them further and they can simply be left alone until they mature and are ready to be harvested. Revivals are usually held in August after the crops are laid by. "Till you are laid-by" (*AILD* 32; *GDM* 67) means "till you have laid by your crops." He aint laid by no crop yit, has he?" (*Sanc.* 40) means "He hasn't made you pregnant yet?" Cf. "laidby crop" (*LiA* 356; also *LiA* 358, 394).

laying (*WP* 300): sexual intercourse. In *Mans.* 73, it means "talk about sexual intercourse."

laying-by time (*Sart.* 199; *Reiv.* 62): the time when people LAY BY their crops, about midsummer.

lead (*Mans.* 39): to aim ahead of (a moving target), at the spot where it will be when the bullet or shot get there.

lead rope (*Unv.* 15, 148; *GDM* 244): a rope attached for leading an animal.

leadsman (*WP* 238): a man at the bow of a boat who takes soundings with a lead weight on a line wherever there is danger of running aground.

leaf worm (*Ham.* 111): measuring worm, looper.

leash (*Race* 183): lease. (Really, the expression is not this simple. The boy has, of course, substituted *leash* for *lease* in a standard expression. But he knows what a leash is, and in his mind the metaphor is doubtless that of getting life under one's control as one gets a hound under control by putting a leash on him.)

leathern cup (*Fable* 156): leather dice-cup, used to keep the player from manipulating the dice in his hand.

leathers (*Reiv.* 169): stirrup leathers, the straps from which the stirrups hang.

leave (*Ham.* 198; *CS:TS* 83, 88; *CS:MV* 750): let.

leave ... be (*AILD* 60; *Sanc.* 65): let alone.

leave ... holding the sack (*Fable* 176): leave holding the bag. The expression comes from the practical joke of the snipe-hunt. A naive person or a greenhorn is invited to go on a night snipe-hunt. He is taken to a remote swamp, given a wide-mouthed bag or sack, and shown how to hold it open on the ground, while the rest of the group fan out, supposedly to surround snipe and drive them into the sack. Actually, they simply go home and leave their victim holding the sack. Hence the expression means to desert someone and leave him in an exposed position.

Leavenworth (*Sanc.* 57, 268; *Mans.* 52): a Federal prison in Leavenworth, Kansas.

Lee (*Sart.* 13, 16; *Abs.* 276, 348): Gen. Robert E. Lee, commander in chief of the Confederate armies.

leff (*GDM* 139, 148): let.

leffen (*GDM* 68): letting.

Le Fleur's Bluff (*RfaN* 106): a bluff and trading post on the Pearl River which ultimately became Jackson, Miss.

Leflore (*RfaN* 106). The reference is to Greenwood Leflore, for whom Leflore Co. and its county seat, Greenwood, are named. He was an educated and "progressive" Indian and helped arrange for the final sale of the Choctaw lands at the COUNCIL OF DANCING RABBIT—apparently because he realized that the alternatives were to sell and profit or to refuse and be gradually swindled and forced out of everything. Leflore's plantation was named Malmaison—a name which Faulkner seems to have confused with *Maintenon*.

Leland (*GDM* 361): a town in the Mississippi DELTA 12 m. E of Greenville and 100 m. SW of Oxford.

le'm (*CS:MV* 764): let me.

lessen (*Sart.* 8, 235; *AILD* 61; *Unv.* 90): unless.

lessen (*Unv.* 139): less, minus.

less-than-one-percent (*Mosq.* 54). This probably should be *less than one-half percent,* since that was the limit (by volume) of alcoholic content of legal beverages fixed by the Volstead Act.

let to (*WP* 262): allowed to.

levee. 1. (*Reiv.* 304): a continuous embankment along or near a river, to contain its floodwaters and keep them from inundating the surrounding country—especially any part of the vast levee system of the Mississippi River (*GDM* 340). The inner face of the levee is so standard a place for boat landings that *levee* can be used for a similar natural slope, as at Memphis (*Mans.* 286). The levees of the Mississippi have a much gentler slope on the river side than on the land side; hence "the almost perpendicular landward slope of the levee" (*WP* 250). When the river is in flood stage, boats are

above the level of the land outside the levee, and if the river is near the top
of the levee, they can be seen moving along against the sky (*WP* 28). **2.**
(*Mosq.* 174): an embankment of raised earth, a fill, on which a road or
railroad crosses a creek, river bottom, valley, etc. Often a bridge is only as
wide as the stream itself, and is approached by a levee (*AILD* 117, 118, 176).
The levee the Negroes climb to the road (*S&F* 363) is the embankment on
which the road runs across "a broad flat dotted with small cabins whose
weathered roofs were on a level with the crown of the road" (*S&F* 362–63).
(This flat, much altered, is in Oxford, and the road that crosses it is University Ave. [Miss. State Route 6], just east of South Lamar.)

Lexington (*Fable* 165): Lexington, Ky., where the old Negro comes from. It
is more or less the center of the Kentucky horse-breeding and racing business.

Liberty Loan (*Sart.* 120): the name given during World War I to the government bonds sold to help finance the war, and to the drives, promotion, etc.,
connected with them.

lick (*Mans.* 6): a blow. To get (or get in) one's licks is to accomplish something
or to have one's fair turn or chance, to have one's innings.

lick dog (*Reiv.* 145): probably a misprint for *lick log*, a log with troughs cut
into it that are filled with salt for cattle. In the southern Appalachians this
term enters into various place-names, as in the several Licklog Gaps.

lid (*S&F* 332; *LiA* 14): STOVE LID.

lief (*Reiv.* 209; *Mans.* 430; *WP* 166): leave, permission. See also GIVE-ME-LIEF.

lief (*Sanc.* 295; *Ham.* 27; *Mans.* 145): soon (expressing preference). "I'd just
as lief" is "I'd just as soon."

liefer (*AILD* 190): rather.

lift (a horse) (*Sart.* 306; *AILD* 137; *LiA* 196; *Unv.* 83): to make him throw up
his head and neck in beginning a jump, covering rough ground, or changing
gaits. ("Lifting" for jumps and rough ground is considered ineffective and
actually deleterious by some horsemen.)

lift a rifle-ball offen a hot stove-led (*Sart.* 221). To do this, one would
obviously have to have steady nerves and a steady hand. Why anyone would
attempt to do it is another question. It sounds like a sort of challenge game,
perhaps played around the stove at country stores, but I have no evidence
for this. Such a game would be like that (which was standard in my boyhood) of demonstrating strength and nerve by holding a full-sized axe
vertically, by the end of the handle, at arm's length, and then, with wrist-
action only, lowering it till the blade rests on one's forehead, and then
returning it to the original position.

light-long (*WP* 233): lasting as long as there is daylight.

lightning bug (*Sart.* 178; *S&F* 38; *Town* 315): FIREFLY.

light out (*Sart.* 63; *Ham.* 264; *Mans.* 125): to start somewhere, hastily and
informally.

light-palmed hand (*GDM* 69). The palms of Negroes' hands are light-
colored, no matter how dark the skintone elsewhere. Cf. FLAC-SOLED.

light-wood (*Unv.* 149; *GDM* 84): fat pine, so called because it is used for lighting fires. The club with which the tall convict hunted alligators was a "lightwood club" (*WP* 255, 266), because a knot of fat pine is both heavy and hard.

like (*AILD* 183; *Unv.* 129; *GDM* 77): to lack.

like Christ (*AILD* 141). One end of the log hangs on some obstruction caught at the FORD, and the current forces the log into a vertical position before it falls over and is carried on down the river. Thus for an instant it appears to stand on the surface, like Christ walking on the water.

Limited (*Reiv.* 46): a luxury, fast passenger-train making a limited number of stops.—Lucius's parents, going to Bay St. Louis, would take the southbound train (p. 43) to Grenada, Miss., 40 m. SSW of Oxford, where they would catch the crack Panama Limited (Chicago-New Orleans) to New Orleans. From there they would take a local train along the coast to Bay St. Louis.

Linda already opening the door (*Mans.* 358). The point is that Charles has been brought up to the chivalrous obligation of a gentleman to open the car door for a lady to get out and to accompany her to her front door rather than merely drop her at the curb; but Linda, with her long absence and metropolitan-Communist connections, doesn't expect these things and doesn't really give him a chance to do them.

line a wild bee (*Ham.* 225). The wild bee is simply a honeybee gone wild. Once a bee has a load of pollen and nectar, it takes a straight line—a "bee line"—for the hive. The way to find bee-trees is to find a place where bees are foraging and mark as closely as possible the line of flight when they leave. By following this line (and sometimes checking for confirmation from other returning bees) one will come eventually to the bee-tree. (Sometimes an enterprising person sprinkles flour on a few bees to make them easier to see and follow.)

line out (*Town* 369): to determine the direction of a source of sound and thus to make a straight line for it. The expression is probably transferred from LINE A WILD BEE.

lines (*S&F* 311; *Unv.* 120; *Ham.* 352): reins, whether of leather or rope (see PLOWLINE). In *Mans.* 118 the lines are wrapped around the whipstock (of the buggy) or the horn (of the saddle) so that they will be out of the way and the horse or mule can be free to go on home under his own guidance.

lining out the words (*Town* 41): reading the words of a hymn a line (or occasionally two) at a time. Many small churches did not have hymnbooks, and the congregations knew the tunes but not all the words. Therefore someone would read a line of a hymn, and then they would all sing it, going through the whole hymn in this fashion. This is known as lining out a hymn.

lint (*Ham.* 160): loose wisps of cotton—always in evidence around a working COTTON GIN.

list slippers (*WP* 13): slippers made of list, a material resembling selvage.

literary clubs (*Flags* 165): women's clubs ostensibly dedicated to literature, but devoting their meetings largely to refreshments and gossip, which is why Faulkner describes them as "so-called literary clubs." There were many such clubs, but the Browning Clubs led the pack.

little-built (*KG:Smoke* 28): small, little in build.

Littlejohn (*Ham.* 10, 100; *Dust* 149): an old Lafayette Co. name. For more than sixty years there has been a Littlejohn's Store on the New Albany road (Miss. route 30) a few miles NE of Oxford.

Little Rock (*Sanc.* 238): the capital of Arkansas, 150 m. W of Memphis.

liveoak (*WP* 175; *Miss.* 11): a magnificent evergreen oak (*Quercus virginiana*), growing to 60′ high and 5′–6′ in diameter, with a very large, wide-spreading crown and long branches that frequently curve down almost to the ground. It is not a Yoknapatawpha tree but is confined to the coastal region. Liveoaks are usually draped with SPANISH MOSS.

livery (*GDM* 285): LIVERY STABLE.

livery barn (*Ham.* 28): LIVERY STABLE.

livery lot (*Ham.* 85): the barn lot of a LIVERY STABLE.

livery man (*SP* 62): a man hired as a driver with a hired rig from a LIVERY STABLE.

livery rig (*GDM* 276): a conveyance of some sort and one or more horses to pull it, hired from a LIVERY STABLE.

livery stable (*S&F* 161; *Ham.* 32): a business that rents horses, carriages, etc. (Faulkner's father operated one for a number of years.)

lizards (*Mosq.* 190, 205). The lizards Pat and David saw on the sandy road would be sand-lizards or "racerunners" (*Cnemidophorus sexlineatus*). They are slender, streamlined lizards, grayish brown with six thin yellow longitudinal stripes, and grow to a length of about 1′. The "hissing" that they made is simply the sound of their scales against the dry undergrowth. These lizards are very common and can run with incredible speed.

Llewellin setter (*Reiv.* 284): a breed of setter built much like an Irish setter but white with black ticking.

lobby of a Memphis . . . hotel (*Miss.* 11). See PEABODY.

loblolly (*Sanc.* 118): mudhole.

local freight (*Sart.* 214): a freight train making local deliveries and stopping at every town, as distinguished from a through freight, used for hauls between urban centers.

locking our nigh wheel with another wagon's (*Ham.* 38): steering so that our hub projected between two of the spokes on the other wagon's wheel.

locust. 1. (*Sart.* 6, 45; *Sanc.* 107): black locust (*Robinia pseudoacacia*), a tree with sharp spines and fragrant, showy white flowers, often miscalled acacia in Europe, where it has been imported as an ornamental tree. The "ragged snow" of *Sanc.* 107 and the "foamy screen" of *Sanc.* 108 both refer to its flowers. Locust wood is extremely durable in contact with the soil and is therefore used for fence-posts whenever possible (*Mans.* 18). **2.** (*LiA* 33):

CICADA. **3.** (*GDM* 291): biblical (true) locust, a grasshopper that sometimes comes in plagues.

log-crotched rifle (*Miss.* 14): a rifle rested, for greater accuracy, in the crotch of an upended log.

log house (*LiA* 2; *Unv.* 52): a frontier-style house with walls made of logs 8″–12″ in diameter, crudely morticed by notches at the corners and made airtight by CHINKING with clay (or, later and occasionally, mortar) between the logs.

log-line (*GDM* 354): a temporary railroad-line built for logging.

logger-head (*CS:BB* 16): a double-ended, **U**-shaped hook used (one on each side) to fasten the TRACES to the HAMES. The hames have a series of holes (illogically called a ratchet), and the loggerhead's two hook-ends are fitted into two of these. The choice of holes permits variation of the line of draft and hence of the depth of plowing. (This term seems to be unknown to lexicographers.)

log-yard (*Unv.* 224): the place where logs are piled to await sawing at a SAWMILL.

longer (*Reiv.* 220): later, farther away.

long-handled shovel (*GDM* 90): a shovel with a straight handle, like a hoe-handle, instead of a shorter handle with a **D**-shaped grip at the end.

Long, Huey (*Mans.* 161, 301, 305; *KG:KG* 229): Huey P. Long, known as "the Kingfish," held various minor political offices before being elected governor of Louisiana in 1928 and U.S. senator in 1930. He was shot and killed by a young doctor in the State Capitol on Sept. 8, 1935, Long was a shrewd, power-hungry, rabble-rousing politician and managed to make himself virtually a dictator in his home state. In spite of his obvious faults, he seems to have had a genuine sympathy for the poor, and he used his dictatorial powers to achieve some necessary reforms and improvements. "One of the best literary magazines anywhere" (*KG:KG* 229) is the *Southern Review*, published at Louisiana State University from 1935 to 1942. A brief account of its origin can be found in the introduction to *An Anthology of Stories from the Southern Review*, ed. Cleanth Brooks and Robert Penn Warren (Baton Rouge, 1953). Brooks and Warren, the two original managing editors, record that the president of the university first proposed the idea of the magazine to Warren. In a private conversation (Lubbock, Texas, Jan. 24, 1973), Professor Brooks told me that he knows of no direct connection between Long and the *Southern Review*, but he conjectured that Long, with his presidential ambitions, might quite possibly have told President Smith to do anything he could to give the state favorable national publicity and that he would pay whatever it cost. Brooks thinks that Faulkner's guess that Long never saw the magazine is probably right: only one issue had been published before Long's assassination.

long hunter (*RfaN* 218): a man living in a settlement on the frontier and habitually disappearing into the wilderness for long periods of continuous hunting.

long-leaf pine (*Miss.* 32): a species of pine (*Pinus palustris*) having bright green needles 8″–18″ long. It grows to a height of 120′ and tends to have an open crown which is little more than a tuft on the end of a long, clean trunk. It grows in the southern half of Mississippi.

long-rifle (*Mans.* 346). **1.** Twenty-two-rifle cartridges are made in three lengths: short, long and long rifle. The long rifle is the most powerful and will carry up to a mile, though it is not accurate for that distance. **2.** (*CS:MV* 745): Kentucky rifle, a small-caliber, long-barreled flintlock that was long the standard type of frontier gun.

Longstreet (*GDM* 286; *Dust* 194; *CS:MV* 760): Confederate Gen. James Longstreet, "General Lee's war-horse." PICKETT's brigade was a part of his corps at GETTYSBURG. In the Battle of the WILDERNESS he had the enemy on the run when by mistake his own men fired on him and seriously wounded him.

Looeyvul (*Sart.* 338): Louisville, Ky. There is a Louisville, Miss., only about 100 m. from the McCallums' place, but in this context the Kentucky center of the bourbon whiskey industry is obviously meant.

look cross-eyed (*Ham.* 163): look askance, view with disapproval.

Look out of here (*GDM* 19): apparently an excited blend of *Look out* and *Get out of here*. It is not a standard expression.

loon (*S&F* 58): a stupid or erratic person. Though this word can be confused with LOONY, the two terms are distinct. *Loon* is a term of more-or-less good-natured abuse, but *loony* refers to a definite mental deficiency.

loony (*S&F* 12, 60; *Unv.* 83): a lunatic or idiot.

lope (*AILD* 178): an easy, swinging gait of a horse, in the nature of a gallop or canter.

Lord-to-God (*GDM* 202): pileated woodpecker, a magnificent crow-sized bird (*Drycopus pileatus*) colored black and white, with a large, flaming-red crest in both sexes. The usual rural and Negro name is *Lord God* (without the *to*) and is probably a folk etymology of the old name, *logcock*.

lotmen (*GDM* 83): men in charge of the lot, and hence of the horses and mules, on a large farm or plantation.

lous— (*Sanc.* 203): the beginning of *lousy*, to be followed by some derogatory noun. *Lousy* is part of Miss Reba's idiom; *louse*, as a term of abuse, is not.

low-pressure piston (*Town* 18): a secondary piston, with its own cylinder, on a steam engine. The steam which has already driven one piston at high pressure is routed to this cylinder to do further work at a lower pressure.

Lufbery (*SP* 33): Maj. Raoul G. Lufbery, a French-born American flier who transferred from the French to the American forces. He is generally recognized as the first American ace of World War I.

lug (*WP* 116): stupid person, dope.

lumberjack (*Race* 192): lumberjacket.

lunge (*Reiv.* 33): to longe, to exercise and train a horse by putting a long rope ("longe") on him and making him run in circles around his trainer.

lyron (*CS:Fox* 599): lion.

M

mac (*Mans.* 266): a vulgar and mildly contemptuous form of address to a person whose name one does not know.

machine lace (*Sanc.* 150): lace mass-produced by machines.

machine-made bread (*Town* 247; *Mans.* 265): bread made by a commercial bakery, as opposed to home-baked bread.

machines in railway waiting-rooms (*Ham.* 199): machines like modern gum-ball machines except that they contained a miscellaneous bunch of cheap trinkets.

Mackaill, Dorothy (*Mosq.* 204): a British-born movie star who went to Hollywood by way of the London Hippodrome and the Ziegfield Follies. She was born in 1903 and was at the height of her popularity in the late 1920s.

mad, *n.* (*Mans.* 84; *CS:MGM* 667): anger, fury.

madam (*LiA* 120, 362): the matron in charge of an orphanage. This is a strange usage, since *madam* with a definite or indefinite article normally means a brothel-keeper.

made them pop (*Mans.* 281): cracked the heels together when coming to attention.

Madison (*Unv.* 143): a town in Mississippi N of Jackson and 140 m. SSW of Oxford.

magic-lantern (*Sart.* 171; *Town* 163; *Mans.* 367; *Reiv.* 247): slide projector.

magnolia (*Sart.* 42): Southern magnolia (*Magnolia grandiflora*), a favorite tree around large old Southern houses. It is a large evergreen tree, up to 80' high and 3' in diameter, with large (about 3" × 8") leaves, glossy dark green above and brownish below. It bears huge, fragrant white flowers, 6"–10" in diameter. As the petals die they assume a beautiful shade of light tan, and this is the point of describing Charles Bon's octoroon mistress as "a woman with a face like a tragic magnolia" (*Abs.* 114—cf. also 193 and 312). The petals show marks if they are roughly handled (*SP* 105).

mail was in and the window had opened (*SP* 111). In one-man post offices, when the mail arrived the postmaster shut the service window while he put it up in the boxes, and then opened it again when he had finished.

Main Street (*Sanc.* 137; *GDM* 234): the actual main street of Memphis. To the west of it, the land falls away sharply to the Mississippi River.

make. 1. *v.i.* (*AILD* 31, 65; *LiA* 379; *Abs.* 356; *Ham.* 307): to develop, to mature. This is the same general sense as that in the last line of Robert Frost's "Mowing": "My long scythe whispered and left the hay to make"—i.e. cure. One critic, completely misunderstanding the word, refers to the "awkward inversion" in this line; apparently he thinks that the scythe was automated and that it left to make the hay by itself. **2.** *v.t.* (*CS:Hair* 136, 137): to arrive at (a place) and, more specifically, to arrive at and "work" it as a traveling salesman. **3.** *v.t.* (*KG:Tomo.* 103): to grow, to produce as a crop.

make a crop (*S&F* 119; *Ham.* 313; *CS:MGM* 667): to go through the whole
cycle from planting to successful harvesting of a crop.

make a foot (*GDM* 124): to make a footprint, leave a track.

make . . . an out of (something) (*Mans.* 63): to succeed at something, do it
competently.

make by (*AILD* 128): get by (financially).

make game (*Town* 310): to find and point game (used of a BIRD DOG).

make his lick (*Town* 261): strike his blow.

make one's manners (*Town* 111; *Reiv.* 77, 100, 168): to perform whatever
social ritual is called for at the moment, such as greeting a guest or thanking
someone for a gift.

make out. 1. (*AILD* 125; *CS:Hair* 135): to pretend. **2.** (*AILD* 182–83; *KG:
Tomo.* 94) to get by, manage, cope.

make the rise (*Mans.* 133): be promoted to the next grade in school.

mammy (*S&F* 2, 3, 33, 36, 364): mother. This is usually a Negro term. Versh,
T. P., and Frony use it for their own mother, and refer to the white
children's mother as "your mommer" (*S&F* 19), as does Dilsey (*S&F* 32).
Note that when Roskus refers to Benjy's "mammy" (*S&F* 37) he is speaking
to Dilsey and not to any of the whites.

Manassas. 1. (*Sart.* 9; *Miss.* 12, 15): the name usually given in the South to
the two Civil War battles (July 21, 1861, and Aug. 29–30, 1862) which are
called Bull Run in the North. **2.** (*Reiv.* 284): obviously a race-horse, but I
have not been able to identify him—and a horse eminent enough to have a
bronze figure made of him and to be known to a small boy when his owner
was not, should be easy to find in the records of the turf. It is possible that
Faulkner invented him, but this seems unlikely because the other famous
horses, dogs, and sportsmen in *Reiv.* are authentic. Perhaps he was thinking
of a horse named Manasseh which, in 1913, set a record for a mile in $1:37\frac{1}{5}$.

Mandeville (*Mosq.* 136, 144, 169): a town directly across Lake PONTCHAR-
TRAIN from New Orleans.

Mann Act (*WP* 27): an act passed in 1910 making it a Federal offense to
transport women or girls across state lines for immoral purposes. Though
intended to curb the "white slave traffic," it has often been used to harass
private, noncommercial lovers.

Manuel Street (*Sanc.* 9; *RfaN* 141; *CS:UncW* 237): a fictional street in the
Memphis red-light district on which Miss Reba's brothel is located.

market hunter (*Mans.* 408; *Reiv.* 265): one who hunts game in order to sell it.
The reference to lawbreaking in the next paragraph reflects the fact that, not
only does a market hunter usually pay scant attention to seasons and bag
limits, but the selling of game animals is itself illegal.

Marse (also Mars') (*Sart.* 114, 367; *Unv.* 6; *CS:MV* 754): master, a title of
respect used by elderly Negroes for their employers (or, earlier, owners) and
for their male children. It is occasionally extended to other white men of
some authority or position.

marshal (*Sart.* 158; *S&F* 161; *Unv.* 229): a small-town policeman, especially a night-marshal, who served as a sort of combination policeman and nightwatchman around the square.

marster (*Sart.* 367; *S&F* 107, 120; *Abs.* 25): master, a slave's regular title for his owner, often retained after Emancipation as a title of respect.

Marster Major Soshay Weddel (*CS:MV* 746): Master Major Saucier Weddel. The Negro's piling up of titles is not standard usage but indicates his pompousness and self-importance.

marster marse gerald (*S&F* 132). This is, of course, an utterly impossible expression, saying the *master* twice. It is a parody of Mrs. Bland's pretentiousness and her exaggeration of the devotion and servility which she thinks she and her son should inspire.

(Mary Buie Museum), described (*CS:SNP* 110–11). This is an accurate account of the Mary Buie Museum, on University Ave. in Oxford. Mrs. Buie (née Skipwith) was a miniature-painter who lived and worked in Chicago. The museum was built next door to the home of her sister, Miss Kate Skipwith.

Mary Montrose (*Reiv.* 166): "Peerless Mary," a white-and-liver pointer bitch and the first Triple National Champion, winning the NATIONAL FIELD TRIALS in 1917, 1919, and 1920. Cleanth Brooks has pointed out that she was not owned by Horace Lytle (her owner was actually William Ziegler, Jr., of New York City), and that the anecdote is true, but that she was not the dog involved in it (Brooks, p. 446).

Mason (*RfaN* 5, 103, 104, *Miss.* 14, 28). See NATCHEZ TRACE.

mast (*AILD* 69): mask.

match-box (*WP* 230): a standard type of hunter's matchbox. An empty 16-gauge shotgun shell, filled with matches, can just be forced into an empty 12-gauge shell, and will make a tight enough fit to be waterproof.

matched team (*S&F* 52; *LiA* 446; *CS:Rose* 124, 125): a team of horses or mules matched in weight, strength, and color. A matched team is worth more than two unmatched animals of equal individual value. Pat Stamper says that he will get three times as much for his matched team as he would selling them singly, i.e. three times what each individual would bring. He is sales talking, of course, but this figure of 50 percent more for a matched team than for two unmatched animals of equal quality sounds about right.

mat-faced (*Sanc.* 21, 62): having a mat (of hair) over the face. Faulkner describes Tommy as having "a sunburned thatch of hair matted and foul" (*Sanc.* 10).

maul (*AILD* 58; *CS:SftL* 27, 29): any heavy piece of wood designed for use as a club or sledgehammer. Sometimes it is in the form of a mallet. The mauls used for driving steel wedges to split logs in my childhood were made of a single section of a hickory log about 4′ long and 8″–10″ in diameter. The last foot of this was left alone, and the rest was cut down to a handle of heartwood about 2″ in diameter. A wooden maul does not spread the back of a wedge or a FROE blade, as a sledgehammer does. Using an ax for this purpose soon ruins the ax by spreading the eye into which the handle is fitted. The maul used with a froe may be either the type described above, or a mallet; in either case, it will be a relatively small one, to be swung in one hand.

Maurepas (*WP* 58). See HAMMOND.

Mayesfield (*CS:MV* 769): an imaginary town in Tennessee.

mayfly (*Fable* 170). Mayflies (Order *Ephemeroptera*) live for only a day or two in the adult form and do not eat. The males often congregate in swarming, dancing flights. The adults live only long enough to reproduce.

McClellan saddle (*Reiv.* 168, 233): the type of saddle used by the American cavalry, developed during the Civil War. It is a sort of compromise between the English and the cowboy types, though leaning toward the cowboy.

Meade (*GDM* 286). See STUART, James Ewell Brown.

meal-mouth (*KG:Smoke* 7): obviously the sort of mouth that a mealy-mouthed person has, but this usage is not standard.

meat-eating (*Mans.* 53, 58): Ratliff uses this term in the sense of "fierce, ferocious."

meat-plow (*Sart.* 63): not a recognized name for any implement. I would guess that it is Caspey's improvised term for a butcher's cleaver.

mechanical piano (*Sanc.* 153, 188): a player-piano, operated pneumatically by perforated paper rolls. Such pianos were the predecessors of the jukebox in places of entertainment.

mellomax tree (*WT* 28, 32, 38): an imaginary tree invented by Faulkner— or by the little old man.

melt. 1. (*Sart.* 330): dissolve. **2.** (*CS:Court.* 372): milt, spleen.

Memphis. In the southwestern corner of Tennessee, it occurs constantly in Faulkner's works, always under its real name. It is about 75 m. NNW of Oxford and is the urban center for all northwestern Mississippi.

Memphis Junction (*Mans.* 34, 179): HOLLY SPRINGS, Miss., 30 m. N of Oxford.

Memphis papers (*KG:Monk* 47). Oxford, being only a very small town, had a weekly county-seat newspaper but until recently no daily, and the Oxford *Eagle* is still published only from Monday through Friday. The regular newpapers of the town have always been the two Memphis papers, morning and evening.

merciful blow of the axe (*Abs.* 79). When a hog is butchered he is suspended by the heels and his throat is cut, but first he is killed, or at least stunned. The blow of the axe here is not a cutting blow, but a stunning blow with the back of the axe.

Meridian (*Miss.* 32): a city 90 m. E of Jackson and 10 m. W of the Alabama line. With a population of about fifty thousand, it is the largest "city" in Mississippi.

mesmered (*Abs.* 140): mesmerized.

mess with (*GDM* 136, 145): fool with, interfere with (in the general sense of meddling and causing trouble).

metal gangways clashed (*KG:Monk* 46). Since railroad couplings are flexible, there is a good deal of clashing of the floor-plates in the gangways leading from one car to another as the train moves.

metal torpedo containing change (*WP* 51). Department stores (some until quite recently) kept all money and made all change at a central location. The customer's money and bill were sent in, and the change was returned in metal containers traveling in a system of pneumatic tubes.

mete (*RfaN* 218): erroneously used for *meet*: "fitting, appropriate."

Michigan City (*Reiv.* 194): a small town in Mississippi, on the Tennessee line, 6 m. S of Grand Junction (PARSHAM).

middle (*Mans.* 22, 49, 92; *Reiv.* 89): the open space between two rows of cotton. Since, when cotton is first planted, the middles are higher than the rows, and since the Mississippi floods in the early spring, the middles are the last part of a field to be submerged by the rising water (*Miss.* 26).

middle buster (*Ham.* 44; *Reiv.* 84; *CS:BB* 17): middle-breaker, a shallow plow that throws earth to both sides, used to bank earth from the MIDDLES between the rows against the cotton plants, after they have attained a fair size. Mink would use a middle buster when he "opened out the middles" (*Mans.* 22).

middle-thigh cotton (*KG:Tomo.* 95): cotton high enough to reach the middle of one's thigh.

middle-year (*Dust* 71): middle-aged.

milk dry (*S&F* 36): to cause a cow to go dry (cease giving milk) by not getting all the milk but leaving a bit more each time she is milked. This process imitates the natural one that causes a cow to go dry when her calf is weaned. A careless or negligent milker can milk a cow dry simply by not doing a thorough job.

milking stool (*AILD* 210): a low stool on which one sits while milking. It may be three-legged, so that it will not teeter on any terrain, or better still, it may be one-legged, shaped like a carpet tack, so that it will be upright on any terrain and the milker can lean in any direction.

mill-yew (*Mans.* 139): milieu.

mimosa (*Abs.* 113; *Mosq.* 14, 49, 324): *Mimosa pudica*, a tree with feathery compound leaves sensitive to touch, and profuse, feathery, spherical pink blossoms, about 1″ in diameter, throughout the summer. Though originally imported, it is now common throughout the Gulf states, but in recent years has been much reduced by a fungus disease.

mind 1. (*AILD* 66; *Abs.* 283; *KG:Monk* 48): to remember. **2.** (*AILD* 203): to notice, pay attention to. **3.** (*S&F* 28, 29): to obey.

Minié (*Sart.* 14; *Miss.* 15): Minié ball, a lead bullet with a hollow base, used in Civil War rifles.

minor (*Sart.* passim): plaintive music. This is a special Faulknerian meaning, apparently due to musical ignorance. Faulkner uses it repeatedly in *Sart.*, and on p. 148 we have proof of the special meaning: "They played 'Home, Sweet Home,' and when the rich minor died away. . . ." The song is, of course, in the major mode, and there is nothing to suggest that the serenaders were not playing it straight. Another piece of evidence is Belle at the piano: "Her hands trailed off into chords; merged, faded again into a minor in one hand" (*Sart.* 195). But Belle was certainly not the sort of pianist who might be experimenting with polymodality.

Minute (*S&F* 75). In addressing Caddy as "Minute," Dilsey is alluding to the common expression that a small child is "no bigger than a minute."

miration (*Dust* 130): the noise made by the wind in pine trees. The context makes the meaning plain. I may have heard this usage in my childhood but cannot be sure; nor have I found it attested anywhere. *To mirate* is a standard rural verb meaning "to express admiration or wonder to a high or excessive degree, to carry on admiringly about or over" something. The *n. miration* is derived from this *v.* A typical use would be "Aunt Sally made a great miration about the new preacher." From this to the "carrying on" of the pines would be a logical extension.

mis'ry (*Sart.* 27, 272): misery, pain, ailment.

Miss: a title with various special uses when employed with the given name rather than the surname. It is used by servants for the daughters of their employers (*S&F* 9; *Miss.* 42). It is a general term of respect from younger to older (*Sart.* 270), and since the given name does not change with marriage, it continues to be applied to married women. My mother, who was considerably younger than Faulkner's mother and was named for her, called her "Miss Maud" until the latter's death at the age of about ninety. It is regularly used by school children for teachers who have grown up in the community. (Looking back over my own teachers in the Oxford schools, I can see this distinction plainly: Miss Kate [Kimmons] and Miss Ella [Wright] were from Oxford, but Miss Lindsey and Miss Furr came to Oxford as mature teachers.) As soon as Miss Reba learns Temple's name, she calls her (in Temple's presence) "Miss Temple," when speaking to Minnie (*Sanc.* 142) because that is the form of address that Minnie will be expected to use. (Miss Reba herself usually calls Temple "honey"—*Sanc.* 142–45.) The point of Rosa Coldfield's elaborate comments about the fact that Clytie "had called me Rosa" (*Abs.* 139) is not the use of the first name, but the use of it without the title: Clytie would have been expected to call her "Miss Rosa," as Judith does when speaking to Clytie (*Abs.* 150). The same point is made in a different way in *Abs.* 204: "your grandfather thought how he could not say 'Miss Judith,' since that would postulate [Bon's Negro] blood more than ever . . . . So he said Miss Sutpen."

miss (*Mans.* 8): to fail to conceive (applied to livestock).

Miss Hestelle (*Miss.* 42): Faulkner's wife, Estelle Oldham Faulkner.

Miss-ippi (*Unv.* 52; *GDM* 12; *Mans.* 52): Mississippi.

miss-out dice (*GDM* 156): MISS-OUTS.

miss-outs (*GDM* 153): crooked dice designed to lose for the person rolling them. We cannot be sure which type Birdsong was using, but it is clear that he was switching (or busting, depending on the nature of the dice) them in and out of the game, and Rider knew it and caught him at it. For details on miss-outs and their use, see John Scarne, *Scarne's Complete Guide to Gambling* (New York, 1961), pp. 280–92.

missus (*Ham.* 290): a form of address (Texas, not Yoknapatawpha) for a married woman. "Missus Judy" (*Abs.* 151) is a very strange usage, probably a slip: if *Miss* is intended, *Missus* is not a form of that title; if *Mrs.* is meant, not only is it wrong, since Judith is unmarried, but it would have to be used with the last name instead of the given name. Mr. Saunders' "my missus" (*SP* 117) is, of course, "my wife."

missy (*Sart.* 241; *Unv.* 112, 130; *Ham.* 215): diminutive of Miss, used both as a title with a given name and by itself in direct address.

Mister (also Mist') (*Sart.* 33, 149; *Town* 360): a title of respect regularly used (like Miss) with the given name by servants for the children of their employers (or, formerly, owners). It is also used in this way generally by Negroes for whites whom they know primarily by their given names, and similarly by whites of lower class to upper class (*Sart.* 142). Rosa Millard is simply sticking to the forms when she tries to insist that Ringo call Ab Snopes (whom neither she nor Ringo respects) "Mister" (*Unv.* 143, 151). When, "even as a child the boy remarked how Lucas always referred to his father as Mr Edmonds, never as Mister Zack, as the other negroes did" (*GDM* 104), the nuance is that Lucas is being formally respectful but not familial or affectionate. Under some circumstances there may be a choice as to whether to use the given name or the surname with the title (*Race* 198). See *Reiv.* 10, 55, 131 for some discussion of usage.

Mistis (*Sart.* 367; *CS:MV* 753; *KG:Smoke* 31): a form of *Mistress*, a term used by Negroes for the wife of the owner of the plantation on which they work. It is a proper name, not a title, in that it is never used with any form of a personal name.

M'I've (*SP* 203): May I have?

mixed train (*LiA* 3): a train made up of a mixture of passenger and freight cars.

mixtry (*Reiv.* 294): mixture.

Miz (*Sart.* 106; *Sanc.* 176; *LiA* 20): Mrs. The normal Southern pronunciation of this title is exactly what Faulkner's spelling indicates, though a formal pronunciation is sometimes two syllables: miz-iz. I. O. Snopes's use of this title with a given name (*Town* 243) is not normal usage.

mizzable (*CS:BH* 69): miserable.

mizzling (*CS:SftL* 28): muddled, confused.

moan (*S&F* 39): to mourn, but also with the meaning of *moan*. It is probable that the speakers consider *moan* and *mourn* to be the same word.

moaner's bench (*Sart.* 24): MOURNERS' BENCH.

moccasin (*Sart.* 226; *Sanc.* 19; *Ham.* 282; *GDM* 205; *CS:SftL* 31): COTTON-
MOUTH (MOCCASIN). Popular terminology is highly confused about the venomous cotton-mouth and some half a dozen species of harmless water snakes of
the genus *Natrix*. The general tendency among people who know snakes
in Faulkner's country is to reserve the name *moccasin* (or *water moccasin*—
Miss. 11) for the venomous snake and to call the others water snakes. Faulkner knew the difference, and this seems to be his practice, since in his usage
moccasin always carries some suggestion of menace. This distinction is confirmed by his making two categories of "moccasins and water-snakes" (*GDM*
205). (Such usages are highly localized. In Georgia, for instance, the distinction is usually between moccasins [which are harmless] and cotton-mouth
moccasins [which are venomous].) The "sluggish thrash" of moccasins (*Fable*
156) and the "thick body" and "flat head" of the one in *WP* 229 make it
clear that they are cotton-mouths.

mocking-bird: a slender gray-and-white bird (*Mimus polyglottos*) about 9″
long, an excellent mimic of other birds and of all sorts of other sounds. It is
a fine and tireless singer, frequently singing at night in the spring and summer
(*Sart.* 26, 41; *Ham.* 277) and well on into the fall (*Unv.* 278, 291). This night
singing is delightful at a distance, but can become maddening when the bird
is too close to one's window (*Town* 310, 334). In 1956, while Faulkner was
working on *Town*, he wrote about one mockingbird in a letter: "We hear him
all the time, during the day and at night. He can imitate anything: other
birds, horses, even trucks changing gear . . . . He's a real nuisance" (Blotner,
p. 1606).

Model T (*Miss.* 34). The Model T Ford had no battery or generator: electricity
for ignition and lights was supplied by a magneto. Consequently, the faster
the engine was turning over, the brighter the lights were. It was a common
practice to go into neutral and race the engine briefly when one needed to
see farther ahead.

modren (*CS:SftL* 30): modern.

Moisant, John (*Miss.* 38): an early barnstorming aviator and member of a
prominent flying family. In October 1910, he and his brother Alfred signed
up a troup of French and American aviators to tour the United States and
Mexico. The following December and January he was flying in races against
a Packard car in New Orleans. His sister Matilde was the second American
woman to earn a pilot's license.

molasses (*Dust* 24): frequently used as a plural. Here it is the antecedent of
they and *um* (them) in the next paragraph.

molasses bang (*Sart.* 182): not a kind of haircut. *Molasses* is used to describe
both the straight flow and the color of the hair. This point is made clear by
the references to Frankie's "straight hair . . . not brown, not gold" (*Sart.*
186) and "the simple molasses of her hair" (*Flags* 173).

mold board (*Mans.* 348): the curved plate on a plow which turns over the
strip of earth that has been cut loose by the PLOWSHARE.

molded bullets (*Abs.* 234). See BULLET MOLD.

mommer (*WT* 13, 20): mamma, mother. Note Versh's distinction between *mammy* for his own mother (*S&F* 2, 3) and *your mommer* for the white children's mother (*S&F* 19). In *SP* 313 the word has the sense of "girl, mistress" —a slang usage of the period. Cf. HOT MAMMA.

mon (*S&F* 371; *Reiv.* 71, 162): man. This is always an exclamation or intensive, never a noun.

monkey nigger (*Sanc.* 184; *Abs.* 232; *CS:SNP* 104): bell-hop. This is a fairly standard term, and comes from the resemblance between a bell-hop's uniform and the costume worn by an organ-grinder's monkey. The "monkey-dressed nigger butler" (*Abs.* 231) expresses the same general idea, applied to the butler's livery.

mont' (*Sart.* 290): months.

Monteagle (*Reiv.* 277): a Tennessee mountain resort 30 m. NW of Chattanooga.

moonless sky of corn-planting time (*GDM* 42). It is a widespread, though by no means invariable, folk-belief that corn should be planted in the dark of the moon.

moonshine (*Town* 173): illicitly distilled, non-taxpaid whiskey.

moonshiner (*Sanc.* 104, 113; *RfaN* 12): an illicit distiller of whiskey. Many people confuse *moonshiner* with BOOTLEGGER (an illegal distributor of liquor), but Faulkner never does. The distinction is clearly made in his reference to "the town bootleggers and the moonshiners in the adjacent swamps" (*Flags* 342).

Moorhead (*WP* 69): a Mississippi town about halfway between Greenwood and Greenville, and some 30 m. S of PARCHMAN.

moren (*S&F* 25): more than (pronounced *mourn*).

Morgan (*GDM* 287; *Unv.* 17): John Hunt Morgan, dashing Confederate cavalry leader famous for his raids and sometimes known as Morgan the Raider. See CAPTURED WARSHIPS WITH CAVALRY CHARGES.

Morgan (*Reiv.* 183): an American breed and dynasty of horses named for the horse Justin Morgan (d. 1821), who founded it and was himself named for his owner.

morticed-log (*RfaN* 4). The logs of a LOG-HOUSE are morticed at the corners. If they were not, the adjacent logs on any side would have gaps between them as wide as the logs on the two sides at right angles to them.

mosey (*Ham.* 158; *Town* 318; *Reiv.* 177): to walk or go in a casual and desultory way.

mosquitoes (*WP* 251, 263). In bad seasons, the mosquitoes along the Gulf Coast can exist in swarms and be a real plague, especially since they are mostly large, vicious, salt-marsh species. They have been known to kill cattle pastured on the islands in Mississippi SOUND. Though Faulkner never mentions them by name in *Mosq.* (except in the title itself), they play an important part in that novel. In the Yoknapatawpha country mosquitoes are usually negligible, though they sometimes reach alarming concentrations in creek and river bottoms after spring floods.

moss (*Mosq.* 169) : SPANISH MOSS.

mossback (*Mans.* 429): ancient, antiquated. This word also picks up and extends the comparison of the ancient pistol to a COOTER.

mother songs (*Sanc.* 240): a sardonically formal version of *mammy songs*, i.e. Negro songs or songs in a Negro style.

motoring bonnet (*CS:Dry* 174): a tie-down bonnet with an attached veil, part of the early special motoring costume.

motor-robe (*CS:Elly* 207): a blanket, usually gaudy and often with a fringed edge, designed to be carried and used in a car but actually a general-purpose article. As the 1927 Sears catalogue says, "Motor robes are so useful and practical that every household should have at least one. Use them for blankets, for the boys' den, for steamer rugs, for covers on couches or day beds, for camping, picknicking and all outdoor sports."

Mott County (*Dust* 189): Calhoun County. See CROSSMAN COUNTY. It is interesting to note that MOTTSTOWN (Faulkner's name for Water Valley) is not in his Mott County. Water Valley is the county seat of Yalobusha (Faulkner's Okatoba) County. That this relationship is no oversight is shown by the reference to "Mottstown, the seat of Okatoba County" (*KG : Hand* 72).

Mottson (*AILD* 176, 187; *S&F* 378 ff.) : MOTTSTOWN.

Mottstown (*LiA* 321; *Unv.* 138; *Ham.* 263): Water Valley, Miss., a town some 20 m. SSW of Oxford by highway Miss. 7 and by rail. This is clearly the same as the Mottson of *S&F* 378 ff. In both *Lia* and *S&F* the identification is accurate even to the train schedules of the time (see Appendix). The Mottson of *AILD* 176, 187, like most of the geography of *AILD*, is incommensurate with that of the other Yoknapatawpha novels. There is also an incongruous use in *Town* 253, since "take it right on up to Mottstown" implies that Mottstown is N of Jefferson.

Mottstown junction (*Town* 101): no connection with Faulkner's MOTTSTOWN, which is Water Valley, Miss. This junction would seem to represent either Grand Junction, Tenn. (the PARSHAM of *Reiv.*) or Jackson, Tenn.

mought (*Sart.* 34; *LiA* 24; *GDM* 76) : might (rhymes with *out*).

Mound's Landing (*WP* 30): Mound Landing (also called Stops Landing), on the Mississippi side of the Mississippi River, just across from Arkansas City, Ark. It is 14 m. N of Greenville and 40 m. SW of PARCHMAN. The great 1927 flood began for the Mississippi DELTA when the levee went out at this point about 11 :00 P.M. on April 21.

"Mountain Victory" (CS: 745–77). This story is set in the Tennessee mountains, probably in East Tennessee, where there were many Union sympathizers and members of the Union forces. The family presented here are genuine Appalachian mountaineers, using the language of the mountaineers (*you-uns*, etc.), which Faulkner sharply differentiates from that of his Mississippians.

This fact should be noted by some critics who have confused the hill-men of Yoknapatawpha with Appalachian mountaineers.

Mount Vernon (*Sart.* 312, 330; *AILD* 112): a settlement on the route between the McCallums' and Jefferson. Since Faulkner never mentions Abbeville (10 m. N of Oxford), and since there was a Mount Vernon church and school just north of it, it seems likely that he used Mount Vernon as his name for Abbeville.

mourners' bench (*Sart.* 24; *LiA* 305): a front bench or pew (or sometimes a whole section) at a revival or camp meeting reserved for the mourners—those who publicly repent their sins. The camp meeting frequently produces a state of hysteria in those who "get religion."

mout (*GDM* 151): might (rhymes with *out*).

Mouth of Ishatawa (*AILD* 107): a fictional place that would have to be where an Ishatawa Creek empties into a river. Cf. Mouth of Tippah.

Mouth of Tippah (*CS:Red* 336): the point and surrounding area where the Tippah River flows into the Tallahatchie, some 15 m. NNE of Oxford. The area is regularly called by this name. The McCallums lived in the hills to the S of this area.

mou-tin (*CS:MV* 747, 774): mountain.

movie subtitles (*Flags* 345): the skeleton dialogue flashed on the bottom of the screen in silent movies. Since it was minimal, it consisted largely of clichés.

Mr. van Man (*Reiv.* 298): a combination of Mr. van Tosch (part of whose name Ned remembers) and the standard *Mr. Man* for a person whose name the speaker cannot remember.

much obliged (*Mans.* 71, 74): often used with the meaning of "No, thanks."

mud-chinked (*RfaN* 4, 16, 214; *Reiv.* 61). See CHINKING.

mudguard (*Town* 66): fender (of a car).

mulberry (*S&F* 331, 363; *Ham.* 316; *GDM* 370): red mulberry (*Morus rubra*), a large tree, often 70′ high and 3′ in diameter, frequently grown around houses. It has edible blackish red fruits much loved by birds and children. The leaves are large (often 3″ × 6″ or larger), many of them shaped like mittens, both right- and left-handed. The size and shape explain why Faulkner compares them to the palms of hands (*S&F* 331).

Mulberry Street (*Town* 48; *Mans.* 62): a short street in Memphis in the same section, and with the same reputation, as BEALE STREET and GAYOSO. It deadends into Beale.

mulehead (*S&F* 61): a stubborn or difficult person.

mule-pen (*Town* 102): not anything specific or particular, like a pigpen, but simply any sort of enclosure in which one or more mules can be penned up.

mule-prints (*Dust* 172). The tracks are identified as those of a mule by the fact that mules have proportionately much smaller hooves than horses (and probably also by the fact that mule-shoes are less curved on the sides than horseshoes). The difference in the size of the feet explains why the mule in

Reiv. 246 is "raising barely half as much dust as a horse would," as well as the reference to "delicate mule-legs and narrow deer-like feet" (*Ham.* 48).

mule shears (*Sart.* 199): shears used to trim the manes and tails of mules. Some are like large scissors, but the more common type is like the one-piece, hand-operated grass-shears which have long triangular blades joined behind the grips by a curved spring.

mumble peg (*CS:Just.* 346; *CS:Lo* 391): mumblety-peg, a boys' game in which a knife must be thrown and stuck into the ground from each of a standard sequence of positions. The loser has to dig a wooden peg out of the ground with his teeth.

Murrel(1), John (*RfaN* 5, 103, 226; *Miss.* 14, 28; *Fable* 168). See NATCHEZ TRACE.

murderer (*Town* 80). Ratliff is just amusing himself with the alleged social difference between an authentic top-class murderer and mere crap-shooters. Murderers could and did work on chain gangs, but Mink would not have been on one at this time because he was not a convicted felon but was simply in jail awaiting trial.

mush-melon (*Mans.* 123): muskmelon, cantaloupe, or similar melon. Ratliff compares the sound of the weighted whipstock on skulls to that of thumping a ripe melon.

mushrat. 1. (*Reiv.* 78; *Miss.* 12): muskrat. **2.** (when applied to a person) (*WP* 238, 245): SWAMP RAT.

music box (*Ham.* 159; *Dust* 245): hand-wound pre-electric gramophone.

musket (*Sart.* 11; *Abs.* 344; *Unv.* 28): a smooth-bore gun with a very long barrel, used primarily for military purposes. When rifling became generally accepted, some muskets were rifled, so that the term *rifled musket* is occasionally encountered.

muskrat (*WP* 262): a brown, semiaquatic, fur-bearing mammal (*Ondatra zibethica*), growing up to 2′ long. Muskrats are not found in northern Mississippi but are common and extensively trapped in the bayous of Louisiana. It was presumably this unfamiliar animal when the tall convict "saw something else swimming toward the mound, he didn't know what—a head, a face at the apex of a vee of ripples" (*WP* 229).

my kitchen (*Sart.* 191; *S&F* 318): a standard expression of the old-style Negro cook, who considered the kitchen her personal domain and had a highly developed sense of territoriality about it.

N

nah (*Sanc.* 302; *WP* 214): no.

nail keg (*CS:BB* 3). Nails are packaged in 100–1b. kegs which, when empty and inverted, make convenient seats.

name: often used as a symbol of self-respect, or identity, in the modern sense. "Remember your name and don't take nothing from no man" (*CS : TM* 53) does not refer to the name's being famous or distinguished; it simply means "keep your self-respect." The idea is similar when Ned tells the boy, in order to prepare himself for a supreme effort, to "say to yourself *My name is Ned William McCaslin* and then do it" (*Reiv.* 263). The concern for protecting the good name of the Snopes clan (*Ham.* 201 ff.) is a parody of this concept.

Nancy (*S&F* 40, 42, 191): obviously a horse, and doubtless one of a MATCHED TEAM with the horse Fancy (*S&F* 13, 33, 42, 186). Similar names for matched teams were not uncommon. Incredibly, it has been suggested that the bones belong to the Nancy of *CS:TES*, and that thus we know that her husband did return and kill her. This assumes that it would be a matter of course for a murdered family servant simply to be thrown into a ditch and not buried!— in spite of the well-known Negro emphasis on funerals. Various critics have parroted this silly suggestion, and others have guessed that Nancy is a cow.

nannies (*Mans.* 196): nursemaids (Briticism).

nappy gleams (*Sanc.* 140). I have no idea what this means unless it be that the gleams of reflected light from the metal strips holding down the carpet were interrupted by or mingled with the nap of the carpet. This is totally unconvincing, but none of the other possible meanings of *nappy* is any better.

nara (*KG:Monk* 58): ne'er a, never a, not any.

narra (*Abs.* 290): negative of ARRA: not any.

narrow-asted (*Reiv.* 15): narrow-assed.

narrow . . . wheels (*LiA* 318): wagon wheels, not car tires.

nary a (*Rfan* 59): never a, not a single.

Natchez. 1. (*RfaN* 217): a town on the Mississippi River, 220 m. SSW of Oxford and 125 m. NW of New Orleans. Founded in 1716 as Fort Rosalie, by 1729 it had a population of 750. It was an old center of gracious plantation-culture when Oxford was still raw frontier. **2.** (*RfaN* 101; *Miss.* 12, 13): a tribe of Indians living in the vicinity of Natchez.

Natchez en de Robert E. Lee (*CS:BH* 79). The race between these two boats was the most famous and the greatest of all the Mississippi River steamboat races. It was prearranged as a sporting event. (Most races were simply impromptu affairs when two boats found themselves in the same reach of river and raced to the next port to get the freight waiting there.) The race was followed with close interest and frequent telegraphic reports, both nationally and internationally, and it is said that friends of the two captains alone bet over a million dollars on it. The two side-wheelers left New Orleans at 5:00 P.M. on June 20, 1870, with St. Louis as the goal. The captain of the *Natchez* treated it as a normal trip except for a furious insistence on speed. But the captain of the *Lee* stripped his boat down to a bare minimum of superstructure in order both to lighten her and to reduce wind-resistance. He also had a small steamboat waiting at intervals to bring coal barges alongside and unload them while he merely reduced speed, instead of having to stop and lash them together—an early instance of refueling in flight. These stratagems enabled the *Lee* to win the race and set a record of 3 days, 18 hours, 14 minutes. This record stood until some sixty or seventy years later, by which time changes both in boats and in the river itself were so great that to break it was really meaningless.

Natchez Trace (*RfaN* 5, 103): an early road (at first merely a trail) leading from Nashville, Tenn., to Natchez, Miss. Since much of it passed through Chickasaw lands for a generation before these lands were ceded to the whites, arrangements were made with this tribe (in 1801) providing for friendly treatment of travelers and guaranteeing to the Indians a monopoly of stopping-places along the route. These arrangements were upheld, but travelers were often at the mercy of white outlaws, of whom the most notorious were Big Harpe, Little Harpe, Samuel and John Mason, and John Murrel (spelled in various ways). The Natchez Trace did not actually pass through Oxford but through the Indian towns in the vicinity of Pontotoc, 30 m. to the E. The phrase "between Natchez and Nashville" (*CS:Court.* 365) alludes to the trace by naming its two terminals.

National Trials (*Reiv.* 193). See PARSHAM.

nature-minded (*Reiv.* 134): sex-minded.

near (with respect to wagons and teams) (*Unv.* 72): NIGH, lefthand.

near a (*CS:MV* 747): ne'er a, never a.

near-silk (*Ham.* 141): imitation silk, probably some fabric like silkalene.

neck-yoke (*AILD* 65): a wooden bar connecting two mules or horses to the tongue of the vehicle they are pulling.

needs (*Fable* 204): need.

negro burying-ground (*Sart.* 372–73). In the country, Negro and white churches have their own burying-grounds in the churchyard. In towns, the Negro burying-ground is a separate section of, or adjacent to, the white cemetery. Negro graves are frequently adorned (as are their flower-beds) with broken crockery and colored glass. Benjy's play-graveyard (*S&F* passim) imitates this custom.

negroid English and flat hill dialect (*GDM* 172). Though these dialects have a good deal in common, there are significant differences between them. For example, Faulkner distinguishes between the two pronunications of *towards*: the Negro one-syllable *to'ds* (*Sart.* 30; *CS:BH* 74) and the white hill-dialect two-syllable *to'a'ds* (*Sart.* 21).

negro's job (*LiA* 31): a job requiring little skill or responsibility, often assigned to or reserved for Negroes. Shoveling sawdust is such a job.

negro store (*Abs.* 209; *Flags* 251). Stores were never strictly segregated, but some stores catered primarily to Negro trade. These were frequently, but not necessarily, run by Negroes.

nekkid (*LiA* 75, 306; *Ham.* 71; *Mans.* 116): naked.

nekkidness (*Sanc.* 207): nakedness.

nemmine (*Unv.* 112; *GDM* 323; *Reiv.* 96): never mind.

nem you mind (*GDM* 13): never you mind. The form of the expression is influenced by NEMMINE.

nere a (*LiA* 364, 408; *Town* 255; *Mans.* 119): never a, not any (negative of ERE A).

Neshoba Indians (*Miss.* 32): not a tribe, but a group of CHOCTAWS. Some 3,000 of them stayed on in Mississippi, and Neshoba Co., with its Choctaw reservation, is the center for their descendants.

net (*Sart.* 35). This is a strange usage. It looks almost like a technical term, but I have found none that fits. Mr. Dick Dodd, of Marshallville, Ga., who has a lifelong acquaintance with both the practice and the literature of bird-dog training and hunting, assures me that there is no such technical term in this field. He suggests, as a wild possibility, that *net* could be an error for *zest*, which is used as a semitechnical term for a dog's eagerness and determination. Another possibility, equally desperate, is that Faulkner uses *net* idiosyncratically and metaphorically for the winding and criss-crossing route taken by a dog to hunt over an area.

never (*Unv.* 189; *GDM* 179, 231; *Mans.* 122): didn't: an emphatic negative that frequently has no temporal sense. "He saw you never had your gun" means "He saw that you didn't have your gun [at that time]." "We never always had the time" (*CS:MV* 750) means "We did not always have the time." "You never forgot to load that gun. You had done already unloaded it a purpose!" (*Race* 197).

new approach to Jefferson (*Mans.* 403): not merely because it is now a paved, numbered highway, but because it approaches from the north, whereas the road from Varner's Store approaches it from the southeast.

new axe (*Reiv.* 28): to be used for cutting large saplings for pry-poles when the car is stuck in the mud or in deep ruts.

new ground (*AILD* 128): land that has never been cultivated before. Before the day of tractors, cleaning up and plowing new ground was notoriously back-breaking labor, since it called for a great deal of grubbing out of the parts of stumps that wouldn't burn, cutting and breaking roots, etc.

New Hope Church (*AILD* 102, 107, 112). There have been at least four churches of this name within a 20-mile radius of Oxford, but none of them will fit the use here. The geography and place-names of *AILD* are, in general, inconsistent with those of the actual countryside and the other Yoknapatawpha novels, and Faulkner seems to have attached a common name to a purely fictional church.

new moon holding water (*S&F* 105). If the horns of the cusp are turned up so that the moon will "hold water," the weather will be dry; otherwise, it will pour out water, and there will be rain.

New Orleans (*Abs.* 70). The southern part of Mississippi was settled long before the northern part, and places like NATCHEZ had fine, established plantations when Oxford was still raw frontier. The metropolis of this culture was New Orleans, and it was only after the Civil War that Memphis began to take over this role for north Mississippi.

news butch (*GDM* 231): a person who goes through the cars of a train selling newspapers, magazines, candy, fruit, etc.

Newt Knight (*Miss.* 33). See KNIGHT, NEWT.

nickel lamp (*LiA* 137): a lamp with the metal parts nickel-plated.

nigger: Negro. This is the only form or pronunciation of the word that many people know, and hence is not necessarily contemptuous, as in the narrator of "Was" (*GDM* 5), for example, or as used by Gavin Stevens (*GDM* 378). When used by one Negro to another, it is always contemptuous (*Sart.* 66, 233; *S&F* 67, 344).

nigger freedom agent (*RfaN* 63): not a standard term, and never explained. I would guess that it is Gowan's designation for Nancy's lawyer or someone else working for her defense.

nigger graveyard (*S&F* 251): NEGRO BURYING-GROUND.

Nigger Hollow (*S&F* 377; *CS:TES* 289). Though at the time of most of Faulkner's novels a good many Negroes still lived in servant-houses on the premises of the older and larger white houses, there were two main Negro section of town, FREEDMAN TOWN and Nigger Hollow. The latter is the valley crossed by University Ave. (Miss. 6) just after it crosses South Lamar, headed east toward Tupelo. This section of town, now largely taken over by urban sprawl, is described several times in Faulkner, notably when Dilsey and the others walk through it to church in *S&F* 362–63. The road is now generally level with the entrances of buildings, but it used to cross the valley on a LEVEE that was level with the roofs of many of the cabins.

nigger in the woodpile (*Abs.* 72): a proverbial expression indicating a suspicion of something devious or concealed. "There's a nigger in the woodpile" is roughly equivalent to "There's a catch in it somewhere" or "There's something crooked about it."

niggerlover (*CS:Dry* 170, 178): a term of opprobrium applied by REDNECKS to whites who try to protect Negroes from them.

Niggertown (*LiA* 333): a generic name for the Negro section of a town.

nigh (with respect to wagons and horses) (*Unv.* 73, 77; *Ham.* 272): NEAR, lefthand. The whole point of Ratliff's application of the term to one of Ab Snopes's daughters (*Ham.* 14) lies in the implied comparison with a lazy team.

nigher (*CS:Queen* 732): more nearly.

nigh hind (*Fable* 196): left hind foot.

nightie (*S&F* 31, 89; *Sanc.* 148; *Mans.* 73): nightgown, NIGHTSHIRT—usually a women's and children's term.

nightshirt (*AILD* 209, 210; *S&F* 248; *Ham.* 210): a knee-length shirt worn by men and boys as a sleeping garment. It is a problem to get horses and mules out of a burning barn, since they seem to feel that a stall is a natural place of safety, and refuse to leave it. The standard way to get them out is to blindfold them. This is accomplished here by wrapping nightshirts around their heads.—Being a Baptist preacher, Whitfield had to go down into a lake or creek for the total immersion of his converts, and he wore a nightshirt for this task (*CS:SftL* 40).

nigra (*Town* 84): Negro. This spelling represents the normal pronunciation of many Southerners who do not say *nigger*. (The *knee-grow* pronunciation, with both syllables stressed, is not indigenous to most Southern speech.) Faulkner's mountaineers use *nigra* where a north Mississippian of the same class would use *nigger* (*CS:MV* 751, 756, 758).

Nine-Mile Branch (*Dust* 4, 69, 149): an invented name, based on Four-Mile Branch, which crosses the road to Yocona (and to Varner's) approximately 4 m. SE of Oxford, and then flows into Yellowleaf Creek. Only the names are similar, since Nine-Mile Branch is in a different direction.

nipple (of a gun) (*Unv.* 29): a raised, hollow stem, on which a percussion CAP was placed, to be struck by the hammer. See CAP-AND-BALL REVOLVER.

nits (*S&F* 142): louse-eggs or young lice.

noble experiment (*Miss.* 19): Prohibition. The phrase is usually attributed to Herbert Hoover, but what he actually called Prohibition was "an experiment, noble in motive and far-reaching in purpose." Oxford outlawed liquor in 1848. Various other communities acted similarly, and a state law closing saloons, though not entirely banning liquor, was passed in 1880.

No bloody moon (*Unv.* 282, 285). See BLOCKADE RUNNERS.

nome (*S&F* 6; *Sanc.* 201; *Abs.* 20; *Unv.* 88): no, ma'am (a respectful form of *no*, addressed to a woman).

nooky seat (*Abs.* 148): a seat in a garden nook—Miss Rosa's coinage.

normal term (*Ham.* 103): a summer term in which the university functioned as a "normal school," teaching only what was then called pedagogy and now masquerades as "education."

Norman Thomas (*Mans.* 272): the perennial Socialist candidate for the presidency.

norrer-asted (*Reiv.* 15): narrow-assed.

norrer-headed (*Reiv.* 15): narrow-headed.

nose glasses (*Sart.* 68; *Sanc.* 242): *pince-nez*.

noseying around (*Ham.* 233): nosing around, going around inquisitively (back-formation from the *adj. nosey*).

notch (*LiA* 308). A notch is sometimes cut into a gunstock to mark the killing of a man.

not creased through the legs, but flat across them (*Ham.* 323): an old rural way of pressing pants. I worked on an Arkansas plantation near Helena in the summer of 1926, and was astonished when a Negro washerwoman pressed a pair of my pants this way.

nothing on the bit (*Reiv.* 169): not pulling on the bit.

notify themselves (*Reiv.* 173): report to the authorities and make their presence known.

not on the mule (*Reiv.* 80). The implication is that a horse will stand for overloading but a mule will not.

Now I lay me (*Reiv.* 251): a standard children's bedtime prayer, now largely forgotten or perverted by the censoring of the possibility of death. It runs:

> Now I lay me down to sleep;
> I pray the Lord my soul to keep;
> If I should die before I wake
> I pray the Lord my soul to take.

Now you're tooting (*Reiv.* 181): now you're talking sense; now you're on the right track.

N.R.A. (*Mans.* 213, 306): National Recovery Administration.

nubbin (*CS:SftL* 39): CORN NUBBIN.

Number Four (*GDM* 378). See NUMBER TWENTY-THREE and Appendix.

Number Eight (*Mans.* 37). See NUMBER TWENTY-THREE and Appendix.

Number Eleven (*Mans.* 64). See NUMBER TWENTY-THREE and Appendix.

Number Five (*Mans.* 63): a southbound evening train in Oxford. See NUMBER TWENTY-THREE and Appendix.

Number 17 (*S&F* 256, 276). See NUMBER TWENTY-THREE and Appendix.

Number Six (*Mans.* 62): an early-morning northbound train in Oxford. See NUMBER TWENTY-THREE and Appendix.

Number Six shot (*Town* 55). See SHOT SIZES.

Number Ten lead shot (*Mans.* 338). See SHOT SIZES.

number-three mule-shoe (*Town* 19). A number three is a medium size (numbers usually run from 0 through 5) for a mule, and hence a large size for a magnet.

number three shot (*GDM* 324). These are somewhat large for rabbits but utterly inadequate for a bear. See SHOT SIZES.

Number Twenty-three (*Town* 365; *Reiv.* 43). Trains have official numbers, as do airline flights, and in small towns these numbers were known and frequently used. Cf. *Thirty-nine* (*Sart.* 131). Trains were normally identified either by number or by approximate time of arrival. Number Twenty-three in Oxford was the "eleven o'clock train," which actually ran at about 10:30 A.M., southbound. See Appendix.

Number-Two and -Five and -Eight-shot shells (*Mans.* 38): shotgun shells loaded with no. 2, 5, and 8 shot. See SHOT SIZES.

nummine (*Sart.* 367; *Unv.* 47; *SP* 170): never mind.

oblige (*Race* 191): obliged.

O.D. (*Sart.* 30, 166): olive drab.

off (with respect to wagons and teams) (*Sart.* 205; *AILD* 48, 65; *Unv.* 72): righthand.

offcolors (*LiA* 192): probably dresses made of cloth sold cheaply as "seconds" because the dyeing had not come out perfectly. Cf. *off-color clothes* (*CS:Hair* 135).

offen (*Sart.* 5, 208; *GDM* 76; *Town* 351): off, off of.

office (*Sart.* 34; *Abs.* 7; *Unv.* 17; *GDM* 192): a room of a large house (or often, on a plantation, a small, detached one-room house) used for business matters and records.

oh you kid (*Town* 56): a popular slang catch-phrase of the early twentieth century. It was originally more or less equivalent to a wolf-whistle but soon ceased to have any definite meaning.

Okatoba County (*Dust* 189; *KG:Hand* 72): fictional name for Yalobusha Co., immediately S of the western half of Lafayette Co. See CROSSMAN COUNTY.

Old Frenchman Place (*Sanc.* 7, 101). In an interview in 1940, Faulkner told Dan Brennan that this ruin was not based on any actual place (*Lion in the Garden*, p. 49). In the middle 1960s I asked an elderly lifelong resident of Tula (a couple of miles across the river from the location of Frenchman's Bend) if she knew of any place answering to this description, and she said flatly that there was none. The present showing of the Jones place south of Taylor as the original of the Old Frenchman Place is mere tourist business.

Old Joe (*Abs.* 346, 355): Confederate Gen. Joseph E. Johnston.

old man (*Abs.* 236, 261): father.

Old Man (subtitle in *WP*; *Miss.* 17, 24): Old Man River, the Mississippi.

Old Marster (*Sart.* 104, 113): Old Master, God. The term is a transfer to the religious sphere of the slave's designation for his master.

Old Moster (*RfaN* 43; *Mans.* 5, 128, 398): Old Master, God, See OLD MARSTER.

Old Point Comfort (*RfaN* 234): a point of land across Hampton Roads from Norfolk, Va.

Old Wyottsport (*Mans.* 206): WYOTT'S CROSSING.

ole (*Abs.* 215): old. When Temple uses this form (*RfaN* 157), she is deliberately parodying the sentimental tradition.

olé (*CS:Red* 335): presumably the Spanish exclamation, which could have gotten into CHICKASAW, although I know of no evidence that it actually did.

oleh (*GDM* 184): OLÉ.

Ole Man (*WP* 72): Old Man, the Mississippi River.

on (*GDM* 153, line 3): doubtless a misprint for *one*.

on (*GDM* 224, line 20). This word should evidently be deleted. The text, as it stands, seems to be a confusion between something like "the day on which it was now becoming traditional to hunt Old Ben" and "the day which it was now becoming traditional to save for Old Ben."

one-gallused (*Town* 278): having only one side of a pair of suspenders (GALLUSES) functioning. The term implies sloppiness and general shiftlessness in the person to whom it is applied.

one-room-and-leanto cabin (*Fable* 196): a cabin consisting of a single real room and another more or less improvised room added to it, with a sloping roof coming much lower than that of the cabin proper.

onliest (*GDM* 139; *Town* 245; *Reiv.* 219, 232): an emphatic form of *only*.

Opera House (*Town* 72; *Reiv.* 8): a standard name for a hall or building used for dances, public assemblies, occasional plays, etc. Most opera houses remained virgin of opera.

orange gleam of banknotes (*Sanc.* 218). See YELLOW ONES.

orange-stick (*Sanc.* 18, 104): an orangewood stick used in manicure.

ore-trammer (*WP* 128): a laborer who pushes the trams (small carts running on rails) in which ore is brought out of a mine.

orneriest (*Sart.* 224): *super.* of *ornery*: mean, cantankerous, hard to manage.

or there ain't a hog in Georgia (*KG:Hand* 65): a standard formula used for strong affirmation of the preceding statement.

otto'bile (*Sart.* 208): ignorant attempt at *automobile*.

ourn (*AILD* 18; *Ham.* 301): ours (*poss. pro.* only, not *adj.*).

ourn'll (*Sart.* 111): ours will.

out, *n.* (*Reiv.* 277): freedom, release from jail.

outhouse (*Sart.* 107): any sort of small structure in the vicinity of a house—tool-shed, smokehouse, kennel—including, but not restricted to, a privy. In *CS:MGM* 675, it is specifically a privy.

outside barrier islands (*WP* 16): The mainland Gulf coast of Mississippi is not directly on the Gulf of Mexico but on Mississippi Sound, a body of water some 6–8 m. wide that is separated from the open gulf by a line of barrier islands, primarily Cat, Ship, and Horn Islands.

outside rein (*Reiv.* 182). Since the horse is being ridden on an elliptical track, the outside rein must have a little slack to permit him to follow the curve instead of going in a straight line.

out with, *v.t.* (*GDM* 235): to produce, draw (a weapon).

oven (*S&F* 86, 218; *Mans.* 14). The oven of a kitchen range is only 10″ or so above the floor, and it is possible to open the door and put one's feet into it in order to warm or dry them.

over-halls (*Ham.* 54; *Mans.* 384; *CS:TS* 91): overalls.

overreach (*AILD* 174): to reach or get at (a person or thing), to get within reach of it. Jewel slips past the effective kick and gets in close, where a kick cannot damage him. As *The Farmer's Practical Horse Farriery* (New York, 1860) puts it: "The man . . . who must come within reach of a kicker should come as close to him as possible. The blow may thus become a push, and seldom is injurious."

Overton Park (*Reiv.* 111): a big park in Memphis containing extensive woods and the city zoo.

over-topped (*Ham.* 289): outbid.

overturned stack of bricks (*Sanc.* 86). Since there was only one andiron, these bricks had evidently been used to replace the missing one—a common practice.

owls (*GDM* 206; *Reiv.* 78). Other species might be involved, but in the river bottom these would primarily be barred owls (*Strix varia*), birds 18″ long with a conspicuous series of eight hoots, all on the same pitch except for a descending slur on the last one: "hoo-hoo, hoo-hoo, hoo-hoo, hoo-hooaw." Owls regularly bolt their prey and later disgorge, as "owl-balls," the compacted indigestible parts (*Mans.* 304).

Oxford (*Sanc.* 25, 161; *Abs.* 311; *Ham.* 112): Oxford, Miss., Faulkner's home and the seat of the University of Mississippi. Oxford is the original of Faulkner's Jefferson, which follows most details of its layout and topography (see Appendix). When Faulkner refers to Oxford by name in his fiction, however, he makes it a different town some 50 m. from Jefferson, at which the university is located. Jefferson is not a university town.

oysters (*WP* 103): testicles.

oyster shells (*WP* 295, 299): used like gravel to surface roads along the Gulf coast.

P

package (*S&F* 305): shipment of liquor. Before national prohibition, it was possible for a person in an area that was dry by local option to order liquor from outside and have it shipped to him by express.

packs (*Ham.* 39): pacts.

pair (*Mans.* 189): a team of two horses, especially a MATCHED TEAM.

pairsawl (*Unv.* 90): parasol.

paling fence (*Abs.* 177; *GDM* 49): PICKET FENCE.

pallet (*AILD* 10, 182: *S&F* 249; *Abs.* 40): a bed made by laying bedding directly on the floor, without any bed-frame or legs. A Negro slave or servant sleeping in the same room with a white master or mistress would normally sleep on a pallet (*Abs.* 140). The caste and racial implications of the bed, trundle bed, and pallet (complicated by personal relationships), are discussed in *Abs.* 197–98. See also *Unv.* 19, 27.

palm (*WP* 13, 307, 324; *Mans.* 248): CABBAGE PALM.

palm leaf fan (*LiA* 4, 7, 138): a fan made of a dried and trimmed palm leaf, with the stem for a handle and some sort of binding to keep the edges from fraying. These fans were bought in stores, since there are no palms in Faulkner's country. Sometimes the edges were re-bound, and this is obviously the case with Lena's (*LiA* 9).

pander with a tin cup and a rubber glove (*Fable* 163): a man collecting semen from a stallion for use in artificial insemination.

panel fence (*KG:KG* 154): a fence made of posts set in the ground with planks between them. A favorite design uses horizontal top and bottom planks, with two planks crossing each other to form an **X** between them. Panel fences are usually painted white and are characteristic of horse farms, pretentious estates, etc.

panther (*Unv.* 222; *GDM* 213; *RfaN* 101): catamount, puma, mountain lion, cougar (*Felis concolor*), a large, tawny cat attaining a length of 8' and a weight of 200 lbs. The early settlers called the animal a tiger, and it figures under that name in Bartram's *Travels*, Goldsmith's "Deserted Village," and the town of Tiger, Ga. It was once common in Faulkner's country but has long since disappeared. When Darl says that Jewel's horse is "wilder than a cattymount" (*AILD* 98) he is making a traditional comparison rather than speaking from personal experience. One of the sounds made by the puma is a piercing and terrifying scream (*GDM* 341).

paper bull, horse, etc. (*Mans.* 17, 25; *Reiv.* 232): pedigreed animal, on which the owner has the "papers."

paper suitcase (*CS:Hair* 140): cheap suitcase made of cardboard, usually colored to imitate leather. This is the same suitcase that was called "imitation leather" on p. 137.

papier-mâché Easter toys (*Sanc.* 67): Easter rabbits, etc., filled with candy. The head was the lid, and had a cardboard sleeve on which it fitted snugly into the neck. The head was normally turned as it was put on or removed, and hence it assumed impossible and "excruciating" positions with respect to the body.

parched corn coffee (*Abs.* 190): substitute coffee, made of parched corn, was a common expedient during the privations of the Confederacy. Acorns were also used in the same way (*Abs.* 276).

Parchman (*Ham.* 320; *GDM* 33; *Town* 78): the state penitentiary of Mississippi, in Parchman, 75 m. SW of Oxford. It is located in the DELTA, and the convicts do extensive cotton-farming. See *WP* 23–24.

Parchman county (*GDM* 70): not a county but a figurative expression. See PARCHMAN.

parlor (*S&F* 26): a room in a large house that was used primarily for formal occasions. With hard times and increasing informality, a parlor often fell into disuse. The account of the Sartoris parlor (*Sart.* 59–61) provides a full and typical case history. The "shrouded parlor" of Sutpen's had its furniture covered in the same way (*Abs.* 204).

Parsham (*Reiv.* 119, 193): Grand Junction, Tenn., a railroad junction point some 65 m. NE of Oxford, the site (since about 1900) of the annual National Field Trials for bird dogs.

partridge (*Ham.* 274): QUAIL.

Pascagoula. **1.** (*Mans.* 245, 246): a town on the Mississippi Gulf coast, 5 m. from the Alabama line. It has large shipyards that were very busy during World War II. **2.** (*RfaN* 101; *Miss.* 13): a small tribe of Indians formerly living on the Mississippi Gulf coast.

passel (*Sart.* 226, 329; *AILD* 99; *Ham.* 32): (parcel), considerable number or quantity.

passenger yard (*Reiv.* 144): a railroad yard where passenger-trains are made up and switched.

past gone (*WT* 71): past. (The *gone* is redundant.)

patch fence (*Mans.* 117): fence around a garden-patch.

patroller (*Unv.* 18, 25; *GDM* 278): a member of a patrol operated by each county to apprehend slaves who were off their owner's property too long without a written pass. Like many other laws, those governing these matters were strict in theory and usually lax in practice. See Charles S. Sydnor, *Slavery in Mississippi* (New York, 1933), pp. 77–83.

Patrol-riders (*GDM* 262): PATROLLERS.

patter-roller (*CS:MGM* 688): PATROLLER. A "patter-roller nigger" (*CS:MV* 752) is a Negro hiding out from, or trying to dodge, the Patrollers.

paving the sidewalks (*CS:Rose* 124). Before concrete sidewalks were laid, most of the sidewalks in Oxford consisted of planks nailed to and resting on transverse two-by-fours every few feet. Others were made of bricks laid on the ground without mortar (*Sanc.* 118).

Pawmp (*LiA* 452): Pomp, short for *Pompey*.

pawn (*Ham.* 246): an ordinary man (as opposed to a king) in checkers. Faulkner apparently borrowed the term from chess.

pawpaw (*GDM* 178; *CS:Red* 331): a small tree or large shrub (*Asimina triloba*) with leaves up to 1' long and fruits looking somewhat like chunky bananas. The fruits are faintly edible, and children and possums like them. Pawpaws tend to form thickets.

pay mind (*S&F* 193, 258; *CS:SftL* 42): to notice, heed, pay attention to.

pay off (of a boat) (*WP* 146): to veer to the leeward.

p.c. (*LiA* 430; *RfaN* 105; *Mans.* 278): post of command.

Peabody (*Reiv.* 96): a Memphis hotel, originally on the NW corner of South Main and Monroe. In the 1920's it was replaced by a new Peabody (now the Sheraton-Peabody) on Union Ave. between S. Second and S. Third streets. The Peabody was for years *the* elegant hotel of Memphis. Faulkner seems to use both GREENBURY and TEABERRY as covernames for it. The Peabody is the hotel in whose lobby "Mississippi begins" (*Miss.* 11).

peace (*GDM* 266): PIECE (2).

peakling (*AILD* 17): **1.** sneaking, skulking: **2.** drooping, being sickly. Either meaning, or a combination of them, is possible here. When asked about this word twenty-seven years after he wrote it down, Faulkner implied that he had the second meaning in mind. He explained the word (quite incorrectly) as "probably a corruption or contraction between *puny* and *weakly*" (*Faulkner in the U.*, p. 126).

peanut-parcher (*GDM* 320; *Town* 18): a device for parching (roasting) peanuts, mounted on wheels and pushed about the streets by men who hawked peanuts. It had an oil-flame which provided heat for the parching and steam to power a little engine that tumbled the peanuts as they parched. It also had a little steam-whistle to attract attention.

peanut-whistle blast (*WP* 196). See PEANUT-PARCHER.

Pearl River (*RfaN* 109): the river on which Jackson, Miss., stands. It flows S into the Gulf of Mexico, and forms the boundary between Mississippi and Louisiana from the Gulf to the 31st parallel.

peart (*Sart.* 224): pert, energetic.

peckerwood. 1. (*Race* 188): a woodpecker. **2.** (*GDM* 360; *RfaN* 43): an ornery rustic, a REDNECK.

Peddlers Field Old Town (*Dust* 34): " 'Pedlar's Field, Old Town,' in the fiction perhaps comes from Pedlar's Field, an old abandoned farm section frequently used by fox hunters" (Cullen and Watkins, *Old Times in the Faulkner Country,* p. 68, n. 1). I do not know of this place. *Old Town* occurs in a good many place-names, designating a former town site or the remnants of a town when the real town, keeping the same name, has shifted to a new site. Cf. BURTSBORO OLD TOWN.

pee a noler (*Reiv.* 112, 142, 154): PIANOLA.

pegged-out hide (*WP* 261). The alligator hide had been "spread on the platform" (previous page) and pegged out with nails or wooden pegs to hold it stretched while it cured.

pegs (*Mans,* 156). Wooden shoe-pegs were still used by some cobblers long after nails came into general use.

Pemberton, Gen. John C. (*Unv.* 7, 20; *Miss.* 17): the Confederate general who conducted the unsuccessful defense of Vicksburg.

Pemberton or Johnston or Forrest (*Miss.* 17). The three Confederate generals go with the three battles Faulkner had just mentioned, but not respectively. John C. Pemberton was the unsuccessful defender of Vicksburg, Albert Sidney Johnston was mortally wounded at Shiloh, and Nathan Bedford Forrest won a great victory at Brice's Crossroads.

penance bench (*Sart.* 24). There seems to be no such thing as a penance bench, as distinguished from a MOURNERS' (moaner's) BENCH. Prof. F. G. Cassidy suggests that the terms are intended to be synonymous, and that the sinner rises from the bench where he has been sitting, jumps onto it, and stands on it to get a vantage-point from which to launch his accusation at the preacher. Songs of this sort are often elliptical and puzzling, and this is the most satisfactory explanation I have found.

Pensacola (*Sanc.* 248): a seaport in the Florida panhandle, 350 m. from Memphis.

pepper tree (*WP* 209): a large South American shrub (*Schinus molle*) grown as an ornamental in the subtropical parts of the United States. It has large bunches of red berries in the winter.

persimmon (*Mans.* 417; *CS:TWBF* 287): common persimmon (*Diospyros virginiana*), a tree growing to about 60' high, with bark showing much the pattern of alligator-hide. The spherical fruits, about $1\frac{1}{2}''$ in diameter, are very astringent when green but sweet when ripe, at which time they are orange or purplish-colored ("miniature suns," *Sart.* 276). Persimmons are much attacked by the Eastern tent caterpillar (*Malacosoma americanum*), which leaves its conspicuous "tents" of webs in the "caterpillar festooned branches" *(Sart.* 276). Persimmons come up promptly in abandoned fields *(LiA* 402; *Abs.* 214).

phaeton *(Abs.* 25; *Reiv.* 96): a four-wheeled carriage with a front and a back seat.

phenagling *(WP* 45): finagling, devious or dishonest maneuvering.

Philadelphia *(Unv.* 126; *Miss.* 32): a Mississippi town 130 m. SSE of Oxford and 35 m. W of the Alabama line. It is the principal town of the Indians remaining in the state.

phosphorus *(Miss.* 29). Various tiny marine organisms in the Gulf of Mexico are luminescent when disturbed, so that any disturbance in the water produces a flash or a trail of light.

phut *(Unv.* 143): an exclamation signifying impatience with or dismissal of an idea.

Pianola *(Reiv.* 100): a brand of player-piano. It had a pneumatic action, and the power for it was supplied by a person sitting at it and "pumping" alternately on two pedals. Sometimes, in public places, it was coin-operated *(WP* 211).

pick *(S&F* 271): win from. (This is a guess from the context. I do not know of such a usage, nor have I found it attested elsewhere.)

picket fence *(Abs.* 21; *Ham.* 147, 158). See FENCE PICKET.

Pickett *(Dust* 194): Confederate Gen. George Edward Pickett, who led Pickett's charge at the Battle of Gettysburg at approximately 3:00 P.M., July 3, 1863. This charge, often called the high-water mark of the Confederacy, was a desperate and almost successful gamble, but it was beaten back with more than 75 percent casualties. Pickett's brigade was a part of Gen. LONGSTREET's corps.

pick it up *(Mans.* 428, 429): speed up, move along.

picquet *(Abs.* 63, 82; *Unv.* 267; *GDM* 15): picket, sentry, group of sentries.

piece. 1. *(LiA* 1, 7; *GDM* 17; *Reiv.* 76, 119): distance, way. **2.** *(Ham.* 46; *GDM* 42, 61; 266—*peace*): piece of land, field. **3.** *(WP* 334): a woman, considered sexually: a "piece of tail."

pieceways *(LiA* 9): an indefinite distance. The word is a combination of "up the road a piece" and "up the road a ways."

pigeon-tailed coat *(Town* 83; *Reiv.* 82, 285; *CS:Court.* 364): dress coat, tail coat.

pigpen *(S&F* 241; *GDM* 248): a small enclosure, usually about 10′–20′ square, in which pigs are kept.

pigsty *(S&F* 347): a dirty and disorderly place. This is a purely figurative expression. In Faulkner's country, a place where pigs are actually kept is always a PIGPEN.

pilot (of a locomotive) *(Unv.* 260): cowcatcher, the wedge-shaped projection at the front which just clears the tracks and serves the purpose of throwing obstacles out of the way so that they will not get under the wheels. It usually has a small platform on which a man can stand.

pin down (a covey of birds) (*Mans.* 230). A bird dog must get close enough to a covey of quail so that they stop running around and are poised, ready to fly at the least further alarm. He thus pins them down until the hunter comes up and flushes them.

pine branches to sleep on (*Unv.* 188): small pine branches can serve the double purpose of padding and a ground-sheet.

pine headstone (*LiA* 2): a pine board used in place of a headstone on a grave.

pine knots (*Sart.* 53; *Abs.* 51, 98; *GDM* 88). Being both hard and resinous, pine knots burn fiercely and long, and can therefore be used for torches and general emergency lighting.

pink dogwood (*Town* 310, 334). See DOGWOOD.

pin oak (*Unv.* 13; *Ham.* 225; *RfaN* 101): not the pin oak (*Quercus palustris*) of most tree handbooks, which does not grow as far south as Faulkner's country, but the willow oak (*Q. phellos*), which is also called pin oak. Its leaves are shaped like those of a willow, and average about 3/4″ wide and 4″ long. The tree grows best in river bottoms, where it reaches a height of well over 100′ and a diameter of more than 4′. It is also often grown ornamentally along streets. Most of the large oaks on North and South Lamar in Oxford and along the road between the bridge and the Confederate monument on the University of Mississippi campus are willow oaks.

p'int (*WT* 54): to point, aim.

pipe down (*Mosq.* 175): quiet down, make less noise, This is the normal meaning, but Pete seems to use the expression here to mean "calm down, collect yourself."

pistol hammer, taut as a (*Unv.* 118). Hammers of Civil War pistols rose high above the gun and were curved forward. The comparison is, of course, to the hammer of a cocked pistol, leaning forward and ready to fire at a touch of the trigger.

pistol sound (*GDM* 239). Jim had been holding the dogs on a leather leash (p. 237). Now he is cracking the leash like a whip.

pitch game (*Ham.* 129): any game operated at a stand or booth by a pitchman.

pitching dollars (*Sart.* 167; *Sanc.* 157, 160; *SP* 112; *CS:Hair* 141): a game played much like horseshoes, except that instead of pitching horseshoes at a stake, the players pitch silver dollars at a hole in the ground not much larger than a dollar. In a common variation, the dollars were simply pitched at a line scratched in the ground. The game was called pitching dollars even when (as was usually the case) large washers from the hardware store were used instead of dollars.

Pittsburg(h) Landing (*Abs.* 124, 270, 339): a battle (also known as the Battle of Shiloh) fought near the junction of Mississippi, Tennessee, and Alabama, April 6–7, 1862.

pizen (*GDM* 148; *CS:MV* 752, 771): poison.

planing mill (*LiA* 9, 46, 408). The original of the one used by Faulkner in *LiA* operated for some years in the late 1920s and early 1930s by the railroad about a mile or so S of Oxford. Thus the courthouse, the Burden house, and the mill formed a triangle and the route from the cabin to the mill was entirely different from the route between the cabin and town.

Plank Road (*GDM* 286): Orange Plank Road, running through the battlefield of CHANCELLORSVILLE.

plantation bell (*GDM* 48): a large bell, often as much as 1' high, placed on a post outdoors and used to signal the beginning and end of work. It is also used as a general alarm bell.

plantation saddle (*GDM* 78): a wide, comfortable saddle, designed for a man who must spend a great deal of time in the saddle, riding around and inspecting or supervising, but not doing any hard riding.

planter. 1. (*GDM* 75; *WP* 72): any of several types of mechanical devices for planting seeds, usually the seeds of such row-crops as corn and cotton; cf. SEEDER. A planter's wheel covers the seeds and firms the soil about them, so that the crop does spring up in the planter's wheel-print. Faulkner qualifies his statement with *almost* (*GDM* 75), because his hyperbole implies that it springs up almost immediately. **2.** (*Dust.* 24): a person who owns and operates a farm (usually a fairly large one), but who does not himself work in the fields, a "gentleman farmer." The term is used in contrast to *farmer* (or, more specifically, DIRT FARMER), which applies to a man who works in his fields. The contrast is specifically stated in the case of Mr. Ernest, whose face "usually did have a smudge of mud or tractor grease or beard stubble on it, because he wasn't jest a planter; he was a farmer, he worked as hard as ara one of his hands and tenants" (*Race* 194).

planting year (*Ham.* 264): the farming year, from planting-time in early spring to harvesting in the fall. Many rural schools opened after cotton-picking and other harvesting was finished in the fall, and closed early in the spring when the children were needed to help with the planting.

play out (*S&F* 229, 289): to play hookey, to stay away from school without one's parents' knowledge or permission.

play pretty (*S&F* 36): any small toy or trinket with which a child plays.

plow-bolts (*Ham.* 239: *GDM* 255): nuts and bolts used for fastening the various parts of a plow together. The term is generic: plow-bolts are of various lengths, sizes, and configurations, but the term is used only for bolts fastening shares, moldboards, etc., to the PLOWSTOCK. These bolts are countersunk, so that the head of the bolt is flush with the surface of the plowshare.

plow bridle (*Ham.* 9): a heavy leather bridle, usually with blinders and PLOW-LINE reins.

plow-collar (*GDM* 255): any mule-collar used for plowing—not a special kind.

plow-galled (*Ham.* 363): having TRACE-GALLS produced by plowing.

plow-gear (*Ham.* 56): a general term for anything needed in connection with plowing: plowlines, harness, plowshares, nuts and bolts, etc. More specifically, the complete harness put on a mule for plowing: bridle, collar, hames trace-chains, and plowlines (*Ham.* 248; *Reiv.* 84). There is a specific contrast between the plow-gear of *CS:BB* 15 and the wagon gear mentioned two pages later. For an explanation of "plow gear merely looped over the hames" (*KG:KG* 154), see TRACE CHAINS.

plow hand (*KG:KG* 233): a general term for a field-worker, often (as here) with a suggestion of *yokel*.

plow handles (*WP* 336; *KG:Tomo.* 92): the two handles by which a man walking behind a mule-drawn plow controls it. They slope upward from the PLOW STOCK to a comfortable height (about waist-high), and are curved to fit the hands.

plowline (*AILD* 41; *Ham.* 7; *GDM* 17, 96, 255): light rope, usually cotton, used for guiding a plow-animal and also as the general-purpose light rope around a farm. The plowlines run from the two ends of the BIT through rings on the HAMES, and from there back to the plowman. A well-trained mule needs little guidance in plowing and cultivating, and some plowmen hold one line in each hand along with one plow handle. Others tie the lines together and loop them over the head, keeping a bit of tension on them against the back of the neck (*Mans.* 84).

plow-marks (*AILD* 128): not a standard word. Since Addie was going back from the field to the house, "stumbling a little on the plow-marks," it probably refers to the cuts made in the soil by a plow being dragged on its side to the field. These are not nearly so big as the furrows made by actual plowing, but would be quite enough to make a woman blinded by tears stumble. The term might also refer to the marks made where the plow is turned around in the TURN-ROW.

plow point (*GDM* 168): a detachable point fastened onto a PLOWSHARE.

plowshare (*Abs.* 181): the steel blade which cuts the earth when it is plowed. This is a generic term. There are many different shapes of plowshares, each with its own name and function.

plow stock (*Ham.* 31; *RfaN* 218): the basic frame of a plow, to which plow-shares, handles, etc., are attached.

plow-tools (*Town* 294): plows and parts of plows: plow stocks, plowshares, sweeps, etc.

plow-trace (*Fable* 176): TRACE-CHAIN.

plug hat (*Abs.* 231; *Town* 83; *Mans.* 156): high silk hat, top hat.

plum (*Sart.* 87): entirely, completely.

po'house (*Sart.* 2): poorhouse.

poison oak (*S&F* 300): poison ivy (*Rhus toxicodendron* or *R. radicans*), two very similar plants which, on contact, cause serious skin eruptions in susceptible people. They grow profusely on the ground and climb even tall trees. In general, the term *poison oak* is used for both species, and *poison ivy* is seldom used by Yoknapatawphans.

pokeberry (*Unv.* 87, 142): pokeweed, or scoke (*Phytolacca decandra*), a large, hollow-stemmed weed growing 5'–9' high. The "berries" are about the size of English peas and grow in clusters much like grapes. Their juice is a dark crimson-purple and can be used as an emergency ink. Children paint their faces with pokeberry juice to imitate Indian war-paint.

poll-tax (*Ham.* 349): a head-tax, as the name itself says. But since the only penalty for not paying it was forfeiting the right to vote, it came to be considered a voting-tax. The point here is that Eustace Grimm should have been a political supporter of Will Varner.

po'ly (*Sart.* 26): poorly. As used by Simon, this is a routine Negro reply to an inquiry about one's health or well-being, the idea being to avoid presumption before the Lord. In fact, the formula is often "Po'ly, thank the Lawd."

pone (*Unv.* 70): CORN PONE.

pony (*Sanc.* 148): a literal interlinear translation, especially of a school Latin text. The use of a pony was considered a form of cheating but was quite prevalent among sorry and lazy students.

Pontchartrain (*WP* 58; *Miss.* 30): Lake Pontchartrain, a shallow, roughly circular body of water some 30 m. in diameter lying N and NW of New Orleans. Actually, it is not a lake but a land-locked salt-water bay. The cruise in *Mosq.* takes place here.

Pontotoc (*Mans.* 62): Pontotoc Ave., in Memphis, parallel to BEALE STREET, intersecting MULBERRY, and sharing the shady reputation of both.

poor white (*Abs.* 380): white TRASH. A poor white is a lower-class, shiftless, hand-to-mouth type, not merely a white who is poor. Sutpen's parents and Wash Jones were poor whites, but Rosa Coldfield and Judith Sutpen, for all their dire poverty, were not. It is often said of someone that no matter how much money he may make, he will still be a poor white. Flem Snopes is a fine example.

popcorn and molasses (*Sanc.* 182; *GDM* 231): a confection packaged in waxed-paper boxes, each containing a little trinket as a "prize," and usually sold under the trade-name of Cracker Jack. The product and package have remained unchanged for at least seventy years except for a great reduction in the size of the package and a corresponding rise in price. Cracker Jack is eaten almost exclusively by children, and hence implies childishness or rusticity when used by adults.

Pope, General (*Sart.* 10, 13, 19). See HALLECK, GENERAL.

popgun (*Sart.* 46): childish, ineffectual weapon (here applied collectively to both the outclassed plane and its armament). The child's popgun, to which the comparison is made, consists of a section of CANE without a joint, so that it is open for its whole length, and a plunger having a handle with a shoulder and, extending beyond that, a rod about half an inch shorter than the cane. The ammunition for it is any hard fruit (usually holly berries or chinaberries) slightly larger than the bore. A fruit is forced into the rear of the cane and then pushed through it until the shoulder stops the plunger, with the charge close to the front end. Then another fruit is put into the rear end and sharply pushed forward. It serves as a piston and builds up air pressure, firing the other fruit out of the end with a very satisfactory "pop" and considerable force. The piston of one shot remains in the cane as the projectile for the next one.

poplar (*Sanc.* 291): possibly SILVER POPLAR or Lombardy poplar, but more likely tulip tree, which is commonly known as yellow poplar. The poplar "strong through very absence of strength" (*SP* 80) is evidently the tall, flexible Lombardy poplar (*Populus nigra italica*), as are the poplars of *SP* 283, 286, *Mosq.* 27, and the "spindling poplars" of *Flags* 346.

popper (*CS:TES* 304). The old-fashioned corn-popper for use over an open fire consisted of a solid metal box fitted with a screened top and mounted on a handle about 3′ long. The top slid in grooves at the top of the box and had a wire attached to it so that it could be pulled back to empty the corn after it was popped. It was presumably this wire which was missing and which Nancy replaced to "fix" the popper.

pop stand (*Ham.* 129): a stand at a fair for selling carbonated soft drinks ("soda pop").

Porcellian (*Mans.* 193): an undergraduate social club at Harvard, founded in 1790. A recent history of the University describes it as "Harvard's snootiest social club."

porter (*Sanc.* 168; *Town* 359; *Mans.* 405). A PULLMAN car has its own Negro porter, who makes down and puts up the berths and sees to the passengers generally. His duties include placing the step-stool (FOOTSTOOL) by which they leave the train, and helping them down. At this point he is supposed to be given a generous tip. It is typical of Clarence Snope's cheapness that he gives the porter only one of his own cheap cigars (*Sanc.* 173). A single porter sees to the needs of all the passengers on day-coaches, unless the train is a very long one. Note the distinction between the Pullman porters (plural) and the day-coach porter (singular) in *Town* 359.

portmanteau (*Abs.* 45; *Ham.* 140, 336): a clothes-case designed to be carried by a man on horseback.

Possum (*Reiv.* 118): PARSHAM.

'possum (*Abs.* 188; *Unv.* 251): opossum (*Diadelphis virginiana*), an omnivorous marsupial about the size of a large house-cat, with a white face, gray fur, hairless pink paws, and a ratlike, prehensile tail. Only zoologists pronounce the initial *o* of the name. *Sart.* 285 gives an excellent description. Possums are great raiders of henhouses (*LiA* 19) and eaters of persimmons (*CS:TWBF* 287). They are also carrion-eaters, and one finds Houston's body promptly (*Ham.* 224).

possum hunting (*Sart.* 281–89; *S&F* 141–42). Possums are hunted with dogs (largely hounds) in the late fall and winter. Kerosene lanterns or (later) flashlights are used for light. The hunters take the dogs into the woods, and the dogs scatter out. When one of them hits a trail, he begins to follow it, with a characteristic baying. The other dogs come and join him, and the hunters try to follow or intercept the pursuit. The dogs are urged on by whoops and called back by a horn. The possum, unlike the coon, is not a fighter: when the dogs get close, he climbs a tree. When the dogs tree (*v., t.* and *i.*), they stop baying and begin a sort of excited barking or yapping. The hunters then make their way, by ear, to the tree. The possum is found by "shining" his eyes. A light is held close to a hunter's eyes, and when the possum looks into it, the hunter sees points of light reflected from the possum's eyes. It is necessary to do this in order to be sure that the possum is really in the tree, and, if the tree is large, just where in it. If the tree is small, it is chopped down—hence an axe is a regular part of a possum hunt. If it is large, someone climbs it, chasing the possum out toward the end of a branch, where he can be shaken until he loses his grip and falls. (Since he has claws on the fore-feet, opposable thumbs which enable him to grip with the hind feet, and a prehensile tail, this takes pretty violent shaking.) Attempts (usually vain) are made to get the dogs away from the spot where he will fall, but they usually have to be driven away after the event. When the animal falls, he "plays possum," i.e. feigns death. He is put into a sack for carrying. A possum is never shot out of a tree. He is killed by putting a stout stick (on a hunt this is usually the axe-handle) across his neck, standing on its ends, and pulling the tail to break the neck. Often, however, he is taken back alive and fattened before he is eaten (*Sart.* 317). The possum is roasted or baked, traditionally with sweet potatoes. The flesh is much like pork, but sweeter and greasier.

possum-rich bear pork (*CS:BH* 68). Being somewhat greasy, bear meat is sometimes called bear-pork. Possum meat is rich and greasy. Hence the meaning is "pork-like bear meat as rich and greasy as possum meat."

post (*Abs.* 287; *Ham.* 12, 349): a small, unpretentious support for a porch-roof. See COLUMNS.

postol (*LiA* 352): misprint for *pistol.*

potato grater (*LiA* 316): any large, coarse kitchen grater.

potlicker (*Dust* 5): a mongrel dog, one allowed to lick cooking pots and fed on table scraps (sometimes called a pot-hound). It is possible that *potliquor* (the water in which greens and fat meat have been boiled) may enter into this designation and that in the following entry.

potlicker possum hounds (*Mans.* 417). See POTLICKER.

potlickin' (*Sart.* 282). See POTLICKER. Caspey uses the term here with a mixture of affection and derogation.

pot still (*Town* 316): a still in which the fire is applied directly to the pot (or KETTLE) containing the mash. This is the general type to which all moonshine stills belong. In its simplest, basic form it consists of a "pot" with a broad, rounded base under which the fire is built and a head (top) with a tapered neck which is connected to the "worm," a spiral of copper (or, earlier, pewter) tubing which is immersed in cold water to serve as a condenser.

potty (*Sart.* 170): none of the regular senses, such as "not quite right mentally" and "dirty as a pot," seems to fit here. My guess is that it means pot-shaped: short and dumpy.

pound-fee (*Ham.* 192, 242): a fee of one dollar which the owner of any strayed livestock must pay to the person who takes up the animal and returns it to him.

pound law (*Mans.* 331). See POUND-FEE.

powder, gun. The black powder of the Civil War era made thick clouds of smoke which cut visibility to zero and (especially with the leakage around the NIPPLES or breeches of guns) blackened the faces of soldiers. This effect, combined with the blackness of unexploded powder around the mouth from biting off the ends of paper CARTRIDGES, explains the "powder-blackened faces" (*Abs.* 189). The powder that Bayard smells so strongly when he finds Rosa Millard's body is, of course, the burned powder of the shot that killed her (*Unv.* 175).

powder-monkey (*WP* 128): a member of a blasting crew.

powder-shooting gun (*Dust* 125): a real, adult gun, as distinguished from BB guns, etc.

power (*WT* 71): a large number or quantity (confined to the expression *a power of* something).

power plant (*Sart.* 165; *Town* 9). The Oxford power plant used to be on the railroad a hundred yards S of the station, and this is where it is always located in Faulkner's novels. This is not the plant where Faulkner had a night job and wrote AILD. That was the university power plant, which is still functioning in the same building and, until 1974, with the same main dynamo.

prayer meeting (*Abs.* 88; *Mans.* 74, 121; *Reiv.* 97): an evening service, usually on Wednesday night, but also sometimes a Sunday night service. It is used both ways in *LiA* 346.

preacher's coat (*Fable* 166): FROCKCOAT.

precher (*GDM* 264): preacher.

presented (of a gun) (*Ham.* 230): held in both hands, with the barrel raised, ready to be thrown down and fired instantly.

prince's feather (*GDM* 49): an annual flower with bright green foliage and long, drooping spikes of red flowers, like plumes.

prissy (*S&F* 49): prim, priggish, affectedly elegant.

prob'ly (*Race* 192): probably.

Professor. 1. (*S&F* 224): a high-school principal, or even the single teacher of a one-room school (*Ham.* 69, 102; *Town* 37). **2.** (*Town* 72): a bandleader, cf. next entry. "W. I. Swain, the King of Tented Theatricals" used to visit Oxford every summer during the early 1920s and put on sentimental plays. The master of ceremonies always referred to the leader of the band as "Professor." This is an old usage. It occurs on the second page of the third chapter of Faulkner's great-grandfather's novel *The White Rose of Memphis* (1880).

Professor Handy (*Town* 72): W. C. Handy, "the father of the blues."

projecking (*S&F* 10, 67): fooling around in an irresponsible or officious manner (derived from the *n. project*).

proud (*Reiv.* 77): glad, happy. ("I'm proud to meet you" is a standard response to an introduction.)

prove on land (*RfaN* 37): to show that one has met all legal conditions for acquiring a clear title to it.

provost marshal (*Abs.* 68): an officer in charge of military police.

prowl, *v.t.* (*Town* 24): to TOMCAT after (a woman).

pudden (*LiA* 215). This bit of doggerel is obviously one of the unintelligible children's, and especially Negroes', songs which either arise as nonsense or, often, are corrupted beyond recognition (like many parts of play-party songs) by a long process of rote repetition without understanding. But there is an intelligible phrase in it. *Pudden* ("pudding") is sometimes used (like the Negro *jelly-roll*) in the sexual senses (both anatomical and abstract) of *pussy*. That seems to be the meaning here.

pugnuckling (*Reiv.* 140, 154, 156): fornicating, screwing. Apparently a nonce-word invented by Faulkner for this novel. Since the story of *Reiv.* is told by a grandfather to his young (and presumably fairly innocent) grandson, neither a learned, clinical term nor a crude, earthy one would be appropriate, and Faulkner seems simply to have made up a word for the purpose.

puke-stomached (*Ham.* 241): inclined to puke, squeamish.

Pullman (*Sanc.* 168; *Reiv.* 136, 198): a railroad passenger-car with berths and/or small cubicles for sleeping. It has its own CONDUCTOR (*SP* 11) and its own Negro PORTER.

pump gun (*GDM* 225, 236; *Reiv.* 23; *Race* 177): a repeating shotgun operated by first pulling and then pushing (i.e. "pumping") a slide under the barrel, between shots. The slide is a sort of sleeve over the magazine. When it is pulled back it ejects the shell that is in the CHAMBER, whether it has been fired or not (*GDM* 253), and when it is pushed forward again, it puts another shell into the chamber (*GDM* 325). When the gun is loaded, the shells are put into the magazine from the end nearest the breech, and they are pumped into the chamber from the same end; hence they are fired in the reverse order from that in which they were loaded (*GDM* 324, 325). The sound of a pump gun being worked is represented as *snick-cluck* (*Race* 189), the *snick* being produced when the slide is pulled back to eject a shell, and the *cluck* when it is slid forward to chamber the next one. The sound is later (p. 190) *click*, *snick-cluck*, as Mister Ernest pulls the trigger of the unloaded gun, making the click, and then works the slide as if trying to put a shell into the chamber.

pump house (*LiA* 30): a shelter over a pump, primarily to keep surface water out of the well.

puncheon (*Ham.* 102; *CS:MV* 756): a log split into halves. A puncheon floor is made of such logs, with the flat sides up.

Punkin Creek (*Mans.* 27, 28): Pumpkin Creek, a stream about $7\frac{1}{2}$ m. SE of Oxford, and hence between Jefferson and Frenchman's Bend.

pure, *adv.* **1.** (*AILD* 37, 218, 223; *LiA* 332): really, very, utterly. **2.** (*CS:BH* 67; *CS:TS* 96): simply.

purely (*Town* 258): really, surely.

pussel-gutted. 1. (*AILD* 13; *Ham.* 232; *Mans.* 55): big-bellied and flatulent. (In northern Florida, the pot-bellied little mosquito-fish, or gambusia, is called the pusselgut.) **2.** (*AILD* 39): to cause to be big-bellied and flatulent.

put in (*AILD* 66, 121): to harness and hitch a horse, team, etc. (to a wagon, plow, etc.). Lucas applies the term by analogy to a machine (*GDM* 81): "put in the machine" means to do whatever is necessary to start working with it.

put into (*Unv.* 48; *Ham.* 193, 195; *GDM* 244): to harness and hitch a horse, team, etc. (to a wagon, plow, etc.). The difference in construction from the preceding entry is illustrated by "He got ready to plow and put the team in," and "He put the team into the plow."

put (something) **on** (someone) (*Ham.* 22): put something over on someone, get the better of him.

put to (*GDM* 47, 75): PUT INTO.

putty (*Sart.* 223; *superl.*, *Sart.* 225): pretty. The *u* is pronounced as in *put*.

putty-face (*Sanc.* 57): one whose face is the color of putty, a dirty grayish white. Cf. "putty-colored face" (*Sanc.* 60): "puttycolored flesh" (*LiA* 370); "face the color of putty" (*Town* 241).

Q

Q'Milla (*Mans.* 81). In the early 1920s there was a girl in the Oxford schools with this strange given name. It is presumably a form of *Camilla*.

quail (*Sart.* 206, 282; *Abs.* 187; *Ham.* 172): bobwhite (*Colinus virginianus*). In spring and early summer it constantly gives the call for which it is named. In the winter it collects into covies of about ten to thirty birds, which all fly up at once with a startling roar of wings, when flushed. Quail are prime game-birds and are hunted with BIRD DOGS that indicate their presence and location to the hunter, who then flushes them and shoots them on the wing— or tries to. Then the dogs retrieve them. In any sort of hunting context, *birds* always means "quail." In fact, any Mississippi farmer, asked if there are any birds on his place, will answer about quail; he would never suspect his questioner of inquiring about towhees or chipping sparrows. Shooting quail on the ground (instead of on the wing) is a standard metaphor for unsportmanlike conduct (*Mosq.* 306).

quality (*Town* 245; *CS:Queen* 732, 734): upper-class people, real gentlemen and ladies—usually contrasted, by implication at least, with TRASH.

quarters (*Sart.* 367; *Abs.* 342; *Unv.* 161; *GDM* 169): the slave-quarters, the cabins grouped together where the slaves lived on an antebellum plantation.

quick. 1. *n.* (*Ham.* 64) : the living, sensitive, inner part of a horse's foot. A shoe is supposed to be nailed to the insensitive wall of the hoof. **2.** *v.t.* (*Town* 37; *Fable* 196) to strike (a horse) in the sensitive part of his foot with a nail.

Quick (*Ham.* 57, 70) : an old Lafayette Co. name. Quick's Lakes are three artificial ponds about 7 m. NE of Oxford.

quoil (*Sart.* 87, 231; *S&F* 142) : to quarrel.

R

rabbit (*Sart.* 118; *AILD* 63; *Ham.* 172) : either the cottontail rabbit (*Sylvilagus floridanus*) or the swamp rabbit (*S. aquaticus*). The former is grayish, the latter more brownish and larger. The cottontail is found in the hills, and the swamp rabbit in swamps and river bottoms. Most hunters are aware of the distinction between the two but seldom bother to make it. A rabbit caught by dogs or other beasts of prey frequently screams (*WP* 174). Ratliff calls his horses "rabbits" in affectionate appreciation of their liveliness and speed (*Ham.* 50).

rabbit foot: a good luck or protective talisman sometimes carried by superstitious people, both white and black. It is particularly effective if it comes from a "graveyard rabbit" at a propitious time—here the dark of the moon, but sometimes midnight (*Sart.* 118–19). Rubbing the foot with a hand, or rubbing it on oneself, activates it or increases its potency. The "hardish lump about the size of a pecan" that Ned gives Lucius (*Reiv.* 239) is probably a rabbit's foot.

rabbit-grass (*Ham.* 79) : apparently used as another name for SEDGE because rabbits frequently take cover in it.

rabbits, hunt the canebrake (*Unv.* 59) : cowards, take cover.

race (as a hunting term) (*Sart.* 331, 332; *GDM* 5; title: "Race at Morning") : a race between the dogs and their quarry; hence, a pursuit, a chase.

racing on two wheels (*Abs.* 24). A four-wheeled carriage will race on two wheels only when going fast on a curve. As Faulkner's map for *Abs.* shows, the church in question is the College Hill church—where, incidentally, Faulkner was married. It is evidence of his close visualization of his localities that this church has a semicircular driveway.

rack (*Ham.* 21; *Dust* 238) : a gait of a horse, also called SINGLEFOOT.

rack. 1. (*AILD* 68) : to overstrain. "If this team don't rack to pieces" (*AILD* 187) means "If this sorry team doesn't come apart from being overtaxed." **2.** (*Unv.* 13) : to stack up, as in a rack. This verb effectively describes the stacking of the rails of two adjacent panels of a SNAKE FENCE alternately on each other.

raddled (*Mans.* 277) : worn, ravaged, the worse for wear.

R.A.F. (*Mans.* 209; *KG:KG* 197) : Royal Air Force.

Rafe (*Sart.* 122) : archaic form and pronunciation of *Ralph*.

rail (*AILD* 8; *Unv.* 135; *Ham.* 5). In Faulkner's more primitive settings, normally a rail of a rail-fence (the sort that Lincoln split in his youth), not a railroad rail. A fence rail is normally about 10′ long and 2″–4″ in diameter, though the accidents of the grain and splitting make the cross-section almost any conceivable shape.

Rainey, Paul (*Reiv.* 166, 194): a wealthy sportsman who, in 1898, bought an 11,000-acre tract at Cotton Plant, Miss. (35 m. NE of Oxford) and stocked it with game, including wolves and bears, as a hunting preserve. Later, he spent six years in Kenya, riding to hounds in pursuit of lions, with devastating success (see Daniel P. Mannix, "The Playboy Lion Killer," *True: The Man's Magazine*, October 1957, pp. 69–70, 108–12). The reference to Rainey as "just a few miles down Colonel Sartoris's railroad toward Jefferson" (*Reiv.* 194) shows Faulkner's characteristic merging of his great-grandfather's railroad through New Albany with the Illinois Central railroad through Oxford (Jefferson). The point of view here is from Parsham (Grand Junction, Tenn.). Cotton Plant and Rainey were actually on Col. Faulkner's railroad between Ripley and New Albany, Miss.; that railroad did not come to Grand Junction, but to Middleton, Tenn., a few miles to the east. The Illinois Central main line (at that time) ran from Grand Junction through Oxford, but did not come within 30 m. of Cotton Plant.

raise (*CS:SftL* 41): to build. Originally the term was more specific. A single family could cut the logs or timbers for a house or barn but could not raise them and fasten them into place. Hence when the timbers were cut, the neighbors would be invited to a barn-raising or a house-raising, and the community would do that part of the work which the individual family could not do for itself. Cf. *raising* (*GDM* 262). Note that *four* slaves "put up the final log" in *RfaN* 34.

raising (*GDM* 262). See RAISE.

Raleigh (*Reiv.* 193): a former watering-place just N of Memphis.

ramshack (*Reiv.* 13): to ransack.

ramshag (*Mans.* 272): to ransack.

rat (*WP* 40): a slang term for a college freshman.

ratchet (*Sart.* 263): the notched (to prevent slipping) quadrant on which the hand-throttle lever of early cars rested. The arrangement was essentially that found on modern tractors. When Bayard "jerked the throttle down the ratchet," he suddenly accelerated to full throttle. His car seems to have had a foot-pedal accelerator as well, since he once "jammed the throttle down to the floor" (*Sart.* 117).

rattlesnake (*LiA* 29; *Unv.* 201): cane-brake rattlesnake (*Crotalus horridus atricaudatus*), a subspecies of the timber rattlesnake. Ike McCaslin's meeting with the big rattler in "The Bear" (*GDM* 329) is detailed and exact. The snake did not coil, but when startled threw itself into a lateral striking loop— a position as effective as a coil, and more mobile. It was over 6′ long, an accurate length for a very large specimen. Hence the raised head was at knee level. A rattler this length would have an effective striking range of more than two feet, and the head was "less than [Ike's] knee's length away";

hence the snake was within easy striking distance, and hence the best thing that Ike could do was to remain "frozen" and let the snake decide that he was no threat. When the snake did this, it retreated, keeping ready for defense if necessary. The address to the snake (in the Chickasaw language) as "Chief, Grandfather" is interesting. Many Indian tribes called rattlesnakes by these names, "chief" referring to their position as chief of serpents. They also applied similar names to other totem animals, including bears, deer, and pumas, so that the echo of Sam Fathers's address to the great stag (*GDM* 184) is entirely appropriate on a factual level. (For a condensed rundown on Indian reverence for rattlesnakes, see Laurence M. Klauber, *Rattlesnakes: Their Habits. Life Histories, and Influence on Mankind* [Berkeley, 1956], 2: 1085–96.) The only thing in Faulkner's account that depends on legend rather than accurately observed natural history is the strong cucumber odor of the snake. A rattlesnake in the wild cannot be smelled by any normal human nose.

rawhide-bottomed chair (*Town* 294). Such a chair might be made with a single square of rawhide for a seat, but the usual construction uses interwoven rawhide strips 1″–2″ wide.

raw-hiding (*AILD* 112): a beating or, figuratively, a severe lecture. The expression comes from the use of a rawhide whip, not from the idea of beating until the hide is raw.

razor-hedged (*Sart*, 62): hedged about with razors. To a considerable extent in practice, and even more in legend, the straight razor is the traditional concealed weapon of the Southern Negro.

razor strop (*Reiv.* 300): a leather strap about 2′ long and 2″ wide, used for stropping (sharpening) straight razors. One end is attached to a hook on the wall; the other (shaped into a handle) is held, and the strop is stretched taut with one hand while the razor is stropped with the other. A razor strop was a standard implement for a pretty severe whipping.

razor-thrower (*Dust* 31): one who uses a straight razor as a weapon. A razor is not literally thrown: the word is used much as a boxer is said to "throw" a punch. This usage is also influenced by the fact that the blade is usually not rigidly held: the sheath is held, and the blade is slung on its pivot as the razor is swung.

reading (*Mans.* 154): printed or typed material, as opposed to "writing," which is handwritten material. This distinction between "reading" and "writing" is a common one. The Warden is making it when he asks Mink, "You cant read writing, can you?" (*Mans.* 97.)

readin' words (*Abs.* 215). Luster is distinguishing between the vocabulary of his reading (probably restricted to such things as signs) and a technical term—a "lawyer word" like *bond*, which he has heard but never seen.

reaper (*Unv.* 165; *Reiv.* 31): a machine for cutting grain. When the lieutenant says, "You were too busy running a reaper to count the ——," the next word would be something like *stalks*; i.e. you were too busy with a wholesale operation of mule-stealing to worry about petty individual cases.

rear-backted (*KG:Smoke* 11): reared-back. The verb-adverb combination, *to rear back*, is taken as a single word, and a *p.p./adj.* is coined on this assumption.

reave (*Town* 265): to snatch, take by force. Cf. title *The Reivers*.

Reb (*LiA* 231): Rebel, a YANKEE name for a Confederate.

receiver (*Mans.* 38): the part of a shotgun or rifle containing the firing mechanism. (This definition is oversimplified but will work for Mink's double-barreled shotgun.)

recinches his saddle (*Town* 262). The traveler has unfastened the cinch (the strap under the horse's belly that holds the saddle in position) in preparation for removing the saddle and stopping for the night, but changes his mind and fastens the cinch again.

recite (*CS: UncW* 227): to do anything orally as a pupil in a school: recite memory-work, answer questions, etc.

red (*Sart.* 125): red fox.

Red Banks (*Reiv.* 194): a Mississippi town 25 m. SW of Grand Junction, Tenn. (PARSHAM).

redbarred trousers (*LiA* 106): not a special term but simply a reference to Brown's suit, which was "tan, with a red criss-cross" (*LiA* 36).

redbird (*Sart.* 337; *WT* 77): cardinal (*Richmondena cardinalis*), a brilliant red (male) or dull red and gray (female) bird with a short conical beak and a sharp crest on both sexes. The term *redbird* is also sometimes applied both to the summer tanager (*Piranga rubra*) and the scarlet tanager (*P. olivacea*), but since these birds are rarely noticed by people whose ornithology is so loose, it usually refers to the cardinal.

redbone (hound) (*Dust* 5): a fast, medium-sized American hound, colored dark red, often with a mixture of tan, and used especially as a coon-dog. Its status as a distinct breed is not clearly established.

redbud (*Sanc.* 134; *Mans.* 26; *CS:MGM* 697): judas tree (*Cercis canadensis*) a shrub or small tree bearing profuse small pink flowers in the early spring.

red dirt (*Unv.* 179, 181): heavy red clay, the primary soil of the north Mississippi hills.

redneck (*S&F* 242, 263; *Abs.* 122; *CS:MV* 771): contemptuous name for a white countryman or farmer.

red tie (*S&F* 289, 291). In the 1920s ties in Oxford were generally restrained and quiet. There was a persistent schoolboy legend to the effect that perverts wore red ties for mutual recognition.

reducto absurdum (*S&F* 93, 105, 111): *reductio ad absurdum*. This impossible form is probably an unintended reflection on Faulkner's Latinity rather than an intended one on that of Mr. Compson or Quentin.

redworm (*Abs.* 377): earthworm.

reel-backing (*Mans.* 346; *Reiv.* 181): a heavy (often old) length of fishing-line wound as the first layer on a fishing reel, and hence the last piece if the entire line is reeled out.

reely (*Sanc.* 245, 250): a pseudoelegant pronunciation of *really*.

refuse (of a horse) (*Reiv.* 147, 266): to refuse to attempt a jump or other obstacle. When a horse refuses, he simply stops at the obstacle without attempting to negotiate it. He may also run out, i.e. swerve around the obstacle or veer away from it.

regiment of infantry which John Sartoris raised (*RfaN* 230). Faulkner's great-grandfather organized the Magnolia Rifles at Ripley, Miss. He was elected colonel of the regiment at Corinth in May 1861. The troops from Tippah County became Company F of the 2nd Mississippi Regiment, Infantry.

reinfest (*Sart.* 274): malapropism for *reinvest*.

reins (*S&F* 200; *Unv.* 282): leather straps fastened to the two ends of a horse's BIT and held by the rider or driver, who uses them to control the horse. Since reins are normally of leather (rope used for the purpose is included in the generic term LINES), "rope reins" (*Ham.* 9) is something of a contradiction in terms, and emphasizes the poverty of Snopes's outfit.

render (*Abs.* 155). Faulkner apparently extends the usual meaning—"to melt, clarify, fat, lard, etc."—to include the home processes of pharmaceutical extraction.

Renfro (*CS: UncW* 241): an imaginary place near Memphis.

renter (*Ham.* 206). Houston's Negro renter is not clearly explained. He could merely have rented a house and made his living elsewhere, but with the remoteness of the region this is unlikely. A SHARECROPPER or share-tenant is not usually called a renter. Hence it would seem that this Negro was a cash tenant: one who pays a fixed money rent for a piece of land and a house, and owns all that he produces. This is the highest form of farm tenancy. However, since Faulkner later says that Mink and his new wife "rented a small farm on shares" (*Ham.* 238), he may not be observing these distinctions.

rentire (*WT* 47): entire.

resert (*Sart.* 114): malapropism for *assert*.

reservoy (*Mans.* 316; *CS: TS* 81): reservoir. In *TS* the reference is to the Sardis Reservoir, which Faulkner places (as he does the university) at Oxford rather than Jefferson. See Appendix.

resin (*Sanc.* 277). The resin escaping from a wound on a pine tree eventually dries into hard reddish lumps—hence the comparison to Temple's "tight red curls."

resk (*Mans.* 89, 262; *CS: TS* 92): risk.

revenuers (*Fable* 191): men from the Bureau of Internal Revenue looking for illicit stills and non-taxpaid liquor. The word is not applicable to men from the bureau when they are working in any other capacity, such as checking on income taxes.

reversed teams (Sanc. 107; *Ham.* 322; *Reiv.* 234): teams tethered to the rear-ends of wagons.

reverted to the state (*Abs.* 213). The Sutpen estate could have reverted to the state because Judith died intestate and (with Henry a vanished fugitive) there were no known heirs, but it is more likely that it was simply taken over, some time after her death, for the unpaid taxes.

R.F.C. (*Mans.* 190, 209): Royal Flying Corps.

rib-gaunted (*Unv.* 118): so emaciated (GAUNTED) that the ribs are conspicuous.

ricklick (*S&F* 60): recollect, remember.

ricklickshun (*S&F* 368, 369, 370): recollection.

ricollick (*Sart.* 233): recollect.

Rider (*GDM*, "Pantaloon in Black"). The physical model for Rider may well have been a Negro who loaded crossties at the railroad station in Oxford not long after World War I. There was a great demand for crossties, and there was a big business in them for a while. The loading was piecework, with payment of a nickel for each crosstie carried up an incline and loaded into a boxcar. Normally, Negroes worked in pairs: a strong man could load a few by himself, but he couldn't keep it up long. This Negro, however, was a magnificent physical specimen who loaded crossties alone all day long. People used to go to the station to watch him. The crossties used for rail-junctions have to be much longer and heavier than the standard ones. Out of sheer exuberance he once picked up one of these, shouldered it, walked up the fairly steep incline into the boxcar, and laid it in place. It had just been weighed at 450 lbs.

ridge-pole (*S&F* 141; *WP* 63; *Fable* 190): the timber of a house that supports the ridge of the roof, and consequently the ridge itself.

riding his crops (*GDM* 99): riding about the farm inspecting his crops.

rifle-crotched log (*RfaN* 102). When Faulkner revised this passage for use later (*Miss.* 14), he changed this phrase to "log-crotched rifle." This is what it really meant: a rifle rested (for greater steadiness and accuracy) in the crotch of an upended log.

right smart (*Sart.* 27; *LiA* 7, 24, 25; *Ham.* 212): a considerable amount, number, period of time, etc.

Rigolets (*Miss.* 30): the passage leading from Lake PONTCHARTRAIN to Lake Borgne, which then opens out into Mississippi SOUND.

riled up (*S&F* 67): irritated, angry.

ring (*Fable* 196): a hitching-ring, to which a horse is hitched while being shod.

ring-bolt (*Ham.* 318): a bolt having threads for a nut at one end and a movable ring passing through an eye at the other end.

ringer (*Mans.* 121): a player or horse fraudulently entered in some competition; hence, an outsider.

rinktum (*S&F* 86): whatchamaycall it—here a jocular euphemism for *butt, ass.*

rive (*CS:SftL* 31): to split.

River, the (*Abs.* 35, 44; *Unv.* 3; *GDM* 340). The Yocona River is in the southern part of Lafayette Co., and the Tallahatchie is in the northern part. Either one may be referred to as "the river" in a context which explains the reference. But the Mississippi, 60 m. away at the closest point, is *the* river, or the River, with a capital R.

roach. 1. *n.* (*S&F* 177): a curve of hair brushed upward from the forehead. **2.** *v.t.* (*GDM* 10): to comb or trim hair into a roach. **3.** *v.t.* (*Race* 181): to trim a horse's or mule's hair (usually the mane) so that it stands on end.

roach campaign (*Sanc.* 162): campaign to exterminate cockroaches, i.e. vermin.

road-company drammer (*Mans.* 205): road-company drama, sentimental and melodramatic plays of the sort performed by traveling companies. W. I. Swain, "the King of Tented Theatricals," came to Oxford for a week every year well up into the 1920s.

road-gaiting (*GDM* 20): striking or holding a gait suitable for a long journey.

roasting ears (*Mans.* 63): corn on the cob, either before or after cooking.

rock (*Town* 66): grindstone. It works best when wet, and hence Top not only turned the handle, but poured water on it from time to time. Some grindstones are provided with a trough around the lower part of the stone for water, but this one evidently was not.

rocking chair (*Race* 175): humorous metaphor for a large, many-branched pair of antlers.

Rockyford (*Town* 296, 298; *Mans.* 142): an imaginary village, apparently in east-central Yoknapatawpha Co.

rode part of the way in wagons (*CS:Hair* 138). Hitchhiking antedates automobiles, with the difference that the early hiker walked when he wasn't riding, whereas the modern one simply stands by the side of the road and waits.

rook-party (*GDM* 155): a party to play rook, a card-game played with a deck of 56 cards in four suits distinguished only by color. The cards have only numbers on them—no pips or faces. The game is played primarily by churchly old ladies who think ordinary playing cards are wicked.

rootbound (*Dust* 119): having the roots compacted and matted together. This is a common condition in old, untended shrubs, and calls for separation and transplanting.

rooting hog (*Mans.* 330). Nothing grows in a pigpen because the pigs root it up and eat it, and the soil in a pigpen is usually foul and sour from excrement and spilled slops and other food. But it is not true that a rooting hog in itself does anything more than mechanical damage to the soil or to plants.

rope-burn (*Dust* 159, 172): a mark where the skin has been chafed by a rope.

rose, bled (*GDM* 45): probably a textual error for *resembled*. See Meriwether, p. 24.

rosin (*Unv.* 81): resin, the heavy sticky sap that oozes from cut pine or similar woods.

Roskus (*S&F* 9, etc.). The name was probably originally Roscius, classical names being, in slave-times, frequently given to Negroes.

rotgut (*Reiv.* 13): bad whiskey.

rotting bricks (*LiA* 327; *WP* 36). Porous or poor-quality bricks used for brick walks disintegrate fairly rapidly with weathering, especially constant freezing and thawing.

rouge and paint (*CS:Hair* 134): usually synonymous when applied to cosmetics. *Paint* here may mean specifically "lipstick."

round up (*Town* 319): to make the rounds of.

rove (*CS:SftL* 31): *p.p.* of RIVE, "to split."

rucks (*GDM* 320): presumably a misprint for *trucks*, the frameworks containing two pairs of wheels on which each end of a railroad car rests.

rumble (*WP* 99): rumble-seat, an automobile seat, with a fold-down top which forms the backrest, placed where the trunk is on most present-day cars.

rum toddy (*GDM* 286): a TODDY made with rum instead of the usual bourbon whiskey.

run (of a still) (*Sart.* 123): the process or act of distilling (once) the still's capacity of mash. Here the term is used loosely to mean "batch," since McCallum's good liquor would certainly be run through twice and hence would, technically, involve two runs. *Fun* (*GDM* 35, line 2) is obviously a misprint for *run*.

run, *v.t.* (*GDM* 210): to range over, have as one's range.

Run (*Unv.* 17; *Fable* 193): a word used for a small stream in the Virginia area (e.g. Bull Run), but not in Mississippi.

runabout buggy with bright red wheels and a fringed parasol top (*Ham.* 89, 132). A runabout is a sporty, one-horse buggy. The parasol top is literally that: a parasol rather than a conventional top. An illustration of such a runabout, fringed parasol top and all, may be seen in Jack D. Rittenhouse, *American Horse-Drawn Vehicles* (Los Angeles, 1948), p. 14.

run a furrow (*Abs.* 154; *Mans.* 20, 21): to make a furrow by running a plow the length of a field. "He ran out that furrow too" (*Mans.* 20) means that he ran it to the end, not stopping short because of his visitors.

run a (trot)line (*KG:Hand* 63, 81): to inspect a TROTLINE, remove the fish that have been caught, rebait hooks, etc.

runaway (*Abs.* 24; *Ham.* 191): runaway horse or team. When horses panicked and ran away they were a great danger not only to their passengers, but to pedestrians and other vehicles on the street.

running backward (of a stream) (*WP* 62, 153). See YAZOO RIVER.

running-board (*Sart.* 115, 158; *SP* 86; *CS:Dry* 178): a flat section of metal outside the doors of a car and joining the bases of the front and rear fenders. It was 8″–10″ off the ground and parallel to it. It was used as a step for getting into and out of a car, and it was possible to ride standing on it and holding on to the car-top. See also FENDER.

running gear (*CS:Red* 324; *Dust* 220): the chassis of a wagon or carriage, on which the body, seats, top, etc., are mounted.

run on sight (*GDM* 8; *Race* 183): to pursue game one sees instead of relying on tracks or dogs. When a dog runs on sight, he is close enough to follow the game by eye instead of trailing it, and he gives tongue with a different sound which tells an experienced hunter what the situation is.

run out (*Reiv.* 147). See REFUSE.

ruptured duck. 1. (*Mans.* 333): an honorable-discharge button. **2.** (*Mans.* 309): a returned veteran.

rush— (*Town* 358): the first syllable of *Russian.*

ruther (*Sart.* 159; *GDM* 59): rather. "I ruther" is "I'd rather."

ruts (*Sart.* 304). The red clay roads of north Mississippi are extremely slippery when wet. One can get stuck in mudholes, but the great danger is sliding off the crown of the road. The only real protection against this is to stay in the ruts made by previous cars. Once out of the ruts, the driver is in a serious predicament.

rutting (*AILD* 124): pursuing females, like an animal in rut.

S

sack. 1. (*AILD* 26; *WP* 277): cotton-picker's sack. See COTTON PICKING. **2.** (*Sanc.* 124; *WP* 162, 309): tobacco sack in which cigarette-tobacco is sold, for the use of those who roll their own cigarettes. These sacks are closed by a draw string, and it is standard practice, after pouring enough tobacco into a cigarette-paper held in one hand, to draw the string with one's teeth and hold the sack thus while using both hands to roll the cigarette. **3.** (*Fable* 176). See LEAVE . . . HOLDING THE SACK.

sacked up (*Mans.* 280): in bed, or at least sleeping or ready to sleep.

sacque (*S&F* 350). See DRESSING SACQUE.

saddlebag (*Abs.* 33, 333; *RfaN* 10): a bag hung on the side of a horse, just behind the saddle. Saddlebags were usually used in pairs, with one hanging on each side of the horse.

saddle-bow (*GDM* 242, 317; *Dust* 91): the arched front of a saddle, with the pommel at the top of it.

saddle girth (*Dust* 177; *Race* 184): GIRTH-STRAP.

saddle horn (*Race* 184): a high pommel (raised and rounded front end) of a saddle.

Sad-dy (*Town* 151; *Reiv.* 154): Saturday.

sage (*Sart.* 307; *S&F* 287; *Unv.* 75): variant of SEDGE.

sagegrass (*WT* 46; *Dust* 157): SEDGE.

Saint Andrew's cross, starred (*Unv.* 112): the Confederate Battle Flag.

Saint Elmo (*Ham.* 318): the title and name of the hero of a popular sentimental novel by Augusta J. E. Wilson (1866), for which the child was evidently named.

Saint Looey (*S&F* 362): Saint Louis, Mo.

salt sack (*Town* 233). Salt was sold in cloth sacks of various sizes, containing various weights. The empty sacks were useful for all sorts of purposes.

Sambo (*Dust* 149, 153, 154): a common generic name for the Negro.

same fingers (*Dust*. 231): the fingers of the same hand as the thumb, so that "rubbing his thumb against the tips of the same fingers" means making the conventional gesture for demanding money.

Samson's Bridge (*Sart*. 332; *AILD* 105; *LiA* 13): a fictional bridge that is vague even in Faulkner's imagination. In the first reference it seems to be on the Tallahatchie River, and in the other two on the Yocona.

sandbags (*Miss*. 25): bags filled with sand, used in emergencies for repairing breaks in a LEVEE or for raising its general level.

sandboil (*WP* 28; *Miss*. 25). When the water inside a LEVEE is much higher than the land outside, water may be forced underground for considerable distances, and begin to come up, bringing sand with it, on the landward face of the levee, or even at some distance inland from it. The place where it comes up, and the phenomenon itself, are both called sandboils. A sandboil must be neutralized promptly. This is done by building a wall of sandbags around it so that a column of water will be built up above it to equalize the pressure.

sandbox (*Fable* 192): a box of sand in which the stove of a store, waiting-room, etc., is frequently set. The sand protects the wooden floor from the heat of the stove and from any hot coals that may fall out when the ashes are being removed. It serves as a spittoon, too. Such a sandbox is also mentioned in *Ham*. 84, 124.

sandbox (*CS:Lo* 395): a box, usually made like a saltshaker, used to sprinkle sand on freshly written documents to dry the ink.

sand darkened (*Ham*. 336, 363). Since wet sand is darker in color than dry sand, the color changes as the water is approached, and changes back (is "lightened," p. 363) as the road again becomes dry.

sand ditch (*S&F* 301; *GDM* 149; *SP* 125): a ditch that has a sand bottom and is dry except during and immediately after heavy rains. Such ditches are common around Oxford. They may be anything from 2' wide and 6' deep to 20' wide and 2'–3' deep. On hillsides they may be much larger than this, but there they are usually called gullies. Since the banks of a sand ditch are usually grown up profusely with weeds and briars, it forms a fine hide-out. The "ravine" by which Ratliff et al. approach the Old Frenchman Place (*Ham*. 337) is a deep sand ditch with steep banks, though it is not called one.

Sande, Earl (*Reiv*. 233): the "Handy Guy," called by one historian of the turf "America's most famous jockey." He won the Kentucky Derby three times, was three times the biggest money-winner for a specific year, and later was once the biggest winner among trainers. At the age of fifty-five he came out of retirement to ride a winner at Jamaica, and then retired again. Actually, at the time of *Reiv*. he was only seven years old. Though Sande was a jockey and DAN PATCH was a harness horse, there is no incongruity in linking them here, as the use of *both* shows: the meaning is that by now

McWillie thinks that he could dominate the world of horse-racing in all its aspects.

Santa Claus (*Sart.* 345; *S&F* 107): Christmas presents or delicacies.

santer (*Reiv.* 64, 65): saunter.

sap-sweating, axe-ended rails (*Unv.* 12). Rails split from a large log would be much better and more durable than any made from saplings, but this is a rush job. The rails are sap-sweating because they have just been cut down, and axe-ended because they have been chopped with an axe. If they had been split from a log, it would have been sawed into rail-lengths first, and the rails would have smoothly sawed ends.

Sartoris (*Unv.* 51, 80). The name of the family is frequently used for the name of the plantation. (*Sartoris* is accented on the first syllable.)

Sartoris Station (*Town* 116, 244): College Hill Station, a former flag-stop on the railroad 4 m. N of Oxford.

sass. 1. (*Reiv.* 106): impertinence, smartiness. **2.** (*S&F* 67): to be impertinent to, smarty to (someone).

sassafras (*Unv.* 251; *Mans.* 417): a tree or, more usually, a large shrub (*Sassafras albidum*) with aromatic twigs, inner bark, and roots. Sassafras tea, used both as a vaguely medicinal tonic and as a drink, was normally made by boiling the split roots and adding cream and sugar. From her reference to sassafras (*Sart.* 153), it seems that Aunt Sally's "bark tea" (*Sart.* 151) was sassafras tea. Sassafras moves promptly into abandoned fields (*LiA* 402).

Satan (*S&F* 54). Dilsey's address of Caddy as "You, Satan" is equivalent to "you little devil." Dilsey seems to have a habit of addressing Caddy with terms appropriate to the immediate situation: cf. her use of MINUTE (*S&F* 75).

satchel (*CS:SNP* 105): HAND SATCHEL, lady's handbag.

Saturday: the traditional day for country people to come to town and spend the afternoon, whether they have any business to transact or not. *Sanc.* 107–08 describes a typical Saturday afternoon on the Oxford square about 1930.

Saturday night shaving customer (*CS:Hair* 132). Many men got shaved once a week at the barbershop. Each had his own barber, whose client he was, and no one else shaved him.

Saulsbury, Tennessee (*LiA* 480): a town 75 m. E of Memphis and 5 m. N of the Mississippi line.

sawbuck 1. (*Mans.* 266): an **X**-shaped frame for holding small logs while they are being sawed by hand. **2.** (*AILD* 236): a ten-dollar bill, so called because the Roman numeral **X** on the old-style bill was fancifully taken as a sawbuck seen end-on.

saw-carriage (*Town* 32): a platform on slides or rollers, parallel to and just clearing the blade of a circular saw in a sawmill. The log being cut into planks is placed on this carriage, which carries it against the saw-blade.

saw chunk (*Abs.* 369; *Unv.* 142, 241): a piece of tree trunk or heavy timber sawed off square at both ends. It is used as a substitute table or seat.

saw-edged grass (*WP* 251): the sawgrass (*Cladium jamaicense*) of the Everglades and of coastal swamps along the Gulf of Mexico as far as Texas. It grows in dense, solid stands, and it is such a stand which the convict saw (pp. 250–51) from the top of the levee. It grows 4'–10' high, and the very sharp-edged leaves cut anyone trying to force his way through it.

sawgrass (*Dust* 171): not the sawgrass of the Everglades (see SAW-EDGED GRASS), but a local name for various grasslike sedges (genera *Carex* and *Scirpus*) that have edges capable of cutting bare hands and arms.

sawmill: an outfit for sawing logs into timbers and lumber. It may be of any size or complexity. Doane's Mill (*LiA* 2–3) is a big commercial operation that creates a temporary village, builds brick foundations for its machinery, and will take fourteen years to "destroy all the timber within its reach" before packing up and moving on. The sawmill at which Drusilla and Bayard work (*Unv.* 221) is a temporary family affair set up to provide the lumber to replace the Sartoris house, which the Yankees have burned. It is powered, not by boilers, but by a mule attached to a sweep and walking in circles around the BANDSAW (*Unv.* 224–25). A sawmill may be more or less anything between these two extremes.

sawmill advocate (*Ham.* 150): an unqualified person pretending to be a legal authority—much as we might call someone a pool-hall lawyer.

saw-milling (*GDM* 137): working at a sawmill.

sawmill shed (*LiA* 146): a crude shed which had protected some part of the sawmill's machinery. It would be a rectangle open at one end (it had a "sagging doorway" but no door), with a sheet-iron roof and sides probably made of slabs. Cf. *mill-shed* (*GDM* 322).

sawn-oak wheels (*Unv.* 139): solid wheels made by sawing a section off a good round oak log.

saw-set (*AILD* 155). The teeth of a saw are not in a straight line. Some are bent to the right, some to the left, and some are straight. Those which are bent cut slits in the wood slightly farther apart than the thickness of the saw blade; those which are straight knock out the bits of wood (grains of sawdust) between these slits. A saw-set is a device for setting the angle of the bent teeth accurately and uniformly.

saw the mules about (*Ham.* 274): maneuver them by pulling back and forth on the reins. For the locking of the wheels, see CRAMP (a wheel).

scairy cat (*CS: TES* 293, 309): 'FRAID CAT, one easily frightened.

scalded flour sacks (*GDM* 138): scalded both to kill any flour-mites and to remove any coloring that might run.

scalding hogs (*Ham.* 21). Immediately after a hog is killed, the whole carcass is scalded, after which the hair can be scraped off.

scale-beam (*Ham.* 59): beam of a platform-scale. The wagon-load of cotton is driven onto this scale and weighed. The platform of the scales is under the SUCTION PIPE by which the cotton is unloaded. Then the empty wagon is weighed, the difference between the two weights establishing the weight of the load of cotton.

scaly bark (*CS:Red* 329): the nut of the scaly-bark, or shagbark, hickory (*Carya ovata*).

scat! (*Sanc.* 243; *Town* 237): Get out!—an expression properly addressed to a cat. The misapplication to a dog and a mule is intentional and humorous on Faulkner's part.

school-satchel (*Ham.* 208): book-satchel.

scoop (*LiA* 28, 34; *Town* 18): a large shovel with a flat bottom, a straight front edge, and turned-up sides and back, used for moving large quantities of loose material like grain, coal, and sawdust.

Scott (*Abs.* 80): Sir Walter Scott. The stallion was named for someone or something in his works.

scraper (*Sart.* 170): a steel scoop with two handles behind it like wheelbarrow handles. This was the standard earth-moving equipment before the bulldozer. The earth was plowed; then a mule dragged the scoop, and a man operating it lifted up the handles to make the front edge bite in. When it was full he dropped the handles and let the mule drag the loaded scoop to its destination, where he picked up sharply on the handles as the mule advanced, so as to catch the front edge on the ground and dump the load. This implement was also called a slip or slip scraper (*GDM* 155).

scrap up (*Reiv.* 120): scratch up, scrape up, piece together.

screech owl (*S&F* 34): a small "eared" owl (*Otus asio*) about 8″ long which has both reddish and gray-brown color-phases. Its call is, as Faulkner says, "a liquid tremolo" (*Sart.* 26), "plaintive and tremulous" (*KG:Error* 130), not, as the name would imply, a screech. Its cry is often thought to foretell a death. In the spring, when it has young just out of the nest, a screech owl will swoop at an intruder and even rip his scalp if he refuses to leave. The owl of *Sanc.* 7 is presumably a screech owl with young in the vicinity.

screen hooks (*S&F* 243): screw-hooks and screw-eyes used to fasten screen doors and window screens.

screening vines starred with motionless pallid blossoms (*SP* 314): moon-flowers (*Calonyction aculeatum*). They are frequently planted at the edges of porches and trained on improvised string trellises to form a screen. They grow very fast and bear many large, fragrant white flowers that open at night. These morning-glory-shaped flowers grow 4″–5″ long and flare out to about the same diameter at the bell.

scrooched up (eyes) (*Sart.* 282): screwed up, nearly closed.

scrouge (*Sart.* 226; *Ham.* 307): to push, crowd, press.

scrub (*Sart.* 294): an unpedigreed, mongrel domestic animal. Dr. Peabody is distinguishing between the "registered" Negroes that officially work for him and the "scrub" stock of informal hangers-on.

scrubbing-board (*Sart.* 138): WASHBOARD.

scrub oak (*Flags* 257): not the scrub oak, or bear oak (*Quercus ilicifolis*) of

botanists, which does not grow in Mississippi. *Scrub oak* is a general term for
small, scrubby oaks of any species, whether they will never be much more,
like the BLACKJACK, or are merely crowded saplings or second-growth of
larger species.

scrunched back (*Reiv.* 158): huddled back, cringing back.

scuppernong (*Abs.* 26, 125; *Reiv.* 56): a bred-up form of the muscadine,
normally grown on arbors some 5'–6' above the ground. Since the vines
grow very thickly and form a solid shade, a scuppernong arbor is a fine
outdoor sitting-place. Scuppernongs make excellent wine (*Abs.* 123).

scuttle (*Ham.* 263; *Town* 233, 242): coal-scuttle, a bucket (usually of galvanized iron) with a flaring top and a handle, in which coal was brought into the
house. It sat by the fireplace or stove. Ashes were carried out in an empty
scuttle. Cf. *scuttleful* (*Sart.* 219).

scythe (*Abs.* 172, 177): a two-handed implement with a curved handle, two
projecting hand-grips, and a wide, slightly curved blade, used for reaping
grain, cutting weeds, etc. It is the implement with which personified Time is
regularly equipped, and is to be distinguished from a sickle, which is the
one-handed, sharply curved narrow blade used as an emblem by the
U.S.S.R.

Second Manassas (*Unv.* 56, 255; *RfaN* 231; *Miss.* 20): the Second Battle of
Manassas (Bull Run), Aug. 29–30, 1862.

seconds (*AILD* 232): the right or privilege of having something if someone
else does not want it, or after he is through with it. The meaning here is:
"Aren't you going to let me have Dewey Dell when you're through with
her?"

second trigger (*Ham.* 218, 230). See SHOTGUN.

Secretary Hoover (*WP* 29): Herbert Hoover, who, as secretary of commerce,
was placed in charge of relief measures for refugees from the Mississippi
flood of 1927.

section (of land) (*Sart.* 222; *Reiv.* 20): a piece of land one mile square.

section hand (*Sart.* 5, 37; *Town.* 359): a member of a railroad maintenance
crew. A section is the stretch of railroad for which a specific crew is responsible, and each member of this crew is a HAND, or laborer.

section lines (*WP* 62; *Dust* 146): the survey-lines dividing a township (6 m.
square) into 36 SECTIONS, each one m. square.

sedge (*Sart.* 286, 308; *Sanc.* 133; *CS:Red* 313): any of various species of the
genus *Andropogon* (especially *scoparius*, *virginicus*, and *ternarius*), grasses growing 2'–4' high, often in solid stands in abandoned fields or open spaces along
the edges of swamps. It is light green in summer, turning grayish- or reddish-brown in the fall, and standing through the winter. It is also called
sage (*Sart.* 307), sage grass (*S&F* 287), sedge grass, and broom sedge. It
frequently grows so thick that an animal in it, like a bird dog, cannot be
seen at all but can easily be followed by the movements of the tops of the
grass (*Abs.* 187).

seeder (*AILD* 180): any of several mechanical devices for planting seeds. There is a tendency to use *seeder* for a device that sows seeds broadcast (hay, oats), and *planter* for one that accurately controls their placement (cotton, corn), but the usage is not consistent.

see you in the funnypaper (*S&F* 137): a smarty catch-phrase for "I'll be seeing you."

Seminary Hill (*Town* 312, 349): College Hill, a little settlement 5 m. NW of Oxford. It was originally an exclusively Presbyterian settlement, in spite of Faulkner's remark about Baptists and Methodists. College Hill Station (Faulkner's Sartoris Station) was a flag-stop on the railroad $2\frac{1}{2}$ m. from College Hill itself. The "church which Thomas Sutpen rode fast to" (map at end of *Abs.*) is in College Hill. The view of Yoknapatawpha Co. to which Faulkner devotes a purple patch (*Town* 315–317) is actually there. One reaches it by driving to College Hill from Oxford and turning right (E) on a paved road at the College Hill Presbyterian Church. Nine tenths of a mile past this turn-off, the road makes a sweeping curve to the north. From this curve the view (partially obstructed by farm buildings) is visible.

Senator (*Sanc.* 169): a senator in the state legislature, not in Congress.

sentry-box (*CS:MGM* 676). See BACK HOUSE.

separator (*Ham.* 30, 45): cream separator, a centrifuge operated by a hand-crank, for separating cream from milk. When it is being used, the gears make a high-pitched, whining sound (*Ham.* 46).

serenading (*Sart.* 145–57): a not uncommon activity of young men on spring and summer evenings early in this century. It was a group activity: several young men would get together and serenade a school dormitory or several individual young ladies in turn. It was not a matter of individual courtship but of a sort of combined pastime and social tribute. The serenaders might provide their own music or bring musicians with them (as Bayard Sartoris does), or both. They might be greeted from a window, or invited in, or ignored.

serve the plates (*Dust* 114): put the food on the plates.

set of threes (*CS:BH* 67). Apparently the major holds three threes—triplets, three of a kind. If two threes were meant, "a pair of threes" would be the standard and almost inevitable expression. Four threes would be too phenomenal and sensational, but three would be good enough to make the major curse the disruption of the game.

set up (of cement) (*AILD* 197): to set, harden. *Set up* is an intensive form: Cash, as a carpenter and a practical man, foresees the trouble he will have with a concrete cast.

seven-eight (*Ham.* 25): seven or eight.

Sewanee (*S&F* 243; *Flagg* 163): an Episcopal college in Sewanee, Tenn., officially named The University of the South, with considerable social pretensions.

shack (*Sanc.* 33): a student hang-out of the late 1920s and early 1930s, actually called The Shack. It was much as Faulkner describes it and was located where he places it, just on the town side of the railroad, on Jackson Ave., in Oxford.

shackle chains (*GDM* 143): the chains (one at the front and one at the back) passed around a load of logs on a truck, to hold them in place.

shadow (*S&F* 110, 111): reflection.

shafts (*Abs.* 108; *Ham.* 148): the two poles, one on each side of the horse, of a one-horse carriage or wagon. They correspond to the TONGUE of a two-horse vehicle, and are propped up in the same way.

shake (*RfaN* 30, 34): hand-split shingle, without the taper at one end that characterizes commercial shingles. Though the word is not used there, the shingles being made in *CS:SftL* are shakes.

shake-down (*RfaN* 4): properly, a makeshift bed made up on the floor; hence, by extension, anything improvised or makeshift.

shake it and break it (*SP* 197, 200): a popular song of the period shortly after World War I. I have been unable to trace it but, as I remember, the chorus ran:

> Oh you shake it and you break it
> And you hang it on the wall,
> And you make it and you take it
> But you don't let it fall.

It was never identified. Johnson (p. 16), speaking of expressions like *shake it* and *shake that thing*, says: "Such expressions are very frequent in the blues. Ostensibly they refer to dancing, but they are really Negro vulgar expressions relating to coitus." See EASY RIDER.

shake it up (*Reiv.* 42; *Mosq.* 57): hurry, get a move on.

shake one's foot (*Mans.* 81): to clear out (without paying).

shale, *v.i.* (*Sart.* 18, 147, 208; *Sanc.* 32; *Ham.* 196; *Dust* 173, 174; *Flags* 289): to give way in small bits, or scale off, especially as earth does on a steep bank. (This is a rare, old word of which Faulkner makes considerable use.)

shanty-boat (*Reiv.* 102): a small, crudely built houseboat.

share (*Sart.* 137): PLOWSHARE.

share-crop, *n.* (*Town* 150): Ratliff's humorous coinage for an extorted share of one's profits. Cf. SHARES, FARMING ON.

share-crop, *v.t.* (*Town* 246): to rent (land) to someone on shares.

share-cropper (*Town* 278; *Mans.* 90, 305). See SHARES, FARMING ON.

shares, farming on (*Sart.* 277; *S&F* 298; *Abs.* 209; *Ham.* 238): any of various forms of farm-tenancy in which the tenant pays his rent in the form of an agreed upon share of his crop. Such arrangements often, but not always, include credit at a farm store or commissary. The share of the crop given to the owner depends on the nature of the tenancy, the ownership of the tools and animals used, and the particular crop involved (see THIRD AND FOURTH). Faulkner refers to the three basic classes in his referecne to "the Negro tenant-

or share- or furnish-hand" (*RfaN* 245). The tenant simply rents the land for cash and keeps whatever he produces. The "share-hand" provides his own equipment and pays one third of his corn and one fourth of his cotton as rent. A "furnish-hand" (more often called a sharecropper) is dependent on the owner for equipment, seed, food—everything—and pays one half his crop. This payment includes the use of equipment, but food is simply charged at the commissary, to be paid for when the crop is sold.

Sharpsburg (*GDM* 286; *Miss.* 12, 15, 20): a village in Maryland involved in the Battle of Antietam, Sept. 17, 1862. *Sharpsburg* is therefore frequently used as a name for the battle.

Shatter Theory (*Mans.* 76): Château Thierry, a town that played a prominent role in the Second Battle of the Marne.

shave a note (*Mans*, 124): to buy a note at an exceptionally or illegally high rate of discount.

shedding snake (*Abs.* 60). A snake sheds the transparent scale over the eye, along with the rest of its skin. A few days before it sheds, there is a separation of the old and new scales, a milky fluid appears between the two eye scales, and the snake is almost blind. During this time it can detect danger approaching but cannot tell just what or where it is. Hence snakes that normally slip away quietly—racers, for instance—are likely at this time to stand on guard in alarm and strike at anything that moves in the vicinity.

sheep sorrel (*Dust* 26): not the 1'–2' high red sorrel (*Rumex hastatulus*) commonly known by this name, but the much smaller violet wood sorrel (*Oxalis violacea*). It grows 1"–3" high, with three greenish-bronze leaflets on each stem, and is eaten by children in the spring for its pungent sour taste. The pink flowers, growing two or three to a stem, are particularly delectable.

sheer (*Ham.* 173, 216). Faulkner, apparently making a *n.* from the *adj.* in such expressions as *a sheer cliff*, uses the word in the sense of "a vertical or nearly vertical drop."

sheer (*GDM* 223): share.

sheet-iron churn (*Reiv.* 71): Ned's name for the specially made gasoline can (p. 65), which is more like a CHURN than anything else familiar to him

sheet-iron heater (*GDM* 349): a stove made of sheet iron rather than cast iron. It is much lighter, has a larger surface for radiation, and heats up much faster than a conventional stove; hence it is ideal for camp use.

Shegog (*S&F* 361). It is interesting to note that the last name of the preacher from St. Louis is actually an old Lafayette Co. name. Faulkner's house in Oxford was the old Shegog place.

shell (corn) (*CS:TES* 305; *CS:Red* 323): to remove the grains from the cob.

shell (shotgun) (*Ham.* 217, 218; *GDM* 236). A shell is to a shotgun what a CARTRIDGE is to a rifle or pistol. It is a cylinder of waxed cardboard or (recently) plastic, with a brass base. The base contains a primer, which the hammer or firing-pin strikes. The cylinder contains a charge of powder next to the primer, then a wad, then a charge of shot, and then another wad, over which the front end of its cardboard is crimped. The casings of shells are reusable and can be loaded by hand (*Ham.* 223). *Shell* and *cartridge* are normally differentiated but are occasionally used interchangeably (*Ham.* 277; *Man*s. 415, 429). Ammunition kept too long deteriorates, and not only may not fire (*GDM* 325), but may dangerously fire after a considerably delay (*GDM* 326).

Sheridan (*CS:TM* 54): Gen. Philip H. Sheridan, Federal cavalry commander. See VALLEY.

sheriff (*Unv.* 254): not only a pursuer and arrester of criminals but also an officer who attaches property for debt. When Col. Sartoris, building his railroad on borrowed money, is "keeping just two cross-ties ahead of the sheriff," he has committed no crime but is barely able to keep going financially.

Sherman (*Abs.* 130, 355; *Unv.* 25; *Reiv.* 285): Federal Gen. William Tecumseh Sherman played a key role in many important battles of the Civil War, but he is chiefly remembered in the South for his ruthless tactics in burning Atlanta and then making his infamous "March to the Sea," in the course of which he systematically destroyed everything in his path between Atlanta and Savannah.

shift (*Sart.* 177; *CS:Red* 320; *KG:Monk* 42): a woman's undergarment, a slip.

shikepoke (*CS:TS* 88): a variant form of *shitepoke*, a common name of several species of herons. In Faulkner's country it is usually the little blue heron (*Florida caerulea*), a medium-sized (2′ high), dark-colored heron nesting in low bushes over the water of ponds and sloughs.

Shiloh (*Abs.* 343, 344; *Unv.* 101; *RfaN* 247). See PITTSBURG LANDING.

shimmy (*Mosq.* 30; *Flags* 173): a slang form of *chemise*.

shimmy (*SP* 192, 193): to dance the shimmy, a popular dance of the years just after World War I. It can best be described as a form of belly-dance. Faulkner's phrases are loosely quoted from a song of the era, "I Wish I Could Shimmy Like My Sister Kate." *Johnson* (p. 16, n.), indicating that "shimmy" is an alternate pronunciation of *chemise*, says that originally the phrase *shake the shimmy* "described the effect produced when a woman made a movement or did a dance step which caused her breasts to shake."

shine (*LiA* 212): Negro. This is not Southern slang: note that it is used in the North and reinforces a specifically non-Southern attitude.

shingle (*Abs.* 162). The simile for a struggle to achieve the impossible is clear enough, but it is not clear whether the shingle is envisioned as an improvised substitute for a shovel or as a hopelessly inadequate barricade.

Ship and Horn and Petit Bois (*Miss.* 29): three of the barrier islands separating Mississippi SOUND from the main body of the Gulf of Mexico. Ship Island is slightly E of a line directly S from Gulfport, Petit Bois is S of the Alabama-Mississippi boundary, and Horn lies between them. They are 7–12 m. offshore.

ship-lap (*WP* 19): sheathing made of planks with the edges cut so that the edge of one plank will overlap the edge of the next one.

shirttail (full) (*Town* 149, 274; *Mans.* 171; *CS:TS* 84): a very small quantity. a "shirttail boy" (*Mans.* 377) is a small boy.

shock of the gun butt (*GDM* 163): a shotgun loaded with buckshot kicks hard, especially for a small boy.

shoeing box (*Unv.* 67): a box in which the tools needed for shoeing a horse are kept. It has no specific size or shape.

shoe-peg (*WP* 119): a wooden peg formerly used to fasten shoes together, and now replaced by nails and adhesives. Shoe-peg knights would be industrialists who had prospered by manufacturing such a trivial article and been knighted as a result.

shooting gallery (*Sanc.* 248): brothel, whorehouse.

short-coupled (*Unv.* 189; *GDM* 7): short-bodied, having the front legs relatively close to the hind legs.

shortening twilight (*Ham.* 23). As the sun comes nearer to the zenith with the approach of summer, its descent is more nearly vertical, and hence the twilight is shorter. In the tropics there is hardly any twilight. Cf. Coleridge, in "The Ancient Mariner": "The Sun's rim dips; the stars rush out: / At one stride comes the dark," with its marginal gloss, "No twilight within the courts of the Sun."

shote (*Unv.* 189; *CS:Court.* 373): shoat.

shotgun (*Ham.* 229): a smooth-bore gun that fires a charge of pellets (shot) instead of a single projectile. A double-barreled shotgun has two triggers, one for each barrel, so that the finger must be moved from one to the other to fire the second barrel (*Ham.* 218, 230). Old-style shotguns had two hammers that were pulled back (cocked) by the thumb, simultaneously if both were to be cocked (*Ham.* 230; *GDM* 182). If a barrel has been cocked but not fired, it can be uncocked by holding the hammer back with the thumb, pulling the trigger to release it, and then easing it down (*Ham.* 230; *GDM* 183, 196).— The suitors who "ran from the smell of Will Varner's shotgun" (*Town* 7) when Eula turned up pregnant were afraid of being forced into a "shotgun wedding."

shotgun cabin (*Reiv.* 84): DOG-TROT CABIN.

shotgun house (*Ham.* 238): a narrow house with a long hallway running down the middle and rooms on each side of it—usually a cheap, slumlike construction.

shotgun shack (*RfaN* 245). Faulkner apparently uses this term for a two-room cabin built on the principle of the SHOTGUN HOUSE. Thus it refers to a typical "dog-trot cabin," consisting of two rooms with an open breezeway between them.

shot sizes. Shot for shotguns are numbered by their size, the higher numbers designating the smaller sizes. There are some variations between systems, but they are all essentially the same. The largest shot are buckshot, in several sizes from #000 to #4, ranging from about 1/3″ to 1/4″ in diameter. Then come a couple of odd sizes, including the familiar BB (.18″ in diameter). After this come the regular numbers, by hundredths of an inch from #2 (.15″) to #12 (.05″). The largest buckshot run about 4 to the ounce; #12 (dust shot) run about 2,200 to the ounce. There are a few intermediate sizes, notably a #7½. The size of shot to be used is determined both by the size of the game and by the shooting conditions—whether short- or long-range, brush or open land, etc. Buckshot are used for large game, #4–6 for squirrels and rabbits, #6–8 (bird shot) for quail, doves, etc. The smallest sizes, #10–12, are used primarily by naturalists for collecting small birds, lizards, and even large insects without ruining them as specimens.

shovel (*S&F* 272): a small shovel for removing ashes. It is the sort which, together with tongs and poker, forms the standard set of accessories for an open fireplace.

shovel (*Mans.* 26): SHOVEL PLOW.

shovel plow (*WP* 333): a plow equipped with one or more shovel-shaped plowshares that operate like reversed shovels, the convex surface being the working surface. Shovel plows are also called shovel cultivators, and are used for cultivating crops rather than for plowing.

showfer (*Mans.* 156): chauffeur.

Showmont (*Mans.* 76): Chaumont.

shown (*LiA* 134): an error for *shone*.

shrinking-tub (*Ham.* 64): a large tub of water used by blacksmiths in putting tires on wagon and carriage wheels. The tire is a hoop of iron which, when expanded by heat, will just go over the wooden wheel. It is heated, driven into place, and then contracted in the cold water of the tub so that it makes a very tight fit.

shrouded (furniture) (*Sart.* 60; *Abs.* 204; *Reiv.* 195, 196): furniture protected with HOLLAND covers against dust and fading. Little-used furniture is often so protected. See PARLOR.

shuck. 1. (*Sart.* 342): to remove the corn SHUCKS from (an ear of corn). **2.** (*Town* 335): to remove and cast off, like a corn shuck.

shuck mattress (*Ham.* 238; *Reiv.* 38; *KG:Hand* 75): mattress stuffed with SHUCKS.

shucks. 1. the husks that cover an ear of corn. They are rounded at one end and pointed at the other, about 3″ wide at the base and 10″ long. When dry they are very tough and springy, and can be put into ticking to make mattresses. Corn-shuck mattresses are extremely comfortable, but they make hissing or crackling sounds with every movement (*Sart.* 319; *AILD* 8; *Sanc.* 68 ff.). Because of their ubiquity and general uselessness, shucks are a standard symbol of worthlessness (*Abs.* 291). **2.** (*Sanc.* 226; *Ham.* 264, 265; *Reiv.* 105): an exclamation expressing mild deprecation or amused and tolerant dismissal of something.

Shuqualak (*Miss.* 33): a town (pronounced SHUCK-a-LACK) 115 m. SE of Oxford and 15 m. from the Alabama line. It is a center for bird-dog breeding and is the location of important national field trials for bird dogs.

shurf (*GDM* 67, 68; *Dust* 62; *Reiv.* 173): sheriff.

shut (*Sart.* 293; *AILD* 183; *Sanc.* 20): rid, in the phrase *get shut of*.

shut it (*Sanc.* 228; *LiA* 95): shut it off, stop it.

S.I.A.A. (*RfaN* 111): Southern Intercollegiate Athletic Association, the athletic conference to which the University of Mississippi and Mississippi Agricultural and Mechanical College, or A. and M. (now Mississippi State), belonged until it was replaced by a different organization.

sic (*Town* 343; *Mans.* 242): to set (a dog, or something compared to a dog) on someone or something.

sick (*LiA* 286): to sic.

side-boards (*Ham.* 45): removable boards that can be added on top of the sides of a wagon to make the box deeper.

side curtains (*CS:TWBF* 282). Buggy tops were equipped with both side and back curtains that could be put on for privacy or protection from the weather.

side meat (*Sart.* 346; *Abs.* 289; *Ham.* 31): salted pork or bacon. Side meat is the typical meat of the poor, and Col. Sartoris's meal of "side meat and greens and . . . cornbread and milk" (*Unv.* 13) indicates the privations of the Civil War.

sides (*GDM* 151, 229; *Unv.* 130, 143): besides.

sidewinder (*Ham.* 272): a rattlesnake of the sandy deserts of the Southwest (*Crotalus cerastes*), named for its way of progressing over loose sand. The Texan would know about sidewinders (though they do not get as far E as Texas), but the word would not be in the vocabulary of Frenchman's Bend.

sifter (*S&F* 336): a fine sieve for sifting flour. From the verb *ground*, it is plain that Dilsey had the type of sifter with a crank which can be turned to scrape wires on the top of its screen, under the flour, thus releasing a small quantity of flour at a time.

sight. 1. (*AILD* 135; *Ham.* 64): a large quantity or number. **2.** (*AILD* 184; *Ham.* 200): a person, viewed with amused condemnation or indulgent disapproval.

silage (*Ham.* 182): fodder kept green in a silo, ensilage.

silver poplar (*Sart.* 136): white poplar, abele (*Populus alba*), a European ornamental tree with leaves dark green above and downy white underneath. The leaves are tremulous in the slightest wind, and if unpruned the tree sends up suckers and forms thickets. The unnamed tree "with tiny white-bellied leaves like a mist, like a swirl of arrested silver water" (*SP* 109; see also 247, 252, 254, 291) is clearly a silver poplar.

Silver Shirts (*Mans.* 161, 303): the name generally given, because of the uniform, to the Silver Legion, an American fascist and anti-Semitic paramilitary group organized by William Dudley Pelly, who was its first national commander, early in 1933. It reached its highest point in the following year, with possibly fifteen thousand members, but soon ran into both legal and financial difficulties. It was finally disbanded in 1940.

single action (pistol) (*LiA* 267; *Dust* 37): a pistol with a hammer that must be drawn back (cocked) by hand before it can be fired.

single ball (*GDM* 225). A shotgun may be loaded with a single ball instead of a charge of shot, for a special purpose. This makes it something like a small cannon. A single ball for a 12-gauge shotgun will weigh 1.33 oz.

single bar'l (*Sart.* 332): single-barreled shotgun.

single-foot (*AILD* 102; *Ham.* 99): a gait of a horse in which the four feet come down singly, those on the same side striking in succession.

single-tree (*Ham.* 289; *Mans.* 106; *Dust* 20): WHIFFLETREE.

sir. 1. (*Unv.* 245; *GDM* 67, 274): a respectful form of address used by children to father, and by children and young men to older men generally, or by strangers treating each other with formal courtesy (*Unv.* 268). Lucius's use of this form of address to Uncle Parsham (*Reiv.* 247, 251) is an exceptional and unstudied tribute to the latter's dignity and authority. **2.** a form of threatening or stern address to a social inferior (*Sart.* 271), but also used between social equals (*Town* 47). **3.** (*GDM* 68, 74): a stressed word following *yes* or *no* and serving to make the affirmation or negation more emphatic.

sireen (*Town* 363; *Mans.* 151): siren.

sister (*Sart.* 97; *S&F* 155; *Flags* 184): a familiar and affectionate form of address not implying actual kinship.

sisters in the Lord (*Sart.* 25): women members of the same church congregation.

sivving (*Mans.* 269): sieving, sifting through a sieve.

six-bit dollars (*Ham.* 8): dollars worth six bits, or $.75. Ab Snopes assumes that, since he will be forced to get his supplies from Varner on credit, the prices will be exorbitant.

sixteen (*Sart.* 332): a 16-gauge shotgun.

skeer. 1. *n.* (*Town* 258, 366; *Mans.* 117, 435): fear, terror. **2.** *v.t.* (*Sart.* 332; *Town* 100, 299): to scare.

skeleton cotton- and corn-fields (*GDM* 177): fields with only the bare stalks left (in November), looking like skeletons of plants. Similarly *GDM* 195; *Mans.* 13.

skid (*KG:Tomo.* 93): to drag (logs) end-on out of the woods to a place where they can be sawed or loaded for normal hauling.

skid-poles (*GDM* 244): poles leaned against something to form an inclined plane.

skidway (*GDM* 143, 144): an inclined plane of logs or heavy timbers by means of which logs are unloaded from trucks at a sawmill. The top of the skidway is about the height of the bed of a truck, and the logs are rolled down it one at a time, if possible. Men on the ground take advantage of the momentum thus acquired to roll the logs farther and get them out of the way of those which are to follow. When Rider "rode the log down the incline" (*GDM* 144) he had to be "balanced erect upon it in short backward-running steps" to cancel out the effect of its forward rolling and stay on top of it.

skillet (*Sart.* 345; *LiA* 312, 382; *Town.* 251): frying-pan.

skim ice (*Unv.* 196; *Dust* 6): a very thin surface layer of ice.

skim or a veil (*Dust* 136): the nictitating membrane, a sort of transparent extra eyelid.

skizzard (*S&F* 26, 42): apparently a private term of abuse among the Compson (and Faulkner?) children. The reply to it—*knobnot*—seems to be the same sort of thing.

skull and bones (*CS:Rose* 126): a warning label formerly required by law on commercially sold poisons.

skun the hen-house (*GDM* 23): raided the women's quarters. Mr. Hubert knows, of course, that Uncle Buck went into Miss Sophonsiba's room by mistake and that he had no designs on her, but he is insisting that by all accepted conventions Uncle Buck has compromised her and must marry her. The metaphor of the chase runs throughout "Was" and is maintained here. First the metaphor is that of a hunter entering a bear's den; then it is shifted to that of a fox that raids the HEN-HOUSE (both meanings) once too often and then is run down.

slatted cattle frame (*Dust* 180): four sides made of slats with spaces between them, mounted on the truck bed for hauling cattle.

slaughterhouse (*Reiv.* 164): a low, cheap brothel.

sleep-raddled (*GDM* 356): confused by, the worse for, sleep. See RADDLED.

sleeve-garters (*Ham.* 130): elastic bands worn around the upper arm to regulate the effective length of shirt sleeves.

slide (*GDM* 253). See PUMP GUN.

Slidell (*WP* 59): a Louisiana town 30 m. NE of New Orleans, on Lake PONT-CHARTRAIN.

slingshot (*CS:TS* 88; *Race* 185): a device for shooting small stones, consisting of a forked stick, two rubber bands, and a leather "basket" in which the stones are placed: British *catapult*. *Not* the ancient biblical and classical sling, in which a stone was whirled around the head and then released.

slip scraper (*GDM* 155). See SCRAPER.

sliver (*Sart.* 11): a long splinter of wood, about a third as thick as a pencil and perhaps 2′ long, kept by a fireplace, lighted at the fire, and then used for lighting candles, pipes, etc. It is extinguished by thrusting it into the ashes (*Sart.* 311), and is used over and over.

slop jar (*Sart.* 108; *Sanc.* 151): a large, bucket-shaped chamber pot used, in the absence of plumbing, both for urine and for waste water from the wash-basin. Sometimes there was a separate chamber pot (*Ham.* 362).

slough (*AILD* 93): to slew, slue, turn, or pivot.

slough (*Sart.* 64; *Unv.* 195; *Town* 80): a body of stagnant water in a swamp or flood-plain, often an ox-bow lake left by a stream's changing its course. *Slough* rhymes with *too*.

sluggish thrash or vicious buzz (*Fable* 156). The sluggish thrash is made as the COTTON-MOUTH (a heavy-bodied snake) either makes away or throws his body into the **S**-curve from which he strikes; the vicious buzz is made by the rattle of the rattlesnake.

smart, *v.t.* (*S&F* 73): to hurt.

smelling-bottle (*Abs.* 195): a bottle containing smelling-salts.

smithy (*RfaN* 223): blacksmith shop. (The recent use of this word for *black-smith* comes from a misunderstanding of Longfellow's "Under a spreading chestnut tree / The village smithy stands.")

smoke (*WP* 188): a Negro, black.

smoke-blackened iron pots (*Dust* 146). See WASH-POT.

smokehouse (*Abs.* 39, 346; *Unv.* 3; *CS:Just.* 343): a tight building with small vents at the top, in which meat was cured by woodsmoke. The meat was hung from the rafters, and the "festooned smoke house rafters" (*Ham.* 97) were festooned with hams.

smoker (*Sanc.* 171): a railroad passenger car, or part of a car, in which smoking is permitted.

smoke stack (of a locomotive) (*Unv.* 112). Early locomotives had a high smokestack, flaring out to a much greater width at the top than at the bottom.

smore (*Dust* 33). This seems to be an inaccurate use of the (primarily Scottish) *smore*: "stifling air, dense smoke, smother," etc.

smouch (*Mans.* 67). See SUCKING AND SMOUCHING AROUND.

snaffle (*Unv.* 14; *RfaN* 124; *Mans.* 39): a slender BIT, jointed in the middle.

snaffle (*Reiv.* 4): to steal, purloin.

snafu (*Mans.* 280): a World War II "codeword" standing for *Situation Normal: All Fucked Up.* (In polite civilian use the *v.* was said to be *fouled.*)

snag (*WP* 75): a stump, branch, log, etc., just below the surface of the water, or sticking up slightly above it.

snakebit (*GDM* 148, 152): doomed. In Rider's uses of the word (which are standard expressions), the idea is, "I am already doomed and consequently immune to anything further that may happen to me." The tone is that of an exuberant defiance of fate to do its worst.

snake fence (*Abs.* 214; *Unv.* 74; *Reiv.* 69): a zigazg fence made of wooden rails, without posts. The rails of each panel rest on and alternate with those of the next. An opening can be made at any point simply by throwing the rails aside at an angle of the fence. This is done in *Unv.* 165 ("Throw down some fence"). Since this does no damage and the fence can be put back up easily and promptly (as Joby does on p. 166), the payment of $10 for damage to the fence is a form of sarcasm.

snap-brim hat (*GDM* 86, 90): the present standard type of man's hat, with a front brim that can be snapped to stay either up or down. For a long time country people associated such hats with city slickers.

snap in the peak (*Sanc.* 242). Peaked caps regularly had a snap-fastener by which the fullness of the cloth over the forehead could be fastened to the peak, or left free.

snap-mouth wallet (*Town* 246): a large pocket-purse having a metal mouth closed with a snap.

snapper (*Unv.* 188): a cracking or snapping tip on the end of a whiplash.

snapping turtle (*Ham.* 282): a savage turtle (*Chelydra serpentina*) which snaps with lightning speed and hangs on tenaciously. It weighs up to 30 1bs., and can be dangerous to fingers and hands. (The similar alligator snapping turtle, *Macrochelys temmincki*, attains a weight of 120 1bs. and is often not distinguished from the ordinary snapper.)

snap-purse (*Dust* 244; *Reiv.* 180, 262): SNAP-MOUTH WALLET.

snatch without whistling (*Reiv.* 191). Butch is such a continuous and smarty talker that context does not mean much in his speech. The only meaning I can suggest for this phrase is that it is a steamboating expression. *To snatch* a steamboat means to spin the wheel, causing it to veer suddenly. It would make a perfectly good maxim, then, that one should not change course suddenly without first blowing the whistle to warn other craft of the maneuver. But I have not been able to find the phrase anywhere else, and this is only a guess.

snick-cluck (*Race* 189). See PUMP GUN.

snuff (*AILD* 10; *KG:Tomo.* 96): extensively used by Negroes and lower-class whites, but always in the mouth—never inhaled in the eighteenth-century fashion. It may be poured into the lower lip or used with a SNUFF STICK. The snuff-box is a pocket-sized, round tin box in which snuff is sold, not an elaborate and permanent possession. The one in *CS:Red* 313 is an exception, obviously being a European eighteenth-century one. To take snuff is to *dip* (*AILD* 17).

snuff-stick (*Sart.* 120; *Ham.* 365): a small stick about the size of a large kitchen match, made of green wood, often of BLACKGUM. One end of the stick is chewed until it is moist and soft; then it is dipped into a box or bottle of snuff, and the end is either chewed or rubbed about the teeth and gums. This practice is known as "dipping snuff."

so—— (*SP* 316): the first syllable of *son of a bitch*.

soap (*Town* 170): soft soap, in the sense of "smooth talk, flattery."

s.o.b. (*Reiv.* 99): son of a bitch.

socket (*Mans.* 126): WHIP SOCKET.

sockm (*WP* 214): sock him, hit him.

sod (*Mans.* 74, 83). Though abbreviated from *sodomite*, this term has lost all reference to perversion. It merely implies affectionate derogation.

soda-jerker (*Town* 156; *Mans.* 187): a clerk who makes and dispenses drinks at a soda-fountain.

soda pop (*Sart.* 122; *Mans.* 264; *Dust* 18): SODA WATER.

soda water (*Sart.* 122; *S&F* 44): carbonated soft drinks generally.

sod cabin (*LiA* 232): a cabin made with blocks of turf or sod for the walls, used by pioneers on the plains in the absence of stones or wood for building.

sody (*Mans.* 261): SODA POP, soft drink.

sody pop (*RfaN* 267; *Town* 114, 366): soda pop, SODA WATER.

sody straw (*Town* 17): soda straw, straw for drinking soft drinks, etc.

so far and no mother (*CS:Elly* 208): a fairly common wisecrack variant on *so far and no further*. A woman afraid of pregnancy will let a man go so far and no mother.

soft soap (*GDM* 138): a form of homemade soap that is a viscous liquid and hence must be kept in a container.

sojer (*Sart.* 5: *S&F* 369): soldier.

something to eat (*Reiv.* 200): food. This is a regular noun-phrase, and is often used in combinations like "some something to eat."

son (*CS:Dry* 171, 172, 177): short for *son of a bitch*, with perhaps a play on *son* as an affectionate form of address to a small boy in *CS:TS* 94.

sonabitch (*CS:BH* 72, 77): son of a bitch. In *Dust* 175 it is not an epithet applied to Gavin Stevens (whom Gowrie is addressing) but simply an expression of incredulous outrage.

sonnen bitch (*Sanc.* 111): son of a bitch.

Sonny Boy (*Sanc.* 240): a maudlin song popularized by Al Jolson in the film *The Singing Fool* (1928).

son of a bitch (plural forms). There are two plural forms: a logical one, *sons of bitches* (*Unv.* 59; *Mans.* 87, 271, 282, 429, 430), and a unitary form, *son of a bitches* (*AILD* 219; *Mans.* 82, 85, 414). Both these forms are in actual use. Faulkner does not make any clear distinction between them, though he does have a slight tendency to assign the logical plural to his more literate speakers.

son-of-a-bitching (*Mans.* 8, 11, 78, 319): an *adj.* form of *son of a bitch*, conveying no meaning beyond a general sense of the speaker's indignation, condemnation, or contempt. It is used when one wants to call something a son of a bitch but at the same time needs to identify it more clearly than that term alone could do. For example, Mink, speaking of Houston's horse, wants to apply the term but to make it clear that it refers to the horse and not to Houston; so he says "sooner or later the son-of-a-bitching horse would kill Houston too."

sont (*Sart.* 8; *S&F* 337; *Unv.* 143): sent.

sorghum. 1. a large tropical grass (*Sorghum vulgare*) grown in many parts of the world in many varieties for seed and syrup. That mentioned by Faulkner is a sweet sorghum cultivated for syrup. It grows about 8′ high and generally resembles corn. The jointed stems, 1″–2″ in diameter, contain a central pith with a sweet juice. The juice is extracted by crushing between rollers. Faulkner's *grinding* (*Sart.* 278) is not a very accurate term; it is probably suggested by the fact that the whole mechanism is called a sorghum-mill. Power is furnished by a mule harnessed to a pole about 15′ long, which turns the rollers. The mule walks in a circle around the mill, and his path is covered with already crushed sorghum stems as a means of keeping down the dust. The extracted juice is boiled in kettles or specially shaped shallow vats until it is reduced to a heavy molasses that is known as sorghum molasses, or simply sorghum. **2.** (*Sanc.* 12; *Flags* 249): sorghum molasses. It is not unknown for rural people to pour sorghum over a whole plateful of food, as the old man does in *Sanc.* 12.

S.O.S. (*Flags* 67): Service of Supply.

Sound (*WP* 303; *Miss.* 29, 30): Mississippi Sound, the body of water between the mainland and the line of barrier islands on the Mississippi coast.

souple (*Race* 179, 182): supple. "Souple up": limber up. "Soupled out": stretched out (in fast running).

soupled (*GDM* 8): suppled, stretched out.

sour dean (*Reiv.* 286, 298): sardine: Cf. *LiA* 24.

southron (*Sanc.* 258): southern. Probably not connected with Scottish *southron* but simply a pronunciation paralleling "modren" for *modern*.

South Street (*Unv.* 17): old name of South Lamar, in Oxford.

sowbelly (*Mans.* 29, 38, 65): salt pork, SIDE MEAT.

spaced shots (*GDM* 244): a standard signal. The usual form of it is three shots with equal intervals (about three seconds) between them. Two shots, from a double-barreled gun, might come from any sort of hunting, as three might from a pump-gun or repeater, but three *equally spaced* shots are clearly recognizable as a signal.

span (*AILD* 175; *LiA* 8; *Unv.* 126): a team of two horses or mules, considered as a single unit.

Spanish moss (*Miss.* 28): an air-plant (*Dendropogon usneoides*) that grows on trees, telegraph wires, or any other support, hanging down in long gray-green, beard-shaped pendants. It does not grow as far north as Faulkner's country (in spite of Hollywood!), but is a striking feature of the landscape of southern Mississippi and throughout the Gulf area. Cf. "bearded cypresses" (*Mosq.* 82, 83).

spanned mules (*KG:KG* 239): mules hitched two abreast, as a SPAN.

spark, *v.t.* (*CS:TS* 83): to date, court.

sparrow (*S&F* 309; *Abs.* 7; *Ham.* 294): English sparrow, house sparrow (*Passer domesticus*)—the familiar worldwide pest. When the droppings of horses and mules provided an almost inexhaustible supply of food, these sparrows swarmed in incredible flocks around town squares and the barns of large farms.

spashing (*WP* 310): apparently a misprint for *splashing*.

spavined (mule, ox, etc.) (*Abs.* 205, 224; *Ham.* 148; *RfaN* 109): lamed by either a bone deposit or an excessive collection of lymph in the hock joint. Since spavins are often caused by work or activities for which the animal is not prepared, and since they yield readily to treatment in the early stages, a spavined animal is likely to be an abused and neglected one.

special (*Sanc.* 31, 54): a special train; here, a special train to a baseball game.

spell (*AILD* 75, 226): an indefinite period of time, anything from ten minutes to a month or more, as in a rainy or dry spell.

Spick (*KG:KG* 137): Spaniard or Spanish-speaking person.

spikehorn buck (*CS:TM* 55). When a buck is a yearling, he grows his first antlers, which are usually straight spikes. In later years they become larger and heavier, with more "points." Hence a spikehorn buck is a yearling, still skittish and kittenish.

spile (*WP* 278): post, pile.

sp'ile (*Sart.* 220; *Sanc.* 45): spoil.

spill (*GDM* 245; *RfaN* 9; *Dust* 10, 29): a twisted strip of paper, or something similar, used to transfer a light from a fire to a lamp, pipe, etc.

spindle of a lathe (*Dust* 167): one of the two shaftlike parts between which the work is held while it is rotated and worked. The point of the comparison is that the two spindles must be precisely aligned with each other.

spindles (*Sart.* 7; *Abs.* 370; *Ham.* 3): the thin, vertical supports of a banister.

Spintrius (*GDM* 265). This name could be derived from Latin *spintria*, "a male prostitute," with the ending loosely taken from the accusative plural, *spintrias*. Burton uses the word in this form in *The Anatomy of Melancholy*, pt. 1, sect. 3, mem. 2, subsect, 4. This explanation is not very convincing, but since the name is obviously supposed to mean something, it is possibly better than nothing.

spiraea (*Abs.* 295): a genus of ornamental shrubs most of which have profuse small pink or white flowers.

spit (*Abs.* 285): likeness, replica.

spitting (*LiA* 20, 21): the constant spitting of Faulkner's characters, especially the more rural ones, is due to the habit of tobacco-chewing.

splat (*Mans.* 270): literally, a thin, flat piece of wood; here used for something resembling a splat.

splint chair (*LiA* 118; *Ham.* 13, 227; *Reiv.* 84): a chair with seat and back woven of long thin flat strips of wood, usually split WHITE OAK. The "splint chair hammocked with deer thongs" (*CS:Red* 322) is puzzling, since the thongs of deer-hide would have the same function as the wooden splints. Perhaps the seat had worn out and been replaced with thongs.

split (wood) (*Unv.* 180). To split wood is to separate it along the grain. Wood of any real size—logs, for instance—will normally be sawed into lengths according to its purpose (anything from fence rails to stovewood), and these lengths are then split into pieces of the proper thickness. *To chop* normally means to cut with an axe across the grain, especially if it is contrasted with *to split*, but it is sometimes used generically for any sort of axe-work. In "wood to cut and split" (*Unv.* 180), *cut* refers to the felling of trees and cutting them, whether by sawing or chopping, into proper lengths, after which they will be split.

splosh (*CS:BB* 21; *CS:TES* 298): a blend of *splash* and *slosh*.

spook. 1. *v.i.* (*GDM* 237; *Mans.* 360): to become alarmed, to panic. 2. *v.t.* (*Town* 12, 291; *Mans.* 83): to cause to become alarmed or to panic.

spool (*CS:BB* 4): the spool on which barbed wire is rolled consists of a solid core with two short planks at right angles to each other forming a flange at each end. The standard spool contains 80 rods of wire.

sport (*Sanc.* 48): a good-natured or obliging person, usually in the phrase *Be a sport*.

sporting house (*RfaN* 116, 141): brothel, whorehouse.

spot (a railroad car) (*Reiv.* 165): to place it at the proper spot (opposite a ramp, cattle-chute, etc.) for loading or unloading.

spotting shot (*Abs.* 279): an artillery shot to check aim and range.

spread blanket (*Fable* 155, 156, 194): an improvised surface for rolling dice. It serves not only to keep the game out of the dirt but to keep it relatively honest, since the friction and irregularities of a blanket spread on the ground largely cancel out a player's skill in controlling the dice.

spreader (*KG:Tomo.* 96): a cross-brace with its ends fastened to the inner faces of PLOW HANDLES, between the PLOW STOCK and the grips of the handles. Many plows have two spreaders. They give greater strength and rigidity, and spread the handles the proper distance apart.

spreading adder (*CS:TES* 298): hog-nosed snake (*Heterodon contortrix*), a short, thick snake about 2 1/2′ long. Though harmless, it puts up a great bluff, flattening the head and neck and hissing terrifically. If this does not succeed, it turns on its back, drags its body through its opened jaws with dramatic writhings, and plays dead.

spring. There are many springs in Faulkner's country, almost invariably at the base of the hills, just where they come down to a creek or river bottom. Since beeches seek out underground water, a spring often flows out from the roots of a beech (*Sart.* 138; *Sanc.* 3; *Unv.* 231). If the spring is regularly used by people living nearby, it will have a wooden frame or a large ceramic pipe let into the sand to provide a place where a bucket can easily be filled without stirring up mud or sand; this frame will be cleaned out periodically, as the spring washes sand into it. A spring near the house will also be used for washing, hog-killing, etc. (*S&F* 15), and will often have a WASH POT there for the purpose (*Sart.* 138). Sometimes a springhouse is built over a spring. (*Sart.* 316; *GDM* 9, 13; *Mans* 171). Its main purpose is to protect milk, butter, etc., being refrigerated in the spring from contamination and animals. The stream carrying off the water from a spring is a spring-branch (*Sart.* 225; *Ham.* 37; *Reiv.* 222). It is seldom more than a couple of hundred yards long, since the spring is at the edge of a bottom and the spring-branch soon flows into a creek.

spring bottom (*LiA* 33): the BOTTOM adjoining a SPRING, through which the spring-branch flows. As a thickly grown-up place, it is a good hideout for a horse that does not want to be caught.

springs (of wagon). See WAGON.

sprinkling-cart (*RfaN* 241): a cart for sprinkling unpaved streets in dry weather, to keep the dust down. A sprinkling-cart was a horizontal cylindrical tank mounted on the running-gear of a wagon, with a horizontal pipe across the back, pierced with a series of small holes through which the water was released. It was very similar to the contrivances now used to spray tar onto roads.

sprung (*Sanc.* 303): gotten out of jail.

spung (*Sanc.* 8): a crook who preys or lives on other crooks. The word is a variant of *sponge*.

square. 1. (*Sart.* 348; *S&F* 108; *AILD* 224): a square surrounding the court-house of a Southern county seat. It normally has most of the stores in town around its four sides. Since it is almost invariably the only square in town, "the square" is a specific expression that needs no further explanation. **2.** (*AILD* 150): a carpenter's square, for making and checking right angles.

squat (*Sart.* 138, 139): to take or maintain a typical countryman's position, sitting on his own heels, with his weight resting on the balls of his feet. This is a restful position for those used to it, but very tiring after a minute or two to anyone else (*Sart.* 140–41, 333–34; *GDM* 80). To assume this position is to "hunker down" (*S&F* 319).

squinch. 1. (*LiA* 386): to squint, screw up the face. **2.** (*GDM* 158): to crouch.

squinch owl (*S&F* 34, 46): SCREECH OWL.

Squire (*Dust.* 34): a title of respect given to a man prominent in a rural community. He is often, but not always, a justice of the peace.

squirrel (*GDM* 216; *Mans.* 105): unless a FOX SQUIRREL is specified, the Eastern gray squirrel (*Sciurus carolinensis*).

squirrel shot (*Town* 130; *KG:Error* 120): ♯4–♯6 shot. See SHOT SIZES.

squirt (*S&F* 166, 217): an impudent or conceited nobody.

stable lantern (*Town* 247): not a specific term, but presumably applicable to any lantern designed to be relatively safe for use around hay, even if dropped or turned over. (Remember Mrs. O'Leary's cow!) Lanterns of this sort were frequently advertised. One old ad begins: "Don't fire your barn! Drop a common lantern and it's done."

stage (*Sanc.* 140): a landing of a staircase.

stalag (*Mans.* 295, 352, 354): German abbreviation of *Stammlager*, a prison camp for enlisted men and noncommissioned officers (World War II).

stall-fed (*Mans.* 136): fed in a stall instead of being merely left to graze in a pasture; hence, specially or luxuriously fed.

stamped tin (*Sanc.* 4): tin stamped out by machine, as in tin signs. Faulkner explains the metaphor more fully when he describes Ab Snopes as a figure that "against the serene columned backdrop" of a mansion, "had more than ever that impervious quality of something cut ruthlessly from tin, depthless, as though, sidewise to the sun, it would cast no shadow" (*CS:BB* 10). Cf. also the town boys watching a dance through the gymnasium windows: "like a row of hatted and muffled busts cut from black tin and nailed to the window-sills" (*Sanc.* 29).

stanchion (*Sart.* 87; *AILD* 4; *Ham.* 59): almost any sort of more-or-less vertical support on a wagon or carriage, especially one of the supports of the seat or the top. The surrey in which the sheriff took Mink Snopes to Jefferson had a folding top, with at least two stanchions radiating from a single point. It is in the **V** between two of these that Mink wedges his neck (*Ham.* 256; *Town* 80).

stand. 1. (*AILD* 35; *Abs.* 179): growing plants of the same kind, considered collectively: "a stand of corn." **2.** (*Mans.* 9): service from an animal at stud. Since Mink had paid for one service and his cow had MISSED, he was entitled to another stand without further payment. **3.** (for deer hunting) (*GDM* 176, 196): not the platform in a tree used for still-hunting (where the hunter merely waits for game to come along), but simply a standing-place along a game trail, past which the dogs may drive the game.

stand (of a horse) (*Unv.* 102, 279; *GDM* 200): to hold still. In the *Unv.* uses, *stand for* is not a verb-adverb combination. *Stand* is the verb and *for* is a preposition.

standard-bred (*Reiv.* 121): bred to conform to the standards of a particular breed.

standers (*Mans.* 31; *Race* 179, 181): people placed at STANDs for a hunt.

stand holder (*Race* 177): STANDER. (The word here should obviously be plural, as is shown by the use of *them* in the following line.)

stanhope (*Reiv.* 96): a type of light, open carriage.

Stanley Steamer (*Reiv.* 259): a steam-propelled car built from 1897 to 1924. In the first decade of the century it set several world's speed records.

star (*Fable* 162): a white spot (of any shape) on a horse's forehead, a blaze.

Starkville (*Sanc.* 27): a town in Mississippi about 75 m. SE of Oxford, the seat of Mississippi State University, formerly Mississippi Agricultural and Mechanical College, known as A. and M. It is the traditional athletic rival of the University of Mississippi. At the time of *Sanc.*, college baseball commanded as much interest as football, with special trains, bands, etc.

starred Saint Andrew's cross (*Unv.* 112): the Confederate battle flag.

start a rabbit out of a brier patch (*Abs.* 281). The rabbit knows where the hunter is, but a noise coming suddenly from a different direction may make him bolt. In Faulkner's country there are few stones; hence a clod (or a stick) is the natural missile to use.

starter (*SP* 86). In earlier cars, the starter was not wired to the ignition-switch, but was activated by a button on the floor, about where the light-beam switch is on many modern cars.

State Penal Farm (*Ham.* 333): PARCHMAN.

State University at Oxford (*Abs.* 67): the UNIVERSITY OF MISSISSIPPI, "Ole Miss."

stay (*Reiv.* 13): to live, reside.

steady (*Town* 245): constantly, always.

steamboat-gothic (*Reiv.* 166): an elaborate, fancy, ornamented style of house architecture resembling that used on river steamboats.

steamboat whistle (*CS:Court*. 366, 380). Steam used for the whistle decreases the pressure in the boilers. For a large steamboat, this does not matter, but it can have a noticeable effect on a small one that is having heavy going.—In the late 1920s the students at the University of Mississippi went in a body to the home of Chancellor Alfred Hume to demand a holiday in celebration of a big football victory. Dr. Hume refused, telling them that as a boy he had known a small steamboat that was a laughing-stock because when it was headed upstream, every time it blew its whistle it lost ground. He got them to agree that the university was a big enough steamboat to be able to blow its whistle without having to back up. Faulkner unquestionably knew this story.

steel-bowed spectacles (*CS:Lo* 390): glasses with frames of thin steel wire.

steeple (*CS:TWBF* 276): staple, the projecting metal **U**-shaped part over which a slot in a HASP passes, and through which it is padlocked.

steering sweep (*WP* 164): a large oar mounted at the stern of a boat and used as a rudder.

stereopticon (*GDM* 298; *RfaN* 254): an early form of slide projector, often with double lenses to produce stereoscopic effects.

stern (*AILD* 232; *Ham*. 14, 69): a jocular expression for *butt, ass*.

stern engines (*WP* 238): reversed engines, and hence engines pulling the boat in the direction of the stern. The boat is enabled to "hang there" by using just enough power to hold it against the current.

St. Francis River (*Fable* 162). The route went across most of Missouri and into Arkansas. The St. Francis empties into the Mississippi 35 m. SW of Memphis. Since the general course of the former is slightly W of S, and that of the latter is SW, they form a **V**. This general area of southeastern Missouri and northeastern Arkansas was the theater of operations of the outlaw band of Jesse James.

stid (*Unv*. 229): instead.

still (*GDM* 34; *Town* 168, 173; *Sanc*. 123): an illicit still for making MOON-SHINE.

still-frozen (*Ham*. 348): presumably "not yet liquidated."

still-hunting (*GDM* 210): hunting by lying in wait in a favorable spot, without the use of dogs, horses, etc.

stirrup (as aid to a runner) (*Unv*. 9, 65; *Dust* 84). A person holding a horse's stirrup can be pulled along by the horse and hence can run farther and faster with less effort. This is a standard way of helping a runner.

stirrup (*Reiv*. 244): a small step used for getting into a surrey or buggy. (Note that Butch's foot is described as being *on* it, not *in* it, as it would be if it were the stirrup of a horse.)

St. John's (*S&F* 395): a church on HURRICANE CREEK just where it enters the Tallahatchie River bottom. It had a good spring and used to be a favorite picnic spot. (Faulkner once went on a picnic with my family there.)The old site is now under water when the Sardis Reservoir is high, and no sign of the church is left there. When the Reservoir was built, the church itself was moved. It is now next to the pumping-station on the pipeline on the College Hill-Abbeville road, 3 m. from its old location.

St. Mihiel (*Mans.* 280): a town on the Meuse, scene of an important battle in 1918.

sto'-bought (*Sart.* 332): store-bought. This is a common term among people living far from settlements and producing most of what they need, or buying or bartering from each other. Under these circumstances, store-bought things are usually regarded as special treats or extravagancies.

stocking (of a horse) *GDM* 78, 123): a white coloring extending from the hoof to above the fetlock.

stocking-foot (*Ham.* 286): a horse's foot with a STOCKING.

stockings (*Reiv.* 66, 211). Since boys wore knee-breeches until they graduated to long pants more or less at adolescence, they also wore stockings, which were invariably black.

stock-trader walking-sticks (*Dust* 134). A stock-trader carries a walking-stick with which to feel animals, prod them to make them turn around, etc. It is not any special kind of walking-stick, but simply a stick carried, in his temporary capacity as a stock trader, by a man who probably would not normally carry one.

stock whip (*Ham.* 68): a whip with a short, rigid handle and a long lash.

stomp (*S&F* 8): stamp.

Stone, Mr. (*Town* 326): Faulkner's friend and early literary mentor, Phil Stone, to whom *Town* is dedicated. Since the character of Gavin Stevens is in many ways based on Phil Stone, it is interesting that Faulkner introduces him separately and by name as a minor character who never actually appears.

Stonewall Jackson (*CS:TM* 54; *KG:Monk* 46). See JACKSON, GEN. THOMAS J.

stool (for milking) (*AILD* 121). See MILKING STOOL.

stool (*Sanc.* 173). See PORTER.

stop my clock with a nose spray (*S&F* 243). This phrase is a total mystery. From Jason's character, we would expect it to be something hateful, and probably nasty as well. But it means nothing to me, no reference books give any lead, and the many people knowledgeable about Faulkner's times and idiom whom I have asked have not even had any good guesses to offer.

stouter (*Reiv.* 82): stronger.

stove-led (*Sart.* 221): STOVE LID.

stove lid (*S&F* 318; *CS:MV* 749): a round piece of iron about 10″ across that fits into an opening in the top of a stove. It is removed and replaced by means of a special handle which fits into a recess in the lid.

stove wood (*Sart.* 83, 107; *S&F* 335; *Abs.* 202): wood cut and split into lengths of about 15″ and a thickness of about 2″, to be fed lengthwise into a wood-burning kitchen range. The illustration in *WT* 42–43 is wrong, since it shows Alice about to throw a piece of firewood, not a stick of stovewood. A stick of stovewood would be somewhat longer and much smaller in cross-section, and for throwing it would be grasped by one end, as one grasps the handle of a hammer. The comparison of *Unv.* 65, "like when you run with a stick of stove wood balanced on your palm" is clear enough as a simile, but I have no explanation as to why anyone would do this. Perhaps it was a private game of the Faulkner children, like racing with an egg in a spoon. But this is only a wild guess.

stove-zinc (*AILD* 68): a square of galvanized iron on which a stove is set. Its function is to keep any sparks or hot ashes from coming into contact with the floor.

straddle of (*AILD* 80; *Unv.* 210): astride.

straighten out (game) (*GDM* 18): to disentangle its confused trail.

straight stock (*Ham.* 31; *CS:BB* 16): a straight PLOW STOCK, used for fairly light work, as opposed to various types of curved ones designed for heavier jobs.

strap oil (*Abs.* 123): oil for HARNESS STRAPS.

strapped like a suitcase (*Mans.* 29). Suitcases were normally fastened shut by straps and buckles, and entirely separate straps were often fastened around them.

straw cow (*GDM* 185): error for *stray cow*. See Meriwether, p. 23.

straw tick (*Fable* 195): straw-filled mattress.

streaked lantern (*Sart.* 281): not a specifically prepared lantern but merely a dirty one. Cleaning a kerosene lantern is a messy task, frequently neglected. There is a long discussion of how seldom Louis Hatcher cleaned the lantern with which he hunted possums (*S&F* 141–42).

streak off (*Reiv.* 89): to lay out (a MIDDLE) by plowing a furrow on each side of it.

stretchers (*Mans.* 22, 23): implements for stretching wire taut before it is fastened to fence-posts.

strike (*Race* 180): a dog's act of striking a trail or scent. "It wasn't even a strike, it was a jump" means that the dog did not strike a scent at all, but simply came upon the deer by accident and JUMPed it.

striking snake (*CS:Queen* 736). The comparison is not to a snake withdrawing after a strike, but to one preparing to strike, jerking the head back and throwing the neck and forebody into an **S**-curve which is suddenly straightened out to produce the strike. The comparison is fully explained in *CS: Elly* 211: "she . . . saw the grandmother, without moving below the hips, start violently backward as a snake does to strike."

string tie (*GDM* 373; *SP* 112): an extremely narrow necktie, tied in a bow.

strip (a horse) (*Reiv.* 267): to take off his saddle, bridle, etc.

struck and jumped (*Race* 178): struck a scent and JUMPed a deer.

Stuart (*GDM* 286, 288): Confederate General and cavalry commander James Ewell Brown Stuart, known as Jeb Stuart (*Sart.* 10) because of his initials. After a brilliant career he was on a raid and unable to get back to GET-

TYSBURG for the battle, and Lee was thus handicapped by the loss of his scouting services. It was on this raid that he rode around the Union army. The Union Gen. George Gordon Meade sent Winfield Scott Hancock to occupy Cemetery Ridge, and Faulkner assumes, probably rightly, that if Stuart had been there these movements would have been known to Lee sooner.—There seems to be a textual problem on p. 286: "Lee should have known of all of Meade just where Hancock was" is clear in its general meaning, but will not work syntactically.

studding (*Reiv.* 255): behaving like a stud-horse—in a sexually aggressive fashion.

study. 1. *n.* (*Sart.* 220): thought, concern. **2.** *v.t.* (*GDM* 68): to consider, think about.

studying (*S&F* 16, 17; *GDM* 77; *Reiv.* 10): concerned with, bothering about, considering, usually in the negative: "I ain't studying. . . ."

stump up (*S&F* 136; *Mans.* 197): to hand over money, "cough up."

sturb (*S&F* 70, 395): disturb.

sucking and smouching around (*Mans.* 67). To suck around is to curry favor, use flattery, etc. To smouch is to trick or cheat. Thus the general meaning is "trying to work by indirect, devious, discreditable means."

suction pipe (*Ham.* 59, 60): a sheet-iron pipe which operates like a huge vacuum cleaner to unload cotton from wagons and convey it directly into a COTTON GIN. It is swiveled so that it can move to any part of the wagon, and is telescoped so that it can be pulled down as the level of the cotton in the wagon is lowered.

sugar up (*Reiv.* 219): to soften up (a woman) by sweet talk.

sugar-tit (*GDM* 50): a piece of cloth containing sugar, tied up in the form of a nipple, for an infant to suck.

suh. 1. (*Sart.* 8, 116; *S&F* 120, 227): sir. **2.** (*Sanc.* 143): the initial sounds of *son of a bitch*, which Miss Reba starts to say, but changes her mind.

sull (*Sart.* 332; *S&F* 87, 349; *Mans.* 10): to become sullen, to sulk. "Sulled up" (*LiA* 337): having adopted a sullen expression.

Sullivan, John L. (*Abs.* 46): world's heavyweight boxing champion, 1882–92.

Sullivan's Hollow (*Miss.* 33): a long, narrow valley extending S from Mize, which is 35 m. SE of Jackson, Miss. It is (or was) pretty much as Faulkner describes it, and derived its name from a large family of Sullivans who dominated it. Everyone in the state knows the tales of lawlessness there. The town of Mize used to be known as "No Nigger." Since my earliest childhood I have known the tale of the revenuer caught in Sullivan's Hollow and made to pull a plow. Though many of the stories are probably apocryphal, there is no doubt about the general clannishness and violence of the place. It is a definite fact, for example, that in 1924 a quarrel about a disputed call in a baseball game left two people dead on the field. There is no way in which Sullivan's Hollow could properly be said to extend into Faulkner's section of the state as a geographical entity. He must mean that, spiritually, the northeastern hills of Lafayette Co.—the Beat Four of *Dust* (see BEAT)—can be considered as an extension of Sullivan's Hollow.

sumac(h) (*Abs.* 214; *Town* 354; *Mans.* 104): staghorn sumac (*Rhus typhina*), a large shrub with compound leaves, striking red foliage, and masses of small fruits in the fall. It appears profusely in abandoned fields. The name is pronounced SHOE-mack.

sunbonnet (*Sanc.* 93, 273; *LiA* 9, 141; *Ham.* 20): a wide-rimmed BONNET with a flap to protect the back of the neck, worn by women as a protection against the sun.

Sunday, Bill (*Fable* 181): the evangelist William Ashley Sunday, usually known as Billy Sunday.

Sunflower River (*GDM* 340; *RfaN* 45): a river in the Mississippi DELTA. Faulkner is not strictly accurate here. The Tallahatchie and the Yalobusha join to form the Yazoo, and the Sunflower empties into it much lower down. Thus a steamboat going from Vicksburg to Ikemotubbe's landing would not go "up the Yazoo and Sunflower and Tallahatchie," but up the Yazoo past the mouth of the Sunflower, and up the Tallahatchie.

sup (*Sanc.* 56): to drink, swallow up.

sup (*AILD* 175; *Sanc.* 44, 145): a small drink.

supper (*S&F* 22, 81; *AILD* 175; *Unv.* 233): the normal name for the evening meal, DINNER being at midday, except for an elaborate social event. Dinner is the main meal because Negro cooks normally see to breakfast and dinner, and then leave about the middle of the afternoon. Sunday night supper, particularly, is simply a snack made up of leftovers from the heavy noon meal (*Reiv.* 109).

supper-bell (*Ham.* 82): a small hand-bell, rung to announce that supper is ready.

suption (*Ham.* 23; *Mans.* 46): taste, flavor, goodness.

Surrender (*Reiv.* 89): Lee's surrender at Appomattox, which ended the Civil War.

survey (*Sart.* 22): the right of way surveyed for a railroad.

suspenders (*Abs.* 239, 244): elastic straps used to support the trousers, braces. Faulkner leaves it to the reader to figure out "why the suspenders." The architect had climbed one tree and then used his sapling pole to vault into another he could not otherwise have reached because of the intervening space. If he had simply done this, his pole would have been left leaning into the tree into which he had gone, or lying on the ground between the two trees, and in either case it would have shown where he had gone. But he tied the top of the pole to the first tree with his suspenders, and they had enough elasticity to let him vault to the second tree and to snap the top of the pole back to the first tree when he released it.

sut (*Town* 21): soot.

Sutpen's Hundred (*Abs.* 16 and passim). The hundred-square-mile size of Sutpen's holdings rules out any possibility that it is closely based on any actual plantation in its area. There were large plantations like it, except for size, in the appropriate place. It was located on the old Sardis road, which crossed the IRON BRIDGE over the Tallahatchie River. This road has been shifted several times, but its general course is that of the present State Route 314, which peters out at the Sardis Reservoir. Sutpen's house would have been in the hills overlooking the creek and river bottom somewhere near the end of this road. Aunt Mitty, who cooked for my family during my childhood, had been a slave on the Corbin Place in this vicinity, and when we got a second-hand Model-T Ford about 1922 she got us to take her out to the site of the old place. There were no buildings left, but she easily found and showed us the foundations of the house, smokehouse, etc., and showed us how her master could overlook his fields in the creek and river bottom from the house. In 1972 I was unable to locate this site, but found another in the vicinity which obviously represented a very large establishment, with the sites of a main house and a large series of outbuildings behind it. The house site, with the cedars and the long sedge-grass-covered open slope leading up to it, perfectly fits the description in *Abs.* 187—but there is no way of knowing that Faulkner knew this spot, or, for that matter, that it would have fitted his description as perfectly at an earlier date. All we can say with confidence is that Faulkner placed Sutpen's in an area and with a general topography fitting the approach of Davidson's Creek to the Tallahatchie River, where there had actually been establishments like his, though by no means as large.

swag. 1. (*Race* 189) : a hollow, depression. **2.** (*AILD* 117; *KG :Hand* 69) : to sag.

swallow (*S&F* 309; *Ham.* 294). There are several species of swallows around Oxford, but the "swallows" of Faulkner are evidently chimney swifts (*Chaetura pelagica*), which are especially active and conspicuous as they twitter and hawk for insects in the early evening. The normal local name for them is CHIMNEY SWEEPS.

swamp-rabbit (*GDM* 185). See RABBIT.

swamp rat (*Reiv.* 102, 136) : a special breed of poor white living in a shack or SHANTY-BOAT in river bottoms or on bayous. He typically supports himself primarily by hunting and fishing, without regard for the niceties of seasons and bag-limits. He may also do a bit of moonshining or bootlegging, or both, and may even plant a few vegetables or a patch of corn. He is solitary and fiercely independent, and may be a very decent sort of fellow according to his lights.

swangdangle (*GDM* 119) : to hornswoggle, to do someone out of something by trickery or sharp practice.

sweater (dark blue, with a big red *M*) (*Ham.* 104). The sweater given to Labove was, of course, the Ole Miss sweater given to an athlete who "makes his letter" on a varsity team, and Faulkner describes it accurately.

sweep (*Mans.* 49; *CS:SNP* 102) : a plowshare shaped like a curved triangle, used for shallow cultivation of row crops. The name comes from the fact that it sweeps a little soil to each side instead of actually plowing it. "The plow and then the sweep" refers to the fact that the plow is used to prepare the field for seeding, but the sweep is used after the plants have come up and attained some size.

sweet biscuits (*Sart.* 168): biscuits in the British sense of the word, cookies.

sweetening: any sweet food or flavoring, whether table syrup or molasses (*LiA* 231), candy (*Ham.* 317), or honey (*Miss.* 14).

sweet gum (*Ham.* 14; *GDM* 322): a large tree (*Liquidambar styraciflua*) which exudes, from wounds or cuts, a viscous, highly aromatic gum that is chewed like chewing-gum by children and country people.

sweets (*Mans.* 155): suites.

swept yard (*Unv.* 99; *GDM* 49; *Reiv.* 167). The yards of Negroes and lower-class whites living in the country regularly consist of packed, bare earth, swept clean from time to time with a broom of twigs bound together. See *Dust.* 8 for a detailed account.

swing. 1. (*S&F* 56, 185): a yard-swing. It has two seats facing each other, and each seat will accommodate two persons. The seats are connected by a lattice floor-board, and the whole assembly is hung by wooden strips from a rigid wooden frame standing on the ground. One swings it by pushing with the feet on the floorboard. Such a swing can be placed in a secluded place in the yard, and is a great favorite of lovers, being much less public than a porch-swing, which has to be where everyone comes and goes. Though there is no proof, I take it that this is the sort of swing in the Compson's yard in Caddy's time, since it is what would normally be expected. In Miss Quentin's time, it was a BARREL-STAVE HAMMOCK, and it is not normal usage to call this a swing. A yard-swing, being exposed to the weather, would not last for even a short generation, and it would be in keeping with the decline of the Compson household to replace it with a rural type of hammock. **2.** (*CS:Elly* 210): a porch-swing, consisting of a single seat, 4'–5' long, suspended by chains at each end which hang from heavy hooks screwed through the ceiling into the rafters.

swing door (*S&F* 342): a swinging door, standard between kitchen and dining room, so that a person with a load of dishes can open it with a push from either side. It has a spring which, after a few diminishing swings, brings it to rest in a closed position. This is why, when Luster left by the dining room door, "after a while it ceased to flap" (*S&F* 336), and why "the swing door slapped behind her in dying oscillations" (*Flags* 298).

swinged (*Ham.* 17): singed.

swinging hands (*Sanc.* 166): couples walked together, but some distance apart, holding hands and swinging their joined hands between them as they walked.

swipe (*Fable* 178): HOSTLER, groom, one who cares for horses.

switch-cane (*Miss.* 17). See CANE.

swivel (*Town* 115): to shrivel.

swivet (*RfaN* 43): normally a *n.* meaning a harried and confused attempt to do too many things at once, and usually confined to the phrase *in a swivet*. Faulkner's use as a verb meaning "to be in a swivet" is a neologism.

swurging (*Ham.* 38, 43; *CS:BH* 67): surging.

symmetrical squared barkless logs (*GDM* 319): crossties.

syringa (*Sart.* 25, 42; *LiA* 52): mockorange, any of several varieties of flowering shrubs of the genus *Philadelphus* (not to be confused with lilac, which actually belongs to the genus *Syringa*).

T

———t (*Ham.* 62, 161; *Reiv.* 140, 155; *WP* 339): shit.

tack (*Reiv.* 178): a collective term for the equipment used in riding: saddle, pad, bridle, etc.

tack up (*Reiv.* 178, 270): to put the TACK on a horse.

tahrs (*CS:BH* 71): tires.

tail gate (*AILD* 225; *Unv.* 148; *Ham.* 274): the removable plank forming the back of a wagon box.

take (*WP* 217): to conceive.

take and (*Sart.* 141; *AILD* 41; *GDM* 67): used with a following verb to give a mild sense of precipitate or unreasonable action. "Tull taken and cut them two big whiteoaks" (*AILD* 135) has much the same sense as "Tull up and cut them."

take a pill (*Sanc.* 304): apparently a variant of *take a powder*; i.e. get out.

take earth (*Abs.* 218): to stop running and take refuge in a hole or burrow—a fox-hunter's term.

take out. 1. (*AILD* 117; *LiA* 13; *Ham.* 35; *Unv.* 41): to unhitch (a horse or team) from a wagon, plow, etc., and possibly unharness it. **2.** (*AILD* 112, 176; *S&F* 310): to start out. These two meanings can be confusing, since (1) normally ends a journey and (2) normally begins it.

talking-machine (*Sart.* 106): phonograph, gramophone, record player.

talk (someone) **low** (*AILD* 70): to speak ill or contemptuously of someone.

Tallahatchie Crossing (*CS:MGM* 689, 690): the point about 12 m. N of Oxford where Miss. 7 and the Illinois Central Railroad cross the Tallahatchie River. There was fighting between Generals FORREST and Smith over this crossing during the Civil War.

Tallahatchie River (*Unv.* 173; *GDM* 169, 340; *RfaN* 45): a river some 12 m. N and NW of Oxford, now disguised, below the Illinois Central Railroad crossing, by the Sardis Reservoir. The COTTON COMPRESS where Rosa Millard was killed, being on this river 60 m. from Sartoris (*Unv.* 173), would have been about 10 m. N of Greenwood.

tallow dip (*Unv.* 175): a candle made by dipping a string into melted tallow.

Tanguay, Eva (*Mosq.* 240): a star of vaudeville and musical comedy (1878–1947), widely known from about 1910 to her retirement in 1929. She made a special furore because of her risqué costumes and songs. For Faulkner's simile, see LAMP.

tapstick (*Dust* 5). Faulkner describes the object adequately but has forgotten how it is made. Since the nut is threaded on the inside, it is impossible to drive it onto a stick so that it will hold. The section of broomstick (or any other tough stick) is whittled down until it can barely be inserted into the opening of the nut, and is then screwed in, with the threads of the nut cutting their own threads in the stick. We usually called this a throwing-stick. It was used not only for hunting rabbits but also to knock nuts and lodged objects out of trees, etc.

tarnation (*Unv.* 78; *CS:BH* 75): damnation (or any other slightly profane idea). In the expression "what the tarnation hell" (*CS:BH* 67, 75), it is a pure intensive.

tarpaulin (*Abs.* 45). Sutpen wrapped this around the legs of his only pair of pants to protect them from the mud splashed up by his horse's hooves.

tarpollyon (*Reiv.* 71): tarpaulin.

tarred bob-wire cuts (*Ham.* 35). Cuts on a horse are normally tarred to prevent infection and, even more, parasitization. The faked barbed-wire cuts would imply a spirited animal that took little account of fences.

Taylor (*Sanc.* 31): a village 8 m. from Oxford, the first railroad stop to the S.

Tchufuncta river (*Mosq.* 277): Tchefuncta River, a stream flowing S into the northernmost point of Lake PONTCHARTRAIN.

Teaberry (*Mans.* 71, 77): a fictional hotel in Memphis. See GREENBURY.

tea gown (*Flags* 167, 292): a gown of expensive material with flowing lines, worn for semiformal afternoon social occasions.

team (*S&F* 381): normally a team of horses or mules. When Jason Compson thinks it's going to rain on him, and drives on, "thinking of himself slogging through the mud, hunting a team," the idea is that it will rain hard, the road will get muddy, he will get stuck, and then he will have to walk down the muddy road looking for a team that can be hired to pull him out.

tear meat or squeal (*Abs.* 287). The meaning is clearly that Wash has Sutpen in a situation where there is no satisfactory course of action. I have never heard the phrase, nor found it attested elsewhere, but it would seem to come from the situation of a hog caught by the ears: he can either squeal and stay caught, or he can pull off his ears ("tear meat") and escape.

telephone crank (*GDM* 60): a small hand-crank on the side of an early telephone. It was turned several times to ring the operator.

telescope bag (*Ham.* 144; *KG:Error* 124): a suitcase made of two separate parts, the top sliding down over the bottom, so that the total height is adjustable. The handle is on the top section, and the bag is held together by straps.

temerious (*Mans.* 147): temerarious.

tenant- or share- or furnish-hand (*RfaN* 245). See SHARES, FARMING ON.

ten-gauge (*Ham.* 217, 232; *Town* 79; *Mans.* 30). The gauge of a shotgun measures the size of the bore. The smaller the number, the larger the bore, since the gauge is actually the number of lead balls of that size that it takes to weigh a pound. The common shotgun gauges of the time of *Ham.* were 12 and 16. (The so-called 410, really a .41 caliber, has come into favor more recently.)

Tennessee Junction (*Unv.* 271): probably HOLLY SPRINGS, Miss. (also called MEMPHIS JUNCTION), since it is within a day's wagon-trip of Sartoris.

terrapin (*S&F* 96): the common box-tortoise (*Terrapene carolina*). He has a shell about 5″–6″ long, which he can close tightly. The comparison of Spoade to a tortoise works two ways: (1) Spoade is placid among the rushing students like a tortoise among blowing leaves; (2) Spoade, "his collar about his ears," resembles a tortoise with his head just protruding from the fold of skin into which he withdraws it before closing his shell.

tetchous (*Mans.* 58): touchy, sensitive.

texas (*CS:Red* 323): part of a steamboat, just behind the pilot-house, containing the officers' quarters.

Thatim? (*WP* 213): (Is) that him?

That's a boy (*Reiv.* 192): that's right, that's doing what you should. The original form of the expression is *That's the boy*, and it is sometimes reduced to ATTABOY.

That's three, thank the Lawd (*S&F* 36). Roskus thanks the Lord because the third death completes the expected series and means that there is no particular reason to fear still another one. The idea that deaths come in threes, which Roskus has expressed on p. 34, is a more specific form of the very widespread belief that misfortunes come in threes.

they. 1. (*Sart.* 20; *AILD* 132; *S&F* 28): there (expletive, not *adv.*). **2.** (*Sart.* 23; *S&F* 2, 37): their.

thin (cotton, corn, etc.) (*WP* 25, 30): to chop out superfluous plants with a hoe, so as to leave a properly spaced STAND.

third and fourth (*GDM* 68; *Ham.* 8). One who pays at this rate is a "share tenant" rather than a sharecropper. He supplies his own equipment (Ab Snopes has his own mule). Then he pays one third of the seed and fertilizer for his corn crop, and pays one third of the crop as rent. He pays one fourth of the seed and fertilizer for cotton, and pays one fourth of his crop as rent. (A sharecropper supplies nothing but labor and normally pays half his crop.)

this-here (*Town* 83): this.

thisyer (*GDM* 324): this here, this.

th'oat (*Sanc.* 220): throat.

Thoms, Captain Joe (*Miss.* 37): apparently (and understandably) a cover name or invented name. I have not been able to find an original for him.

thon bitch (*Sanc.* 243): a childish lisping of *son of a bitch*.

Thoroughbred (*Reiv.* 232; *Fable* 157): not merely a purebred animal (as many people think), but a specific breed of horse developed in England around

1700 from native mares and Arabian stallions. Practically all race-horses and jumpers are Thoroughbreds.

three-four (*AILD* 175; *S&F* 121; *Sanc.* 46): three or four.

Three Mile Bridge (*Ham.* 35): the bridge over Four Mile Branch, on Miss. 334 some 3 1/2 m. SE of Oxford.

three on one (*Unv.* 199). Ab Snopes is protesting the fact that he is outnumbered. His exclamation derives from the standard children's "Two on one's no fair."

three-quarters bred (*Reiv.* 125): having three pure-bred grand-parents and one of inferior or questionable stock.

threw down upon them with the old gun (*GDM* 252; cf. *Unv.* 83): pointed the gun at them quickly. The expression comes from the situation of a hunter who, for safety's sake, carries his gun (in any of several ways) with the muzzle aimed upwards, and who literally throws the muzzle down onto the line of his game as he aims.

threw me up (*Reiv.* 169, 171, 181). Ned interlaced the fingers of his two hands, and Lucius put his left foot in them ("Hand/give me your foot"— *Reiv.* 171, 181; *CS:BB* 14). Then, as Lucius stepped upward on this foot, Ned tossed him, so that he could throw his right leg over and land in the saddle. Lucius was too small to mount unaided without wasting a great deal of energy.

thriblets (*CS:TM* 55): triplets.

throttle (*Reiv.* 52): a hand-throttle, a lever sliding on a notched quadrant (see RATCHET) placed on the right side of the steering column, a few inches below the wheel.

thrush (*Sart.* 26, 56, 169; *SP* 160, 309). Two very different birds are often lumped together under this designation: the brown thrasher (*Toxostoma rufum*), a reddish-brown bird with a streaked breast, related and very similar to the MOCKING-BIRD; and the wood-thrush (*Hylocichla mustelina*), a more grayish-brown bird with a spotted breast. From the references to the song and to singing at twilight, I would guess that all these references except probably *Sart.* 26, are to the wood-thrush.

thumps (*CS:SftL* 27): an affliction of various domestic animals, marked by spasmodic contractions of the diaphragm like those in human hiccups.

ti' (*S&F* 381): tire.

ticked (hound, setter, etc.) (*Sart.* 24, 35; *Ham.* 62): having small markings of a different color from the ground color.

Tidewater (*Abs.* 222, 380): the coastal areas of Virginia, roughly as far up the rivers as the tide is perceptible. This is the area of the most magnificent plantations and landed gentry.

tie (*LiA* 172): to match, equal. "Can you tie that?" "Can you match that; did you ever hear of such a thing?"

tie-rope (*Dust* 86): halter-shank, a rope used to tie a horse in his stall. One end has a metal snap that can be snapped over one of the rings of the bridle; the other end is tied to a wall-ring: a RING-BOLT through the stable wall.

tie-up (*AILD* 121): a place where cows are tied up for the night.

tight. 1. (*AILD* 128): difficult, leaving a scant margin for safety. **2.** (*AILD* 49): a difficult situation.

Tillatoba (*GDM* 341): a tiny town in Yalobusha Co., Miss., 35 m. SW of Oxford.

timber (*Abs.* 53): any wooden obstacle or jump, like a gate, fence, or stile.

time and time (*AILD* 20): time and time again.

tires (of wagon) (*Sart.* 316; *Reiv.* 11; *CS:BB* 19). See WAGON.

tire tool (*Town* 67; *Reiv.* 65): a type of pry-tool used (in pairs) to remove the tire-casings and replace them on early cars. Since there were no demountable rims or wheels, when a tire went flat the casing and tube had to be removed, repaired, and replaced on the spot.

to: frequently used for *at*, e.g. "down to the bridge" (*AILD* 29), "like he was to a circus" (*AILD* 118), "down to the house" (*S&F* 10).

to'a'ds (*Sart.* 21, 22): towards.

tobacco-sack (*S&F* 242; *Ham.* 344; *Dust* 246). Smoking-tobacco is regularly sold in pocket-sized cloth sacks with draw-strings. The empty sack is a handy container for coins or any other small articles.

tobaccostained . . . beard (*LiA* 348; *Unv.* 60): from chewing and spitting tobacco. Cf. the columns of the courthouse, "stained with generations of casual tobacco" (*LiA* 393) and the stove, "stained with fading tobacco" (*WP* 69–70).

toddy (*Sart.* 37): a drink made of water, lemon (optional), sugar, and bourbon whiskey. It can be hot or cold. The McCallums, living far from town, did not use lemons (*Sart.* 313), nor did Ratliff (*Mans.* 231), but Gavin Stevens did (*Mans.* 372). The question of the proper way to make a cold toddy is crucial in *KG:Error* 127.

toddy-time (*Sart.* 29): late afternoon, the time to have a TODDY. Cf. modern *cocktail-hour*.

to'ds (*Sart.* 30; *CS:BH* 74): towards. This is one syllable, whereas Will Fall's *to'a'ds* (*Sart.* 21) is two syllables.

told. 1. (*S&F* 22, 352): to tell. **2.** (*Fable* 180): have told.

tole (*Unv.* 23; *GDM* 150): tell.

to let's move/get away (*Sanc.* 158; *LiA* 357): not "to let us (permit us to) move away." In each case, the wife was telling her husband "Let's get away," and in the narrative she makes an infinitive of the whole expression.

toll (*Sart.* 299): to lead (an animal) by holding food in front of him. In *CS: MGM* 684 and *Miss.* 31, the sense is extended to become "to lure, decoy."

Tombigbee (*Miss.* 18): a river in northeastern Mississippi that ultimately empties into Mobile Bay.

tomcat (*GDM* 61; *Town* 23, 26; *Reiv.* 13): to prowl around at night in sexual pursuit of women.

tongue (of wagon) (*Sart.* 112; *Ham.* 38, 298): the pole projecting from the front of a two-horse wagon, to which the animals are attached, one on each side. A drop-tongue swivels vertically where it is attached to the wagon, and hence the front end rests on the ground when it is not attached. A slip-tongue is rigidly fastened and cannot drop. The wagon of *Unv.* 67, with its team stolen and "the wagon tongue sticking straight out ahead," obviously had a slip-tongue. Anyone who takes good care of a vehicle with a drop-tongue will prop the tongue up to keep it off the ground when the wagon is standing idle for any length of time (*Ham.* 53).

tongue (*GDM* 14): to give tongue, to bay.

tongue-and-groove box (*WP* 3). The hall was not plastered or panelled or papered, but the whole thing—floors, walls, ceiling—was simply made of tongue-and-groove lumber.

top. *v.t.* (*Mans.* 14): a bull tops a cow when he mounts her, breeds with her.

torch (*Abs.* 370): flashlight (one of Faulkner's Briticisms).

tote (*Sart.* 22, 334; *AILD* 69; *Abs.* 151): to carry.

tother (*AILD* 224; *CS:MV* 773): the other. "Right tother of the brush" is impossible and is evidently a misprint by omission. The first published version of the story (*Saturday Evening Post*, no. 205, Dec. 3, 1932, p. 45) differs slightly; it has a pleonastic *the*, but does contain the needed and missing word *side*: "It's on the tother side of the bushes."

touch (a horse) (*Race* 184, 187): to touch him with the spur, to spur him slightly.

tourist camp (*LiA* 471; *CS:UncW* 241): a place provided by a municipality, in the early days of car-travel, where travelers could camp. A section of a city park was often set aside for this purpose. Other tourist camps were private and charged a fee.

towhead (*RfaN* 104): a sandbar or low island in a river, with at least a fringe of trees.

towing cleat (*WP* 273): a cleat on the stern of a boat to which the rope of an object to be towed is fastened. The skiff's painter was fastened to this cleat, and then the loose end, "after it had passed the towing cleat," was given to the convict. Thus he was holding onto and bringing back the skiff only symbolically.

town and swamp and farm (*Fable* 162): these words are all *adjs.* modifying the preceding *people*, so that the meaning is "townspeople, SWAMP RATS, and farmers."

town-marshall (*GDM* 316; *Town* 23). See MARSHAL.

town nigger (*Sart.* 87, 234). As a retainer of the landed gentry living on their hereditary estate, Simon regards the town Negro as the ultimate in worthlessness.

Trace (*RfaN* 6): NATCHEZ TRACE.

trace chains (*GDM* 11, 78; *Reiv.* 84): chains used as TRACES. When Tull "taken the mule out and looped up the trace chains" (*AILD* 117), he unhitched the mule and hung the unattached back ends of the trace chains over the HAMES on the mule's back, so that the chains would not be dragging underfoot.

trace gall (*Unv.* 138, 163; *Sart.* 278; *Ham.* 130): a sore place or callus on the flanks of a horse or mule, made by the TRACES. Trace galls come from hard work like plowing, and they are much more likely to be caused by TRACE CHAINS than by leather traces. When trace chains are used, they should be passed through a trace pipe (a leather tube about 30″ long) to protect the animal's flanks, but this precaution is ignored more often than it is followed. These facts explain why the pampered pedigreed horses on the Harriss place would have been so horrified by trace galls (*KG:KG* 154–55).

traces (*Unv.* 118; *GDM* 244): the chains or leather straps that connect a horse or mule to the vehicle or implement he is pulling. They are connected to the HAMES or the breast-strap at the front, and run along the animal's sides. Straps are normally used for carriages, and TRACE-CHAINS for plows and similar implements. Either may be used for wagons. Since the Yankees "unfastened the traces and cut the harness off the mules" (*Unv.* 66), this wagon must have had trace-chains, which could not be cut with pocket knives. In the simile of *Unv.* 136, to have someone "in the traces" means to be trying to get work out of him.

trade days (*Dust* 235; *Reiv.* 14, 17): special days (usually once a month) set aside for auctioning and trading in livestock. The Lafayette County Live Stock and Trade Day Association was organized in 1912. Some north-Mississippi communities to this day have signs on the highways saying "Trade Days: second Saturdays" (of the month) or something similar.

train conductor (*SP* 15). See CONDUCTOR.

traipse (*CS:TWBF* 274; *CS:Queen* 730): to gad about. When one woman accuses another of traipsing around, it always means going around giddily, brazenly, wantonly, and up to no good.

trammer (*WP* 188). See ORE-TRAMMER.

transformation (*Dust* 60): woman's wig.

transparent film (*Unv.* 266): the nictitating membrane, a transparent sort of extra eyelid found, for example, in all the cats. Col. Sartoris's acquisition of it is, of course, metaphorical.

trap (*Abs.* 108, 111; *Reiv.* 96): a type of light, well-sprung, two-wheeled carriage.

trap (*Sanc.* 45, 98): an opening at the top of a wall-mounted ladder by which one enters the loft of a BARN. It is not a trap-door, in that there is no way of closing it.

trap-line (*GDM* 222, 248): a series of traps set along a fixed route, which the trapper follows periodically to check on them.

trash (*Sart.* 5, 367; *S&F* 362; *Town* 245): low-class people, specifically, low-class whites. The antonym is QUALITY.

traveling in a circle (*Abs.* 245). This general tendency of a person lost or traveling without any specific bearings is much stronger in thick undergrowth at night. While hunting bullfrogs in the Tallahatchie bottom at night, I once quite inadvertently returned to my starting point to find that I had made a circle less than a hundred yards in diameter.

tree. 1. *v.t. (Sart.* 282; *LiA* 234): to chase up a tree or to a similar refuge. **2.** *v.i. (GDM* 5, 8): to take to a tree or similar refuge in order to escape pursuit. **3.** *n. (GDM* 30): the act of treeing (sense 1).

tree frogs *(S&F* 192; *SP* 99; *KG:Error* 129): frogs of the genus *Hyla* (several species), which live in bushes or trees. They have "suction disks" on their toes to aid in climbing, and are much more vocal in wet weather than in dry. The notion that they are venomous *(SP* 234) is pure superstition.

trees *(Unv.* 126): the wood-and-iron members at right angles to the line of march to which TRACES are fastened, and which are themselves fastened to the wagon or implement that is to be pulled. A "set of trees" would be the two WHIFFLETREES and one doubletree which a SPAN of mules requires.

trigger-set *(Ham.* 243; *Town* 132): set as on a (HAIR) TRIGGER, ready to go off at a touch. The corn was dry and ready to rustle at a touch. Similarly, the covey of quail was alert and ready to fly at the slightest alarm.

Trigg foxhound *(Dust* 159): a strain of American foxhound developed by Col. Haiden Trigg in Kentucky, about the time of the Civil War.

tripled mules *(KG:KG* 239): mules hitched three-abreast.

trolley *(Reiv.* 95): the electric contact of a streetcar. It is a pole held against the overhead electric cable by a spring, and ending in a grooved wheel that runs on the cable. There is a trolley at each end of the car, and it always slants backward; thus, when a car is reversed at the end of the line, the trolleys have to be changed.

tromp *(Sart.* 65; *Sanc.* 45; *Ham.* 16): to tramp, trample.

trotline *(Mans.* 323; *Mosq.* 279; *KG:Hand* 65, 78): a heavy cord or light rope to which fish-hooks on short lines are attached at intervals. A trotline is often strung across a small river or arm of a lake, and checked ("run") once or twice a day. See *KG:Hand* 64 and passim for detailed descriptions.

truck. 1. *(S&F* 68): junk, rubbish. **2.** *(Mans.* 81): dealings, relationship. **3.** *(WP* 69, 245): the wheel-axle-and-spring assembly under each end of a railroad car. **4.** *(Flags* 343): the four-wheeled, flat-bedded, long-handled cart, the height of the floor of an express-car, on which express is taken to and from trains.

trumpet vine *(Miss.* 28): trumpet creeper *(Bignonia radicans)*, a creeping and climbing vine that forms dense tangles in thickets and climbs even high trees. It has showy trumpet-shaped reddish-orange flowers, about 3″ long, blooming throughout most of the summer and well into the fall.

trustle *(Fable* 157): trestle.

try oneself *(S&F* 70, 80, 320): to be offensive or insubordinate, seeing how far one can go and get by with it.

Tulane *(Sanc.* 14): Tulane University, in New Orleans.

tumbler of snuff *(Dust* 22). Snuff is normally sold in tin boxes or wide-mouthed bottles. The snuff in a tumbler was probably a special gift-item, like some of the present-day decanter-bottles of whiskey.

turban (*S&F* 330; *Sart.* 26, 371; *GDM* 379): HEADCLOTH.

turkey (*GDM* 196, 204; *Mans.* 283): the wild turkey (*Meleagris gallopavo*), a bird very similar to the domestic turkey but smaller and more slender. (The domestic breed is based primarily on a Mexican subspecies.) Turkeys are fairly weak fliers and prefer to run, but they roost in groups in trees. Hunters ambush them at these roosts before dawn. The bare red skin on the neck of the gobbler (male) gets even redder when he is angry—or such, at least, is the common belief (*Town* 131). Ratliff's "turkey's neck" (*Ham.* 160) presumably refers to its being sunburned to a similar shade of red—the characteristic that has given rise to the use of REDNECK as a derogatory term for Southern rural whites.

turkey-buzzard (*AILD* 26). See BUZZARD.

turkey-roost (*GDM* 171). See TURKEY.

turkle (*Sart.* 64): turtle.

turn (*Ham.* 114): to plow. Cf. "turned earth" (*LiA* 137), for freshly plowed earth. A plowshare is so constructed that it does not merely stir up the earth but actually cuts a strip of earth loose and turns it over.

turnip greens (*Ham.* 61): the tender young leaves of turnips, boiled and seasoned in various ways.

turn-row (*Town* 126; *Mans.* 20, 21; *Reiv.* 223): an unplanted strip at the ends of a field to make room for turning plows and cultivators around.

turn the dogs loose (*CS:SftL* 28): to release them so that they can attack an intruder.

turpentine (*CS:Hair* 144): an all-purpose folk-remedy among rural people.

Tutwiler (*Mans.* 377): a town and road junction point 6 m. N of PARCHMAN.

tweaky (*Mosq.* 64, 220). This should be British slang, but I have been unable to find it attested anywhere. The meaning is obviously "commercially cute, in a tawdry sort of way."

'twell (*Sart.* 62, 287; *S&F* 338; *Unv.* 229): till, until.

Twenty-three (*Reiv.* 43): train NUMBER TWENTY-THREE.

twenty-three skiddoo (*Town* 56; *Reiv.* 140, 141): a popular slang catchphrase of the early twentieth century. It originally meant "get out" or "go away" but soon ceased to mean anything at all.

twenty-two calibre rogue (*Town* 347): petty rogue—as a .22-calibre rifle is a small-bore, light gun.

twister (*Ham.* 248): a device (adequately described by Faulkner) used to control a dangerous or unruly horse, much as a nose-ring is used to control a bull. The loop of rope is slipped over the horse's nostrils, and the stick is twisted to tighten it and cut off his breath.

twisting stockings at the knees (*SP* 133): The tops of the stockings are rolled in a tight roll to just below the knees. Then the slack of the roll is pulled sidewise, twisted tight, and tucked into the top of the stockings.

two and seventy-five percent (*SP* 199). The Lever Act outlawed malt liquors containing more than 2.75% alcohol by weight, beginning Jan. 1, 1918. This was the legal limit until the Volstead Act cut it to 0.5% by volume, beginning Oct. 28, 1919.

two bits (*S&F* 288; *Ham.* 267; *GDM* 79): twenty-five cents.

two-sing games (*Ham.* 127): obviously the party games in which couples pair off, to an accompanying song, and usually with kissing. But I have never heard the phrase itself, and the authorities on play-party games do not know it.

two State Colleges (*Ham.* 111): the University of Mississippi at Oxford and the Agricultural and Mechanical College (now Mississippi State University) at Starkville.

two-time (*AILD* 232): to be unfaithful to in love.

Ty Juana (*CS:Fox* 595): Tijuana.

U

U.D.C. (*RfaN* 240): United Daughters of the Confederacy.

umbrella (*LiA* 138, 333; *Abs.* 88): parasol.

umbrella stand (*Town* 190): a stand some 2' high and 8"–9" square or in diameter, for holding umbrellas, particularly wet ones. The sides might be either solid metal or open metal-work, but the bottom was always a pan that would catch and hold water running down the folded umbrellas. An unbrella stand by the front door was standard equipment in most homes and offices.

umptieth (*SP* 7): an indefinite ordinal number.

umpty-nine (*Mans.* 354): an indefinite number. *Umpty* is based on *twenty*, *thirty*, etc., in the same sort of formation as the more familiar *umpteen*.

umumuh (*Sart.* 64). Faulkner seems to be awkwardly trying to represent a type of grunt signifying admiration and astonishment. It can be described as the sound made in humming a tune, divided into two syllables, with a heavy stress and a sharp rise in pitch on the second syllable.

unbitted (*Ham.* 205; *Mans.* 117, 119): not yet beginning to be subject to discipline. The first real step in breaking a horse to the saddle is to get the bit into his mouth, since it is the bit which gives the rider some measure of control. The unbitted horse is not only undisciplined; he is not even potentially disciplined. Cf. BITTED (*Ham.* 214).

unbobbed hair (*CS:Fox* 591): natural, long hair. When it became a craze for women to bob their hair, long hair became for a while a peculiarity to be commented on.

Unc' (*Sart.* 283; *Unv.* 83; *GDM* 150): UNCLE.

unchinked wall (*Abs.* 286). See LOG HOUSE. It is typical of Wash's neglect that the mud between the logs of his cabin has not been replaced as necessary. It is so completely gone that the sun shines through the openings.

Uncle (*Sart.* 270, 283): a title of respect applied (with the given name) by both white and black to an elderly Negro man or, less commonly, to an elderly white one (*Ham.* 77, 340; *GDM* 3; title, "Uncle Willy," *CS* 225–47). See especially *Reiv.* 30.

Uncle Bud (*Sanc.* 243, 244, 245). This boy is clearly nicknamed from a floating folk-song popular in the 1920s. It consisted of an indefinite number of loose tetrameter couplets, with *Uncle Bud* tacked onto the end of each. The tone was generally one of cheerful indecency. Two typical stanzas are:

> Uncle Bud he moved across the water
> To keep the boys from screwing his daughter,
>   Uncle Bud.

> Corn in the crib what ain't been shucked
> And a gal in the house what ain't been fucked,
>   Uncle Bud.

uncooked biscuit (*Ham.* 261): a circle of creamy white dough.

uncooked dough (*Ham.* 22, 255). A pan of uncooked dough presents a slightly rounded and utterly undifferentiated surface.

under leather (*S&F* 138): when saddled. The fine pedigreed horse was, in practice (and changing the metaphor from horses to dogs) a mere cur.

Union depot (*Reiv.* 139): one of Memphis's two railroad stations, located between Second and Third streets. Trains for Grand Junction (PARSHAM) leave from it.

unionsuit (*Dust* 11, 147): a suit of one-piece underwear. One worn for hunting in cold weather would be "long underwear" and would be close-fitting, covering everything from wrists to ankles.

University Grays (*Abs.* 341, 382, 383): a Confederate company organized "at the University [of Mississippi] among the student body" (*Abs.* 119). This company served throughout the Civil War, and suffered 100 percent casualties at GETTYSBURG (see Maud Morrow Brown, *The University Greys* [Richmond, Va., 1940]). It was Company A, Eleventh Mississippi. Faulkner makes no attempt to use the actual military history of this company, which was a part of the Army of Northern Virginia and was in Virginia when the Battle of SHILOH was fought in the northeastern corner of Mississippi on April 7–8, 1862. It was in this battle that Henry was wounded.

University of Mississippi. Chartered by the state legislature in 1844, it began its first session in the fall of 1848, only sixteen years after the Chickasaw lands had been ceded to the United States. Hence it was, when Henry Sutpen went there in 1859, "a small new college in the Mississippi hinterland and even wilderness" (*Abs.* 74), and was (approximately) "a small college only ten years old" (*Abs.* 311). It is "near Oxford" (*Abs.* 313) because it is not actually in the town but is separated from it by the railroad.

Unk (*Town* 65): UNCLE.

Unker (*CS:UncW* 244): UNCLE.

unmuffled engine (*Sart.* 118–119). See CUT-OUT.

unshod mule (*GDM* 83). There is very little stone in Faulkner's country, and mules not intended to work on paved or graveled roads are not usually shod. It is partly because the mule is not shod that she is led along the soft shoulder of the road rather than on its graveled center.

unskeerableness (*Mans.* 125): unscarableness, ability to resist being scared.

untack (*Reiv.* 185): to remove the TACK from a horse.

unto (*GDM* 49, 62): until.

up (*CS: Court.* 380): mounted, on horseback.

up and (*Sanc.* 46). See TAKE AND.

uppity (*Sart.* 233; *GDM* 128; *Mans.* 35, 405): impertinent, disrespectful, not keeping one's place. The word is usually applied by lower-class whites to a Negro who does not "keep his place."

up pon topper (*CS:BH* 78): up on top of.

upwind (*GDM* 179, 207): into the wind. A hunted or wary animal tries to move upwind so as to smell hunters or predators and keep them from smelling him. Though the word is not used there, when Mink tests the wind before approaching the hound (*Ham.* 229), he does so in order to approach it upwind.

urped (*WP* 83): euphemism for *vomited*.

'us (*Sart.* 22): was.

use (*KG:Smoke* 25): to make a habit of (cf. "I used to . . . "). In reply to the question "Do you smoke?" "I never used it" does not mean "I never used tobacco," but "I never made a habit of it; I never got into the habit."

use, *v.i.* (*AILD* 173; *Sanc.* 66): to reside, live.

usquebaugh (*Town* 317): the Gaelic word from which *whiskey* is derived. I have never heard the word in Lafayette Co. except in a learned, jocular use, but possibly Faulkner did, as Gavin Stevens says that *he* has.

V

vagrance (*RfaN* 266): vagrancy.

Valley (*GDM* 288; *CS: TM* 54): the Shenandoah Valley, in Virginia. The first use of the word refers to Stonewall JACKSON's campaign there in 1862; the second refers to the valley itself, geographically. Sheridan's cavalry (strongly supported by infantry) blocked Lee's escape route from Appomattox to Lynchburg, which would have given him access to the valley, and thus forced the surrender of Lee's army on April 9, 1865.

valley . . . where the corners of Georgia and Tennessee and Carolina meet (*Fable* 189). There is no such place. The corners of Tennessee and North Carolina meet almost in the center of Georgia's northern boundary.

vamp (*Mosq.* 273): to get (a man) under one's power by a deliberate use of female charms and wiles.

Van Dorn. 1. (*Sart.* 223, 226; *Unv.* 17): Confederate Gen. Earl Van Dorn rode
to parade once with the wife of a Dr. Peter, who later shot him and escaped
behind the Federal lines. Van Dorn led the cavalry raid on HOLLY SPRINGS
which captured and destroyed the vast Federal stores there, as Faulkner
indicates in *Sart.* 226. This is the raid in which Hightower's grandfather
was killed, and which Faulkner transfers, for the purposes of *LiA*, to Jefferson. Both the raid on Holly Springs and the cause of Van Dorn's death are
alluded to in *Abs.* 346. **2.** (*Race* 187): a fictional settlement or village, obviously named for (1).

Vardaman (*Town* 37; *Sart.* 67; *Miss.* 13): James K. Vardaman, governor of
Mississippi (1904–08) and U.S. Senator (1913–19), a shrewd and ruthless
politician of the same type as BILBO and Huey LONG. It is significant that the
Gowrie twins in *Dust* are named Vardaman and Bilbo.

varmint (*GDM* 253; *Town* 112): originally vermin, then vermin in the sense
of unwanted or injurious animals (predators, to stockmen, for example),
and finally mild jocular derogation when applied to a person (*Abs.* 276).
The word can also mean simply a wild animal (*CS:BH* 69, 74).

Varner's Store (*LiA* 11, 24): the country store at Frenchman's Bend. In *LiA*
it is 12 m. from Jefferson; in other works, it is 20 or 22 m. See Appendix.

vatted (*Sanc.* 162): contained or stored, as in a vat.

verbena: a genus of perennial herbs, often grown in beds for solid masses of
flowers of various colors. Faulkner's classification of verbenas as shrubbery
(*Sart.* 26) is probably carelessness. There are some shrubby species, but
they grow wild and are not garden plants—and the "present owner" in
question is obviously making a perfectly conventional garden. In "An Odor
of Verbena" (*Unv.* 243–93), verbena is the garden flower, and its rich fragrance is the significant characteristic.

vestibule (of a train) (*Sart.* 163; *Sanc.* 36; *LiA* 420): the porch at the end of a
passenger car, with a folding-up platform over the steps by which passengers
enter and leave the train.

Vicksburg (*Unv.* 3; *GDM* 272; *WP* 76): a Mississippi city on the Mississippi
River. It fell to the Union forces after a long siege which involved the near-
starvation of the inhabitants. This is why Old Man Falls says that the horses
were so sorry that he doubts if they would have been eaten even in Vicksburg
(*Sart.* 224). The small steamboat brought freight to WYOTT'S CROSSING
"up from Vicksburg" (*Reiv.* 73) because it would have to leave the Mississippi
just above Vicksburg and come up the Yazoo and Tallahatchie. Presumably
it would load for its trips at Vicksburg. The fact that Vicksburg is on a bluff
high above the river explains how the convict could pass it without knowing
because "he wasn't looking high enough above the water" (*WP* 157–58.)

victrola (*Sanc.* 194; *Town* 215; *Mosq.* 93): gramophone, record-player. This
was originally a brand-name, but soon generalized into a common noun.
Early hand-wound ones had no mechanism for automatically stopping the
turntable when a record was finished; hence the needle continued to slide

in the final circular groove until either someone stopped the machine or the spring ran down completely (*Mosq.* 95).

vieux carré (*WP* 43; *Mosq.* 10): the old French city in New Orleans.

Virginia, University of (*Sanc.* 24): at Charlottesville. Gowan Stevens is a parody of its self-conscious tradition of drinking like gentlemen.

vittles (*Sart.* 294, 331; *Abs.* 135; *Ham.* 313): victuals, food.

voce (*GDM* 119, 128): divorce.

V of Big River and hills (*Miss.* 24): the **V**-shape formed by the Mississippi, flowing south, and the hills, which have been as much as 60 m. E of it about the middle of the DELTA, coming in from the NE to rejoin it just above Vicksburg and below the confluence of the Yazoo and the Mississippi.

voodoo (*Abs.* 252; *CS: TES* 307). The same charm—a pig-bone with a bit of flesh still on it—is cited in both passages, the first being more elaborate, with chicken feathers, pebbles, etc. These charms are widespread, but they are by no means ritually fixed and are subject to a good deal of improvisation.

vote-rousing picnics (*Ham.* 128): political rallies, with candidates making speeches and "dinner on the grounds" from baskets brought by those attending. These, like ALL-DAY SINGINGS, bring out the competitive and exhibitionistic tendencies of housewives and usually produce quantities of elaborately prepared food. These gatherings are a standard rural pastime in the summer after the crops are laid by. It was at such a political picnic that the dog-thicket episode (*Mans.* 314 ff.) occurred.

Vymy Ridge (*Mans.* 76): the scene of violent fighting in World War I.

W

wadding (*CS: Court.* 374): the material used in a muzzle-loader to make a bullet fit tightly and keep the bullet and powder from being lost. Sometimes it was a bit of cloth wrapped around the bullet; sometimes it was cloth, paper—at a pinch, moss, etc.—rammed down on top of it.

Wade Hampton (*Reiv.* 285): Confederate cavalry leader and general who played a large part in the battles of Mechanicsville (June 26, 1862) and of Gaines's Mill on the following day. Late in the afternoon of Gaines's Mill, an all-out Confederate assault broke through the center of the Union forces of Fitz-John Porter, forcing them to withdraw across the Chickahominy River.

waes hail (*Sanc.* 141): Middle English *wæs hæl*, "be in good health"; hence, a toast. *Wassail* is derived from this phrase.

wagon. In spite of superficial variations, farm wagons are basically much alike. The usual one is the two-mule wagon, with a TONGUE that extends forward between the mules and is attached to the pivoted front axle for steering. The running gear consists of the tongue and wheels and the framework that holds them together. The wheels have wooden spokes joined to a projecting metal-bound hub at the center and to a wooden rim. Outside this rim there is a flat iron tire (*Sart.* 316). A loose tire is fixed by driving into a creek or pond so that the wood of the rim swells inside the tire (*Reiv.* 11; *CS:BB* 19). The axle is mounted in a heavy steel-bound wooden beam called an axle-tree (*Sart.* 205, 312; *Ham.* 286). Though proper brakes are made for wagons, many a farm wagon has none. A pole is tied in such a way that, by pulling on a rope, the driver or someone else can press it against the tire of the OFF rear wheel (*Ham.* 35). On a very steep hill a wheel can be locked by wedging a pole through the spokes and over the axle-tree; then the locked wheel will leave an iron-colored mark on the road as it slides (*Sart.* 206). On the running gear is mounted the wagon bed, or wagon box. Strictly speaking, the bed is merely a platform, and the box is this platform with vertical sides attached to it, but the box is often loosely called the bed, or wagon bed (*Sart.* 137, 206; *AILD* 172; *Unv.* 117). There are normally no springs in the running gear or between it and the bed. The seat, however, is as wide as the wagon box and is mounted on springs on the edges of the box (*AILD* 244; *LiA* 10).

wagon gear (*CS: BB* 17): the gear used to harness a mule to a wagon, as opposed to the plow gear mentioned two pages earlier.

wagon hood (*Abs.* 35): the arched covering of a covered wagon.

wagon spoke (*Ham.* 138; *Mans.* 122, 123): the spoke of a wagon-wheel. This is a formidable weapon, being a heavy piece of seasoned wood (probably HICKORY) up to 2′ long, easy to grip at the rim-end and heavier at the hub-end.

wagon stake (*Sart.* 206; *Unv.* 100; *Ham.* 274, 291): a stake driven vertically into a metal bow (stake iron) mounted on the side of a wagon bed or box, or both. Stakes are used on the bed alone, without the box, for hauling logs, lumber, etc. They are used with the box to extend the box upward for hauling cotton, etc. I know of no standard reason for anyone to "knot a green cornstalk around a wagon stake" (*Unv.* 100), but it might be done if the stake was loose, to keep it from rattling or from bouncing out of the stake iron.

waiter (*LiA* 451): a large serving-tray.

wait on (*Reiv.* 231; *Mosq.* 60): wait for.

Wales, Sells (*Miss*, 22 ff.): an at least partly fictional character. Blotner (p. 1455) says that Faulkner "took the millionaire sportsman PAUL RAINEY and turned him into Sells Wells [*sic*]."

Walker hound (*Ham.* 62; *GDM* 10): a breed of foxhound developed by crossing British and American strains. It is named for its developer, John W. Walker.

walking-beam (*Abs.* 36): a horizontal beam that transmits animal-power to a machine. One end is fastened to a vertical shaft, and the mule, fastened to the other end, walks in a circle about the machine, turning the shaft as he goes. The sorghum mill described in *Sart.* 277–80 has a walking-beam.

walking up every hill (*Ham.* 33). It is common practice for a wagon-driver to walk up steep hills, especially if the wagon is heavily loaded, in order to ease the burden on his team. Ratliff has himself and Ab walking up even the gentlest slope as a humorous exaggeration of the decrepitude of the team.

Wall (*Town* 127, 144): a convenient fiction rather than a historical allusion. There was no General Wall in the Confederate army. There were two Confederate colonels of this name, but neither was from Mississippi.

wall-eyed (*Ham.* 287): having eyes showing an abnormal amount of white.

wall-ring (*Dust* 91). See TIE-ROPE.

warmer (*S&F* 346): one or two compartments in a kitchen range in which food can be kept reasonably hot without being overcooked. The range has a solid back, and the warmer projects forward from this, about a yard above the top of the stove. The flue runs through it.

Warwick (*GDM* 5, 9, 306). Miss Sophonsiba, on what was still a pretty raw and crude frontier, is imitating the British gentry to some extent, but even more the established, splendid plantations around NATCHEZ, where such plantation names are common.

washboard (*Ham.* 288): a board with a ridged metal surface on which clothes are rubbed when being washed. It is largely known today as a percussion instrument in washboard bands.

Washington, Miss. (alluded to but not named, *CS:Lo* 398): a small town 6 m. NE of Natchez. It served as Mississippi's second territorial capital and first state capital, 1802–20.

wash pot (*Ham.* 13, 147, 286; *CS:BB* 13): wash boiler, a hemispherical iron pot (shaped like a kettledrum) for outdoor use. It has very short feet (only an inch or so) which serve as stable points on the curved belly and are placed on bricks or stones to raise the pot far enough off the ground so that a fire can be built under it. These pots are used not only for washing but for various other purposes, especially for scalding the carcasses when hogs are killed.

wash-stand (*Sart.* 108; *Sanc.* 151; *LiA* 112): a table in a bedroom, used for washing, shaving, etc., in a house without plumbing. It normally has a basin, often let into a recess in the top but always removable for emptying, and a container of clean water standing on it. Water is poured into the basin, used for washing, and then emptied into a SLOP JAR standing on the floor. The slop jar may double as a chamber pot, or there may be two separate utensils. Mrs. Varner had a washstand with elaborate, flowered, matching accessories (*Ham.* 361–62).

water barrel (*CS:SftL* 39). Barrels of water are frequently kept near a barn, church, or railroad trestle, for use in case of fire. When they are by a building, the gutters usually empty into them and keep them filled. Tow sacks dipped in these barrels and laid on the roof of the crib (*Ham.* 17) would keep its roof from being ignited by sparks from the burning barn.

waterbugs (*Dust* 188; *Mans.* 147). The name is applied to several different families both of beetles and of true bugs. Assuming that he distinguishes them, Faulkner probably intends whirligig beetles (*Gyrinidae*), which are particularly gregarious and attract attention because of their wild gyrations.

water gap (*S&F* 186): a form of fence across a small or intermittent stream. A post is placed on each side, at the edge of the banks. A pole is extended from the top of one post to the top of the other, and a panel of fence is suspended from this pole. It hangs nearly to the ground or to the normal surface of the water, including the plank which is fastened to its lower edge. The plank keeps the fence hanging in place normally, and reacts to water pressure when the stream floods by swinging the fence downstream and upward to let the water under it.

water haul (*KG: Tomo.* 97): any effort or attempt that accomplishes nothing (from fishing, when one makes a haul of the net and catches only water).

water-jointed (*AILD* 235). I have never heard this term and am unable to find any definition of it. Joseph B. Cobb, in his *Mississippi Scenes; or Sketches of Southern and Western Life and Adventure*, 2d ed. (Philadelphia, 1851), pp. 194–95, refers to "a tall, gangling, long-limbed, water-jointed figure of a man," and all further references to this character emphasize his extreme thinness.

water-mark on the bridge piling (*AILD* 80). When in flood, the rivers of north Mississippi are very muddy with red clay, and when the water subsides this mud clearly marks trees, etc., showing how high the water was. Such marks may be visible on trees for several years. On bridge-pilings, which are protected from rain by the bridge itself, they remain almost permanently as a record of the highest the water has been for many years.

watermilyuns (*S&F* 236): watermelons.

water moccasin (*GDM* 15; *Mans.* 373; *Miss.* 11): COTTON-MOUTH (MOCCASIN). See also MOCCASIN.

water oak (*Sanc.* 157; *CS: TES* 289): an oak (*Quercus nigra*) growing naturally in creek and river bottoms and reaching a height of 75′ and a diameter of 4′. It will grow in uplands and is often planted on streets and squares.

watersnake (*GDM* 205): any of some half a dozen nonpoisonous snakes of the genus *Natrix*. See MOCCASIN.

water-tank (*Fable* 160): a wooden tank standing by a railroad track, with a swiveling spout, used to supply steam locomotives with water for the boilers.

Watson, Tom (*SP* 112): Georgia populist politician (1856–1922) and foe of Negroes, Jews, and Roman Catholics. He served in Congress both as representative and as senator.

ways (*LiA* 9; *Mosq.* 202; *CS: MV* 746): an indefinite distance.

W.C.T.U. (*S&F* 121): Woman's Christian Temperance Union.

wear away (of a ship) (*WP* 150): to turn away from the wind in order to come around on another tack.

wear out (a person) (*S&F* 25, 234): to give a good whipping to.

wearying (*Abs.* 223). None of the standard meanings seems to fit here. Most of them are impossible because they are derogatory, and the context is one of praise. The best guess seems to be "longing" (as in Carrie Jacobs Bond's song, "Just a'wearying for you"), but it is not very convincing.

Weatherford, Texas (*Fable* 157, 159): a town some 20 m. W of Fort Worth.

wedding suit (*Mans.* 296): fancy suit, dress-up suit.

wedge (*CS:SftL* 27, 29, 39): a steel wedge about 8″ long and 3″ thick at the thick end, driven with a MAUL or sledgehammer, and used to split logs. (Wooden wedges are also improvised on the spot and used for this purpose, but they last for only one or two uses. The fact that the wedges were carried to the job shows that they were steel ones.) "Cold out as a wedge" is obviously an intensive comparison, meaning "totally unconscious," but I have not seen or heard the expression elsewhere. Perhaps the idea is that a wedge, being constantly pounded by mauls and sledgehammers, will be knocked out as completely as anything can be—but this is sheer speculation.

weekly bath in the barbershop (*Mans.* 182). Before bathtubs became standard equipment in homes, they were one of the facilities provided by barbershops.

weevil poison (*GDM* 116): poison "dusted" on cotton fields from airplanes to kill BOLL-WEEVILS.

wellhouse (*Unv.* 4; *GDM* 139): a shelter over a well to protect a person using it from the rain and to protect the well-water from surface-drippings. A wellhouse normally has no walls or door but is simply a roof supported on posts. Its rafters provide a place to hang the WELL PULLEY. If a wellhouse has sides, they are likely to be latticed (*Ham.* 220; *Reiv.* 97).

well pulley (*LiA* 142; *Abs.* 83; *Ham.* 19): a pulley 12″–18″ in diameter, with a grooved rim in which the well-rope runs. It is suspended in the top of the WELLHOUSE. Such pulleys usually creak, and it is sometimes considered bad luck to oil one. The better type of well has a section of log about 8″ in diameter, with a crank on it, which serves as a windlass, but many wells do not. If there is no windlass, the bucket is pulled up hand-over-hand on the rope, as Ab Snopes's daughter does it (*Ham.* 19).

wellum (*CS:TS* 92): well, ma'am.

were (*WP* 339): we're.

weskit (*CS:Court.* 364): waistcoat, vest.

West Point (*Miss.* 33): a town in northeastern Mississippi 65 m. SE of Oxford and 20 m. fron the Alabama line.

whadya (*WP* 213, 214): what do you.

whang (*Race* 186, 191, 192): thong.

what-ere (*Town* 8): a nonce-word coined by Gavin Stevens to parallel Ratliff's that-ERE.

Wheeler, Gen. Joseph (*CS:MGM* 673). See EARLY, GEN. JUBAL A.

whelp (*Reiv.* 181): welt, weal.

when the cheese begun to bind (*Mans.* 67): when the situation became critical, when the decisive moment approached.

Which? (*Unv.* 45, 83; *CS:MV* 752): What?

which a way (*Unv.* 184; *Reiv.* 165; *CS:Fox* 591): which way. Cf. *that-away*.

whicker (*CS:MV* 754): to neigh, whinny.

whiffletree: singletree, the horizontal bar to which the TRACES of a horse or mule are fastened. The end of the whiffletree projects to the side farther than the mule or wagon-wheel, and hence could be struck by very delicate steering of a car (*Sart.* 204). When Joby is "holding the mules like they were sitting down on the whiffletree" (*Unv.* 65–66), he is pulling back on the reins and forcing them to a sort of crouching position in which their buttocks almost touch the whiffletrees.

whiles (*S&F* 69): while.

whip (*LiA* 134): a buggy-whip, about 5' long and rigid enough to stand upright when the butt is placed in the WHIP-SOCKET.

whipper-snappin' (*CS:UncW* 233): having the characteristics of a whipper-snapper, insignificant.

whippoorwill (*Sart.* 26; *Sanc.* 196; *Ham.* 29): not the true whippoorwill (*Caprimulgus vociferus*), but the chuck-will's-widow (*C. carolinensis*). It is a nocturnal goatsucker seldom seen, but the cry of which its name is an imitation is constantly heard at dusk in the spring and early summer. As a ground-nesting and ground-perching bird, it is frequently seen on dirt roads at night, where its eyes reflect the car's headlights (*Sart.* 149–50). The "whippoorwills" heard in October in *Unv.* 278, 291 are a mistake. The birds stop calling by midsummer and have already migrated by October.

whipsaw (*S&F* 237): to pull back and forth, manipulate two ways at once.

whip socket (*S&F* 311; *Ham.* 136): a socket somewhat like a candlestick, with a cavity 8"–10" deep, mounted on a wagon or carriage. The butt of the whip is placed in this socket for carrying. It is a handy place to which to attach the reins to keep the horses still during a brief stop for which it isn't worth while to hitch them properly.

whip stock (*Mans.* 31, 38, 118): the handle of a whip. Since it would be standing in the WHIP SOCKET, it would be adequate to hold an obedient and well-trained horse.

whistle-britches (*Reiv.* 163, 168): a standard name for corduroy pants, or someone wearing them, because of the sound made when the legs brush against each other. Though the fact is nowhere stated, we have to assume that Otis was wearing corduroy pants. Tallman, *Dictionary of American Folklore*, defines the term as "an expression used in North Carolina for a small boy proud of his first pair of britches." I have never heard this usage. At the Oxford schools, when a boy appeared in his first long pants (instead of knee breeches), at early adolescence, he was ritually "bumped" at recess. He was laid on his back and picked up by four other boys, one for each arm and leg. Then a volunteer bent over, and the victim was swung hard, three times, butt against butt, into the volunteer. It was not a particularly painful process and was at least as hard on the volunteer as on the victim, but the idea seems to have been a ritual humiliation to keep the new young man from thinking himself too smart. With this ritual in practice, if there had been a term in use for a boy proud of his first pair of long pants, I am sure that I would have known it.

white folks (*Sart.* 132, 342; *Sanc.* 35; *LiA* 109): a form of address, either singular or plural, used by Negroes to whites.

white folks and Methodists (*CS:SftL* 42). As a Baptist, Whitfield is contemptuous of Methodists and excludes them from the category of white folks.

white gravy (*Mans.* 65): FLOUR GRAVY.

white hill whiskey (*Ham.* 133): colorless MOONSHINE whiskey, "white lightning." See CHARTERED WHISKEY.

white kitchen (*Fable* 182): the kitchen of a white person.

Whiteleaf (*Ham.* 64, 322; *Town* 167): Faulkner's name for Yellowleaf, a creek, church, and community some 4–5 m. from Oxford on the road to Frenchman's Bend (State Route 334).

Whiteleaf Bridge (*Ham.* 30, 64): the bridge where the road to Frenchman's Bend (State Route 334) crosses WHITELEAF Creek (Yellowleaf Creek) some 4 m. SE of Oxford.

white man's work (*GDM* 169): there have been traditional racial differentiations in types of jobs. See NEGRO'S JOB.

White mountain whiskey (*Fable* 194): WHITE HILL WHISKEY.

white mule whiskey (*GDM* 60, 156; *Mans.* 64): colorless MOONSHINE whiskey, sugar liquor, "white lightning." *Mule* refers to its powerful kick.

white oak (*Sart.* 205; *AILD* 135): a large oak (*Quercus alba*) growing up to 150' high and 5' in diameter. Its wood is very tough and durable, and hence appropriate for a braking-pole for a wagon or for a cudgel (*KG:KG* 206). It is also split into long strips and used for basketry and chair-backs and seats (*RfaN* 34; *CS:Lo* 382).

white people (*Unv.* 152). A Negro's white people ("white folks" is the commoner expression) are his owners, employers, former employers, etc.—those on whom he depends, and who feel responsible for meeting his needs and helping him out of difficulties. This relationship, now almost entirely gone, was quite similar to that between a Roman patrician and his "clients."

White Steamer (*Mans.* 34; *Reiv.* 28): a steam-propelled car, the principal rival of the STANLEY STEAMER. White built cars from 1901 to 1919. President Taft, the first president to own a car, had a White Steamer.

white trash (*LiA* 363; *Abs.* 181; *Unv.* 55): TRASH.

whitewash (*Sart.* 26). It was, and to some extent still is, a common practice of lower-class whites and Negroes to whitewash the trees in their yards, up to a height of about 5'. The purpose is not clear—it seems to be ornamental. Whitewashing the trees is evidence that the man from Frenchman's Bend did not belong socially in this section of Jefferson.

whitewashed fence that has been rained on (*CS:TWBF* 273). Fences are frequently whitewashed instead of painted (cf. Tom Sawyer). Since whitewash is a water-based mixture, it runs easily until it has thoroughly dried.

Aunt Louisa's face with tear-channels through her powder is like a white-washed fence that has been rained on before it has dried and set.

white whiskey (*Town* 357): MOONSHINE, which is practically colorless—whence the names *white lightning, white mule,* etc.

whoa (*S&F* 11, 174): a command to a horse or mule to stop (pronounced *woe*).

whooy (*Sart.* 283, 285): a shout of encouragement or sheer exuberance. It has two syllables, with a heavy stress and a considerable rise in pitch on the second.

whorehouse (*Fable* 163): used contemptuously for a stud-farm.

whup (*Sart.* 265; *S&F* 356, 398): to whip, beat, defeat. Use of a switch or whip is not necessarily implied: Boon "whupped that Law" (*Reiv.* 255) with his fists.

whut (*S&F* 311, 340; *GDM* 13): what. It can be used as a relative pronoun (*Abs.* 215), and may be entirely redundant (*CS:MV* 747).

wick (*Abs.* 309). See LAMP.

widow's bonnet (*Sanc.* 152): mourning bonnet, a black hat with veil worn as a part of formal mourning. Miss Reba's fidelity is out of style: by 1927, Sears was no longer selling mourning bonnets.

Wilcox (*Dust* 195). See GARNETT.

wildcat (*AILD* 227; *S&F* 228; *GDM* 204): bobcat, bay lynx (*Lynx rufus*), a bay-colored wildcat standing nearly 2′ high at the shoulder and weighing 15–30 lbs. The name *bobcat* comes from the absurdly short tail, only 2″–3″ long and tipped with white. The wildcat is a ferocious fighter when cornered, and hence is a standard comparison for anyone fighting fiercely.

wildcat——(*GDM* 64). When Edmonds is interrupted, he may be about to say either *wildcat liquor* (MOONSHINE) or *wildcat piss.* Cf. *panther piss* as a designation for moonshine.

wild-catted (*Ham.* 236): exploited in an irregular, speculative, unsound way.

Wilderness (*RfaN* 247): an intermittent battle (or concentrated campaign) in Virginia during most of May 1864.

wild grape (*Sanc.* 13): any of several species of *Vitis*, all moderately edible. These are the "sweet small grapes" of *Flags* 249. The most edible species of this genus, the muscadine, is always called by that name and is never called a wild grape.

wild plum (*RfaN* 213: *Mans.* 26): either of two very similar species, the American plum (*Prunus americana*), or the Chickasaw plum (*P. angustifolia*). Both have white flowers that appear before the leaves, and both bear edible red to yellowish fruit. They tend to grow in thickets about 5′–7′ high, which is why Boon stands above the crowd "like a pine sapling out of a plum thicket" (*Reiv.* 238).

Willow Springs, Iowa (*Fable* 157): a fictional town. A large gazetteer lists two places named Willow Spring and nine named Willow Springs, but none of them is in Iowa.

window . . . propped open with a stick (*LiA* 216). Many older farm-houses did not have windows equipped with sash-cords and weights; one simply inserted a stick lengthwise under the raised window to keep it open.

window shade (*Unv.* 141). In the absence of paper, especially in any large sheets, the light side (the inside) of a window shade has been used to draw a map on.

wing-shot (*Mans.* 409): a shooter of birds on the wing.

winter. Winter in north Mississippi is relatively mild but unpleasant. Beginning early in December, there is a great deal of steady rain and drizzle. There are few days when the temperature stays below freezing, but there are many nights when it falls into the upper twenties. Snow is very rare: only once every several years is there any accumulation on the ground. About once each winter the temperature may go as low as 12°F or so. The weather described in *Unv.* 186–87 is typical winter weather. By the old folk-accounting, the seasons went by calendar-months, and winter consisted of all of December, January, and February (*KG:KG* 230). I was brought up on this system, and never heard of counting from the solstices and equinoxes until I was grown.

Winton Flyer (*Reiv.* 28): presumably one of the cars made by Alexander Winton, who built cars from 1896 to 1924. He set up the earliest known franchised dealership (Reading, Pa., 1898) and a Winton claimed the first transcontinental trip by car, leaving San Francisco on May 23, 1903, and arriving in New York on July 26. The Thomas Flyer was a famous make of early car, but I have not found any other reference to a Winton Flyer. The first car to pass through Oxford, awaited and watched with great interest by the Faulkner boys, was a red Winton Six in 1908 (*My Brother Bill*, p. 37).

wished (*CS:Queen* 743): wish.

wisht (*Town* 243): wish.

wistaria (*Sart.* 112; *Sanc.* 134; *Abs.* 31): an ornamental vine (*Wistaria floribunda*) bearing masses of fragrant purple flowers in the spring and velvety seed-pods. (The name is sometimes spelled, and usually pronounced, *wisteria*.) If not restrained, it will run wild over houses and strangle even large trees. Along with CRAPE MYRTLE, it is one of the standard signs of old house-sites. The "thick cables along the veranda eaves" of *Sart.* 351 are wistaria vines. Sometimes a wistaria blooms a second time, much less profusely, in the early fall (*Abs.* 7). The "lilac rain of this wistaria" (*Abs.* 148) refers to the falling of the lilac-colored petals as the blooms finally shatter.

wistaria frame (*S&F* 210): a trellis or arbor for a wistaria vine.

without (*Sanc.* 5; *Ham.* 280; *CS:BH* 63): unless.

withouten (*AILD* 179): unless.

wolf (*GDM* 214; *RfaN* 101; *Reiv.* 20): Southern wolf (*Canis floridanus*), similar to the gray wolf but much darker. It was driven out of Lafayette Co. early, but reappeared briefly in the wild hills in the eastern part of the county in the 1930s.

women bright and dark (*GDM* 138): women of various shades of skin-color, ranging from "high-yellow" to black. Cf. *bright-colored*.

woning (*Unv.* 203): warning.

woodbox (*Sart.* 64, 81; *S&F* 335): a box in the kitchen in which STOVEWOOD is kept.

wooden box (*Reiv.* 135): part of an early wall-telephone. The mouthpiece projected from a wooden box mounted on the wall, and the receiver hung from a hook on the side of this box.

wooden hammock (*Ham.* 133, 140): BARREL-STAVE HAMMOCK.

wooden lid of the cellar stairs (*Town* 234). Mrs. Haight's cellar stairs, entering from outside the house, had a hinged wooden cover over the entrance to keep out the rain and cold.

wooden pin (*Abs.* 39): wooden peg used instead of a nail. A great deal of pioneer building was done with such pins, since nails had to be brought from a distance but pins could be made on the spot. Holes were bored in the timbers, and the round pegs were driven through them, like dowels. A good many covered bridges with this type of construction are still standing.

woodhouse (*CS:TWBF* 276): woodshed.

wood landing (*CS:Red* 318; *WP* 278, 334): a landing where steamboats stopped to take on wood for fuel.

woods colt (*Mans.* 4): bastard.

wood tick (*GDM* 296): any of several ticks that hang on bushes and then attach themselves to animals that brush against them, especially the American dog tick (*Dermacentor variabilis*).

wool (*Sart.* 270, 344): kinky Negro hair.

wop, *n.* and *adj.* (*S&F* 121, 155; *Sanc.* 237; *LiA* 211): Italian (always derogatory).

work (*CS:Hair* 136). To work a town, in salesman's jargon, is to do whatever has to be done there from a business point of view.

worm (*GDM* 37, 77): the spiral, copper condensation-coil of a still.

worm (an animal), *v.t.* (*Ham.* 306): to treat for an infestation of parasitic worms.

would bound to get (*Race* 176): would be bound to get, would certainly get.

wound up the wheel (*Town* 67): jacked up the wheel. This is not standard usage but the description of a boy to whom cars and their vocabulary are not yet really familiar.

W.P.A. (*RfaN* 242; *Mans.* 306; *CS:SftL* 29): Works Progress Administration, a governmental organization during the depression of the 1930s which provided employment on public buildings and various other public works, including some things like historical research.

W P and A (*Mans.* 287): W.P.A. The added *and* was a common phenomenon, probably by analogy with railroad names like the *B. and O.* (Baltimore and Ohio).

wrapper (*AILD* 128; *Ham.* 44, 141; *Town* 233): bathrobe, dressing gown, kimono.
wrassling (*Reiv.* 101): wrestling.
writing (*Mans.* 154). See READING.
wroil (*Abs.* 143): apparently an error for *roil*, in the sense "to move about, eddy, vigorously or turbulently."
wrong side (of a horse) (*Unv.* 72): the right-hand side. A horse is trained to be mounted from the left (near) side and only from that side.
wrop (*Sart.* 21; *CS:TS* 88, 95): wrap. In *CS:TES* 295, the meaning is to wrap an arm around, embrace.
wygelia (*WP* 227): weigela—any of several species of the genus *Weigela*, ornamental shrubs bearing tubular red, pink, or white flowers.
Wylie's Crossing (*Miss.* 18, 25): WYOTT'S CROSSING.
Wyott's Crossing (*Town* 172; *Mans.* 220, 316; *Reiv.* 72): Old Wyatt, 12 m. NNE of Oxford, the original head of navigation on the Tallahatchie River. Before the Civil War it was a thriving town with its own bank—I have seen a banknote drawn on it. The railroad through Oxford doomed it. By the 1930s its main street was a huge gully in the bluff above the river, and the approach road from the Oxford side was impassable before the Sardis Reservoir covered it. It is now better known and more accessible than it was in the 1930s, since it is a boat-landing on the reservoir with signs saying "Wyatt Crossing" leading to it. The bluff on which the old town stood is visible some 200 yards NE of the boat-ramp, and the ramp itself is near the site of the old bridge across the Tallahatchie. The town extended N of the river into the hills, but nothing is left of it but deep gullies—one with a fox den in it—where the streets and roads were. Miss Vaiden Wyott (*Town* 145) is a descendant of the family for whom the town and crossing were named.

X

XYZ's (*CS:UncW* 241): a collective term for alphabetical government agencies.

Y

yaas (*CS:Fox* 605): yes.
yah (*WP* 148, 161, 214): yeah, yes.
yaller gal (*LiA* 215): yellow girl, a very light mulatto woman.
Yalo Busha (*RfaN* 21). I know of no settlement by this name. Yalobusha Co. (from the river of the same name) is just S of Lafayette Co.
Yankee. 1. *n.* (*Sart.* 20, 21; *Abs.* 290): a member of the Union forces during the Civil War. **2.** *adj.* (*Sart.* 11, 14; *Abs.* 344, 351): pertaining to the Union forces during the Civil War. **3.** (*LiA* 81, 323; *CS:MV* 746): a person from the

northern part of the United States—never the European meaning of simply an American.

Yaphank (*SP* 7, 9, 11): a nickname doubtless suggested by *Yip Yip Yaphank*, a musical show put together for an army camp by Sgt. Irving Berlin. It had a New York run in 1919.

yardman (*Mans.* 156, 164): a person hired for general work outside the house —raking leaves, mowing grass, chopping wood, etc. He may also double as chauffeur (*Mans.* 203) and butler (*Mans.* 215).

yawl (*Abs.* 213; *Unv.* 24, 47; *GDM* 322): YOU ALL.

yawls' (*Unv.* 47; *CS:TES* 299, 300): *poss.* of YOU ALL, with misplaced apostrophe. It is correctly placed in *CS:MV* 755.

Yazzo (City) (*GDM* 341; *WP* 153): a moderate-sized town on the YAZOO River, some 125 m. SSW of Oxford.

Yazoo (River) (*GDM* 340; *RfaN* 45; *WP* 153): the river that carries the water of all Faulkner's country to the Mississippi. The ceasing to flow and then reversing once a year (*GDM* 340) happens when the snow melts in the northern part of the drainage basin of the Mississippi River, which then rises rapidly and high, and backs up into the local streams that normally empty into it. This is the "running backward" of *WP* 62, 153. The hunting in "Delta Autumn" (*GDM* 335–65) takes place along the lower Yazoo, probably where the river bottoms of the Yazoo and the Mississippi join. The mouth of the Yazoo is 160 m. SW of Oxford as the crow flies but easily the 200 m. that Faulkner mentions (*GDM* 340)by the roads at that time.

Yazoos (*Miss.* 12): a small, warlike Indian tribe once occupying part of what is now Yazoo Co. They disappeared early in the white man's occupation.

year (*S&F* 72): ear.

y'ear (*Sart.* 11): (Do) you hear?

yearling (*Sart.* 294; *LiA* 469; *Ham.* 90): an animal, or by extension a person, between the first and second birthdays.

yearly settlement (*Ham.* 60). Annual accountings were once standard, with debtors as well as tenants, at the end of the agricultural year, about November. This is the occasion of Capt. Joe Thoms's crooked settlement with his tenants (*Miss.* 37).

yearth (*Ham.* 343): earth.

yellin calf (*LiA* 320; *Race* 181): YEARLING calf.

yellow (*AILD* 118): the color of the muddy water of the flooded river. The rivers of southern Mississippi are "no longer yellow or brown, but black" (*Miss.* 29), because they do not carry silt from the red clay hills and flow too slowly to carry much silt of any color. Their water is stained by various plants so that when one looks through it, it is amber but seen from above it appears to be black. (The rivers of Florida have the same effect.)

yellow and stunted stand of corn (*Ham.* 220): a stand not actually yellow but a sickly yellowish-green instead of the rich dark green of a well-nourished stand of corn.

yellow bills (*Sanc.* 258). See YELLOW ONES.

yellowhammer (*Unv.* 208; *Race* 188): yellow-shafted flicker, golden-winged woodpecker (*Colaptes auratus*), a large woodpecker, nearly a foot long, with a great variety of local names. The underside of the wings is a bright golden color. Flickers have several different calls, all loud, cheerful, and unmistakable.

yellow ones (*S&F* 253): yellowbacks, gold certificates. These bills, issued between 1882 and 1922, were bright yellow on the back (or orange for the $20 denomination). The significance of Jason's remark lies in the fact that the smallest yellowback was a $10 bill; hence the handful of bills represented some real money. "The smug orange gleam of banknotes" showing through the platinum mesh of Temple Drake's handbag (*Sanc.* 218) has the same significance.

yellow-wheeled buggies (*Abs.* 304; *CS:Rose* 124). Sporty buggies and carriages often had the wheels and other running gear painted bright red, yellow, or green.

yere (*Sart.* 270): here.

yessuh (*Sart.* 367): yes, sir.

yessum (*Sart.* 189, 373; *S&F* 6; *GDM* 11): yes, ma'am.

yeuh (*Sanc.* 47, 195): yeah, yes (two syllables).

yez (*Sanc.* 141): you.

Yocona county (*Flags* 86, 87). In *Flags*, Faulkner used the present name of the river S of Oxford as the name of the county having Jefferson as its county seat. (In *Sart.* "the county" was substituted in these two passages.) Later he adopted the old name of the river, Yoknapatawpha.

Yoknapatawpha County (*AILD* 193; *Ham.* 34; *Town* 102): Faulkner's fictional name for Lafayette Co., Miss. It is the old name of the Yocona River.

yo'n (*Sart.* 51, 66, 238): yours.

yon (*LiA* 414): YONDER.

yonder, *adv.*, never *adj.* (*Sanc.* 5, 57–58; *Reiv.* 86; *SP* 93). Standard in all Southern speech as an adverb of place usually implying something more distant and less definite than *there*.

yon's (*Sanc.* 45): YONDER is.

you' (*Sart.* 20): your.

you all. This expression is *always* plural. If it is addressed to a single person, it is understood to include others along with him, according to the context— family, business associates, or some other group. *S&F* 41 provides a clear example, when Dilsey says: "Take [Benjy] down home, T. P. Frony fixing him a bed. You all look after him, now." She is addressing T. P., but clearly means that T. P. and Frony and anyone else who is there are all to look after Benjy. Similarly, in *S&F* 397, *y'all* is addressed to Dilsey but refers to the whole group of women that decorated the church.

you alls' (*S&F* 347): a group-possessive built on YOU ALL. It is miswritten here: the apostrophe should precede the *s*.

you better hadn't (*CS:MV* 752): you had better not.

you can haul out the family sock on it (*Mosq.* 258). Since a sock is a traditional place for hiding the family's savings, this seems to be a fancy variant of "You can bank on it."

your (*SP* 246): you're.

your mama don't vote (*Dust* 108): as a general rule, Negroes did not vote in the South until recently, though there were many individual and local exceptions.

yourn (*S&F* 34; *Ham.* 150): yours.

you's (*WT* 13, 46): you is, you are.

you-uns (*CS:MV* 755, 766, 767): you ones, a distinctive plural form of *you* used by mountaineers of the Southern Appalachians and parallel to the YOU ALL of the South generally and the *yous* of Brooklyn.

yr stars fell (*GDM* 269): the year the stars fell. There was a huge and spectacular meteoric shower over all of eastern North America on Nov. 13, 1833.

yuther (*Unv.* 229; *GDM* 77, 143): other.

Z

'zackly (*Sart.* 232): exactly.

Appendix
Faulkner's Geography and Topography

L'état de lieux que nous dressons ici est d'une rigoureuse exactitude et éveillera certainement un souvenir très précis dans l'esprit des anciens habitants du quartier.

—Victor Hugo, *Les Misérables*

In most criticism of Faulkner it has been taken for granted that his Yoknapatawpha County is really Lafayette (accented on *fay*) County, Mississippi, and that his Jefferson, the county seat, is really Oxford. As early as 1961, this view was questioned by G. T. Buckley, who argued that both the town and the county were put together by combining features of several different towns and counties.[1] Ripley (Tippah County) and New Albany (Union County) were, he said, about as important as Oxford. I replied to this in an article pointing out the exact and detailed use of the streets of Oxford and the roads, creeks, and swamps of Lafayette County in many of Faulkner's works. This appendix is based on that article, with some revisions and additions.[2] The question has recently been reopened by Thomas L. McHaney, who essentially adopts Buckley's view and says that my approach "yields too readily to an absolute resemblance."[3]

The difference of opinion is really not serious. Faulkner was certainly not bound by the local landscape, and he felt free to change it whenever it suited his purposes. He removed the university from his

1. Buckley, "Is Oxford the Original of Jefferson in William Faulkner's Novels?" *PMLA* 76 (1961): 447–54.
2. Brown, "Faulkner's Geography and Topography," reprinted by permission of the Modern Language Association of America, from *PMLA* 77 (1962): 652–59.
3. McHaney, "The Faulkners and the Origin of Yoknapatawpha County: Some Corrections," *Mississippi Quarterly* 25 (1971): 247–64. The quoted phrase is from p. 262, n. 45.

Jefferson. He imported from the Ripley cemetery the statue of his great-grandfather (in the guise of Colonel Sartoris) standing on a high column and looking out over his railroad. The "valley road" from Jefferson to Sartoris fits somewhat better in Ripley than in Oxford, though the distance is twice what it should be. And, as I shall show later, he combined three bridges across the Tallahatchie River into one for the purposes of *The Reivers*. But the vast majority of his local references and descriptions apply to Oxford and its environs—so much so that the features from other places, like the statue and the cemetery, frequently run him into contradictions.

It seems proper to go into this question of the localization of Faulkner's settings in some detail, particularly since a good deal of evidence is already beyond the reach of the literary researcher, and much of the rest is fast disappearing. Both the barbershop at the corner of the square and the old jail have gone since my first treatment of the subject, and early in Faulkner criticism local changes began to contribute to literary misinterpretations.[4]

But first of all we must deal with the somewhat metaphysical question of what we mean when we say that Faulkner's Jefferson "is" Oxford—or, more emphatically, "is really" Oxford. In a literal sense, of course, such a statement is a patent absurdity. Jefferson is a fictitious town inhabited by people of Faulkner's creation, no matter how much raw material local scenes and characters may have supplied to

4. For example, in *The World of William Faulkner* (Durham, N.C., 1952, p. 104), Ward Miner says that the parallels between Oxford and Jefferson "make us more easily comprehend what is wrong at the end of *The Sound and the Fury* when Luster turns the carriage to the left at the Confederate monument on the square. Traffic around the square is one way, and Luster is going against it, since the Oxford traffic pattern would demand that he go right at the monument." But this one-way traffic around the square has been legislated since the writing of *The Sound and the Fury*. Under the old system, one could go either clockwise or counterclockwise, keeping to the right in either case. For all Luster's flightiness, he certainly understood traffic patterns better than Benjy did. The actual point is quite different. The drive to the cemetery is a sort of ritual pastime for Benjy. It is described early in the book (pp. 11–13), and at the end, before Luster sets out, Dilsey, knowing that it is a set ritual, lays great stress on his knowing the way, and he promises to go "same way T.P. goes ev'y Sunday" (p. 398). When he turned left at the Confederate monument, Benjy began to bellow. "There was more than astonishment in it, it was horror; shock; agony eyeless, tongueless; just sound" (p. 400). This is not the reaction of a passenger noting a minor traffic violation, but of an idiot snatched from the security of his cosy routine and plunged into the terrors of the unknown. This interpretation is borne out by Faulkner's notation on the map accompanying *Absalom, Absalom!*— "Confederate Monument which Benjy [not traffic] had to pass on his LEFT side."

his imagination. Nor can it be maintained that everything stated about the history of Jefferson is true about the past of Oxford. It has often been noted that Van Dorn's raid and his burning of Grant's supplies, for example, are located in Holly Springs (where they actually took place) in *Sartoris*, but are placed in Jefferson in *Light in August*. This does not mean that Jefferson "is really" Holly Springs—especially since Memphis Junction is Faulkner's usual fictional name for Holly Springs—but merely that, for the purposes of Hightower's monomania, it is convenient to place Van Dorn's raid in Jefferson.

Sometimes things said about Jefferson are not true of Oxford simply because the truth is not important for the novel and hence is not worth running down. Mink Snopes, returning to Jefferson in the fall of 1946 after thirty-eight years in the penitentiary, has learned that there have been no passenger-trains through Jefferson since 1935 (*Mans.* 179, 406). Faulkner is not a researcher—he is not writing for learned journals. Hence there is no reason for him to check with the Illinois Central Railroad and to be reminded that passenger service through Oxford was actually discontinued on August 16, 1941.[5]

There is one sense, however, in which it can be maintained and proved that Jefferson is Oxford and Yoknapatawpha County is Lafayette County. Faulkner habitually imagines his characters moving about the square and streets of Oxford and the roads, hills, and swamps of Lafayette County. Since he often describes his settings in detail, it follows that anyone who knows the town and country well will frequently recognize these settings, especially if he has known the territory long enough to recall many features and landmarks now either obliterated or altered beyond recognition.

Faulkner himself drew two maps of his domain, the first for *Absalom, Absalom!* (1936) and the second for the Viking Press's *Portable Faulkner* (1946). These maps agree in general, though neither is drawn with pedantic accuracy. For example, if we take the shortest precise measurement as a base—the Burden house in *Light in August*, which is repeatedly stated to be two miles from the square and the courthouse clock—we find that by the same scale Sartoris must be seven and a half miles from town on the earlier map and six on the later one, though Faulkner consistently states that it is four. Actually, the stated distance is right and the maps are wrong. The Burden house was on the old Batesville road (a quarter of a mile or so north of the present

5. Letter to the author from Mr. Arthur C. Carlson, Press Relations Department, Illinois Central Railroad, Oct. 25, 1961.

Mississippi Route 6), beyond the Negro community of St. Paul, two miles west of town. And Sartoris, with its own little flag-station on the railroad, was at the flag-stop of College Hill Station, four miles north of town. The Viking map is less detailed, but more accurate than the one in *Absalom, Absalom!* For example, it abandons some fanciful ridges which are quite different from the actual watersheds, and it has the main east-west road missing the square, as it actually does.

But all this is anticipating. The first thing is to show that Faulkner's maps actually represent a geographical reality. Even in the relatively early comments on the general similarity between the Oxford countryside and Faulkner's maps, like those in Ward Miner's *The World of William Faulkner*, the issue is confused by the fact that some resemblances have already been obscured by such changes as the rerouting of roads and the building of the Sardis Dam and Reservoir. The best demonstration of the basic identity of Yoknapatawpha and Lafayette counties is a simple confrontation of the right maps. I reproduce here (pp. 228–29) the map of Yoknapatawpha County which Faulkner made for the *Portable Faulkner* and a map of Lafayette County showing the railroad, Oxford, the two rivers, and all the roads leading to other towns of importance—what would now be numbered highways—as they were in 1912, when Faulkner was fifteen. The merest glance will show that Yoknapatawpha County is simply an offhand schematic (and laterally compressed) version of the Lafayette County of Faulkner's boyhood.

The actual topography is usually as accurate as the geography, and the regularity with which the same places recur in different novels bears further witness to their reality. Perhaps it will be best to begin with what, for many modern visitors to Oxford, is the beginning. If one drives into Oxford from the east on Mississippi 6 (not taking the bypass), a mile from town one comes over the top of a ridge and sees, across a broad valley, a striking view of the town on the next ridge. The road has been relocated several times,[6] but it has always come in over this same hilltop, so that the visitor is immediately in the place of Lena Grove in *Light in August* as she first approaches the town,

6. Mississippi 334 (still known to a few old-timers as "Old 6") is, with some minor changes, the road to Varner's as it appears in most of Faulkner's novels. It crosses Yellowleaf (Faulkner's "Whiteleaf") Creek, turns east along the edge of the Yocona River bottom, and, twelve miles from town, passes the little community formerly known as Cornish—Varner's Crossroads—where Mississippi 331 turns off south to cross the river.

"looking ahead, across the valley, toward the town on the opposite ridge" (p. 26). In *As I Lay Dying* Darl tells us that the Bundren family gets the same view. "From the crest of a hill, as we get into the wagon again, we can see the smoke low and flat, seemingly unmoving, in the unwinded afternoon. 'Is that it Darl?' Vardaman says. 'Is that Jefferson?' " (p. 216). At the bottom of the hill, Dewey Dell goes off into the bushes and puts on her town clothes. Then the approach across the valley, between Negro cabins, and up the last hill into town is described in detail (pp. 218–21).

In *The Sound and the Fury* we travel this same stretch of road on foot, in the opposite direction, with Frony, Dilsey, Luster, and Benjy. "A street turned off at right angles, descending, and became a dirt road. On either hand the land dropped more sharply; a broad flat dotted with small cabins whose weathered roofs were on a level with the crown of the road. . . . The road rose again, to a scene like a painted backdrop. Notched into a cut of red clay crowned with oaks the road appeared to stop short off, like a cut ribbon. Beside it a weathered church lifted its crazy steeple like a painted church" (pp. 362–64). The exactness of this description is now blurred since the present road no longer crosses the valley on a high fill, and the Negro church in which they heard the Easter sermon, which formerly stood by the road near the top of the ridge, is gone.

Another instance of the topography of Oxford being clearly used for Jefferson occurs near the end of *Light in August*, in Percy Grimm's pursuit of Joe Christmas. On the way from the jail to the courthouse, Joe breaks loose from a deputy on the square, runs down a street a short distance, and cuts into an alley leading promptly to "a pasture and then a deep ditch which was a town landmark. The tops of tall trees which grew in it just showed above the rim; a regiment could hide and deploy in it" (p. 435). This ditch was in Oxford, exactly as it is described here, and Joe Christmas could have gotten into it, by the route indicated, within less than two hundred yards from the courthouse. It may seem strange to call a gully of such heroic proportions a ditch, but the term here is really a proper name. This gully ran along the back edge of the boys' playground of the old Oxford High School. It was indeed a town landmark, and was known to generations of schoolboys simply as The Ditch. It was off limits but was regularly used for crap games and serious fights. (If the fighters were merely bluffing, they stayed on the playground, knowing that the teachers would soon intervene.) It is worth while to record the existence and genuineness of The Ditch as Faulkner describes it, for large portions of

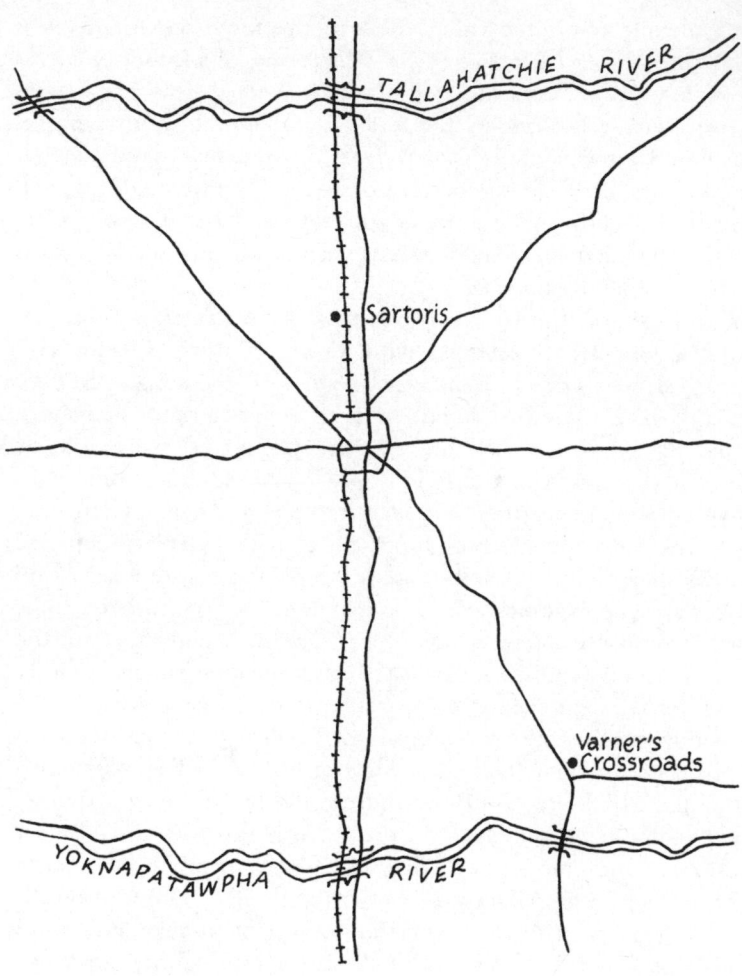

JEFFERSON AND YOKNAPATAWPHA COUNTY, MISSISSIPPI, 1945

As mapped by Faulkner for the endpapers of *The Viking Portable Faulkner* (New York, 1946). This is an exact copy of all the geographical features of Faulkner's map, but it omits all his text except for his names of the rivers and two place-names. Faulkner gives no scale of miles. This reproduction to the original size makes the distance from the center of Jefferson to Sartoris almost identical with that from the center of Oxford to College Hill Station on the facing map. Hence the two maps are on a generally comparable scale, though some other distances, of course, are not in agreement.

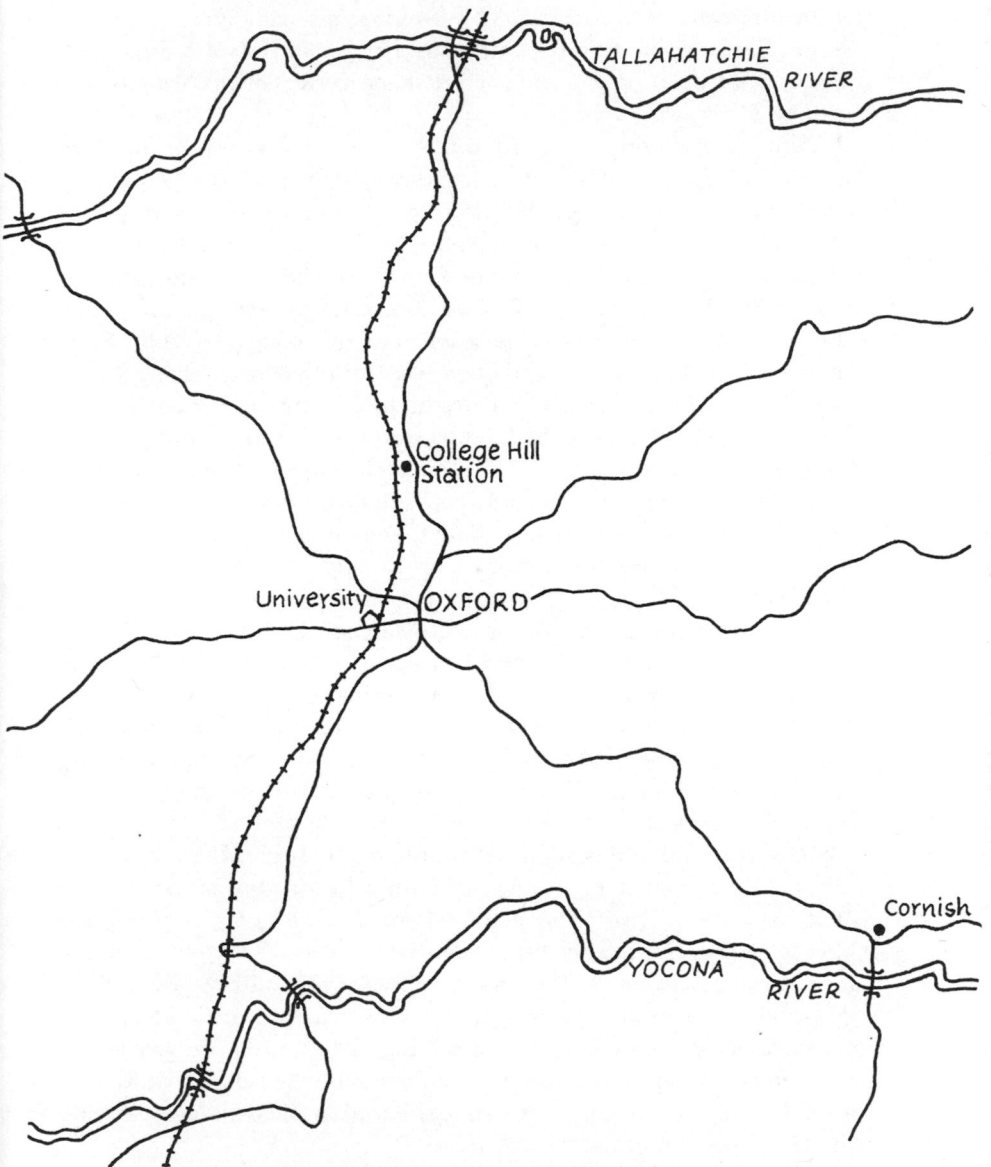

LAFAYETTE COUNTY, MISSISSIPPI, 1912

Mapped from *Soil Survey of Lafayette County, Mississippi* (U. S. Dept. of Agriculture, 1914—Advance Sheets, 1912). This copy is reduced to a scale of four miles to one inch. It shows the principal roads, the railroad, the two rivers, and a few key place-names. It does not include the edges of the county where they extend beyond Faulkner's map four miles to the east, three miles to the west, and from one to three miles to the south.

it have already been sacrificed by bulldozers to subdivisions and the future Faulknerian may find little trace of it. North Ninth Street now crosses it at what used to be the left back corner of the school playground.[7]

Mink Snope's trip from Memphis to Jefferson in *The Mansion*, which has been cited as evidence that Jefferson is not Oxford,[8] is actually a specific and detailed proof of the identity of the two places. Mink reaches the Junction (i.e. Memphis Junction, or Holly Springs) in a truck on which he has hitched a ride. "The truck was going on east into Alabama, but even if it had turned south here actually to pass through Jefferson, he would have left it at this point" (p. 396). Since the time is 1946 and the roads involved have not been changed, the route can be readily checked on any highway map. The truck brought him from Memphis on U.S. 78 and continued on that route toward Alabama. Mink would have left it at Holly Springs anyway because he had to slip into Jefferson undetected in order to kill Flem. "He was in thirty miles of Jefferson now, home, one same mutual north Mississippi hill-country people even if there was still a trivial county line to cross" (p. 396).

Holly Springs is the county seat of Marshall County; Oxford is the county seat of Lafayette County, immediately to the south. The two towns are exactly thirty miles apart. Mink finds that the road to Jefferson is now a properly surveyed black-top road (Mississippi 7), not the meandering dirt road that he remembers from some forty years earlier. This is all perfectly accurate. After a cotton-picking interlude, Mink starts for Jefferson in the cotton-owner's truck, and when he is told that it is eight miles to town, he begins to count off the miles. "Then four miles, a long hill with a branch bottom at the foot of it" (p. 404). This is the point where the road crosses Hurricane Creek, a stream Faulkner often mentions, usually with the common local pronunciation of "Harrykin" Creek, and always with strict geographical accuracy. Mink gets out of the truck here, "following the dense brier-cypress-willow jungle of the creek bottom for perhaps a quarter of a mile, maybe more, when suddenly he stopped dead with a kind of amazed excitement, even exhilaration. Before him, spanning the creek, was a railroad trestle" (p. 404).

---

7. It was also here, "in a cave they dug in the big ditch behind the school house," that "Byron Snopes's children out of a Jicarilla Apache squaw" cooked and ate Mrs. Widrington's five-hundred-dollar Pekinese (*Town* 362–64).

8. Buckley, p. 450.

The Illinois Central Railroad crosses Hurricane Creek bottom on two long fills, connected by a short, high trestle across the creek itself, actually something more than a mile down the creek from the highway. Everything here is precisely as Faulkner describes it, except that the jungle of the creek bottom is, if anything, understated. Mink tests his erratic pistol in the swamp, takes a nap, walks the railroad[9] to "the first quiet edge-of-town back street beneath the semaphore arms of the crossing warning and a single lonely street light" (p. 407), and there, where Washington Avenue[10] crosses the railroad at the edge of Freedman Town, he asks a Negro boy how to find the house of Flem Snopes.

As a final example of minutely accurate topography combined with deliberate alteration, we may take Joe Christmas's walk from town to his cabin behind Miss Burden's house (*LiA* 105–10). It begins with Joe looking into the barber shop in order to let Brown see him. From what follows, this is evidently the barber shop that operated at the northwestern corner of the square for at least half a century.[11] Then he "went on, not fast, away from the square," along a street that "led down through the negro section, Freedman Town, to the station. . . . He went on, passing still between the homes of white people, from street lamp to street lamp. . . . Then he found himself. Without his being aware the street had begun to slope and before he knew it he was in Freedman Town, surrounded by the summer smell and the summer voices of invisible negroes."

The route followed here is unmistakable. From the barber shop he went on west down Jackson Avenue away from the square, between the Episcopal church and (at the time of *Light in August*) the white school, through a white neighborhood, along a gently sloping street. Then, just before North Seventh Street turns off to the right, the street

9. This route along the railroad took him by Sartoris Station (College Hill Station), and as he approached town he passed the crest of the grade where Lucas Burch, alias Brown, hopped a freight train and disappeared from Jefferson (*LiA* 417).

10. To Mink it would still have been College Hill Street, at Stone's Crossing. Some years ago the street names which had grown up naturally in Oxford—North Street, South Street, Depot Street, Hash Row, etc.—were replaced by an arbitrarily assigned set of presidential avenues and numbered streets. For the reader's convenience I use the new names, but I doubt that they seemed real to Faulkner any more than they do to me. The older names show up occasionally in his works. See n. 12 for an example. Stone's Crossing appears again, though not named, in *KG:KG* 241.

11. This barber shop moved from its ancient location (now occupied by the drive-in window of a bank) on May 1, 1972. The Oxford *Eagle* of April 7, 1972, devoted a considerable amount of space to its history and tradition.

began to a slope steeply and passed through the edge of Freedman Town. This is the actual local name of this Negro section, bounded by Jackson Avenue, North Seventh Street, and the railroad, and extending up the railroad past Washington Avenue.

When Joe realized where he was,[12] "he began to run. . . . toward the next street lamp. Beneath it a narrow and rutted lane turned and mounted to a parallel street, out of the black hollow." He "plunged up the sharp ascent . . . and into the higher street," where "the air now was the cold hard air of white people. Then he became cool. The negro smell, the negro voices, were behind him now. To his left lay the square, the clustered lights. . . . To his right the street lamps marched on. . . . He went on, slowly again, his back toward the square, passing again between the houses of white people." From Jackson Avenue he had turned left (south) up South Sixth Street (nameless in the old days, so far as I know; notice that Faulkner calls it a lane), a very short, steep street, not much more than fifty yards long, running up to Van Buren Avenue. When he stopped running (without turning) at the top of this street, the square lay to his left. He turned right (west again) down this gently sloping street, which has white houses on both sides all the way to the station. Here he passed a cotton warehouse with a line of freight cars on a siding by it. Then he crossed the tracks of the main line.[13] "Beyond the tracks woods began. But he found the path unerringly." It went up a hill, from the top of which he looked back at the town. "His way was sure, despite the trees, the darkness. . . . The woods continued for a mile. He emerged into a road," with Negro cabins along it.

In this last passage we have conclusive proof that Faulkner has deliberately removed the University of Mississippi from Oxford in order to create Jefferson. When Christmas crossed the tracks, he would actually have found a concrete sidewalk lighted by street lights and leading through woods up a hill to the campus. When he paused and looked back at the top of this hill, he was standing between the

12. He was at the same place where Charles Etienne de Saint Velery Bon would turn up about once a year "either blind or violently drunk in the negro store district on Depot Street" (*Abs.* 209).

13. Parts of Christmas's route are covered by other characters in Faulkner. Christmas walked from the square halfway to the station on Jackson Avenue and then crossed over a short block and went the rest of the way on Van Buren Avenue. Mink Snopes walked the whole distance on Jackson (*Mans.* 34–35), and Horace Benbow rode—in a trip described in minute detail—the whole way from the station to the square on Van Buren (*Sart.* 165–66).

house in which I was born and raised and the one in which Faulkner lived while his father was employed by the university. (Both houses are now gone.) The university owns a tract a mile square, and Faulkner has simply made this tract into woods crossed by a path. He lets Joe reenter the real landscape when he has crossed this mile, and then come into the road at the edge of the Negro community of St. Paul, about where the university hospital now stands. Half a mile farther down this road is his destination, the cabin behind Miss Burden's house.

By a strange coincidence, we can continue Joe's walk as it actually would have been by leaving Jefferson and going to "Oxford."[14] When Horace Benbow goes to the university there to make enquiries about Temple Drake (*Sanc.* 166–67), he gets off at the station, and Faulkner describes his walk up this sidewalk and on to the campus grove with the three paths running through it, the broader one leading to the post office—where Faulkner once officiated—all exactly as the campus was at the time of both *Light in August* and *Sanctuary*.

In this connection it should be noted that Faulkner offers no description of "Oxford" as such. His Jefferson corresponds to the real Oxford, and his "Oxford" is a nebulous town connected with the state university. His descriptions in *Sanctuary* deal with the university and stop at the edge of town: Doc and his friends break a bottle on the bridge spanning the railway cut that separates Oxford from the university, and Gowan gets drunk at The Shack—which was, in spite of Faulkner's lower-case letters (cf. The Ditch, above), the actual name of a joint of those days adjoining the station at the end of Jackson Avenue (pp. 30–34). Beyond this, we learn nothing about "Oxford" except that it has a square through which Gowan drives on his way to the actual little town of Taylor, seven miles to the south. As a matter of fact, the shortest way from the station to the old Taylor road in Oxford does not lie through the square, and Gowan is in a hurry. The discrepancy may be intentional because Jefferson is Oxford and "Oxford" is not—but it is also true that Gowan is in no condition to plot his course very intelligently.

Faulkner is deliberately vague about the location of "Oxford" as well as about its physical features. He gives us three main points of reference for it: Varner's Store (Frenchman's Bend), Jefferson, and

14. To avoid confusion, I use quotation marks to designate the place called "Oxford" in Faulkner's novels, and use the name without quotation marks to designate the actual town in which Faulkner lived.

Sutpen's. These points lie in a straight line. Jefferson is in the middle, with Varner's store twelve miles to the southeast[15] and Sutpen's mansion twelve miles to the northwest. But "Oxford" is forty miles from Varner's and Sutpen's, and fifty miles (occasionally forty) from Jefferson.[16] Its location is an obvious geometrical impossibility. It is futile to start from Oxford and try to locate Jefferson.[17] Jefferson, the proper starting-point, *is* Oxford, and "Oxford" is a place adjoining a state university and, latterly, a large artificial reservoir[18]—things that Faulkner does not want in his typical Jefferson. They are placed a day's ride away on horseback, and an appreciable journey in cars on dirt roads, and there is no direct rail connection.[19] As far as Jefferson is concerned, "Oxford" is simply somewhere else, and the two places are incommensurable.

It has often been pointed out that the locations of the principal hotel and the jail[20] in Jefferson correspond exactly to those in Oxford. Many other places are readily recognizable to those who knew the town fifty years ago. Among them are the livery stable from which young Bayard Sartoris rode the wild stallion (*Sart.* 131–34), the planing-mill on the railroad south of town where Byron Bunch worked in *Light in August*, Deacon's Café and its proprietor (*Sart.* 122–28), and Christian's Drug Store, which, with its owner, appears repeatedly in Faulkner's works. There is also a perfectly accurate account of the history and nature of the Mary Buie Museum in "Shall Not Perish" (*CS* 110–11).

In addition to such definite institutions as these, there are many places in the county which are precisely described, but which I cannot

15. This is the figure given in *Light in August* and is the map-distance, both on Faulkner's maps (where Sutpen's and Varner's are equidistant from Jefferson), and on the actual county and highway maps. In other works the distance from Jefferson to Varner's is regularly given as 20 or 22 miles, probably in order to make the hamlet more remote. This greater distance would make the impossibility of "Oxford's" position even more striking.

16. See *Ham.* 110; *Town* 290; *Mans.* 141, 202; *Abs.* 128, 311, 319; *Unv.* 245, 248.

17. Buckley, p. 448.

18. Miner (p. 104) sees in the omission of the Sardis Reservoir an example of Faulkner's "resistance to change." But the lake is not ignored. Like the university, it is moved to "Oxford." The boy in "Two Soldiers" refers to "that Government reservoy up at Oxford" (*CS* 81).

19. In *Sanctuary* (pp. 168–73), Horace Benbow makes the trip by rail, with a change at Holly Springs, which is here called by its right name in its accurate relationship to both "Oxford" and Oxford.

20. The present new jail occupies the same site as the old one.

identify. Oxford is small enough so that anyone brought up there could know it thoroughly, but the 664 square miles of Lafayette County will not be known in exactly the same way to any two persons. A good example is Hub's place, where Bayard, Suratt, and Hub go to drink by the spring (*Sart.* 136 ff.). The spring flowing from the roots of a huge beech could be duplicated hundreds of times in the county, but the whole complex of the carefully detailed route of the field road leading to the house, the trees about the house, the road forking between the house and the barn (normally such a road would go past the house and on to the barn), and all the other minute details, convince me that Faulkner had a specific place in mind here, and that I would immediately recognize it if it were a place I happened to know. The same thing may be true of some of the terrain in "The Bear," but someone who had an intimate knowledge of that part of the Tallahatchie River bottom would have to recollect it, for it is now irretrievably lost on the bottom of the Sardis Reservoir.[21]

McHaney has argued for a chronological development in Faulkner's use of the local scene. "It seems clear that particularly at the beginning of his career Faulkner blended Lafayette and Tippah Counties rather evenly; Jefferson and Yoknapatawpha are like an overlay of Oxford/Lafayette on Ripley/Tippah, with the addition of much more from other sources as the need arose. As he grew older, he relied more on Oxford and environs than on Ripley, depending on context, so that the land routes in *The Reivers* are patently those from Oxford to Memphis during his youth."[22] The statement about the route in *The Reivers* is perfectly accurate, but it is hard to see any merit in the argument for a progressively increasing use of the Oxford scene. After all, the detailed examples of the use of accurate details which I have given in this appendix come largely from the early novels—*Sartoris, The Sound and the Fury,* and *Light in August.*

There is, however, one striking exception, for which I can suggest no explanation. The geography of *As I Lay Dying* is unique. It uses many of the same place-names and characters as the other Yoknapa-

21. On the other hand, it is possible that the terrain here is purely imaginary or is a general mixture of features from a number of places. "The camp started around a hundred years ago. . . . The hunters moved from the north around Oxford, following the game, moved on to Batesville, west toward the Big River and south toward the Gulf. By 1938–39 (when Faulkner was writng *Go Down, Moses*) they were close to Onward, not far above Vicksburg, hunting east of Highway 61"—Floyd C. Watkins, "Delta Hunt," *Southwestern Review* 45 (1960): 271.

22. McHaney, p. 263.

tawpha novels, but the generally consistent geography (including Faulkner's own maps) of the other novels will not work. The map in *Absalom* place the Bundrens across the Yoknapatawpha from Varner's, just about where the little town of Tula stands. Hence they would have to cross the river to get to Jefferson. But we find them, before they have crossed it, apparently on the same side as the Tulls, Armstids, and Varners. They also pass Whiteleaf Creek (p. 103), which in Faulkner regularly stands for Yellowleaf Creek, which flows into the Yocona river from the *Oxford* side. A bit later they are trying Samson's Bridge, and one of the MacCallums is there (p. 107). But the MacCallums are in the northern part of the county by the Tallahatchie River, and the one other reference to Samson's Bridge (*Sart.* 125) implies that it is across the Tallahatchie. Then we find the Bundrens going by way of Mottson, which is regularly Water Valley, on the same side of the Yocona as the Bundren house. And so it goes. Only when they get to the vicinity of Jefferson do they come into the otherwise consistent world of the Yoknapatawpha cycle: the view of Oxford from the ridge and other details are all accurate—but only if they have come in on the road from Varner's, not the road from Mottson. Whatever the reason may be, we simply have to concede that, except for the immediate vicinity of Jefferson, the geography of *As I Lay Dying* is inconsistent with that of the rest of the Yoknapatawpha novels.

A particularly good example of the deliberate modification of local fact for an obvious artistic gain is found in the Tallahatchie crossing depicted in *The Reivers*.[23] At the period in which this novel is set, there were three bridges across the Tallahatchie in a northerly direction from Oxford. The map on page 229 will be useful here. The crossing almost due north of Oxford, alongside the railroad, is the Abbeville Bridge. The one to the left of it (on the old Sardis road) is the Iron Bridge. About halfway between these is Wyatt (Faulkner spells it Wyott) Bridge. It is not shown on this map because, in the interest of simplification, only "principal roads" are shown, and by the time of this map the road across Wyatt Bridge went nowhere in particular.

Faulkner's adventurers actually used the Abbeville Bridge, which was the standard route to Memphis at that time. With minor reroutings, it is the present Mississippi 7 to Holly Springs, and the rest of the

---

23. Most of the discussion of this example is taken from my note, "Faulkner's Three-in-One Bridge in *The Reivers*," *Notes on Contemporary Literature* 1, no. 2 (March, 1971): 8–10, which is here reprinted with the editors' permission.

way was on the present U.S. 78 to Memphis. This fact is confirmed by the crossing of Hurricane Creek four miles out of town (p. 68) and the position of Mr. Wyott's house, evidently in Abbeville, "eight miles from Jefferson and still four miles from the river" (p. 69). Hell Creek, then, would stand for Springs Creek.[24] The railroad parallels the road through the Tallahatchie bottom, and the whistle-stop there was evidently the whistle-stop of Spraggins, on the northern edge of the bottom, which was used for logging operations for some years. There was no railroad near either of the other two bridges.

What Faulkner did was to combine the three bridges into one. The Iron Bridge was on the road to Sardis. It was "THE Iron Bridge since it was the first Iron Bridge and for several years the only one we in Yoknapatawpha County had or knew of" (p. 73). It was always called the Iron Bridge, and appears under that name on the Soil Survey map on which the map on page 229 is based. As Faulkner's maps of Yoknapatawpha County indicate, it was also in Sutpen's Hundred, near the site of what later became Major de Spain's hunting camp.

The Wyatt Bridge was more interesting. Before the railroad "destroyed it" (p. 74), Wyatt was really, as Faulkner says, the head of navigation on the Tallahatchie (p. 73). Before the Civil War it was a flourishing town—I once saw a banknote issued by the Bank of Wyatt. It was on a bluff just north of the river, one of the few places where there is any high ground near its course. Faulkner puts Ballenbaugh's just *south* of the river, since the travelers cross the bridge immediately after leaving Ballenbaugh's for Memphis. If it had actually been there, it would have been subject to intermittent flooding all winter. After the railroad put an end to navigation on the Tallahatchie, Wyatt declined and finally disappeared completely, though its picturesque outlaw history was, so far as I know, sheer invention on Faulkner's part. Now "Wyott's Crossing is only a name" (p. 72).

I may have driven the last car across Wyatt Bridge, about 1936. That bridge was still intact, but to reach it from Oxford I had to patch gaping holes in a couple of bridges across sloughs in the river bottom with odd rotten planks and logs. By that time the main street of Wyatt was a gully forty feet deep, though old wells, traces of houses, and odd bits of broken china still marked the site. Last time I was there (1972), there was hardly a sign of human habitation, and in a gulley marking a former street there was a fox den. Lizards in Jamshyd's

24. Faulkner may have borrowed the name (which is perfect for his purposes) from an actual Hell Creek a couple of miles north of New Albany.

courtyard! The bluff is, of course, still there, but the sites of the Iron Bridge and Wyatt Bridge have been under the Sardis Reservoir for nearly forty years. The Abbeville Bridge, toward the upper end of the fluctuating impoundment, is still there.

Faulkner's combination of these three crossings furnishes an interesting example of his free handling of minute local facts. Since the actual route to Memphis in his youth was by Abbeville, he used this route for his roads, creeks, and distances. But since this crossing was prosaic and undistinguished, he combined the other two with it, thus arriving at the picturesque name of the Iron Bridge and, by references to Sutpen's Hundred, Major de Spain's camp, and the ornamented history of Old Wyatt, tying it into the history of both Yoknapatawpha and Lafayette counties.

Many other places are deliberately altered. A few, like the power plant where Flem Snopes stole the brass fittings, seem wrong now because of relatively recent changes. This power plant was on the railroad, a couple of hundred yards south of the station, just as Faulkner describes it, and near it there was a tank whose threatened explosion (caused by the carelessness and averted by the heroism of its watchman) evidently suggested the death of Eck Snopes (*Town* 107 ff.). It was dismantled when the present power plant was built east of town off Highway 6. But there has never been an airport where Faulkner places the one on his map and in "Death Drag." The one from which he did his own flying is in a field south of the Yocona River, and the present commercial one was built relatively recently.

Likewise, there has never been a golf course near the Compsons' section of town. At the time of *The Sound and the Fury*, the university's course near the campus was the only one, and this fact alone is sufficient to explain why Faulkner created a new one in a different location for Jefferson. He also plays fast and loose with the cemetery, even to the extent of committing inconsistencies. This is presumably because he wants the old Colonel's statue to stand on its column overlooking his railroad, as it actually does in Ripley.[25] Consequently, in the *Absalom* map he puts the cemetery between the road in from Sartoris (North Lamar) and the railroad, and hence *west* of North Lamar. In *Sartoris* he has the statue plainly visible from the road (p. 119), and it is by the cemetery that old Bayard dies of heart-failure in young Bayard's car (pp. 304–05). Faulkner has apparently forgotten this when he makes

25. For an account and photograph of this monument, see Maud Morrow Brown, "William C. Faulkner, Man of Legends," *Georgia Review* 10 (1956): 437, 439.

the map for *Absalom*, because there he places old Bayard's death about a mile from the cemetery. Near the end of *Sartoris*, when Miss Jenny visits the cemetery, it is put in its proper place and is reachable by a grassy lane[26] from the edge of town (p. 372). In Faulkner's other works, though no detailed route to the cemetery is given, it is clearly placed in the section of town where the Oxford cemetery actually is, north of the square and several blocks *east* of North Lamar.

The houses in which Faulkner's characters live are never specifically identifiable. In one case, there is a definite impossibility to anyone who knows Oxford. In *Light in August*, Hightower's house backs up to The Ditch, since, from the edge of The Ditch, Percy Grimm can see Joe Christmas run up the back steps into it (p. 438). One of the recurrent themes of the novel is Hightower sitting alone on Wednesday and Sunday evenings and listening to the singing from the Presbyterian church, where he had once been pastor (pp. 75, 345–47, and passim). But these two pieces of information about the location of Hightower's house are contradictory. Any house near The Ditch would not only have been too far to hear music from the Presbyterian church, but would have had to hear it through the intervening Methodists (at this time), Episcopalians, or Baptists. Obviously, the layout of Oxford is not allowed to dictate to Faulkner, and only the local citizen (for whom he is not writing anyway) might find any difficulty about this highly effective use of the evening service.

There are no such inconsistencies about the locations of other houses in Jefferson, but the locations are not specific. There is no question (and would be none, even without the maps) as to the general neighborhood of the Compson and Benbow houses, for example, but the exact positions are never pinpointed. Probably prudential considerations combine with creative ones to produce this indefiniteness. People live in houses and are quite capable of litigation. Furthermore, it is doubtless simpler to invent a house along with its inhabitants than it is to put a set of imaginary people into an actual house already associated with a set of workaday neighbors. This point needs to be emphasized, since Oxford is now beginning to develop a Faulkner-based tourist industry and, as an inevitable part of this sort of enterprise, to give the customers what they want, including the identification of unidentifiable houses.

Further evidence of how closely Faulkner imagined his novels as

26. This lane, paved, has become North Sixteenth Street. Faulkner lies buried close beside it.

taking place in Oxford is his train schedules. The fact has never been noted before, but he always uses the approximate schedules, and often even the actual train-numbers, of the Illinois Central Railroad through Oxford. Until 1912, Oxford had two passenger-trains daily in each direction. Early in that year, a third train each way was added. In the early 1920s this third one was a one-coach generator-electric unit nicknamed The Bilbo. After it was wrecked in about 1924, it was not replaced, and the schedule went back to the two trains. During the period covered by most of Faulkner's novels, these trains varied by not much more than an hour in their schedules, and two of them even kept their numbers unchanged. Here are the passenger-train schedules near the beginning and near the end of this period, taken from the Oxford *Eagle*.

March 28, 1912		*March 14, 1929*	
NORTHBOUND		NORTHBOUND	
No. 6	4:18 A.M.	No. 26	3:58 A.M.
No. 24	3:05 P.M.	No. 24	2:53 P.M.
No. 34	8:22 P.M.		
SOUTHBOUND		SOUTHBOUND	
No. 33	3:04 A.M.		
No. 23	10:35 A.M.	No. 23	10:28 A.M.
No. 5	9:45 P.M.	No. 25	8:42 P.M.

Faulkner refers, with complete accuracy, to "Number Five south-bound" (*Mans.* 63), "Number Six north-bound" (*Mans.* 62), and "Number Twenty-three south-bound" (*Town* 365; *Reiv.* 43). He also uses several train-numbers that do not occur in the schedules given above, but it would be rash to conclude that these are necessarily invented or inaccurate. With the Faulkner background of railroading and interest in trains, they may well be numbers used at various periods or (when passengers are not involved) the numbers of freight trains.

More important than the numbers is the fact that Oxford's basic pair of trains each way, with their approximate times, are the regular trains of Jefferson. Old Bayard sat on his porch at night and heard "the whistle of the nine-thirty train"—obviously No. 5, above (*Sart.* 43). When Horace Benbow left his house at three in the morning to walk to the station and start to "Oxford" (*Sanc.* 163), he was obviously going to catch No. 26. The clearest example, and the most detailed, occurs when old Doc Hines and his wife, in Mottstown (Water Valley, twenty miles south of Oxford), decide to go by train to Jefferson (*LiA* 339–41). "That was about four o'clock"—so they had just missed No. 24. They sat in the courthouse yard until six and then started toward the station, "and the folks knew there wasn't any train due for three hours"—No. 25, "the southbound." When Mrs. Hines asked for tickets to Jefferson, the agent told her "That train is not due until two o'clock in the morning." After the southbound train left, they spent most of the night in the waiting-room and then took No. 26 to Jefferson. Mink Snopes's night in the station at Jefferson, seeing both these same passenger trains (*Mans.* 34–37), is similarly accurate.

Various other points about Faulkner's use of local geography and topography might be raised, and various other specific identifications are made under their individual headings in the glossary itself. Enough has been said here to establish clearly the fact that Faulkner habitually thinks of his characters as moving about Oxford and Lafayette County, and that he often uses the local scene effectively and accurately, though he never bows to it pedantically or slavishly. These facts seem well worth establishing and documenting, and they contribute to an understanding both of Faulkner's methods and of his works. But it is also worth insisting that, interesting as this aspect of his work may be, it is only a minor aspect. The aesthetic qualities that have made works like *Absalom, Absalom!*, *Light in August*, and *The Sound and the Fury* a part of world literature are ultimately rooted in their universality rather than in their localization.